PRESIDENTIAL POLICIES AND THE ROAD TO THE SECOND IRAQ WAR

Presidential Policies and the Road to the Second Iraq War

From Forty One to Forty Three

JOHN DAVIS
Howard University, USA

ASHGATE

Published by
Ashgate Publishing Limited
Gower House
Croft Road
Aldershot
Hampshire GU11 3HR
England

Ashgate Publishing Company
Suite 420
101 Cherry Street
Burlington, VT 05401-4405
USA

Ashgate website: http://www.ashgate.com

British Library Cataloguing in Publication Data
Presidential policies and the road to the second Iraq war :
  from forty one to forty three
  1. Iraq War, 2003- - Causes 2. United States - Foreign
  relations - Iraq 3. Iraq - Foreign relations - United States
  4. United States - Foreign relations - 2001- 5. United States
  - Military policy
  I. Davis, John, 1962-
  327.7'30567

Library of Congress Cataloging-in-Publication Data
Presidential policies and the road to the second Iraq war : from Forty One to Forty
Three / edited by John Davis.
      p. cm.
  Includes index.
  ISBN 0-7546-4769-2
  1. Iraq War, 2003- 2. United States--Politics and government--2001- 3. United
States--Foreign relations--2001- I. Davis, John, 1962-

  DS79.76.P74 2006
  956.7044'31--dc22

                                                                        2006000107

ISBN 0 7546 4769 2

Printed and bound in Great Britain by Antony Rowe Ltd, Chippenham, Wiltshire.

Contents

List of Tables

Introduction

John Davis

Howard University

US Presidential Policies and Iraq: A Myriad of Themes

Since the commencement of *Operation Iraqi Freedom* a veritable cottage industry has developed around a number of themes. Those themes include: the infighting[1] within the administration of George W. Bush that set the stage for war with Iraq, the prewar military planning, assessments of the military operation,[2] and finally, the failure to plan for the postwar peace.[3] These studies in themselves are valuable in that they provide unique perspectives of the multiple stages of the Bush administrations policies that ultimately culminated in regime change in Iraq. In reading these and other studies the overriding impression is that President Bush was prepared from the outset of his administration for the removal of the arch nemesis of the US, Iraq's Saddam Hussein. On this point few would disagree.

A second theme asserts that the administration's intervention in Iraq had less to do with the Bush doctrine, which some assert was utilized as a disguise to hide the president's real intensions. Rather the policy is illustrative of how a cabal had convinced a US president to implement their agenda. The group referenced here is of course the neoconservatives which have argued since the Carter administration that Saddam Hussein represented a threat to regional stability and US and allied oil interests and needed to be removed. The neoconservatives were unrelenting in their quest for regime change. If and when, for example, their agenda had been undercut this group counterattacked. In second example, as the Clinton administration pursued a course indifferent to the Iraq Liberation Act, elements within this faction both inside and outside of government quickly responded. In a notable example, the Clinton administrations apparent unwillingness to implement the act produced swift criticism from neoconservative Gary Schmitt:

> The Clinton Administration of course committed itself to a policy of removal when the president signed the Iraq Liberation Act. . . . Yet there have been persistent doubts about how serious the administration was in carrying out the Act. Its efforts at implementation

---

1   See the following, Glenn Kessler and Walter Pincus, "Bush Team Infighting Could Hurt War Plan," *Washington Post*, 1 April 2003; Dan Morgan, "Deciding Who Rebuilds Iraq Is Fraught With Infighting," *Washington Post*, May 2003.

2   Anthony Cordesman , *Iraq War: Strategy, Tactics, and Military Lessons* (New York: Greenwood Publishing Group, 2003).

3   David L. Phillips, *Losing Iraq: Inside The Reconstruction Fiasco* (New York: Westview Press, 2005).

have been grudging, background statements about the Act by administration figures have been dismissive, and its response to the assessment made by Marine General Anthony Zinni, commander-in-chief of US forces in the Middle East, about the Act's wisdom was indifferent. Now we have been told that National Security Advisor "Sandy" Berger has decided to bring Kenneth Pollack, one of the co-authors of the "The Rollback Fantasy," on board the staff of the National Security Council to handle Iraq policy. In the absence of administration efforts to put forward a coherent and strategically-sound policy toward Iraq, Congress enacted the Iraq Liberation Act. However, if Congress wants to see the law effectively implemented it will need to increase its oversight of the administration's handling of US-Iraq policy and insist on a more faithful adherence to what is, after all, the law of the land.[4]

In the third example, Lawrence Kaplan and William Kristol contend that Clinton's disastrous policy of "avoiding confronting the moral and strategic challenge presented by Saddam, hoping instead that an increasingly weak policy"[5] would avoid a major clash between the US and Iraq. Thus this path according the neoconservatives demonstrates that the resident's policy was indifferent to the spirit of the Iraqi Liberation Act.

These statements are representative of one important aspect of this group: they are relentless in the pursuit of their objective: regime change. When members of this faction filled multiple senior levels positions in the current administration, they mounted another attack that was essential to achieving their goal: the marginalization of Colin Powell.[6] With this task complete they were relatively free to influence President Bush and thus control the formation and implementation of US policy toward Iraq.

A third view holds that US policy toward Iraq is based on "unfinished business." This view of US presidential policy acknowledges that President Bush's efforts of regime change commenced around two views. The first is that Saddam's conspiracy to kill the elder Bush in April of 1993 lingered on the mind of the president for years. The president even hinted publicly why he wanted to end the regime in Iraq with the following statement made at a Houston, Texas political fundraiser in September of 2002: "After all this is the guy who tried to kill my dad." Second, for many of the president's critics this was pivotal because prior to this statement administration official's repeatedly spoke of an Iraq-Al Qaeda connection that produced the devastating attacks on 11 September 2001. That is elements within the administration (Vice President Dick Cheney, Secretary of Defense Donald Rumsfeld, et al. believed that Iraq indeed had a connection to the events of 9/11. This group of administration officials point to Lauren Mylroie's controversial book the *Study of Revenge: Saddam*

---

4   See Memorandum by Gary Schmitt. Subject: Iraq, 3 March 1999, http://www. newamericancentury.org/iraqmar0399.htm. Retrieved 14 September 2005.

5   As quoted in a study by Robert Pauly, *US Foreign Policy and the Persian Gulf: Safeguarding American Interests Through Selective Multilateralism* (London: Ashgate, 200$), p. 5.

6   See James Mann, *The Rise of the Vulcans: The History of Bush's War Cabinet* (New York: Penguin Books, 2004).

Hussein's Unfinished War Against America which supported their view that Saddam provided cover for Al Qaeda in the 1993 World Trade Center bombing and did so again in 2001. Despite this contention few outside the US government accepted the validity of the argument. Many point to the 9/11 Commission report—which noted that a minor relationship existed, but that no substantial evidence existed to support a conspiracy.[7] Equally damaging, the administration's policy of regime change attracted criticism from elements within the British government. British Foreign Office political director Peter Ricketts established that the case of "regime change does not stack up. It sounds like a grudge between Bush and Saddam."[8] Thus regime change in this scenario became synonymous with the unfinished business of the first Bush administration.

Following the release of secret British intelligence reports in the spring of 2005, a fourth view suggests that the Bush administration's policy toward Iraq had been based on obfuscation. The Downing Street memos establish that the administration "has lost faith in containment and is now considering regime change. The end states could either be a Sunni strongman or a representative government."[9] Subsequent statements contained in a memo written by a British intelligence officer marked "SECRET AND STRICTLY PERSONAL," and written eight months before the start of hostilities, makes the case that "intelligence and facts were being fixed around the policy."[10]

This revelation proved damaging to Bush and Tony Blair, the British Prime Minister, each of which were dealing with the aftermath of internal commissions which were tasked to investigate the role of flawed intelligence and the formation and implementation of US-British policies toward Iraq.

The contributors in this study advance an altogether different proposition: that the momentum for war had been in place long before the current administration entered office. In advancing this unique window into the conflict in the gulf, *Presidential Policies and the Road to the Second Iraq War: From Forty One to Forty Three* asserts that after exploring the policies of George H.W. Bush (41), Bill Clinton (42) and George W. Bush (43), a number of variables supplement the contention that a second war with Iraq was inevitable. To add validity to this point, consider the following: on the question of UN inspectors, none of the presidents mentioned in this study had great faith in their utility. This statement is exemplified by statements by officials such as vice president Cheney and civilians in the Pentagon who strenuously argued that Saddam's methods of hiding his weapons programs were well ahead of the UN

---

7   See the National Commission on Terrorist Attacks Upon the United States. 9/11 Commission Report (New York: Barnes & Noble Books, 2005), 334.

8   Thomas Wagner, "British memos show Bush push for an Iraq war soon after 9/11," Associated Press, 19 June 2005, http//deseretnews.com/dn/view/0,1249,600142505,00.html. Retrieved on 15 September 2005.

9   Text of the Iraq Options Paper. March 8, 2002 memo from Overseas and Defense Secretariat Cabinet Office outlining military options for implementing regime change.

10   Walter Pincus, "Memo: U.S. Lacked Full Postwar Iraq Plan," *Washington Post*, 12 June 2005, A1.

inspector's ability to locate them.[11] The only way according these officials to remove the threat was through regime change.

Second, another perspective suggested that by the close of the first Bush administration a growing chorus within the administration concluded that the coalition erected to remove Saddam from Kuwait did not have long term sustainability, and thus the Arab participants, owing to domestic and regional pressures, were unlikely to support a sustained UN-led umbrella of coercive diplomacy erected against another Arab state. Similarly, with key members of the Security Council (Russia, China, and France) themselves having direct economic (oil) interests in Iraq this too militated against a viable international effort to contain Saddam. Viewed collectively, there was a growing perception among key sectors of the national security establishment that multilateral efforts to contain Saddam were unraveling and the costs to the United States were increasing to the point where the reconsideration of a major military response involving the introduction of US ground forces emerged as a significant policy option.

Third, covering 41 through 43, with greater emphasis on Clinton and Bush II, each US president feared the cost of containment. During his first term Clinton utilized a policy of comprehensive containment as the central element of administration policy. Containment was designed to keep Saddam in his box. This policy had a number of imperfections. First the policy represented a liability because "it relied on multilateral cooperation during a period when US allies, as well as Iraq's regional neighbors, were suffering from sanctions fatigue."[12] This point is exemplified by the simmering tension between Iraq and the Security Council over the implementation of UNSCR 687. As a result of this tension Iraq repeatedly precluded UNSCOM inspectors from completing their inspections.[13] Similarly, Iraq challenged the validity of the no-fly zones, eventually placing a series of air defense networks that threatened the safety of coalition aircraft patrolling the no-fly zones. In each of these and other instances, the Security Council had all but turned a blind eye. In the face of growing pessimism of an UN-led multilateral response, the administration repeatedly deployed expensive naval build-ups in the preparation for military hostilities for the multiple occasions when Saddam violated a string of UN Security Council resolutions. Additionally, Saddam's "cheat and retreat" policies forced the withdrawal of UN inspectors and the administration finally reacted in December of 1998. The administration responded by launching of *Operation Desert Fox*, a military operation that utilized US air and surface ship assets to destroy selected weapons of mass destruction targets throughout Iraq.

11　　Ibid. A statement in the Iraq paper validates this point: "distrust of UN sanctions and inspection regimes, and unfinished business from 1991 are all factors" point to reasons for skepticism about the inspections regime.

12　　Robert S. Litwak, *Rogue States and US Foreign Policy* (Washington, DC: Woodrow Wilson Center Press, 2000), 128.

13　　Ibid., 128–9.

In the second Bush administration the burgeoning price tag of containment resulted in a split among the presidents senior advisors. The pragmatic realists, led by Colin Powell, were indifferent to attacking Iraq without any provocations. The second faction, led by the neoconservatives, had pushed for a policy of regime change, based on their contention that multilateralism failed to end the threat posed by Iraq. Unable to agree on a new course of action, after this opening debate concerning the review of Iraq policy concluded, an ad hoc policy of "smart sanctions" was implemented; even so the internal debate for ending containment continued.

Fourth, elements within the executive branch (and also within the Congress, on both sides of the isle) remained committed to military intervention in Iraq. Much of these feelings emerged as a result of the events that unfolded before and after the Safwan agreement and others that developed at the close of the first Bush administration. On the first point, intelligence analysis concluded that after the administration decided to conclude the war it had become painfully obvious that key battlefield objectives were not met, specifically that many Republican Guard units had not been destroyed and therefore Iraq could, if Saddam chose to, again threaten their neighbors. In the wake of the agreement, US forces watched as Iraqi units slaughtered Shiite rebels in southern Iraq. The use of helicopter gunships to kill people that the president himself urged to dethrone the Iraqi leader did not sit well with field commanders, senior military officers in the Pentagon, and with civilians throughout the national security establishment. On the second point, in December of 1992 at the close of Bush I, Saddam tested the strength of the lame duck US president by launching surface to air missiles (SAMs) at coalition aircraft over the no-fly zones. Following a UNSCR that declared Iraq "in material breach" of the post-*Desert Storm* ceasefire resolution, coalition pilots launched a massive attack on Iraqi air defense sites that were in the no-fly zones. Just two days before the commencement of the Clinton administration, undaunted, Iraqi forces on orders from Saddam violated the no-fly zones a second time. US-led coalition aircraft launched another counter attack.[14] In the wake of these events the overwhelming perception was that a second phase of hostilities with Iraq was on the horizon.[15]

The idea of finishing off Iraq was based on a number of additional factors. Politically, the unfinished business in Iraq infuriated republicans who felt that the legacy of George Bush was negatively impacted because he failed to unseat Iraq's dictator. Moreover, for the neoconservatives this failure had another political consequence, the loss of the White House to the Clintonistas. Bureaucratically, the neoconservatives, whose central agenda was based on the toppling of the regime in Iraq, were so incensed by the Bush administration's inability to unseat the regime in Iraq in the wake of first gulf war that elements of this same group openly criticized the president, and some took the unusual step of supporting then Governor Bill Clinton's

---

14   Kenneth Pollack, *The Threatening Storm – The United States and Iraq: The Crisis, the Crisis, and the Prospects After Saddam* (New York: Random House, 2002), 64.

15   See Patrick Clawson, editor, *Iraq Strategy Review: Options for US Policy* (Washington, DC: Washington Institute for Near East Policy, 1998).

bid for the White House.[16] This point is instructive in that those neoconservatives that openly campaigned for Clinton during the 1992 Presidential Election did so with the hope of securing senior positions and thus another opportunity to take out the Iraqi leader. This pattern was again repeated after Clinton's failed covert policies to unseat the regime. Elsewhere within the bureaucracy senior military officers had ongoing discussions about the potential for war with Iraq. Beginning with General Norman Schwarzkopf's military exercises just months before Iraq's invasion of Kuwait[17] through General Tommy Franks invasion plans[18] that culminated in *Operation Iraqi Freedom*, it was clear that a host of Iraq contingencies were underway. Debates such as these were conducted among intelligence officials within the CIA, DIA, and in other areas of the intelligence community. Thus, when a second war with Iraq erupted there was little surprise among these officials (some inside the corridors of government and many former officials outside government).

The aforementioned factors demonstrate that the United States was on a collision course with Iraq. With this background concerning US presidential policies toward Iraq, and the attendant themes, viewed collectively this study involves the consideration of the following issues:

- First, the two previous presidential administrations and the thrust of their policies indicate that the momentum for a second war with Iraq existed long before the arrival of President George W. Bush. And that following the election of Bush, the administrations policies toward Iraq, both pre-11 September and with respect to post-11 September administration policy, evidence exists to substantiate the proposition that war preparations were considered and eventually implemented.
- That the course of policy formation and implementation was greatly influenced by "hawks" scattered throughout the national security bureaucracy and within the Congress that favored war with Iraq.
- That the three US presidential policies toward Iraq were themselves a product of bureaucratic infighting. Similarly, there were numerous warning signs concerning the costs of intervention and the occupation of Iraq that went unheeded or otherwise ignored; and equally significant, similar warnings (and even direct evidence) concerning the politicalization of decision making—in the areas of intelligence collection and dissemination and postwar planning, for example—the latter representing the consequences of failing to plan for peace, were issues that were features of all three administrations.
- That the evolving threat posed by Iraq forced each administration to change

---

16   See John Ehrman, *The Rise of Neoconservatism: Intellectuals and Foreign Affairs* (New Haven: Yale University Press, 1995), 137.

17   See *Newsweek*, 28 January 1990; for more information on the revamping of Pentagon strategy in early 1990, see Michael T. Klare, "Policing the Gulf – And the World," *The Nation*, 15 October 1990.

18   See Bob Woodward's *Plan of Attack* (New York: Wheeler Publishing, 2004).

US military doctrines in recognition of this eventuality and to ensure that such strategies were consistent with presidential policies toward Iraq.

- The dilemmas associated with US intelligence, including the failure to accept the validity of intelligence analysis that warned of Iraqi troop movements that pointed to an imminent invasion of Kuwait during the first Bush administration, along with the prewar intelligence failures during the second Bush administration are illustrative of the problems that hampered US decision making and ultimately US policies toward Iraq.
- There were fatal flaws concerning US presidential policies, such policies were overly depended upon errant perceptions of Iraq; Such misperceptions—such as vice president Cheney's statement that the Iraqi people will welcome US soldiers as liberators—are therefore critical in unraveling the all too many flaws involving US policies toward Iraq.
- A core element of each administration's policies involved the advancement of the cause of Middle East Peace and the export of democracy. Again, the failures to confront the realities posed by Iraq impacted these efforts as well.
- Lastly, a critical flaw that accompanied each presidential policy concerned the ongoing misperception of the "Arab Street" both prior to and in the wake of US military operations against Iraq.

Structure of the Study

The layout of the book is designed to address the aforementioned fundamental issues. In an effort to provide a comprehensive analysis of the multiple dynamics that impacted the evolution of US policy toward Iraq over the course of three presidencies, the opening section of the study begins with **Part I—The View From Washington**. This section begins with Von Hermann's analysis of the presidential decision models utilized by Bush I, Clinton, and Bush II in dealing with the threat posed by Iraq. Of particular interest the author examines the competitive and collegial models and how these approaches influenced the decision making of three presidents associated with this study; the author thereafter provides an extensive analysis of the decision making approach utilized by Bush II and how that model contributed to laying the foundations for war. The second chapter commissioned by the editor explores the controversial role of ideology and its function in the development and subsequent implementation of the US policy of regime change. This chapter's central focus concerns the neoconservative agenda and their efforts to capture a US president and thereafter fulfill their objective of regime change in Iraq and the remaking of the Middle East. In the third chapter Fisher offers a unique perspective on Congress' performance in several functions: the authorization of war in Iraq, the oversight function of presidential covert operations and intelligence. All three according to the author are critical to understanding the role (or lack thereof) of the legislative branch and how three US presidents essentially received a "pass" on Iraq. In the final chapter in this section, the editor examines the role of bureaucratic infighting and how such politics ultimately shaped three presidential policies toward Iraq. The major contention of this chapter is that each of the administration's policies is itself a product of bureaucratic infighting. Similarly, another conclusion is that the intensity of such infighting prevented US presidents from consideration of other policy options, namely an exhaustive review of Iraq policy, intelligence collection, and postwar planning.

Part II—The Diplomatic Perspective—of this study explores the diplomatic perspective of US policy toward Iraq. In the opening chapter, Pauly explores the extent to which personal diplomacy played in the development and implementation of US policy toward Iraq since 1989. Subsequently, this chapter explores the "relative strengths and weaknesses" of the use of personal diplomacy by US presidents in an effort to utilize a series of coalitions to "minimize if not preclude the threats posed by Saddam's regime to US interests in the region." In chapter six, Lansford addresses the role of three US presidents and their efforts to build coalitions to confront a series of challenges posed by Iraq. In the area of multilateral intervention in the first gulf war, the author examines the efforts of the first Bush to erect a diplomatic coalition in the UN Security Council to pass several important resolutions. And when it came to war, the author explores the senior Bush's efforts to build a large military coalition to remove Saddam from Kuwait. With respect to Clinton, the author examines this president's efforts to hold together an ever-shrinking sanctions and inspections regime. Finally, the last chapter of this section uncovers the internal decisions that in the end led to the dissipation of multilateral efforts and the ushering in of unilateralism. El-Khawas' chapter (seven) provides a vivid treatment of three US presidents and the objective of utilizing post-Iraq hostilities as a pivotal period to jump start Middle East Peace negotiations. The central objective of this study is that the US peace efforts—whether the Madrid Conference, Clinton's eleventh hour peace efforts, or "W's" Road Map did not enhance stability, but rather created instability.

The last section of this study—**Part III—The Military Dimensions**—provides a comprehensive examination of the military policies and strategies that emerged as a critical component of US policy toward Iraq. In the opening chapter, Thies examines the evolution of the US policy of containment at the close of the senior Bush administration and how Clinton proceeded to institute a "dual containment" strategy that sought to restrain both Iraq and Iran. Additionally, this study examines the shift from containment to the Bush doctrine and how the latter strategy moved the country on the road to a second war with Iraq. Brattebo's chapter explores the role of no-fly zones that were utilized to contain Iraqi militarism against the Kurds in North and the Shiites in the South. This chapter explores the costs of the no-fly zones, the movement to end them and how the use of no-fly-zones eventually became the defining "opening phase" of *Operation Iraqi Freedom*. The last chapter provides expansive coverage of the multiple military strategies that governed each of the three administrations discussed in this study. As Metz suggests, "from 1991 to 2003, the Iraq conflict validated America's assumptions about the nature of the global security environment and the appropriate strategy for it." Thus in many ways US military strategy is a by-product of the often-shifting and often-fluctuating policies of each of the US presidents and their efforts to confront the Iraqi threat.

The concluding chapter—"Getting There: The Road to and the Aftermath of the Second War in Iraq"—represents and effort to utilize content from selected chapters within this study to provide a sense of how the policies of Bush I, Clinton, and Bush II contributed to the commencement of renewed hostilities in Iraq. Second, this chapter explores the failure of lessons learned in two categories: prewar planning (war termination and postwar planning) and second, post-conflict activities (security, interagency cooperation and coalition participation and nation building) and the Bush II administrations inability to learn critical lessons concerning each doomed the postwar environment in Iraq and set the stage for the evolution of a new and more dangerous insurgency.

PART I
The View from Washington

Chapter 1

Presidential Decision-Making: Three Models and the Road to War with Iraq

Denise von Hermann

University of Southern Mississippi, Gulf Coast

Introduction

Some American foreign policy scholars have noted that the events of 11 September, 2001, began a "transformation"[1] of the Bush presidency. Viewed previously as lacking focus or clarity, the post-9/11 Bush administration took on an air of determination and certainty about its goals and how it might best achieve them. In much the same way that 9/11 brought White House foreign policy goals into perspective, the invasion of Iraq in the spring of 2003 revealed a resolute presidential team: one that appeared publicly to have fallen into near lock-step on a critical and internationally controversial policy.

By the fall of that same year, fissures began to appear. Calls for the resignation of Defense Secretary Donald Rumsfeld were prevalent, and questions about the quality and accuracy of information used to plan and execute not only the war with Iraq, but the rebuilding of Iraq as well were rampant.

Presidents, like any other managers of large and complex organizations, face myriad challenges in making key decisions. Of all decisions a president may face, arguably the decision to go to war is among the most vexing. Studying *how* a president makes such a crucial decision is highly instructive for scholars of presidential decisions, as well as for scholars of American foreign policy.

The principle focus of this chapter concerns an evaluation of the most recent case study: President George Bush and his national security team's decision to launch a full-scale assault on the regime of Iraqi President Saddam Hussein. The chapter begins with a brief overview of the previous literature on the processes by which presidents and their foreign policy teams make decisions. The chapter then provides an in-depth analysis of the last three presidents, with the major focus on George W. Bush, exploring the dynamics that contributed to the road to war in Iraq. Next, the available information regarding the actual decision to go to war with Iraq is

---

1   John Davis, "The Bush Administration Responded Appropriately to the Terrorist Attacks Against the United States," in Tom Lansford and Robert P. Watson, *Debating the War on Terror* (Dubuque, IA: Kendall-Hunt, 2003).

examined, and finally, the record on the Bush presidency is discussed and predictions for the future of the Iraq conflict are offered.

How Presidents Make Decisions

Studies of presidential decision-making during the last quarter-century have revealed three possible models: 1) centralized management through formalistic, hierarchical structures, 2) the competitive model—in which all agencies, departments, and individuals openly compete for presidential attention, and 3) the collegial models which provide for balanced, but structured debate among a relatively small circle of competing policy advocates.

Much of this line of research into presidential decision-making rests upon earlier work by Alexander George[2] concerning the links between personality and presidential decision-making. This model provides indicators on the role of the president's cognitive style, his sense of efficacy, and his level of comfort (or lack thereof) with political conflict, work together to create a unique style of making important decisions.

Another key figure in the development of the presidential decision models was Richard Johnson,[3] who examined six presidential administrations from FDR to LBJ, and discovered the three styles mentioned above. Johnson found that the formalistic approach places strong emphasis on maintaining order, and tends to be favored by presidents who wish to avoid becoming embroiled in political conflicts. Johnson points to the management style of Harry Truman, for instance, where by the president assembled a well-organized and competent staff, served as the final decision authority, and tended to stick firmly to decisions once made. A weakness of this style is its reliance upon solid and generally unified information from key advisors; when these persons disagree, the formalistic president has no sure way to process or respond to the varying opinions. The national security inner circle put together by the first President Bush, for example, has been characterized as a "closed circle" that was hindered by the president's "inability to think through, articulate, and act on a coherent vision of the larger purpose behind his frenetic activity."[4]

The competitive style, on the other hand, causes a president such as Franklin Roosevelt to assemble a team filled with persons whose views differ from his own. Typically, Roosevelt's diverse and openly competitive team would have two solid but differing opinions, and he would charge them with "weaving" these together. The failing of his style was most evident during war, when the competing factions could not come together to adequately plan and react for the longer term.

---

2   Alexander George, (*Presidential Decision-Making in Foreign Policy: The Effective Use of Information and Advice.* Boulder, CO: Westview Press, 1980).

3   Richard Johnson, *Managing the White House* (NY: Harper & Row, 1974).

4   Donald Snow and Eugene Brown, *Beyond the Water's Edge: An Introduction to US Foreign Policy* (New York, NY: St. Martin's, 1997), 122.

The collegial style of such presidents as John Kennedy and Bill Clinton also relied upon a diverse team with divergent opinions. The two presidents shared common traits and outgoing personalities. Both men loved to immerse themselves in the details of foreign policy matters, and both relied heavily upon teams of advisors who were generally more loyal to their president than to the specific agencies for which they worked.[5]

Clinton, unlike the other collegial presidents, operated in a foreign policy vacuum created by the fall of the Soviet Union and the hope that domestic agendas could supplant foreign policy concerns. President Clinton was much more likely than Kennedy to attempt to keep all of his team members happy—which some scholars trace back to his childhood attempts to placate an abusive stepfather.

A related group of studies, especially work by Fred Greenstein, arrives at similar conclusions about presidential leadership by examining presidents' leadership qualities and personal style from a political psychology perspective.[6] Greenstein examines emotional intelligence—a person's ability to control emotions and turn them to productive use—as well as cognitive style, political skill, policy vision, organizational capacity, and effectiveness as a public communicator.

Greenstein has found that the modern presidency places a premium on the external communications expected of presidents. The best public communicators among postwar presidents—Roosevelt, Kennedy, Reagan and Clinton—were all outgoing presidents, he notes. Yet, outgoing personalities often falter with respect to focus and attention to detail. They may easily become bored with routine tasks and detailed policy. He says the flawed presidencies of Lyndon Johnson, Richard Nixon, Jimmy Carter and Bill Clinton all serve as stark reminders of the effects of emotional mismanagement on presidential performance.[7]

George H.W. Bush and the First War with Iraq

The first President Bush's principal focus was foreign affairs, an area in which he was very well prepared, due to his extensive background in foreign policy. The collapse of Communism and the end of the Cold War left America trying to define a new mission for itself:

> Bush was initially criticized for his apparent lack of ideas, and he disarmingly confessed that he was not good at 'the vision thing' ... But by the summer of 1989, events in Europe

---

5   Johnson, 1974.

6   Fred I. Greenstein, "The Changing Leadership of George W. Bush: A Pre- and Post-9/11 Comparison," *Political Science Quarterly*, March 2002.

7   Fred Greenstein, *The Presidential Difference: Leadership Style From FDR to Clinton*, (NY: Free Press, 2002).

were moving so fast that 'the vision thing' became largely irrelevant. All the United States could do, in Bush's words, was encourage, guide, and manage change.[8]

The President's early policies and those of his team of foreign-policy experts led by former National Security Advisor Brent Scowcroft, reveal an internal struggle between what Scowcroft called the "traditionalists" and those who wanted a more transformational foreign policy. Where Iraq was concerned, the first Bush administration initially tried to have friendly relations: "Under National Security Directive (NSD) 26, the Bush administration's goal was to normalize relations with Iraq."[9] Iraq's invasion of Kuwait and forced the administration to rethink its policy.

Critics immediately claimed the real motive for fighting was oil. George Bush insisted he was acting to preserve national interests. Congress held extensive debates over war powers, and finally on 21 January 1991, voted to endorse the UN Security Council resolution calling for use of force. Congress refused to declare war, with votes falling primarily along partisan lines.[10] An overall Iraq policy stressing moderation, practical consideration of national interests, and a limited form of multilateralism was the ultimate approach selected by the administration. The president continued to assert, however, that he did not require congressional approval to expel Saddam Hussein from Kuwait.

Secretary of State James Baker helped the president put together a grand coalition of the willing, an informal grouping that, while clearly headed by the Americans, could nonetheless boast of support that was both deep and wide. Iraq's former ally, the Soviet Union, had voted in favor of the UN authorizing resolution, as did Cuba.

The war itself was brief, but decisive. The ground war began at 8:00 p.m. on 23 February and lasted about four days. Once the war ended, the administration worked with the United Nations to secure passage of Resolution 687, which gave the UN Special Commission broad access to sites in Iraq to search for and destroy weapons of mass destruction.

The Security Council also passed Resolution 688 to allow international relief operations for the Kurds. These actions allowed the Bush administration to proceed with a combination of military and humanitarian programs designed to severely limit Iraq's ability to cause further harm to its citizens or neighbors. Shortly before Bush left office, no-fly zones were extended in Iraq from the 33rd parallel to the southern border, even though no specific authorization for such action had come from the United Nations.[11]

Pragmatic, thoughtful, and both collegial and formalistic in his decision-making,[12] the first President Bush repeatedly demonstrated restraint in his dealings with Iraq.

---

8   Michael Howard, "The Prudence Thing: George Bush's Class Act," *Foreign Affairs* (review of Bush and Scowcroft memoir), 1998 (Nov/Dec).

9   Ryan C. Hendrickson, *The Clinton Wars: The Constitution, Congress, and War Powers* (Nashville, TN: Vanderbilt Univ. Press, 2002), 141.

10   Jean Edward. Smith, *George Bush's War* (New York: Henry Holt and Co., 1992).

11   Hendrickson, 143.

12   Snow and Brown, 120.

Yet some critics of his policies have charged that he left too much unsettled with Iraq. Margaret Thatcher, former Prime Minister of Britain, would later speak of her surprise at the war being ended with Saddam in power. President Bush and others assumed that Hussein would not survive politically in the wake of Iraq's defeat.[13]

But the president always asserted that the war had accomplished its mandate. The mission, he said, the only one approved by the Security Council, was to expel Iraq from Kuwait. President Bush considered it critical to maintain coalition unity. Obviously, keeping the Arabs from viewing the United States as an occupying force remained an important variable. Many Arab leaders showed increasing displeasure over Iraq's reduced stature and now-destroyed infrastructure. Indeed, the threat of force initially was deliberately restricted to removing the Iraqis from Kuwait, "in part because Arab coalition members would not or could not support a more ambitious threat to destroy the Iraqi regime."[14]

Bill Clinton and the Decision Not to Decide

Immediately following the war, the US and its allies had established no-fly zones in both the northern and southern regions of Iraq in order to protect Iraqi minority groups. Throughout his campaign for the presidency, Bill Clinton was critical of the Bush policy on Iraq. At one point he even claimed Bush had carried out a policy of appeasement with Iraq's leader, Saddam Hussein.[15] Thus in January of 1993, Bill Clinton took office as a president with a contained, but very volatile, relationship between Iraq and the US already well-established.

Yet foreign policy was far from a priority for the new president. The 42nd president came to the Oval Office with a clear mandate to fix the economy—something Bush had been unable to convince the voters he could do. Unlike Bush, he brought no significant foreign policy experience to the table. His eight years as governor of Arkansas gave him the credentials to talk about education, about health care, and about federalism, but he had no direct prior military or foreign affairs experience upon which to draw.

A Democratic president with new and convincing, Republican majorities in both the House and the Senate just a year after he took office, Clinton was left to shape a new foreign policy direction in the post-Cold War, post-Gulf War landscape with no clear direction from either inside or outside of the beltway. Indeed, while the Clinton administration was regularly denounced for its lack of leadership or its absence of a coherent world view on the editorial pages of major newspapers and in the elite foreign policy journals, "a second charge is equally grave: the failure to articulate foreign policy objectives clearly or to employ the various foreign policy instruments

---

13   Margaret Thatcher, *The Downing Street Years* (New York, NY: Harper Collins, 2003).

14   Barry M. Blechman & Tamara Coffman Wittes, "Defining Moment: The Threat and Use of Force in American Foreign Policy," *Political Science Quarterly* (1999): 114, 1, 15.

15   Thomas Friedman, "The 1992 Campaign," *New York Times*, 2 October 1992.

effectively in order to attain these goals."[16] Yet despite all the complaining, Congress continued its long-established pattern of deference in foreign policy.

Clinton engaged Saddam's military on numerous occasions. The first was the 1993 strike in retaliation for a failed plot to assassinate former president Bush. Another major strike occurred in 1996, when US forces struck with cruise missiles at several targets in the southern part of Iraq. While the presidential advisors were heavily involved in the decision, neither incident raised much concern from the congress.

Repeated (but limited) air strikes occurred with each violation of the no-fly zones, and there was an incessant cycle of naval buildups in response to various Iraqi refusals to meet UN requirements. As some foreign policy scholars have noted, "the American modus operandi in the Iraqi theater during the years 1992–98 (which was manifested in Washington's repeated willingness to resort to punitive military action in order to guarantee that Iraq fully complies with the United Nations Security Council resolutions),"[17] differs markedly from the last two years of the Clinton Presidency which were characterized by a less combative tone and a growing reluctance to confront powerful UN member states such as Russia and France who were growing increasingly impatient with sanctions and air strikes.

In 1998 Hussein refused to allow American team members to work with the UN Special Commission, (UNSCOM) leading President Clinton to ask the Defense Department to begin planning for military strikes. Clinton, characteristically, consulted with his foreign policy advisors. In mid-November the situation was coming to a head, and Clinton consulted with Secretary of State Albright, Defense Secretary Cohen, National Security Advisor Sandy Berger, and CIA Director George Tenet while traveling to Washington on Air Force One. The passage of a law (The Iraq Liberation Act) designed to provide support for Iraqi regime change came at the height of a year-long series of crises over UN weapons inspections in Iraq, in which inspections were repeatedly halted and restarted after mediation by the United Nations, Russia, and others. On 15 December 1998, UN inspectors were withdrawn for the final time, and a three-day US and British bombing campaign against suspected Iraqi WMD facilities followed. President Clinton then explained to Congress that "on December 16, United States and British forces launched military strikes on Iraq (*Operation Desert Fox*) to degrade Iraq's capacity to develop and deliver weapons of mass destruction (WMD) and to degrade its ability to threaten its neighbors."[18]

This time congressional reaction was mixed. On the first day of the attacks, Congress was "scheduled to begin voting on the president's impeachment for his inaccurate testimony regarding his extramarital relationship with White House intern

---

16   Linda B. Miller, "The Clinton Years: Reinventing US Foreign Policy?" *International Affairs*: (October 1994): 70, 4, and 625.

17   Abraham Ben Zvi, "The Clinton Legacy in the Middle East: Preliminary Lessons," *Strategic Assessment* (November 2000), 3.

18   William J. Clinton, "Letter to the Speaker of the House and the President Pro Tempore of the Senate," *Public Papers of the President*, 3 March 1999.

Monica Lewinsky."[19] The Administration pointed to a 15 December UNSCOM report by Chairman Richard Butler to the UN secretary-general, stating that "Iraq did not provide the full cooperation it promised on 14 November 1998. Iraq initiated new forms of restrictions upon the commission's work."[20] But speculation remained that the decision to embark on the operation was linked to the President's desire to improve his image and deflect public attention from the Lewinsky affair, in part because critical administration personnel seemed not to have been consulted on the matter.

Indeed, the US never sought a Security Council resolution in support of a military action, fearing opposition from Russia, China, and France. Instead, the US and Britain used the Butler report to justify the attack. There was concern that attacks during Ramadan might increase anti-American sentiment in the Muslim world. In all, despite a near complete lack of prior discussion with Congress, little to no support from the UN, rumbling from some disgruntled administration officials about being left out of the decision, and looming questions about personal scandals and a desire to improve the president's image, Congress supported the President overwhelmingly.

A 1999 study examining the use of force in American foreign policy discussed *Operation Desert Fox* in a postscript. Its authors noted ominously that "US unwillingness to undertake clearly and unambiguously the only potent threat in this situation—to remove Hussein by force unless he complies—suggests that the Iraqi-US conflict has not yet run its course."[21]

During 1999–2000, US efforts to rebuild and fund the Iraqi opposition did not end the debate within the Clinton Administration over the regime change component of Iraq policy. In hearings and statements, several members of both parties expressed disappointment with the Clinton Administration's decision not to give the opposition combat training or sufficient military support.

Background to War: Events Leading up to the Iraq Invasion

The second Bush administration, like the Clinton administration before it, faced a tremendous dilemma in Iraq. Existing policy had stopped working after the UN inspection team had been evicted, and the United States seemed unable to deal with Iraq's reported production of weapons of mass destruction. So, like the Clinton administration, the second Bush administration began with a policy of limited air strikes to try to contain Iraq.

Yet early on the stage was also set for a new presidential style. The new President appeared to be consciously attempting to avoid many of his father's mistakes. For example, the choice of Richard Cheney to be Vice President appears in stark contrast

---

19   Hendrickson, 155.

20   Shlomo Brom, "Operation Desert Fox: Results and Ramifications," *Strategic Assessment*: June 2002, 1.

21   Blechman & Wittes, 30.

to his father's choice of Senator Dan Quayle as a running mate.[22] The foreign policy team brings considerable experience both in Washington (Rumsfeld, Cheney, Powell, etc.) and also as high level managers in the private sector (most notably Cheney's days at Halliburton). What this means for Bush is that they are not prone to simply playing out political roles, but instead have a tendency to make decisions and to act rather quickly.[23]

According to one early observer, "Bush's personal and informal manner must not be confused with an informal approach to staff organization and interaction or decision making. Bush favors a more formal White House with more hierarchical organization. Bush insists on punctuality and the Governor of Texas would not let anyone brief him for longer than twenty minutes."[24] The key decision makers met regularly and typically all key players are given time to have their say.

Since Bush ran primarily on a domestic policy platform, and since he brought little to no personal foreign policy experience to the position, many observers initially labeled his presidency as ineffective in the foreign policy realm. Indeed, just after the terrorist attack on New York and Washington, the editorial staff at *The Economist* noted that George W. Bush was "a neophyte whose main contribution to foreign policy…was to invent ingenious ways of irritating his allies."[25]

Several scholarly and journalistic reports have described how candidate Bush assembled his foreign policy team, not to help him form his basic beliefs, but rather to provide details and context to an already-established framework of foreign policy ideas. Bush put together a team of eight GOP advisors. This group, which came to be known as the "Vulcans," was led by would-be National Security Advisor, Condoleezza Rice. Other Vulcans included Paul Wolfowitz, Richard Armitage, Robert Blackwell, Stephen Hadley, Richard Perle, Dov Zakheim, and Robert Zoellick.[26] The team was chosen primarily because its members already supported the basic tenets of Bush's own free trade, hegemonist policy positions.

Bush tends to limit himself and his administration to avoid losing the "vision thing" which so clearly dogged his father's administration. He has become almost single-minded in his pursuit of The War on Terror. This can become a weakness, however, as the nation draws ever farther from the initial emotions of 9/11 and desires from its president a more balanced set of policy objectives.

---

22   Richard Brookhiser, "Close Up: The Mind of GWB," *Atlantic Monthly*, April 2003.

23   Joseph Kahn, "Bush's Selections Signal a Widening of Cabinet's Role," *New York Times*, 31 December 2000.

24   Alexander Moens, "The Foreign Policy Decision Making Process of the George W. Bush Administration," Paper presented at the 2002 annual meeting of the International Studies Association, New Orleans, LA, 2002.

25   "A Leader is Born," *The Economist*, 24 September 2001.

26   John Dean, "An Early Assessment By Leading Presidential Scholars of George W. Bush's Presidency: Part One," 7 November 2004 Findlaw.com. Accessed 5 February 2004 at http://write.findlaw.com/dean/20031107.html.

The 9/11 attacks made foreign policy the administration's top priority and gave George W. Bush a new missionary zeal. The president's friends and advisers described the impact of September 11 on his thinking in similar terms. "I think, in his frame, this is what God has asked him to do,"[27] said one close friend. According to a senior administration official, Bush "really believes he was placed here to do this as part of a divine plan."[28] Clearly the younger Bush had a vision. What he needed was a plan.

When the President was forming his initial reactions to the 11 September attacks, he assembled all the key players at Camp David. In a show of classic collegial model process, Bush ended up going around the room and asking for all opinions. Those he took home with him and on 17 September he announced to the National Security Council his plan for war against supporters of terror in Afghanistan.[29] Bush wanted information, but was not going to be slow in making a decision.

While a majority of American citizens either agree with or are willing to acquiesce to the administration's hegemonist views, the vast majority of our traditional allies—particularly those in most of Europe—are not. In Western Europe, Bush and his foreign policy agenda have never been more unpopular, according to a major American-European poll released in September of 2003. The poll of 8,000 Americans and Europeans found 60 per cent of Americans backed their president, but only in Poland, which has a sizeable troop contingent now in Iraq, did a majority of respondents back Bush. Approval was at 16 per cent in Germany and 15 per cent in France. A full 78 per cent of Europeans polled said they thought US unilateralism posed a possible international threat over the next 10 years.[30]

The issue of a war with Iraq had initially come up in the wake of the terrorist attacks. President Bush had allowed discussion of the possibility of attacking Iraq as part of the initial phase of the war on terrorism, according to various news accounts from his advisors. When Deputy Defense Secretary Wolfowitz and others first suggested that the US go after Iraq, the team clearly debated the options and concluded that Iraq was probably not their primary mission—al Qaeda was.

Yet Wolfowitz, Rumsfield, deputy Secretary of State Armitage and over 35 others had expressed a strong desire to see Saddam Hussein ousted in a 1998 letter to then-President Bill Clinton. Writing about the President's plans a year after he was forced out of the Treasury Department, Paul O'Neill declared that the overthrow of Saddam Hussein in Iraq was "Topic A" at the first National Security Council meeting of the new administration, which he attended, on 30 January 2001. O'Neill also asserts that

27   Frank Bruni, "For President, A Mission and a Role in History," *New York Times*, 22 September 2001, A1.

28   Michael Hirsh, "America's Mission," *Newsweek*: Special Edition, 10 December 2002.

29   Ivo H. Daalder and James M. Lindsay, "The Bush Revolution: The Remaking of America's Foreign Policy," *The Brookings Institution*, May 2003.

30   Tim Harper, "Goodwill Squandered: George W. Bush Prepares to Quietly Mark 9/11 Anniversary with Little to Show for His War on Terror," *Toronto Star*, 7 September 2003.

the NSC never discussed the merits of overthrowing Saddam Hussein, or whether such a US intervention would be legitimate under international law.[31]

The general foreign policy vision of Bush and his inner circle allowed Iraq to emerge as a major threat again in the 29 January 2002 State of the Union speech, in which the President outlined the administration's view that the so-called "axis of evil"—consisting of rogue states Iraq, Iran, and North Korea—constitute a primary threat to US interests.[32]

Confusion over what exactly the administration was seeking hampered efforts to develop a coherent strategy for taking the country from a statement of policy (the "axis of evil" speech) to Saddam Hussein's ouster. In the weeks following the "axis of evil" speech, the administration did nothing to turn its words into deeds. Cheney traveled to the Middle East in March in an attempt to enlist Arab support for confronting Iraq, but his meetings were dominated instead by the escalating conflict between Israelis and Palestinians. That issue preoccupied the administration throughout the spring. Internal debate on Israel-Palestinian conflict was settled only in late June when Bush announced that American involvement in the peace process would be possible only after the Palestinians chose a new leadership that had not been "compromised by terror."[33]

Administration officials generally agreed on the need to remove Saddam from power. They disagreed, however, on how to do it. Cheney and Rumsfeld believed from the start that military force was the only option—though in the flush of the seemingly easy victory in Afghanistan they believed that the combination of precision airpower, local opposition forces, and a small number of US ground troops would suffice. Powell, in contrast, believed that if Washington convinced the international community to force Saddam to choose between his weapons or his rule, he would give up his weapons. That, in Powell's view, would weaken Saddam's hold on power and enable the Iraqi people to overthrow him.[34]

Administration officials also differed about what removing the Iraqi leader from power would accomplish. Cheney and Rumsfeld have argued that removing the Baathist regime and disarming Iraq would eliminate a significant threat to regional stability and American security. In contrast, Wolfowitz saw the opportunity to democratize Iraq as the first step to a reshaping of the greater Middle East.[35]

Many Bush administration officials at that time did not realize that the president had apparently already decided to seek Saddam's ouster. Richard Haass, the director of policy planning at the State Department and a close confident of Secretary Powell, met with Rice during the first week of July as part of regular series of meetings

---

31   Ron Suskind, *The Price of Loyalty: George W. Bush, the White House and the Education of Paul O'Neill* (New York: Simon & Schuster, 2004).

32   George W. Bush,"The President's State of the Union Address," 29 January 2002. Accessed on 20 December 2003 at http://www.whitehouse.gov/news/releases/2002/01/20020129-11.html#.

33   Daalder and Lindsay, 43.

34   Ibid. 40.

35   Ibid, 41.

they held to discuss world events and administration policy. Haass asked whether Iraq really should be front-and-center in the administration's foreign policy. Rice responded that the decision had in fact been made.[36]

As it became clear within the administration that toppling Saddam was a top priority, the debate over how it should be done grew more intense. Powell pushed the President hard, arguing that war could be avoided if the US made it clear to Iraq that it must allow UN weapons inspections and destroy any remaining weapons of mass destruction. He later recalled that there was a "realistic chance that it could have worked, if [Saddam] realized the seriousness of the president's intent."[37]

Powell made his case for coercive diplomacy in a private dinner with Bush and Rice in early August. He argued that by going to the United Nations the United States would be able to gain broad international support for the resumption of tougher inspections and, if necessary, for war. He worried that a military operation would turn the Arab world into a "cauldron."[38]

Nationalists such as Vice President Cheney made the opposite case. "I am familiar with the arguments against taking action in the case of Saddam Hussein," Cheney said. "Some concede that Saddam is evil, power hungry and a menace, but that until he crosses the threshold of actually possessing nuclear weapons, we should rule out any preemptive action. That logic seems to me to be deeply flawed."[39] Not only would weapons inspections fail, Cheney argued, but Saddam could be expected to seek domination of the entire Middle East, attempt to take control of a great portion of the world's energy supplies, and subject the United States or any other nation to nuclear blackmail.

With the administration's internal debate spilling out into public, Bush was forced to choose. In early September he essentially decided that the US would use Powell's general strategy while working toward a goal for which Cheney had argued. He went directly to the United Nations, calling upon its members to stand up to Iraq and enforce the Security Council resolutions it had previously passed. Resolution 1441, imposing tough new arms inspections on Iraq and including precise definitions of what would constitute a "material breach" passed on 8 November 2002.[40] Although some have questioned the genuineness of the administration's push for a UN resolution, Richard Haas later said that Resolution 1441 represented an extraordinary achievement. It got inspectors back in under far more demanding terms. And it didn't tie our hands. We never committed ourselves to another resolution. So it

---

36   Nicholas Lemann, "How It Came To War: When did Bush decide that he had to fight Saddam?" *The New Yorker*, 31 March 2003.

37   Richard Wolffe and Tamara Lipper, "Powell in the Bunker (Challenged Plans for Early, Small-scale War)," *Newsweek/MSNBC* on-line, accessed 24 March 2004.

38   Bob Woodward, *Plan of Attack*, Simon & Schuster, 2004, 332.

39   CNN.com. "Cheney cites 'risks of inaction' with Iraq," 27 August 2002, CNN.com/ *Inside Politics*. Accessed 4 January 2004 at http://www.cnn.com/2002/ALLPOLITICS/08/26/ cheney.iraq/.

40   United Nations Resolution 1441, 8 November 2002. Accessed on 18 December 2003 at http://www.un.int/usa/sres-iraq.htm.

was an extraordinary accomplishment. It gave tremendous legal and political and moral authority to anything that we would subsequently do. I don't see how anyone could fault that. Indeed, any problems that we have today pale in comparison to the problems we would have had if we had not done 1441.[41]

Meanwhile, visits to various intelligence agencies permitted Cheney and his closest aides to have direct exchanges with analysts, rather than asking questions of those conducting the daily brief's, who directed others to prepare responses that resulted in additional papers. According to news reports the goal was to have a free flow of information and not to intimidate the analysts, although some may well have misinterpreted questions as directives.[42]

The *Financial Times*, in a May 2003 article about the events leading to war with Iraq, has asserted that the Bush White House had made up its mind to go to war in mid-December 2002. The "internal moment," the article asserts, occurred when President Bush was briefed "on the contents of Mr. Hussein's 12,000-page declaration" regarding weapons of mass destruction, or WMDs. Bush and his top foreign policy advisors, the article asserts, felt that Hussein had "made a 'strategic decision' not to co-operate."[43]

In the end, the administration, in its 28 January 2003 State of the Union address, articulated four different reasons for going to war with Iraq: the cruelty of Saddam against his own people; his flouting of treaties and United Nations Security Council resolutions; the military threat that he poses to his neighbors; and his ties to terrorists in general and to al Qaeda in particular.[44]

Bush defined the United States' mission more broadly than on previous occasions. This mission, he said, is not just protecting the country from terrorist attacks, and not just ridding the world of "every terrorist group of global reach" (the previous formulation, which he unveiled in his speech on 20 September 2001), but "confronting and defeating the man-made evil of international terrorism." By dropping the qualifying clause "of global reach," he gave the United States enough doctrinal space to declare war, if it wishes, on purely regional overseas terrorist organizations, like Hamas, Islamic Jihad, and the Al Aqsa Martyrs.[45]

These objectives had been clearly spelled out in the 33-page National Security Strategy (NSS) document for 2002, offering the administration's first comprehensive rationale for a new, aggressive approach to national security. The strategy called for preemptive action against hostile states and terror groups. It stated that the US "will

---

41   Lemann.

42   Walter Pincus and Dana Priest, 3 "Some Iraq Analysts Felt Pressure From Cheney Visits." *Washington Post*, 5 June 2000, A01.

43   Quentin Peel, Robert Graham, James Harding, and Judy Dempsey, "How the US Set a Course for War with Iraq," *Financial Times*, 26 May 2003.

44   Lemann, Nicholas. 2003, "After Iraq: The plan to remake the Middle East," *New Yorker*, 17 February 2003.

45   Ibid., 2003.

not hesitate to act alone, if necessary, to exercise our right of self-defense by acting preemptively."[46]

A little over one month following the State of the Union speech, Chief UN weapons inspector Hans Blix reported that Iraq had begun to destroy its Al Samoud missiles. The US delegation to the United Nations stepped up its efforts to press Security Council members to vote in favor of a US-UK proposal authoring military intervention, but only Spain and Bulgaria are reported to have agreed. The US had fallen five votes short of the needed nine votes.

As promised, the US did not hesitate to act alone, and on 19 March 2003, a US-led force began its invasion under the banner *Operation Iraqi Freedom*. Baghdad fell on 29 April and by 1 May the US declared that major hostilities had ended.

After the War: Reflections on the Decision Process

The hybrid Collegial-Hierarchical style of President Bush should have served him well in deciding to go to war. Scholars have noted that the collegial model has worked well under optimal circumstances

> …but in the absence of a coherent presidential vision…runs the risk of excluding outside views and miring the president in the 'trees' of specific issues without providing an overall map of the foreign policy forest he intends to nurture.[47]

George W. Bush had a strong vision and was easily able to share it with key policy officials in his administration. Indeed, the President has consistently asserted the correctness of his policies regarding Iraq, even in the face of tremendous criticism from the international community, from Congressional Democrats, and even from a few key Congressional Republicans.

Was the model a success for the Bush war team? Certainly more time and information will be needed to fully assess this issue. Yet it is clear that the decision to go to war itself appears strongly related both to Bush's personal style and to the inherent flaws of the collegial model. Although much of the internal workings of the Bush national security team's Iraq war decisions are still not publicly known, the available evidence does point to a tendency of team members to work in a generally closed system, where information flowed within the circle, but conflicting information was only rarely allowed inside. In addition, Bush's own insistence upon formality and group cohesion likely lead even those within the group—such as Secretary of State Powell—to self-censor their comments in order to remain within the inner circle.

A year after he made an impassioned speech before the UN Security Council, Powell told a *Washington Post* reporter that he might not have supported the war if

---

46   George W. Bush. *National Security Strategy*, 2002. Accessed 5 February 2004 at http://www.whitehouse.gov/nsc/nss.html.

47   Snow and Brown. 1997, p. 128.

he had been presented with clear evidence that WMDs did not exist in Iraq. However, Powell added that the American people will understand "with that body of evidence, that was the information and intelligence that was available to the president at that time, the president made a prudent decision."

Even those who are generally supportive, such as Donald Kettl, note that Bush's decision to take his concerns about Saddam Hussein into a full-scale military conflict is "stunning in terms of its daring and boldness."[48]

The Bush administration has also generally been praised for its assertion that the "trinity of terrorists, tyrants, and technologies of mass destruction"[49] is the principal threat to American security. Yet the administration's strategy, and particularly the Bush Doctrine itself, remain very much in question. These problems may well lie beyond the reach of individual states, and terrorists are clearly able to wreak havoc long after the states which sponsor them have been overthrown.

Prospects for Bush's Second Term

President Bush's decision to invade Iraq despite overwhelming opposition to his plans abroad "provoked complaints that great power was being wielded without great responsibility, followed by an unprecedented collapse of support for the United States abroad. From nearly universal sympathy in the weeks after 11 September, Americans within a year and a half found their country widely regarded as an international pariah."[50] A major challenge for his second term will be rebuilding the US' role as legitimate leader among nations.

Nascent efforts by Bush to achieve broader support bring him ever closer to a decision style that is reflective of his father and his predecessor. But while Bush "41" was a master at the art of building coalitions while maintaining US sovereignty, and Clinton "42" was sometimes charged with refusing to lead in the absence of clear international support, the internal dynamics of the second-term Bush "43" administration will surely change now that Colin Powell is no longer a player.

Political pressures have also come to bear upon the second-term presidency. The war lasted much longer, and was much more costly in both human and economic terms than the administration had predicted. Early in 2004, even leading conservative Republicans, such as columnist George Will, were criticizing both the Iraq war and the larger goal of democratizing the Middle East. Rising oil prices through the start of his second term make potential charges over "war for oil" much more salient.

---

48   Craig Gilbert, "What if Bush's Style Flops? Training Will Mean Great Success, or Abject Failure," (Milwaukee) *Journal-Sentinel* online, 8 March 2003. Accessed 2 February 2004 at http://www.jsonline.com/news/nat/mar03/124065.asp.

49   Daalder and Lindsay, 47.

50   John Lewis Gaddis, "Grand Strategy in the Second Term," *Foreign Affairs*, (Jan/Feb, 2005).

In the first State of the Union speech following his re-election, Bush shifted his focus from a go-it-alone approach, vowing to build alliances and co-operate with allies.

Bush also issued warnings to Syria and Iran to stop supporting terrorism. These new potential Middle East conflicts pose the greatest opportunity for the Bush foreign policy to test its more inclusive approach.

The most revealing insight into a potential shift in the administration's articulation of foreign policy, at least in tone, came from Condoleezza Rice in her confirmation appearance before the Senate Foreign Relations committee: "Our interaction with the rest of the world must be a conversation, not a monologue," Rice said, adding "the work that America and our allies have undertaken, and the sacrifices we have made, have been difficult and right. Now is the time to build on these achievements to make the world safer, and to make the world more free."

The world is reportedly watching to see if the change is real. Harvard's Joseph Nye wrote in a recent opinion piece that Bush now "seems to realize that hard power alone will not consolidate his reputation, but he remains hostage to incidents and accidents that could drive even his best-laid plans off course."[51] Thus, Bush has pursued multilateral talks on Iran, and has asked Congress for increased funding for key State Department initiatives. While during his first term his administration committed itself strongly to a particular foreign policy—that of unilateral pre-emptive action—this foreign policy has not ultimately proven vastly successful either abroad or at home. With the election of a new Iraqi government, the pressure to withdraw US troops now comes from three sides: from the insurgents, from the new Iraqi government, and from public opinion. Similar pressures kept his father and his immediate predecessor from engaging in broadly ideological foreign policies, and forced both to seek input from a relatively wide circle of advisors. Increasingly, George W. Bush seems destined to do the same.

Conclusion

The problem of Iraq has been a vexing one throughout the presidential administrations of George H.W. Bush, William Clinton, and George W. Bush. The decision styles of each president have shaped American foreign policy not only in Iraq, but in all areas these administrations have associated with "terrorist activities" or "human rights abuses." As the United States holds deposed Iraqi leader Saddam Hussein and contemplates potential human rights criminal charges against him, it is instructive to note that in the span of two decades he managed to move from the status of US ally in the Iran-Iraq war to the primary target of a major military offensive to oust his government.

While the first President Bush viewed containment as a key objective, President Clinton attempted to hold Hussein within boundaries that were increasingly fluid.

---

51   Joseph Nye, "Bush Goes Soft During Second Term," *Korea Herald*, 28 February 2005.

Bush's limited objective in pushing Iraq out of Kuwait was based upon his well-documented cautious and traditional foreign policy-making style. His failure to get a handle on "the vision thing" likely contributed to the lasting and unresolved issues that were left to his successor. As noted above, President Clinton's incessant use of coercive diplomacy failed to achieve the major American objectives, namely to contain the Iraqi leader inside the no-fly zone and to eliminate the chance that he was rebuilding his weapons stocks. But again, Clinton's actions make sense in light of his decision-style, which appears to be based upon assuring that major disagreements be avoided through sometimes excessive collegiality and rare exercises of true authority.

Finally, President George W. Bush brought his own personal history and decision style to the White House and to his foreign policy initiatives. Consciously trying to avoid his father's mistakes, yet determined to organize a hierarchical and efficient policy process, Bush seemed destined to act more decisively and with greater scope (though before 9/11 most assumed those actions would be primarily in the domestic policy sphere). After terrorist attacks gripped the national conscience, Bush strode confidently and assertively into the foreign policy arena, launching successive wars against first Afghanistan and later Iraq, instituting an entirely new foreign policy platform of preemptive military action, and finally toppling the regime that had both directly and indirectly tarnished both his father's and his predecessors' presidential legacies.

Chapter 2

The Ideology of War:
The Neoconservatives and the Hijacking
of US Policy in Iraq

John Davis
Howard University

Introduction

Three American Presidents—George H.W. Bush, Bill Clinton, and George W. Bush—pursued disparate military strategies to confront the divergent threats posed by Iraq's Saddam Hussein. For the elder Bush, he employed a multilateral approach augmented by Security Council approval to "use force."[1] With the support of the international community President Bush commenced *Operation Desert Storm* to eject Iraq from Kuwait.

The latter two presidents employed divergent strategies that shifted from traditional American diplomacy and decision making that resulted in the use of force without UN approval. The consequences of these actions produced condemnation from the international community. In the first example, as the Lewinsky scandal entered the impeachment phase in the House of Representatives, President Clinton launched a unilateral air campaign (*Operation Desert Fox*) that was intended to degrade Saddam's WMD capability and to force the return of UN weapons inspectors. In the case of President George W. Bush, *Operation Iraqi Freedom* commenced with the ostensible purpose of forcing Iraqi compliance with United States Security Council (UNSC) Resolution 1441. Consistent with Clinton, Bush launched a unilateral action that was viewed by domestic and international critics as a violation of international law.[2] The intervention strategy employed by the Bush administration was however far more egregious due in part because the administration invaded a sovereign state in the absence of Security Council support and was belittled further when coalition forces were unable to locate weapons of mass destruction.

In each of the aforementioned cases a small group endeavored to impact US policy. In the pages that follow this chapter is less about the success or failure of

---

1   See text of UNSCR 678, 29 November 1990.

2   Duncan J. Currie LL.B. (Hons.) LL.M, "'Preventive War' and International Law After Iraq," 22 May, 2003. www.globelaw.com/Iraq/Preventive_war_after_iraq.htm. Downloaded on October 2004.

American presidential actions in Iraq but is rather an effort to chart the ascension of the neoconservatives' war ideology and their search for a president to launch their crusade for regime change in Iraq and regional democratic transformation of the Middle East. The chapter begins with the humble beginnings of a nascent war ideology and the neoconservative search for a president to aide their cause. Thereafter the author examines the role of the neoconservatives participation in three administrations—Bush I, Clinton, and "W"—and their efforts to impart an aberrant war ideology whose ultimate objective concerned the capture of US Iraq policy.

Reagan, the Cold War and Iraq: Neoconservative Optimism and Defeat in the Midst of Evolution

German émigré Leo Strauss long ago laid the foundations for the neoconservative movement. For Strauss the goal of the neoconservative movement was not just to reform the Republican Party but to reform the political culture of the United States itself.[3] Specifically, Strauss railed against liberal academicians and their efforts to ostracize those individuals beholden to the neoconservative philosophy. Additionally, Strauss recognized that confronting liberalism required the transformation of Republican philosophy. Having completed this transformation of the Republican elite, the larger objective said Strauss was to end the liberal dominance of the US body politics and thereafter saving America.[4]

One of Strauss' disciplines, Irving Kristol, has been dubbed the modern intellectual leader of the neoconservative philosophy. In an unusual paradox, Kristol drew on the lessons of Leon Trotsky. This point requires clarification. As stated by Kristol, "The neoconservatives are the political intellectuals, and that's what the Trotskyites were."[5] In this analysis Kristol asserts that while Trotsky spoke of the "export of Communism", his group, the neocons, believed that the US should actively "export Democracy" as a counter to Soviet adventurism. As to when this group made their convergence to the Republican Party, Patrick Buchanan makes a revealing observation regarding the evolution and rise of this faction: "When the Democratic Party was captured by McGovern in 1972 these Cold War liberals found themselves isolated and ignored in their own party. Adrift, they rafted over to the Republican

---

3   Leo Strauss, *Natural Right and History* (Chicago:University of Chicago Press,1990); and see also Shadia B. Drury, "Saving America: Leo Strauss and the Neoconservatives," http://www.informationclearinghouse.info/article6750.htm. This article was retrieved on 26 October 2005.

4   Shadia Drury, "Saving America: Leo Strauss And the Neoconservatives," http://www.informationclearinghouse.info/articels6750.htm. Retrieved on 26 October 2005.

5   Gary Dorrien, *The Neoconservative Mind: Politics, Culture, and War of Ideology* (Philadelphia: Temple University Press, 1993), 68.

Party and were pulled aboard as conservatism's long voyage was culminating in the triumph of Reagan."[6]

Even in their infancy, in the words of Kristol, the neocons had an ultimate goal— to capture the Republican Party:

> The historical task and political purpose of the neoconservatism would seem to convert the Republican Party and American conservatism in general, against their wills, into a new kind of conservative politics suitable to governing a modern democracy.[7]

While Kristol may have been the intellectual guru of this political band, the agenda of the group was advanced by Albert Wohlstetter and his protégé Richard Perle, who would later be introduced to Paul Wolfowitz and James Woosley. The three were neighbors in Chevy Chase, Maryland, and according Elizabeth Drew, worked on many panels and served together on numerous commissions.[8]

These individuals and other members of this clique were referred to as "Scoop Jackson Democrats"—named after the late Senator Henry Jackson, who was known to hold strong anti-Soviet views. It is during this period (the 1980s) that the war ideology began to take shape.

The neocon war ideology during the Cold War consisted of the following components: First, like Secretary of State John Foster Dulles, this group called for rollback of the Soviet Empire and an end to Moscow's adventurism; second, this group opposed nuclear disarmament talks and deterrence and openly campaigned for a strategy to "fight and win a nuclear war"; third, they opposed détente and preferred a more confrontational approach to dealing with the Soviet Union. Fourth, they believed that multilateralism, particularly through the UN represented an inhibiter to US policy initiatives and therefore this group called for unilateralism, asserting that American military power used correctly could serve the purpose of promoting US national interests and thus a force for good in the world. Fifth, the vast majority of the group is highly supportive of Israel and untrusting of the "so-called moderate Arabs" in the region, principally, Saudi Arabia, Jordan and Egypt. Finally, and of interest to this study, while serving in the Carter administration and later in the Reagan administration, elements of this group recognized as early as 15 June 1979 that Iraq represented a threat to US policy and had to be dealt with.

Led by Wolfowitz, at the time a Pentagon analyst, a group of mid-level analysts (others include the likes of Dennis Ross and Geoffrey Kemp) were tasked to lead a "top secret study" titled "Capabilities for Limited Contingencies in the Persian Gulf." This study concluded that Iraq represented a threat to the regional states of Kuwait and Saudi Arabia and thus US oil interests. Based on the analysis of regional history, the group presciently concluded that it was only a matter of time before

---

6 Patrick J, Buchanan, *Where The Right Went Wrong* (New York: St. Martin's, 2005), 37.

7 Buchanan, 39.

8 Elizabeth Drew, *Fear and Loathing in George Bush's Washington* (New York: New Review of Books, 2004), 20–39.

Iraq attacked Kuwait. In a revised study, the group boldly asserted that "If the US were to intervene at all, it would be desirable to do so early in the crisis, before hostilities began, and while escalation might still be avoided."[9] The plan required the development of several contingencies, the most important of which called for rapid reaction forces to forestall any preemptive strike by Iraq. The goal of this study was clarified by the following quote: "We should make manifest our capabilities and commitments to balance Iraq's power—and this may require an increased visibility for US power."[10]

Having submitted the document, then Secretary of Defense Harold Brown quickly dismissed the study arguing that Iran not Iraq was the biggest threat to the region and US oil interests.[11] The document was then placed in a draw and remains classified to this day (This was and still is a typical bureaucratic response to a position paper or study that is out of step with a presidential policy or agenda).

In 1982 as the head of the policy planning staff at the State Department, Wolfowitz again turned his attention to Iraq. According to Charles Mann,

> [he] was taking American foreign policy several steps beyond the usual Cold War thinking of the era. When he studied the Persian Gulf in the late 1970s, Wolfowitz had started out with the predictable cold war anxieties about a Soviet drive toward the oil fields of the Middle East, but he then had gone on to focus on a different possibility, the prospect that Iraq might try to dominate the oil fields by invading its neighbors.[12]

In another example, a frustrated Perle became a major advocate of what amounted to the initial phase of the regime change debate. This debate increased after 1986 (more will be said on this point in the Bush I section). In spite of the Iraq initiatives, the neocon agenda was advanced by President Ronald Reagan whose policies fit their plans. This statement is buttressed by a statement by John Erhman, who asserted that Reagan's election victory "fulfilled several neoconservative hopes" particularly in "the overriding importance of resisting Soviet expansionism and Third World leftism."[13]

Equally significant, this group was well positioned within the administration to implement Reagan's policies. A few examples are instructive. One of the most influential members of the group during the Reagan administration was Wolfowitz, who held a number of posts: 1981–82: head of state department policy planning staff, 1983–86; Assistant Secretary for East Asian and Pacific Affairs, and at the close of the administration he held the position of US Ambassador to Indonesia.

---

9   Michael Gordon and Bernard E. Trainor, *The Generals' War: The Inside Story of the Conflict in the Gulf* (Boston: Little Brown, 1995), 8.

10   Ibid.

11   Ibid.

12   See James Mann, *Rise of Vulcans: History of Bush's War Cabinet* (New York: Viking Press, 2004).

13   John Ehrman, *The Rise of Neoconservatism: Intellectuals and Foreign Affairs* (New Haven: Yale University Press, 1995), 137.

Other notables include, Perle who served in the Pentagon as the Assistant Secretary of Defense, Jeanne Kirkpatrick as the US Ambassador to the United Nations, Elliott Abrams who served over at State as the Assistant Secretary for Latin America; and Kenneth Adelman who held posts at the UN and the State Department.

This faction within the Republican Party was instrumental in shaping Reagan's first term agenda and his international image. Dubbed the "cowboy" or "the warmonger", internationally many feared the president both for his discordant rhetoric and his policies. Some twenty years later the neocons would again assist in the development of the persona of another US president—George W. Bush.

Though a relatively small minority, the neocons proved beneficial to the Reaganites. Similarly, the neocons and the traditional conservatives were often united by the cause of the defeat of communism. Throughout what was dubbed "Cold War II" the neocons and traditional conservatives were in an uneasy alliance. The Reagan Doctrine, the trillion dollar modernization of the US conventional and nuclear forces, research on the STAR WARS Defense shield and calls for Gorbachev to "tear down this wall"—a reference to the Berlin Wall—aided their cause. Additionally, in an adroit move the neocons utilized such organizations as Clear and Present Danger (Here the articles of journalist Norman Podhoretz were instrumental) and the Committee for the Free World, along with the *Weekly Standard, Commentary, National Review* and the *National Interest* to promote their causes when in the view of both "the neocon insiders and outsiders," Reagan was faltering or "other elements" within the administration were blocking their initiatives. In short, what might be described as the second generation of neocons elevated a once floundering political theory to a level of operationalization that seemed unimaginable to their critics.[14]

During the second term of the Reagan administration the neocon strategy began to dissipate. The arrival of Mikhail Gorbachev signaled that a new era in the superpower relationship was about to commence. Indeed, the new Soviet leader was instrumental in the transformation of Reagan's worldview.[15] Thus in the course of two years, the neocon war ideology existed no more. The Reagan administration had confronted the Soviets in the periphery, but for the neoconservatives the task was incomplete. That said Reagan's about face ended their influence and desire of witnessing the death of a communist empire that for decades had handcuffed US foreign policy. The resulting superpower summits sealed their fate. Paradoxically, individuals who once used the term "neo-Reaganites"—in respect to the leader who had once championed their causes—had now become the source of their criticism. In one example, Frank Gaffney observed that "Reagan's endorsement of [the] START process was the worst strategic blunder by any American president since the Yalta Accords."[16] Such criticism drew counter claims that the neoconservatives were out of step with the conservative movement, or in the view of others, they were lost in a

---

14   Stefan Halper and Jonathan Clarke, "Twilight of the Neocon: Perle has Begun to Panic," *Washington Monthly*. www.washingtonmonthly.com/features/2004/0403.clarke.html.

15   Dorrien, *The Neoconservative Mind*, 324.

16   Ibid, 13.

cold war time warp. In the twilight of the Reagan presidency many neoconservatives left the administration, hoping to reemerge under another Republican presidency that advanced their agenda.

From Ascension to Bystanders to Detractors: The Neocons and the Elder Bush

In this section the author examines the evolution of the neoconservative war ideology; this time the focus shifted from the former Soviet Union to one of its former client states, Iraq.

With the superpower ideological struggle entering its twilight phase, the neocons had several issues to contend with. First with the Soviet Union in chaos, and their adventurism checked by the Reagan Doctrine, the neocons were in a quandary: a global democratic movement was underway, and second, with the cold war ebbing they were loosing the central framework of their war ideology, an enemy. After nearly a decade of pontificating about the Soviet threat, the neocons were confronting another dilemma: exile. Thus while members of the flock held high ranking positions within the administration of President George H. W. Bush they were at best bystanders: no influence (until Iraq attacked Kuwait) and operating in an administration that lacked a vision and without any ideological zeal.[17]

To be sure a new era in American foreign policy had begun. In a world adrift the new president floundered in his efforts to discern its course, preferring a day to day management of recurring crises rather than defining how the United States would lead a world in disorder.[18] This too posed a problem for the neocons: no enemy, unsure of their footing and ultimately, no influence within the administration. Those outside the administration had little trouble criticizing the Bush administration. In the final analysis, with no discernable American adversary, the neocons and their ideology were out of step with the evolving international realities.

The harsh anti-Reagan criticism that commenced at the close the Reagan era did not serve the interests of the neocons. In fact, a hangover effect existed within the new administration. That said another issue emerged during the Reagan era that impacted subsequent Presidents (Bush I and Clinton) and reached its apex during the administration of George W. Bush. Within the national security bureaucracy their was recognition that the neocons were known for their strength of ideas but with respect to bureaucratic politics, they were often perceived as fanatical, indeed ruthless when it came to promoting their agenda. Indeed, anyone, even if was the president, that was not in step with their agenda the neocons wasted little to time to thwart opponent policy initiatives, or when appropriate, their allies not in government would use their network of journals, newspapers, or access to the broadcast media to ridicule their positions. Such politics had a lasting character. As Dorrien writes,

---

17   See Michael Mandelbaum, "The Bush Foreign Policy," *Foreign Affairs*, America and the World/1990/91.

18   See Lawrence Freedman, "Order and Disorder The New World," *Foreign Affairs*, America and the World/1991/92.

The resentment they inspired during the Reagan presidency did not pass, however—even after a new president wiped the appointment slate clean. With a few exceptions, George Bush studiously avoided the neoconservatives.[19]

The subject of Iraq, interesting enough, provides an illustration of this point. Concerned with the burgeoning threat of Shiite fundamentalism, beginning in 1986 the Reagan administration sided with Iraq in their war with Iran. Not only did the administration provide intelligence on Iranian troop movements, the administration supplemented this assistance by selling "dual use" items to the regime of Saddam Hussein.

This policy decision awakened the neocons within the Reagan administration. Perle led a major bureaucratic fight over US Iraq policy. It should be noted that State, the CIA, and the White House were in agreement that the sales should be approved and any "export-import" regulations should be lifted in cases where such sales could impact of the security of Israel. Perle asserted that "Iraq is a problem country" and an ally of the Soviet Union. Equally significant Perle offered a caveat: the sale of formally prohibitive material could only assist the regime in their development of nuclear, chemical, and biological weapons. He offered one additional argument. In a meeting with then Secretary of Defense Casper Weinberger, Perle noted that in an effort to 'protect our national security interests' it is necessary to tighten all "export controls on Iraq."[20] Like others (mid level officials) throughout the national security bureaucracy Perle asserted that the lifting of the export controls occurred after the administration made the foolish mistake of taking Iraq off the list of sponsors of state terrorism..

After the neoconservative position was exposed, Secretary of State George Shultz, in recognition of an evolving bureaucratic dispute, wrote a terse letter to Weinberger intended to reign in Perle. The letter warned of "impractical positions" that are disrupting US policy towards Iraq.[21] In the end Perle lost the bureaucratic dispute, but left these words that signified that the neocons were not through with Iraq:

> Iraq continues to actively pursue an interest in nuclear weapons, that the large number of Warsaw Pact nationals in Iraq makes diversion in place a real possibility and that in the past, Iraq has been somewhat less than honest in regard to the intended end-use of high technology equipment.[22]

This statement is significant for two reasons. First, it illustrates the unrelenting nature of the neocons; that is, even when it appeared they were defeated, this group took steps to lay the foundations for a future dispute, one which, aided by the events

---

19   Dorrien, 13.

20   Bruce Jentleson, *With Friends Like These: Reagan, Bush and Saddam, 1982–1990* (New York: WW Norton, 1994), 51–2.

21   Ibid.

22   Ibid.

of 11 September, would thrust them into the pivotal position of directing US policy toward Iraq. Second, the unwillingness to end the debate when it appeared they lost (keep in mind the defense department was admonished over its obstruction of high technology sales to Iraq) angered traditional conservatives that were more amenable to the realist approach. Additionally, insiders charged that the neocons within the administration were not team players and instead were labeled as obstructionists.

To his credit President Bush endeavored to end the factional rift among the conservatives (traditional conservatives, neoconservatives and the paleconsrvatives) that quarreled and often caused inertia in the implementation of Reagan's foreign policy. Still, the president lamented and filled several vacancies with neoconservatives. This decision would impact the president's handling of *Operation Desert Shield*, *Operation Desert Storm* and the aftermath of the war with Iraq. Those receiving appointments include Bill Kristol, Wolfowitz, Bernard Aronson, and Constance Horner to name a few.

Most interesting, no overt war ideology existed during the early period of the Bush administration, and this greatly impacted the neoconservatives. This point is instructive. They entered the Reagan bureaucracy with a well thought out strategy but as the Cold War dissipated the neoconservatives were busy during the first two years of the Bush administration developing and later refining a new war ideology that centered not on the Soviet Union but a regional threat: Saddam Hussein.

In order to shift the focus to Iraq, the neocons had to overcome a major hurdle: the accomodationist approach towards Iraq. That is, Reagan adopted a strategic approach. This strategy used Iraq as a buffer to prohibit the spread of the Islamic (Shiite) revolution that commenced under the Ayatollah Ruhollah Khomeni. Reagan's successor, President Bush, with the assistance of National Security Directive (NSD)-26, endeavored to go beyond the Reagan model. Signed by Bush in October 1989 the new directive (NSD-26) went beyond the basic Reagan objective of economic, military, and political assistance to Iraq. Bush intended to utilize the directive to "propose economic and political incentives for Iraq to moderate its behavior and to increase our influence with Iraq" [23] and the policy will "serve our longer-term interests and promote stability in both the gulf and the Middle East."[24] Perhaps more troubling is the directive authorized the administration to "pursue, and seek to facilitate, opportunities for U.S. firms to participate in the reconstruction of the Iraqi economy."[25] Additionally, the directive authorized joint U.S- Iraq military exercises. Unfortunately, this directive became the means by which some three dozen US commercial industries used as a cover to sell millions of dollars worth of technology

---

23   As quoted in Jentleson. To read the full text of the declassified directive, go to http://www.fas.org/irp/offdocs/nsd/nsd26.pdf.
24   Ibid.
25   Ibid.

and military hardware to the regime of Saddam Hussein. As a result of the latter, the administration had to confront an ever widening scandal: "Iraq-Gate."[26]

The Bush administration's policy toward Iraq ended abruptly following Saddam Hussein's invasion of Kuwait. Congressional critics from both sides of isle and the neoconservatives questioned administration policy. Indeed the thrust of this criticism was directed at NSD-26. The administration responded that the directive had a contingency to deal with unforeseen actions on the part of the Iraq. As Secretary of State James Baker explained in his memoirs, "NSD-26 provided for rescinding or curtailing our ties."[27] The contingency Baker spoke of concerned the use of weapons of mass destruction, but the directive did not envision an aggressive Iraqi move to attack a sovereign state. In other words, in spite of administration pretensions the reality is they were caught off guard, even ignoring intelligence of a pending Iraqi invasion of Kuwait.[28]

Thereafter administration policy shifted to a multilateral approach to end the crisis and it was later supplemented by rudimentary war aims: the removal of Iraqi forces from Kuwait, reduction of Iraq's offensive military capacity so that it could not threaten its neighbors, protect westerners being held as human shields, and securing the world's oil supply. The multilateral approach included the use of United Nations sanction's to assist the Bush administrations quest for international support as well as to provide cover for a large multilateral coalition. The use of the UN angered the neoconservatives who were averse to the use of this organization because it slowed the American-led action and provided too many countries—Russia and France, to be sure—with the right to veto administration actions.

The neoconservatives had another issue with the Bush administration: the president refused to explicitly state that they intended to remove Saddam Hussein. The president repeatedly rejected this idea and continued to restate the standard line: the UN did not authorize the removal of Saddam. This point is confirmed by Secretary Baker, but as the following statement indicates this issue infuriated opponents of the presidents decision.

> To this day, controversy endures over whether coalition forces should have continued their offensive all the way to Baghdad and topple Saddam's regime. I believe this idea is as nonsensical now as it was then, and not merely for the narrow legalistic reason that the UN resolutions did not authorize coalition forces to undertake anything beyond the liberation of Kuwait. The entire truth embodies strategic, pragmatic, and political aspects

---

26   For more on this point, see the following works, Robert Hennelly, "Anatomy of a Scandal: How Bush Armed Saddam, Then Painted Him as Hitler and Called for War," *Village Voice,* 11 August 1992, 23–31 and Thomas Blanton, Editor, *White House E-mail: The Top Secret Messages the Reagan/Bush White House Tried to Destroy,* (New York: New Press, 1995).

27   James A. Baker, *The Politics of Diplomacy: Revolution, War and Peace, 1989–1992* (New York: G.P. Putnam's Sons, 1995), 264.

28   Gordon and Trainor, *The Generals' War,* 4–6.

that prompted the President's decision not to go to Baghdad—an absolutely correct judgment on which there was virtually no debate.[29]

This statement did not end the controversy. Moreover, administration actions throughout the war along with statements during the postwar period were indicative of an implicit policy of regime change. Two examples exemplify the point. Irrespective of the public and private statements it was clear that the Bush administration had authorized several plans to eliminate the Iraqi leader. In short, the administration never expected Saddam to survive the conflict. With respect to this point, Baker elicits this contradictory statement:

> It's important to recall that, while it would have been welcome, Saddam's departure was never a stated objective of our policy. We were always very careful to negate it as a war aim or political objective. At the same time, we never really expected him to survive a defeat of such magnitude.[30] As to the strategy of regime change during the war, the administration employed two contingencies. On the first, CENTCOM had considered the use of special operation forces to "assassinate Hussein."[31] Second, on the final night of the air campaign the Air Force delivered two 5,000 pound "special bunker buster" missiles whose task was to destroy hardened strategic command facilities frequented by the Iraqi leader in Northwestern Baghdad.[32]

For the neocons, the administration decision to end the war early prompted Wolfowitz to a mount a bureaucratic effort within the Pentagon, but the generals asserted— Chairman of the Joint Chiefs of Staff General Colin Powell and CENTCOM Commander General Norman Schwarzkopf—that the administrations goals were achieved and it was therefore time to conclude the war.[33] This setback was tempered by the Bush administrations overt and indeed explicit effort of regime change in Iraq. The source of this enthusiasm followed the president's statement on 15 February 1991 in which Bush enlisted "the Iraqi military and the Iraqi people to take matters in their

---

29   Baker, 436.

30   Ibid, 442.

31   See my chapter, "The War on Terrorism and President Bush: Completing His Fathers Legacy and Defining His Own Place in History," in Patrick Hayden and Robert Watson, *America's War on Terrorism* (London: Ashgate, 2003), 43–53; and see the following sources for other relevant information. On the plans to kill the Iraqi leader, see, "The Plan to Kill Saddam Hussein," *Newsweek*, 10 January 1994, V. 123, no. 2, 4–5; Janet L. Seymour, *Operation Provide Comfort* (Alabama: Maxwell Air Force, 2001).

32   See, *US News and World Report: Triumph Without Victory: The Unreported History of the Persian Gulf War* (New York: Times Books, 1992), viii, and In another example of the efforts to kill Hussein in his command bunkers, see Walter Pincus, "Saddam Hussein's Death is a Goal, Says Ex-CIA Chief; Bush Advisers Hoped that Collateral Damage Would Include Iraqi Leader," *Washington Post*, 15 February 1998.

33   For more on this point, see Baker, 410 and 435, and Gordon and Trainor, *The Generals' War*, 475–7.

own hands, to force Saddam Hussein, the dictator, to step aside."[34] The president offered a subsequent statement that reinforced the view that this was indeed an overt campaign orchestrated in Washington to end the regime: "The Iraqi people should put him aside and that would facilitate the resolution of these problems that exist, and certainly would facilitate the acceptance of Iraq back into the family of peace loving nations."[35] These statements and the fact that Wolfowitz was aware of "secret contingency plans by members of Schwarzkopf's staff to take Baghdad"[36] cooled the internal neocon criticism of the administration (This dampened but did not end the criticism of those neoconservatives that were outside the administration). The "Iraqi people" the president spoke of consisted of the Shiites and the Kurds. The results of the president's rhetoric however were not backed by the intent to employ US military forces to assist the opposition forces. These forces were subsequently slaughtered. The neoconservatives were again angered by administration policy and they targeted three individuals: President Bush, Chairman of Joints Chiefs of Staff Colin Powell and CENTCOM Commander General Schwarzkopf.

In the case of President Bush the neocons had had enough. The criticism of the presidents handling of Iraq came in two forms. Joshua Muravchik noted that "Bush kept democracy off the Desert Storms agenda."[37] Other criticisms were more in-depth and therefore are indicative of the neoconservative grievances against the elder Bush. According to Michael Novak, "He [Bush] tried to govern without providing meaning. He was a good man and even exhibited in the Gulf War preeminently, touches of greatness. But he eschewed meaning. He was averse to vision and people of vision [a reference to the neocons]—and ultimately, this was the flaw that did him in. He misunderstood the presidential office."[38] This statement represented an effort to assert that even in his successes in Iraq the president did so in the absence of a vision and only remotely accepted the neoconservative agenda (a reference at least to confronting Iraq, without a concomitant to seeking regime change).

In the case of Schwarzkopf and Powell, Wolfowitz had disdain for both generals. The neoconservatives viewed each individual as obstacles to their war ideology. Second, Wolfowitz remained dismayed by Schwarzkopf's "declaration that the allies had no intension of going to Baghdad." Third, he harbored additional anger toward the general following the signing of the Safwan Treaty, which as it turned out

---

34   Remarks by The President To Raytheon Missile Systems Plant Employees, Raytheon Missile Systems Plant Andover, Massachusetts. Office of Press Secretary, The White House. 15 February 1991.

35   Quoted in Robert S. Litwak, *Rogue States and US Foreign Policy: Containment After the Cold War* (Washington, DC: Woodrow Wilson Center Press, 2000), 123.

36   Gordon and Trainor, *The Generals' War*, 452–3.

37   Originally cited in, Joshua Muravchik, "Conservatives for Clinton." *Commentary*, November 1992, 22; quote taken from Stefan Halper and Jonathan Clarke, *America Alone: The Neoconservatives and Global Order* (London: Cambridge University, 2004), 81.

38   Mark Gerson, *The Neoconservative Vision: From the Cold War to the Culture Wars* (New York: Madison Books, 1996), 249.

represented a major blunder by Schwarzkopf that permitted Iraq to use its helicopter gunships to quell the internal insurrection unleashed by the Shiites in southern Iraq.

From the beginning of their relationship Wolfowitz had had no great affinity for the Powell. Similarly, the two had a running feud that began in the Reagan administration and they would lock horns over the direction of Iraq policy. The source of the rift during the Bush administration, as was the case with Schwarzkopf, was the Safwan Treaty. Among Pentagon and White House staffers, and among some field generals, few were openly critical or bold enough to disparage Powell directly. This was not the case with Wolfowitz who took his criticism of the general to the press. It was then that Powell responded. As Gordon and Trainor explicate, "Wolfowitz received an angry call from Powell, who complained that Pentagon civilians were telling the press the question of enforcing a total ban on Iraqi helicopter flights [an issue that developed as a result of the Safan Treaty] was still open."[39] Thus "shortly after that the issue was closed"[40] the Bush administration moved on and accepted the coalition battlefield successes and was therefore willing to allow the Iraqi internal fighting to run its course, even if that meant that the Shiites in the South were to be massacred.[41]

The results of the internal events in the aftermath of the brief ground war symbolized the neoconservative discontent with the Bush administration. From the beginning of the administration the neocons were treated as bystanders. However, as the administration policy shifted in the wake of the Iraq's invasion of Kuwait, the neocons, in the person of Wolfowitz were situated to shape the war planning and therefore they had a seat on Bush's war council deliberations and therefore an opportunity to advance their war ideology. As the war dissipated the neocons were infuriated by what they viewed as "twin betrayals"—the inability to complete the task of unseating the Iraqi dictator and as a result of presidential rhetoric, and second, the administration stood by and watched the slaughter of people "they felt" the president rallied but allowed them to twist in the wind.

Exile and Lobbying Efforts: The Neocons and the Clinton Administration

As the 1992 Presidential Election season emerged, a vocal minority of disaffected neoconservatives began to express their negative views concerning the Bush administrations stewardship of US foreign policy. Many concluded that the presidents inability to support democratic movements such as those in the Tiananmen uprising in China, to preclude Soviet meddling in the Baltic states during their desperate bid for independence and the absence of similar support as the Yugoslavian state began to fragment represented clear signals that Bush was out of step with the neocons. Then there was another issue: the president's unprecedented pressure on Israel, a country with whom the neocons had pledged their loyalty. Additionally, an offhand

---

39   Gordon and Trainor, *The Generals' War*, 456.
40   Ibid.
41   Ibid.

remark by Secretary of State James Baker, when he was overheard saying "fuck the Jews, they didn't vote for us,"[42] alienated them further. This coupled with the failure to take down Saddam, even after the Iraqi leader launched two dozen scud missiles deep inside Israel (and the fact that American pressure on the Israeli government prevented a counter attack), left them more distraught.

Those neoconservatives not serving within the administration reprised their role that emerged when Reagan, in their estimation, betrayed them: open criticism of the Bush administrations policies. Articles of discontent appeared in the *Commentary, Weekly Standard,* and the *New York Post* with one expressed purpose: to humiliate the president and in some cases hamper Bush's reelection bid.

These issues by themselves provided a series of reasons why the neoconservative movement began to fragment, and it explains why elements within this movement worked publicly and privately to assist the Clinton campaign. The reader needs to understand that Clinton himself wooed them privately and with public statements against Bush that appealed to the neocons. In one example, during the campaign Clinton offered sharp criticisms of the president asserting Bush did not provide military assistance to the Bosnians, or in spite of warnings of an Iraqi invasion of Kuwait, the president and his senior advisors ignored the evidence. Finally, Clinton offered a statement that caught the attention of most if not all neocons: Bush had "left the Kurds and the Shiites twisting" as Saddam moved to violently crush their rebellions.[43]

Some, like Muravchik, openly supported the Clinton presidential bid during the 1992 campaign. In another strange twist, Richard Schifter, a neocon who had served as "a human rights official in the Reagan and Bush administrations"[44] joined the Clinton campaign as a senior foreign policy advisor. According to Dorrien, several more notable neoconservatives such as Samuel Huntington, Edward Luttwak, Peter Rosenblatt, Stephan Morris, Aaron Wildavsky, and others, shifted their support to the Democratic nominee.[45]

Though this group was impressive, there rafting over to Clinton served a purpose: an attempt to secure jobs and access. These efforts produced an admonishment from William Kristol, who observed "Any neocon" that "drifts back to the Democratic Party is a pseudo neocon."[46]

To their big disappointment, the neocons did not fill any vacancies within the Clinton administration. In short, the overt and covert lobbying efforts by this group yielded no positive results. The neocons envisaged a tripartite dilemma: no president who supported their view of the world, at least enough to hire them; and therefore no means by which to promote their agenda, and third, the neocons had no member of their flock to participate in national security meetings. This was the first time in four

---

42   Ehrman, *The Rise of Neoconservatism,* 197.
43   Ibid., 194.
44   Dorrien, *The Neoconservative Mind,* 389.
45   Ibid.
46   Ehrman, *The Rise of Neoconservatism,* 198.

presidencies that the neocons had no direct access to foreign policy decision making. Thus the neocons were confronting a daunting and painful verity, exile.

Shut out of the Clinton administration the neocons were forced to do several things that were antithetical to previous practices. First, most returned to think tanks, others returned to writing for their all-too-numerous journals or dailys, and when that was not enough, some served as foreign policy analysts on network and cable news outlets. Second, some served on panels or commissions that promoted their agenda. Third, when all else failed the neocons became critics of the Clinton administrations policies. In short, collectively the aforementioned usually occur at the close of administrations when their views were no longer welcomed.

This group in exile wasted little time in their criticism of Clinton administrations stewardship of US foreign policy. The most immediate threat to their interests concerned the fact that two former officials of the Carter administration—Warren Christopher (Secretary of State) and Anthony Lake (National Security Advisor)— became senior advisors. And when it appeared that the president was embarking on a multilateral foreign policy with the UN assuming a major role, this caused additional consternation within the group. The neoconservatives, along with republicans in congress and other circles within the Beltway, were equally concerned with Presidential Review Directive-13 (PRD-13) which represented the administrations review of international peace enforcement and was signed in February 1993.[47] While not a statement of policy, the Clinton administration considered the commitment of American forces to an expanded military role for the United Nations.[48] The neoconservatives viewed this consideration as an open ended commitment to multilateralism and an aversion to the use of American military power.[49]

The debacle in Somalia on 3–4 October 1993, along with the paralysis in Haiti and in Bosnia, caused heightened fears that America's credibility was taking a major beating particularly since it had been reestablished during Operation Desert Storm.

In response to this development Wolfowitz asserted that after only one year in office, the president squandered American military prestige on matters not considered in the national interests of the United States:

> The administration has squandered military prestige on issues of little importance in Somalia and Haiti. In Bosnia, it has failed to reconcile American interests with the dangers of military intervention. In his implementation of policy, Clinton has been too wedded to two limited tools of diplomacy: multilateralism and peacekeeping. Neither is as important as is currently fashionable to think. In the future, the real threats to U.S. interests are "backlash states" like North Korea, Iraq and Iran and instability in Europe and East Asia. All require skill, determination and a president truly engaged in foreign policy.[50]

---

47   Halper and Clarke, *America Alone: The Neoconservatives and Global Order*, 86.
48   Ibid.
49   Ibid.
50   Paul Wolfowitz, "Clinton's First Year," *Foreign Affairs*, January/February 1994.

The fact that Iraq was listed as a backlash state is symbolic. It is clear that neoconservative still considered this country the principle target country for invasion. Equally significant this criticism developed as the debate concerning administration policy toward Iraq continued without a discernable policy. Participants in this debate represented two factions. The first group, led by Secretary of State Christopher and National Security Advisor Lake, wanted the administration to continue the containment of Iraq, a policy that began at the close of the Bush administration. There was a minor nuance in the strategy: Clinton wanted a comprehensive containment strategy. The major thinking behind this group is fundamental: they favored a less confrontational approach toward Iraq. Second, this faction observed that more resources should be devoted to a more internationalist agenda where bilateral relationships with Russia, China, India, or the transformation of NATO, would assume priority within administration policy. This group concluded that if Iraq became the central foreign policy priority then time, resources and political capital would be dominated by this pursuit leaving scant time for other more pertinent issues.[51]

The second faction, led by individuals from the Vice President, to elements in the Military, State, CIA and the NSC Staff, and even UN Ambassador Madeline Albright, recognized that a military showdown with Iraq was inevitable. Earlier in the administration Martin Indyk privately argued that dual containment was ineffectual owing to the fact that in the case of Iraq, Saddam would work to defeat it. Indyk argued for US support to Iraqi opposition groups and exiles that with the assistance of the CIA could topple the Iraq leader.[52]

Though this debate continued unabated during the first term, publicly the administration tried to implement its dual containment strategy.[53] This strategy however was problematic from the beginning. First, it was attacked by the French, Russians and Chinese, (each of which hoped at the time to sign major oil or other business related contracts with the regime), which openly called for ending the sanctions regime. This revelation indicated that administration's diplomatic initiative within the UN Security Council was running into opposition. Second, the coalition itself was tired of the Iraqi debate and the attendant obligations. Third, the American military, principally the Air Force and Navy were concerned about the increasing costs of operating the no-fly zones and the strains on their respective pilots.[54]

---

51   Kenneth M. Pollack, *The Threatening Storm: The United States and Iraq: The Crisis, The Strategy and the Prospects After Saddam* (New York: Random House, 2002), 56.

52   Pollack, *The Threatening Storm*, 57.

53   Though the Clinton administration accepted the reality that containment was their policy, but the president went to great lengths to depersonalize US policy via Iraq. Even with this attitude the administration was concerned with the growing perception that Clinton policy toward Iraq was soft. In response to this criticism, then Press Secretary Dee Dee Myers lamented "there is no practical difference" between this administration and the Bush administration. For more on this point, see Litwak, *Rogue States and US Foreign Policy*, 127.

54   Scott Peterson, "US Sliding Into War with Iraq? Airstrikes in the No-Fly Zones— and Iraqi Counterattacks are Intensifying," *Christian Science Monitor*, 8 October 2002.

With respect to US policy toward Iraq, the neocons were, from their perspective, witnessing disaster. They were critical of the Clinton administrations "containment debate" and the appearance that the administration had done little to reduce the Iraqi WMD threat. Similarly, the simple fact that Saddam remained in power and incessantly continued a game of brinksmanship over the issues of inspections, sanctions, and abuses within the no-fly zones, represented unmistakable evidence that the administrations' policies were problematic.

In the second term of the Clinton administration the attacks from the neocons became more frequent and the issue of regime change more insistent (as did the call for utilizing Iraqi exiles). The leading voice in this debate was none other than Perle. On this point Ivo Daddler and James Lindsay observed that throughout the 1990s "he distinguished himself as a relentless critic of the Clinton administration policy toward Iraq and staunch supporter of Iraqi exile groups looking for aid in their bid to topple Saddam."[55]

Second, the neocons were embarking on a dual strategy of their own: attempting to work out a strategy that sought regime change in Iraq, and when the appropriate moment arrived, they attempted to petition the administration on the need for a direct US policy to overtly unseat the regime in Iraq. On the former, members of this group wrote a policy paper on 1 June 1996 for incoming Israeli Prime Minister Benjamin Netanyahu, titled "A Clean Break: A New Strategy for Securing the Realm."[56] The study openly suggested "removing Saddam Hussein from power in Iraq—an important strategic objective in its own right."[57] The paper called for a joint US-Israeli sponsored effort to unseat the Iraqi leader, a clear break from the neocon war ideology which had previously argued for the US military to undertake this task alone. Additionally, this group used this study to call for regime change in Syria, Iran and elsewhere in the region. This represented an early effort to promote the need for the democratic transformation of the Middle East.[58] As for the issue of the US-Israeli preemptive strike against Iraq, such as that advocated by the authors', the issue was too polemical and the Israeli's wisely never considered the matter.

On the latter, in an attempt to reassert their agenda, the neocons tried a more direct approach: they sent a letter to President Clinton in an attempt to push for "regime change" in Iraq. The essential lines associated with the letter are these:

> Given the magnitude of the threat, the current policy, which depends for its success upon the steadfastness of our coalition partners and upon the cooperation of Saddam Hussein, is

---

55   5Ivo Daadler and James Lindsay, *America Unbound: The Bush Revolution in Foreign Policy* (Washington, DC: Brookings Institution Press, 2003), 29.

56   "A Clean Break: A New Strategy for Security the Realm," a report prepared by The Institute for Advanced Strategic and Political Studies' "Study Group on a New Israeli Strategy Toward 2000." The report also urged the new Israeli government to end its support for the Oslo Peace Accords. For more on this and other points, go to www.israeleconomy.org/strat1.htm.

57   Ibid.

58   Ibid.

dangerously inadequate. The only acceptable strategy is one that eliminates the possibility that Iraq will be able to use or threaten to use weapons of mass destruction. In the near term, this means a willingness to undertake military action as diplomacy is clearly failing. In the long term, it means removing Saddam Hussein and his regime from power. That now needs to become the aim of American foreign policy. We urge you to articulate this aim, and to turn your Administration's attention to implementing a strategy for removing Saddam's regime from power. This will require a full complement of diplomatic, political and military efforts. Although we are fully aware of the dangers and difficulties in implementing this policy, we believe the dangers of failing to do so are far greater. We believe the U.S. has the authority under existing UN resolutions to take the necessary steps, including military steps, to protect our vital interests in the Gulf. In any case, American policy cannot continue to be crippled by a misguided insistence on unanimity in the UN Security Council. We urge you to act decisively. If you act now to end the threat of weapons of mass destruction against the U.S. or its allies, you will be acting in the most fundamental national security interests of the country. If we accept a course of weakness and drift, we put our interests and our future at risk.[59]

The letter yielded an invitation from the White House to discuss the issue of regime change. The results of the meeting however between President Clinton and his National Security Advisor, Sandy Berger and Donald Rumsfeld, Wolfowitz, and Perle did not culminate in an outcome consistent with the neocon agenda. In fact the meeting resulted in growing skepticism of the president and his national security advisor. After leaving the White House, Perle quotes Rumsfeld's observations of the meeting:

Did you notice that with respect to every argument we made Sandy Berger's response had more to with how it would look [presumably a reference to a US-led effort of regime change] and not with what it meant for our security? Totally preoccupied with the political perceptions of administration policies and practically indifferent to the situation we were in and the dangers we faced.[60]

For the neoconservatives, this meeting produced a clear sense of urgency. That is there was a strong belief among the neoconservatives that the Iraqi leader had gained from the verbal confrontations with the administration, and when the administration "showed force"—American Aircraft Carrier Battle Groups were sent to Persian

---

59   The except from the letter was obtained from the following web address: www. newamericancentury.org/iraqclintonletter.htm.The information was downloaded on 19 December 2004. The letter was signed by the following individuals: Elliott Abrams, Richard L. Armitage, William J. Bennett, Jeffrey Bergner, John Bolton, Paula Dobriansky, Francis Fukuyama, Robert Kagan, Zalmay Khalilzad, William Kristol, Richard Perle, Peter W. Rodman, Donald Rumsfeld, William Schneider, Jr, Vin Weber, Paul Wolfowitz, R. James Woolsey, and Robert B. Zoellick.

60   Quote taken from the PBS program, *Frontline*, "The War Behind Closed Doors." The quote comes from an interview with Richard Perle on 25 January 2003.

Gulf—but Clinton failed to follow through with planned air strikes.[61] For each event the administration showed force but failed to use it, Saddam Hussein, in the view of the neoconservatives, emerged as a victory and a more powerful symbol in the region. Having attempted a bipartisan approach the neoconservatives were now willing to implement their own brand of brinksmanship. This time the objective was to force Clinton into accepting a definitive policy of regime change. The source of leverage was the republican controlled congress. This time the neoconservatives sent a separate letter that was intended to enlist the support of Senator Trent Lott and Speaker of House Newt Gingrich dated 29 May 1998. The last paragraph of the letter is instructive:

> If we continue along the present course, however, Saddam will be stronger at home, he will become even more powerful in the region, and we will face the prospect of having to confront him at some later point when the costs to us, our armed forces, and our allies will be even higher. Mr. Speaker and Senator Lott, Congress should adopt the measures necessary to avoid this impending defeat of vital U.S. interests.[62]

The measures that the group proposed consisted of establishing "support (with economic, political, and military means) [for] a provisional, representative, and free government of Iraq in areas of Iraq not under Saddam's control" and second, "We should use U.S. and allied military power to provide protection for liberated areas in northern and southern Iraq" and the American military should employ force to "protect our vital interests in the Gulf—and, if necessary, to help remove Saddam from power."[63]

Some six months later, the neocons did receive assistance from the Congress (It remains unclear the degree to which the aforementioned letter assisted in this process. It is a safe bet that it did play a minor role at best). The boost to their cause came in the form of legislation. The important legislation was HR4655, better known as the Iraqi Liberation Act. The act asserted "that it should be the policy of the United States to seek to remove the regime of Saddam Hussein from power in Iraq and to replace it with a democratic government."[64] Though an important gain,

---

61   Bradley Graham, "Clinton's Advisors Split on Attacking Iraq," *Washington Post*, 16 November 1998.

62   See letter to Speaker Gingrich and Senator Lott on 26 May 1998. For the complete neoconservative letter, and its context go to: www.newamericancentury.org/iraqletter1998. htm. The letter was downloaded on 19 December 2004. The letter was signed by the following individuals: Elliot Abrams, William J. Bennett, Jeffrey Bergner, John R. Bolton, Paula Dobriansky, Francis Fukuyama, Robert Kagan, Zalmay Khalilzad, William Kristol, Richard Perle, Peter Rodman, Donald Rumsfeld, William Schneider, Jr., Vin Weber, Paul Wolfowitz, R. James Woolsey, and Robert B. Zoellick.

63   Ibid.

64   The passage is quoted from HR 4655, Iraq Liberation Act of 1998, which was passed. October 1998. For the full text, the reader should consult www.iraqwatch.org/ government/US/Legislation/ILA.htm. The cite was accessed on 20 December 2004. The Senate version is S.2525 which was passed on 7 October 1998.

the US government would be indirectly involved in regime change, by providing eight million dollars in aid to Iraqi opposition groups. As a result of this growing action the neoconservatives were once again players, using the issue of American assistance to fund a covert war to unseat Saddam. Moreover, much of this funding, to the dismay of State and CIA, went to the Iraq National Council (INC), a group led by Ahmed Chalabi, a close associate of Perle and Wolfowitz. In the final analysis, despite this influence the neocons remained wedded to their ultimate objective: direct American intervention. With no direct use of ground forces proposed, this group had to settle for *Operation Desert Fox*, a four day air campaign whose objective was to return UN weapons inspectors back to Iraq and to degrade Saddam's WMD capacity. The cause of removing the Iraqi leader would have to await another president.

The Road to Triumph and Disappointment: "W" and the Neocons

From the outset of the administration of George W. Bush the neoconservatives achieved unprecedented access and influence. Each venue was critical to the promotion and the implementation of their ultimate objective: regime change in Iraq. A few examples illustrate the point. Within the Department of Defense the neocons filled three critical positions: Secretary Defense (Donald Rumsfeld), Deputy Secretary of Defense (Wolfowitz), and Under Secretary for Policy (Douglas Feith). Similarly, the Defense Policy Board was a group utilized as a means to assert additional control and to ensure that this body marched to the drum of the neocons. Perle filled one of the vacancies on this board. In another area John Bolton filled an influential position (Under Secretary of State for Arms Control) within the Department of State, over the objections of Secretary of State Powell. This move was perceived by observers as having a "mole"—a neocon to watch the moves of Powell—within the department.[65] Equally significant, the neocons influence extended into the White House. This is best exemplified by understanding the authority of I. Lewis "Scooter" Libby who held three separate portfolio's—an unprecedented move in of itself—that included the Chief of Staff to the Vice President, the National Security Advisor of Vice President and additionally, he held the position as an assistant to President Bush.[66] Within the National Security Council staff, the neoconservative effort received a boost from Elliott Abrams, who served as the specialist on Near East Affairs. His assistance was particularly useful in the internal bureaucratic battles in the run up to the war with Iraq and matters concerning Middle East policy. The neoconservative evolution was aided further by allies within the White House. Those allied with the movement were none other than Vice President Cheney and Condoleezza Rice.[67] Second, the events of 11 September provided additional movement toward the neoconservative

---

65   For more on this point see, Elizabeth Drew, "The Neocons in Power." Vol. 50, No. 10, June 12, 2003.

66   Bob Woodward, *Plan of Attack* (New York: Simon & Schuster, 2004), 48.

67   The author does not contend that Rice is a neocon. The point here is that she has taken positions consistent with the neoconservatives and has therefore aided their cause.

cause. By this the author asserts that President Bush was sympathetic in a way that advanced the neocon cause of regime change unlike any previous American President. Moreover, Bush was already predisposed to conflict with Iraq due in part to Saddam's conspiracy to assassinate the elder Bush.

Viewed collectively, as the Iraq debate intensified the neoconservatives were positioned to impact US policy like never before. In this section the author will access the neocon impact on US-Iraqi policy during the *prewar period*, the *post-9/11 period*, and during *Operation Iraqi Freedom and the Post-Saddam phases*.

Prewar Phase

The prewar phase of administration Iraq policy was consistent with previous administrations: it represented a period whereby presidents commission a policy review to examine previous policies and then the interagency process suggests minor adjustments in policy, or there maybe calls for radical transformation of existing policy. So it was with the Bush administration. For many of his fathers former advisors—Cheney and Wolfowitz being the most significant—Iraq was perceived as "unfinished business." For others, such as Powell, Iraq was not a priority, other than strengthening the sanctions regime to ensure Saddam's containment.

In the interagency meetings during the period of February 2001 to 10 of August 2002 no formal policy recommendations on Iraq emerged. Instead, what developed were the nascent formulations of the neoconservative designs to unseat Saddam. In one example, in what has been described as the "enclave strategy"[68] Wolfowitz prepared a Pentagon contingency that required US forces to seize 1,000 Iraqi oil wells in the Southern areas of the country.[69] With control of significant Iraqi territory the American military would thereafter be positioned to assist anti-Saddam forces in a bid to unseat the regime. In response to the plan, Powell thought "this was lunacy."[70] According to Woodward, Powell's reaction did not inhibit Wolfowitz's planning efforts: He "was like a drum that would not stop. He and his group of neoconservatives were rubbing their hands over the idea, which were being presented as 'draft plans.'"[71]

The planning for some form of intervention in Iraq could not proceed without presidential authorization. With this reality Powell recognized that he could do little to preclude contingency planning but the secretary of state had one option available to prevent a policy of regime change: take the matter to president. In a private meeting with the president in December of 2002, Powell made his pitch: "Don't let yourself be pushed into anything until you are ready for it, or until you think there is

---

68   Woodward, *Plan of Attack* 22.
69   Ibid.
70   Ibid.
71   Ibid.

a real reason for it. This [invasion of Iraq] is not as easy as it is being presented, and take your time on this one. Don't let anyone push you into it."[72]

What is clear at this point is that a schism was evolving over the future of Iraqi policy. Interestingly, the tension over Iraq was consistent with the struggles of Bush I and the Clinton administration (There were clear lines drawn: those who supported intervention and those who opposed it).[73] Second, the neocons within the administration recognized that there was one central force that stood in the way of their objective: Powell. For now State had won the first round, but the neocons were simply waiting for the right movement to again do battle with the charismatic and bureaucratically astute secretary of state. There was an additional obstacle (a temporary one) to their plan: the president. The president agreed with Powell that Iraq presented no direct threat to the United States.

As to US and coalition planes flying over the no-fly zones in northern and southern Iraq, that was a different issue altogether. This time State, Defense and the President were in agreement that coalition forces must make Iraq pay for using surface-to-air missiles as a threat to allied planes; the response to such threats should send a clear signal to Saddam.[74] That said with Bush on vacation in August of 2001 the interagency process failed to make any formal policy recommendations on Iraq. Subsequent events would place Iraq back on the table.

The Post-11 September World

The post-11 September period caused additional tension among senior advisors over how to deal with Iraq. For the neocons the post-11 September world provided a means to achieve their objectives: regime change in Iraq and securing a transformation of the Middle East. As important as this may appear, it is significant that we illustrate how this group came to dominate the foreign policy agenda of the Bush administration. The point now is to explicate the elevation of the neoconservative war ideology and how this group in the words of then democratic presidential candidate Howard Dean that President Bush has "been captured by the neoconservatives around him."[75]

Immediately after 11 September the neocons moved swiftly to assert their agenda.[76] During the opening war councils, elements inside the administration argued the target was clear, Iraq not bin Laden. Indeed, this group had an "obsessive fixation on getting rid of Saddam's regime."[77] A few examples are instructive. Clarke writes

72   Ibid.

73   Pollack, *The Threatening Storm: The United States and Iraq*, 105 and 108.

74   See Thomas Ricks, "American, British Jets Hit 5Antiaircraft Sites in Iraq: Baghdad Areas Bombed in Biggest Air Strike in Two Years," *Washington Post*, 18 February 2001.

75   Adam Wolfson, "Conservatives and Neoconservatives," *Public Interest* Winter 2004: www.thepublicinterest.com/archives/2004winter/artcel2.html. The information was downloaded on 22 September 2004.

76   Michael Lind, "How the Neoconservatives Conquered Washington and Launched a War," *Salon*, 10 April 2003.

77   Pollack, *The Threatening Storm: The United States and Iraq*, 105.

that on 12 September the neoconservatives made their move. During this opening war council, Wolfowitz and Rumsfeld remained incredulous to the notion of attacking Afghanistan, their alternative concerned Iraq. Clarke asserts from his vantage point the message was clear: they "were going to try to take advantage of this national tragedy to promote their agenda about Iraq."[78] Second, later in the afternoon these same two individuals were talking about broadening the American response (when it appeared that Afghanistan would be the first target in the war on terror) to include Iraq.[79] Woodward observes that "Wolfowitz put forth military arguments to justify an attack on Iraq rather than Afghanistan."[80] Similarly, to justify their position they argued that the Iraqi terrorist menace is equally threatening as the Al Qaeda threat. It was at this juncture that Powell intervened and warned that the central US focus should be Bin Laden not Saddam. The secretary made this additional statement: "This is a long war and it's a war we have to win. We are engaging with the world. We want to make this a long-standing coalition."[81] At this point Clarke was happy to have allies; he privately thanked both Powell and his deputy Richard Armitage and made the following statement in their presence: "I thought I was missing something here. Having been attacked by Al Qaeda, for us now to be bombing Iraq in response would be like our invading Mexico after the Japanese attacked us at Pearle Harbor."[82] In response, Powell acknowledged "It's not over yet."[83]

In subsequent meetings Powell became alarmed at the gall of the neocons and their burgeoning obsessive behavior, a reference to their pursuit of regime change in the face of opposition. Powell was so concerned that the secretary had a private discussion with then Chairman of Joint Chiefs of Staff Hugh Shelton. Powell's words are instructive: "What the hell! What are these guys thinking about? Can't you get these guys back in the box?"[84] Powell had succeeded in delaying intervention in Iraq but once again it was a presidential intercession that would be the deciding factor.

In spite of the internal pressure the neocons were unable to obtain a complete victory. On 16 September the neocons received unwelcome news from President Bush: "We won't do Iraq now, we're putting Iraq off."[85] However, in a sign of the victory to come, Bush authorized Rumsfeld to "continue working on Iraq war plans

---

78   Richard A. Clarke, *Against All Enemies: Inside America's War on Terror* (New York: Free Press, 2004), 30.

79   Ibid.

80   Bob Woodward, *Plan Attack*,

81   See Dan Balz and Bob Woodward, "A Day to Speak of Anger and Grief: After Bush's Pivotal Speech and New York Visit, Time to Decide Strategy (Part Four)," *Washington Post*, 30 January 2002.

82   Ibid. 30–31.

83   Ibid.

84   Bob Woodward, *Plan Attack*, 25–6.

85   Ibid. 26.

but it was not to be a top priority."[86] The bureaucracy went to work and set the stage H-Hour, the formal invasion of Iraq.[87]

The neocons were not finished. The internal lobbying continued in subsequent war councils. Outside the administration other neoconservatives sought and obtained additional leverage; many were dismayed that Iraq was not considered a higher priority and were vocal about the necessity of attacking Iraq. In an open letter dated 20 September 2001, the neocons openly warned President Bush:

Dear Mr. President, We write to endorse your admirable commitment to "lead the world to victory" in the war against terrorism. We fully support your call for "a broad and sustained campaign" against the "terrorist organizations and those who harbor and support them." We agree with Secretary of State Powell that the United States must find and punish the perpetrators of the horrific attack of September 11, and we must, as he said, "go after terrorism wherever we find it in the world" and "get it by its branch and root." We agree with the Secretary of State that U.S. policy must aim not only at finding the people responsible for this incident, but must also target those "other groups out there that mean us no good" and "that have conducted attacks previously against U.S. personnel, U.S. interests and our allies." In order to carry out this "first war of the 21st century" successfully, and in order, as you have said, to do future "generations a favor by coming together and whipping terrorism," we believe the following steps are necessary parts of a comprehensive strategy. We agree with Secretary of State Powell's recent statement that Saddam Hussein "is one of the leading terrorists on the face of the Earth." It may be that the Iraqi government provided assistance in some form to the recent attack on the United States. But even if evidence does not link Iraq directly to the attack, any strategy aiming at the eradication of terrorism and its sponsors must include a determined effort to remove Saddam Hussein from power in Iraq. Failure to undertake such an effort will constitute an early and perhaps decisive surrender in the war on international terrorism. *The United States must therefore provide full military and financial support to the Iraqi opposition. American military force should be used to provide a "safe zone" in Iraq from which the opposition can operate. And American forces must be prepared to back up our commitment to the Iraqi opposition by all necessary means.*[88]

The letter itself was signed by several leading members of this group[89] and representatives of this movement boldly asserted to the leader of their party that Iraq

---

86   Ibid.

87   See the following works for more on this point, Woodward, *Plan of Attack*; for two other inside perspectives consult, General Tommy Franks, *American Soldier* (New York: Regan Books, 20040, Chapter 9 and 10, and Lt. General Michael Delong, *Inside CENTCOM: The Unvarnished Truth About the Wars in Afghanistan and Iraq* (Washington, DC: Regnery, 2004), Chapter 4.

88   The title of the letter is "Toward a Comprehensive Strategy." The letter was obtained from the Project of New American democracy website: www.newamericancentury. org/Bushletter.htm. The complete letter in its entirety may be obtained from this site. The information was downloaded on 19 December 2004.

89   Those neoconservatives and their supports endorsing the letter include the following: William Kristol, Richard V. Allen, Gary Bauer, Jeffrey Bell, William J. Bennett,

had to be part of the opening phase of the first war of the 21st century. If not, they asserted, the war on terror could not be construed as a success. Buchanan a leading critic of the neoconservatives, offers this refrain: "Here was a cabal of intellectuals telling the Commander-in-Chief, nine days after an attack on America, that if he did not follow their war plans, he would be charged with surrendering to terror."[90] Similarly, the critical words in the letter (see italics) were consistent with the enclave strategy; an approach rejected at the deputy level but was now reincarnated to become the leading strategy to unseat Saddam. Equally significant, Michael Ledeen, another neoconservative, had a larger design that argues that Iraq was the key to toppling subsequent dominoes:

> First and foremost, we must bring down the terror regimes, beginning with the Big Three: Iran, Iraq, and Syria. And then we have to come to grips with Saudi Arabia.... Once the tyrants in Iran, Iraq, Syria, and Saudi Arabia have been brought down, we will remain engaged ....We have to ensure the fulfillment of the democratic revolution.... Stability is an unworthy American mission, and a misleading concept to boot. We do not want stability in Iran, Iraq, Syria, Lebanon, and even Saudi Arabia; we want things to change. The real issue is not whether, but how to destabilize.[91]

This statement symbolized the neoconservative effort to make the centerpiece of the design to remake a region they believed were central to war on terror, and with work, could become a linchpin in the unleashing of democracy in the Middle East.

Ideology, Bureaucratic Politics and the Preparations for War

The intensity of the neoconservative efforts, along with the assistance of Vice President Cheney, helped to change the president's mind.[92] In the end, Iraq would be invaded. With the planning for contingences for a confrontation with Iraq underway, the neoconservatives were positioned to win the internal bureaucratic battles even if Powell won the public wars (this is a reference to Powell's victories to shift the strategy away from a unilateral response via Iraq to a multilateral one that would be sanctioned by the United Nations). That is, not only did members of the flock

---

Rudy Boshwitz, Jeffrey Bergner, Eliot Cohen, Seth Cropsey, Midge Decter, Thomas Donnelly, Nicholas Eberstadt, Hillel Fradkin, Aaron Friedberg, Francis Fukuyama, Frank Gaffney, Jeffrey Gedmin, Reuel Marc Gerecht, Charles Hill, Bruce P. Jackson Eli S. Jacobs, Michael Joyce, Donald Kagan, Robert Kagan, Jeane Kirkpatrick, Charles Krauthammer, John Lehman, Clifford May, Martin Peretz, Richard Perle, Norman Podhoretz, Stephen P. Rosen, Randy Scheunemann, Gary Schmitt, William Schneider, Jr. Richard H. Shultz, Henry Sokolski, Stephen J. Solarz, Vin Weber, Leon Wieseltier, and Marshall Wittmann.

90   As quoted in Patrick Buchanan, "Whose War? A Neoconservative Clique Seeks to Ensnare Our Country in a Series of Wars that are Not in America's Interest", *The American Conservative*, 24 March 2003.

91   Ibid.

92   Yossef Bondansky, *Inside the Secret of the Iraq War* (New York: Harper Collins: 2004), 85–113.

(Rumsfeld and Wolfowitz) control planning, other less notable neoconservatives were critical to "getting Iraq done." In one example, Douglas Feith, a major proponent of Al Qaeda-Iraqi ties, called for the creation of a "planning cell in Defense Department," whose sole purpose was to secure postwar reconstruction within the Pentagon.[93] In short order this shrewd bureaucratic move ran into opposition (State traditionally handles postwar reconstruction activities). With the assistance of Cheney the plan eventually received approval. Following the president's signature on National Security Presidential Directive 24 (NSPD-24), the Office of Reconstruction and Humanitarian Assistance (ORHA) was created on 20 January 2002.[94] Additionally, Feith played a role in the implementation of the Office of Special Plans, what amounted to the Pentagon's own intelligence gathering apparatus.

Second, Libby, another neocon, attempted to direct attention to what he perceived as a clear Al Qaeda-Iraq connection in the events of 11 September. This individual assisted the work of the deputies committee on the review of Iraq policy and in the prewar military and postwar planning in Iraq.[95] In short this individual was both a neocon ally and a front man for Cheney in those forums in which the vice president was not a participant.

Though Cheney's role was critical to the success of the neoconservative dominance during the war planning and postwar reconstruction phases, one cannot dismiss the actions of Libby and Abrams, both of whose arguments buttressed those of the vice president, which, in the final analysis, precluded the efforts of Powell and others from delaying or internationalizing the intervention.

On the matter of ideology, the neoconservatives were delighted by the words "axis of evil" and the clear link to WMD ensured that Iraq would be within the strategic calculus of the Bush Doctrine. Similarly, the neocons were cognizant that the argument that a potential bin Laden-Iraq connection to 9/11—even if there was no supporting evidence—along with the presence of Ansar al Islam in Northern Iraq, a known Al Qaeda affiliate, would assist their cause. If one were to add the post-9/11 mood within the country, the neocons would finally have the war with Iraq. Collectively, these dynamics illustrate the evolution of the neoconservative ideology of war.

Postwar Realities

For many commentators, the war on terror, with particular emphasis on the second phase of the campaign, symbolized the zenith of the neocons. Indeed, *Operation Iraqi Freedom* secured a long-awaited victory for the former Democrats turned Republican. In the words of Vijay Prashad the success in the war phase of *Operation*

---

93   Woodward, *Plan Attack*, 282–3.
94   Ibid.
95   Ibid, 50–51, 72, 207, 280–83 and 300–301.

Iraqi Freedom ushered in the "age of neocons."[96] Woodward writes in his book *Plan of Attack* this group celebrated after Saddam Hussein's regime collapsed. In the residence of the Vice President Cheney, Wolfowitz, Libby, and Kenneth Adelman were in celebration mode. They congratulated each other but heaped praise upon their leader, President George Bush for his efforts to withstand the "leftwing critics"—both at home and abroad—and for keeping his promise to the Iraqi people and to their small circle. Speaking for the group Adelman lamented that he had been overcome by the president's determination: "I just want to make a toast, without getting too cheesy: To the President of the United States."[97] According to Woodward, "They all raised their glasses, Hear! Hear!"[98]

The neoconservative triumphalist attitude moved to new heights on 1 May 2003, the date when President Bush flew aboard the *USS Abraham Lincoln* and promptly announced "that major combat operations" in Iraq had ceased.[99] In the view of senior elements The Project for the New American Century, the neocons were on there way to achieving their goals:

> It is also becoming clear that the battle of Iraq has been an important victory in the broader war in which we are engaged, a war against terror, against weapons proliferation, and for a new Middle East. Already, other terror-implicated regimes in the region that were developing weapons of mass destruction are feeling pressure, and some are beginning to move in the right direction. Libya has given up its weapons of mass destruction program. Iran has at least gestured toward opening its nuclear program to inspection. The clandestine international network organized by Pakistan's A.Q. Khan that has been so central to nuclear proliferation to rogue states has been exposed. From Iran to Saudi Arabia, liberal forces seem to have been encouraged. We are paying a real price in blood and treasure in Iraq. But we believe that it is already clear—as clear as such things get in the real world—that the price of the liberation of Iraq has been worth it.[100]

This statement symbolized the euphoria that was rampant among neocons during the *postwar phase*. For the neocons, the "cakewalk" was over. It was now time to secure Iraq, capture Saddam and his two sons, and pave the way for democracy. This triumphalist attitude began to change however as the insurgency in August of 2003 began to increase and when the Iraqi Survey Group was unable to locate any WMD. It was at this point that triumphalist hysteria dissipated. Finally, as the attacks on coalition troops intensified, producing a rapid increase in the deaths of coalition military personnel, as a result the president and the neocons received a wave of criticism.

---

96 Vijay Prashad, "The Age of 'Neocons", www.flonnet.com/fl2102/stories/20040130000506400.htm. Information retrieved on July 2005.

97 Woodward, *Plan Attack*, 409–10.

98 Ibid.

99 See "President Bush Declares Major Combat Operations In Iraq Over," www.cbsnews.com/stories/2003/05/01/iraq/main551946.shtml. Retrieved on November 8, 2005.

100 Robert Kagan and William Kristol, "The Right War for the Right Reasons," *Weekly Standard*, 27 February 2004, www.newamericancentury.org/iraq-20040217.htm.

In a piquant critique of the postwar planning, the instability within Iraq, and the burgeoning insurgency, retired General Anthony Zinni, who served as CENTCOM Commander under President Clinton, stated the source of these failures were the result of the neoconservative ideology. Zinni was shocked by their arrogance, acknowledging that "The more I saw the more I thought this [war] was the product of the neocons" that "didn't understand the region and were going to create havoc there."[101] In his view "these were dilettantes from Washington think tanks who never had an idea that worked on the ground."[102] Additionally, the general observed that cognizance of this group and its ideological zeal with respect to Iraq "was the worst kept secret in Washington. That everybody I talk to in Washington has known … what their agenda was and what they were trying to do."[103] The war according to Zinni was a product of this group of civilians and not the generals within the defense department.[104]

Three setbacks set the stage for the decline of the neoconservative influence over postwar policy in Iraq. The first concerned the cloud of suspicion surrounding Ahmed Chalabi. Perle boasted that this individual represented Iraq's version of a founding father. Thus in his view and those of other neoconservatives (Wolfowitz, Feith, Libby to name a few), Chalabi should become Iraq's first postwar leader. Few outside this group supported this contention.[105] Chalabi's dilemmas, and thus that of his neoconservative benefactors, concerned the "hyped intelligence", particularly with respect to WMD, his false statements regarding how US forces would be greeted once they arrived, his alleged ties with the Iranian intelligence, along with the rumors that he passed on American intelligence secrets to the Iranians, only heightened suspicions he coned senior neocons within the administration.[106]

The second dilemma for the neocons concerned the issue of postwar reconstruction. As mentioned above, the neocons were in complete control of postwar reconstruction. That said a host of errors led to several missteps in the post-Saddam era. First, the neocons, aided by ineffectual CIA intelligence on the strength and strategies of the insurgency, misread the need for larger troop concentrations. While one may question the absence of intelligence, the civilians in the Pentagon were warned by Army Chief of Staff General Eric Shinseki who argued on 23 February 2003 that "Something on the order of several hundred thousand soldiers, are probably, you

---

101   Buchanan, *Where The Right Went Wrong*, 55.

102   Ibid.

103   General Anthony Zinni: 'They've Screwed Up'" May 21, 2004. The article may be obtained at www.cbsnews.com/stories/2004/05/21/60minutes/printables618896.shtml. The article was downloaded on 20 December 2004.

104   Ibid.

105   For a recent study surrounding the role of Chalabi's anti-Saddam activities that caught the attention of the neocons, see Jon Lee Anderson, "A Man of the Shadows" *The New Yorker*, 24 and 31 January 2005, 60–64.

106   John Dizard, "How Ahmed Chalabi Conned the Neocons," *Salon*, 4 May 2004, www.salon.com/news/feature/2004/05/04/chalabi/index_np.html. The article was downloaded on 2 February 2005.

know, a figure that would be required. We're talking about post-hostilities control over a piece of geography that's fairly significant with the kinds of ethnic tensions that could lead to other problems."[107]

In order to deal with this perspective, Wolfowitz testified before Congress that the general had been incorrect. In another attempt to insure that the Pentagon spoke with one voice, Rumsfeld publicly rebuked the general, noting that in the age of transformation an analysis such as that suggested by the general and others were out of touch with reality and the necessity of the new war, which argued that American forces may be needed to fight in another theatre. The secretary provided this additional statement: "The idea that it would take several hundred thousand U.S. forces I think is far from the mark."[108]

Additionally, Rumsfeld and Wolfowitz had to confront the view of Thomas White, the Secretary of Army. White, a retired general, held similar views as Shinseki. Several days later he testified before Congress. In an interview with *Frontline*, in a private conversation before the hearing begins the secretary makes this statement: "I see Sen. Levin before the hearing starts," and he says, "I'm going to ask you the same question." I said: "Good. You're going to get the same answer."[109] White felt that implications for him would be consistent with Shinseki, thus "On the 26th of April, I was called in late on a Friday afternoon and told by Rumsfeld, with Wolfowitz standing there, that I was going to be replaced."[110]

These revelations did not end the criticism of the neoconservative failure in this venue. Indeed, retired general Norman Schwarzkopf, and the former CENTCOM Commander, asserted his disagreement with the civilian leadership of the Pentagon noting that they simply ignored the historical evidence.[111]

The neoconservatives received additional criticism on another matter—the postwar insurgency—from an unusual source, General Tommy Franks. Frank's directed his anger in the direction of Feith, who was a major participant in the planning of the Iraq war and incessantly argued that WMD should be the top item when selling the necessity of the invasion to a skeptical domestic audience. Feith apparently was responsible for a number of postwar tasks including thee dismantling of the Iraqi Intelligence Services, Iraq's prison complex, closing Iraq's 50 plus embassies abroad, de-Baathification of the military and dealing with the insurgency. It was the latter that was crucial in the eyes of Frank's.[112] The prevailing view is that this was perhaps the single greatest failure, one that clearly impacted the

---

107   As cited in David Shuster, "Conflict Within the Pentagon," *MSNBC*, 12 January 2005, www.msnbc.msn.com/id/6814437/. Article downed on 2 February 2005.

108   Ibid.

109   See Interview with Thomas White. *Frontline*. "Rumsfeld's War." This interview was conducted on 1 August 2004.

110   Ibid.

111   Shuster, "Conflict Within the Pentagon."

112   Woodward, *Plan Attack*, 343. Additionally, Frank's asserted in his own book that Feith "was getting the reputation around here as the dumbest fucking guy on the planet." See the general's book, *American Soldier*, 362.

soldiers, both in terms of the number of troop to secure the country and to reduce casualties. On the criticism of Feith and his role in postwar planning, Frank's said the following: "The fucking stupidest guy on the face of the earth."[113] In an effort to explain this comment, Frank's notes in his book *American Soldier* "No one could deny Feith's academic achievements … but Feith was a theorist whose ideas were often impractical."[114]

It has been reported that Feith has become the scapegoat among the troika within the Defense Department. Within Rumsfeld staying on for another term, and Wolfowitz, another neocon that has envisaged significant criticism, is assuming a lower profile but eventually he departed the administration for an opportunity to direct the World Bank. Similarly, Feith resigned in the summer of 2005.[115]

Lastly, another piece of evidence augmented the decline of the neoconservatives: postwar reconstruction funding. In the planning phase of the war (during an early war council gathering) Rumsfeld acknowledged that reconstruction funding would run smoothly if it was under the control of the Pentagon, rather than State. Powell of course objected but the President sided with Rumsfeld's argument. With the chaos continuing to mount within the Sunni triangle in the summer leading up to the US Presidential Election, the president lamented, shifting this authority over to State (a move echoed by congress). In another example of burgeoning displeasure with the Pentagon mismanagement of postwar reconstruction, Congress mandated in a supplemental bill that control of the distribution of the money should be directed by Secretary Powell.[116] Similarly, in a related defeat the political-military issues in Iraq were overseen by Dr. Rice, embarrassing Rumsfeld and the other neoconservatives. In short, these examples illustrate "How the Neoconservatives are Putting the World at Risk."[117]

In the wake of the 30 January 2005 elections in Iraq the neoconservatives were quietly jubilant. This time it was the external elements of the movement—those outside the administration—that carried the torch. In one example, David Frum, a former Bush speechwriter, and recent convert, made this statement: "The leaders produced by last weekend's elections will no doubt have many defects and weaknesses. But they will, as elected leaders always do, boast [of] one supreme strength: the legitimacy that comes from the most direct and obvious possible connection to the wishes of the people. The Sunni Islamists have responded to elections with murder, and that too has been seen globally and in real time on Arab media."[118]

---

113   Ibid, 281.

114   Franks, *American Soldier*, 330.

115   Mark Mazzetti, "Contentious Defense Official to Depart," *The Los Angeles Times*, 27 January 2005.

116   Kathy Kiely, "Congress: Powell should Control Postwar Spending," *USA Today*, 3 April 2003.

117   See, Craig R. Eisendrath and Melvin A.Goodman, Bush League Diplomacy: How The Neoconservatives are Putting the World at Risk (New York: Prometheus, 2004).

118   See David Frum, "A Defeat for the Forces of Fear," *American Enterprise Institute*, 1 February 2005, www.aei.org/news/newsID.21907,filter.foreign/news_detail.asp. Downloaded

Is this the "twilight of the neocons"?[119] Have their multiple failures extinguished their hold over administration Iraq policy for good? If this question were addressed by the neoconservatives in and out of power, their answer would come in two forms. First, they would assert that while they have lost many recent bureaucratic wars for the control of Iraq policy, their view would be that since the president's legacy is tied directly to the success of Iraq there is plenty of time for the vindication of their movement and agenda. From another perspective, the neocons assert that the reelection of President Bush represents the exoneration of their efforts in Iraq.[120] Indeed, some suggest that the survival of Rumsfeld attests to the fact that their council is still required to correct the errors, finish the job, and then move on to the next phase, what many pundits suggest may be Iran or Syria.[121] Finally, there is yet another view that holds that the neocons are under the radar, "lying low until the Iraq storm passes."[122]

The second form concerns the fact that the neoconservatives are publishing frantically in an attempt to protect their fledgling agenda. In one example, Perle and Frum authored *An End to Evil: How to Win the War on Terror*.[123] The study endeavors to make two points: to deflect criticism away from the failures of the neocon agenda and second, bring to light the accomdationists agenda of those within and outside of government that is attempting to defeat the president's war on terror. This negative view illustrates what the neocons refer to "the will to win is ebbing in Washington" and "of a reversion to the bad habits of complacency and denial."[124] In another example, the neocons openly applaud their strategic and operational successes irrespective of the multiple failures. The following excerpt supplements the point:

> The war in Iraq has produced two significant military achievements, one strategic, the other operational. . . The strategic success is the end of the Iraq containment policy that required a large US military presence in Saudi Arabia after the 1991 Gulf War. Significant numbers of US forces were tied down in an increasingly hostile country. Their effect, moreover, on Hussein's conduct was dubious. The operational good news coming out of Iraq was the destruction of the Mahdi army that served the rebel Shiite cleric Muqtada Sadr. The militia had effectively occupied the holy cities of Iraq, including the Imam Ali Mosque in Najaf. The conventional wisdom was that the US military would be unable to

---

on 2 February 2005.

119   Halper and Clarke, "Twilight of the Neocon: Perle has Begun to Panic."

120   Seymour M. Hersh, "The Coming Wars," *The New Yorker*, January 324 731, 2005, 40.

121   Ibid.

122   Howard LaFranchi, "In Foreign Policy Battles, Are Neocons Losing Their Hold? *Christian Science Monitor*, 13 July 2004, www.csmonitor.com/20040713/p01s02-usfp.html. Information downloaded on 23 November 2004.

123   See, David Frum and Richard Perle, *An End to Evil: How to the War on Terror* (New York: Random House, 2003).

124   See Halper and Jonathan Clarke, "Twilight of the Neocons: Perle has Begun to Panic."

expel the rebels from their redoubts without causing an explosion of anti-Americanism in the Shiite world. Yet US personnel combined measured force, diplomatic negotiations and skillful deployments to retake Najaf and recover the shrines without inflicting any substantial damage on them. There was no outcry in Iraq or the Muslim world at large, and some Iraqis even took to the streets to protest Sadr's actions. US and Iraqi forces removed a threat to the development of a peaceful and democratic Iraq.[125]

These examples illustrate that the neoconservatives may be perceived as down or in decline, but this groups' persistent efforts are to ensure that their movement will always be heard and that they remain in close council to the president. Thus as the Bush administration continues its twin efforts of defeating the insurgency and constructing democracy out of the ashes of the Baathist tyranny, one may disagree with the neocons and their agenda but as this study has indicated it would be foolish to count them out.

Conclusion

This study has endeavored to provide a window into the evolution of the neoconservative ideology of war, and their efforts to influence several presidential administrations to complete unfinished business: regime change in Iraq.

On the matter of their war ideology, evidence obtained from this study indicates that through persistence, supplemented by "the right president", set the stage for the adoption of the neoconservative agenda by an inexperienced and vengeful American President, George W. Bush. Long before Bush, the neoconservative war ideology took shape with Wolfowitz's warning of a pending Iraqi invasion of Kuwait in 1979. To deal with this threat, Wolfowitz called for increasing the American military presence in the Persian Gulf. During the administration of Ronald Reagan, Perle was indifferent to administration support of Saddam in the Iran-Iraq war, even warning that the removal of Iraq from the state-sponsored terrorist list and the US support for WMD development could prove costly to American interests. In the administration of Bush I the war ideology shifted, calling for direct removal of Saddam prior to and in the wake of *Operation Desert Storm*. Following a period of estrangement at the close of the administration, the neocon war ideology shifted again. First, in their study "A Clean Break: A New Strategy for Securing the Realm," the neoconservatives called for a joint US-Israeli intervention to unseat the Iraqi leader. When this strategy failed to gain traction with the new Likud government in Israel and with the Clinton administration, they opted for a new approach to promote their ideology. This time they sent a letter to Clinton which openly called for American military forces to end the regime of Saddam Hussein. When this effort failed, they sent a second letter to congressional allies in the form of House Speaker Gingrich and Majority Leader Lott. The republican controlled Congress pushed through supportive legislation that

---

125   Christopher Hitchens, Michael Rubin, Frederick W. Kagan, and Gary Schmitt, "What's Going Right in Iraq," *Los Angeles Times*, 24 October 2004.

called for covert means to end the Iraqi dictatorship. With no victory on the horizon, the war ideology transformed yet again under Bush II, but the objective remained the same: regime change. With unprecedented access to war planning, aided by the post-9/11 environment, by allies in the White House (The NSC Staff), the Vice President, and ultimately, the President himself, there was no stopping their efforts for complete victory.

The evolution of the neoconservative ideology aside, the study has illustrated the clique has proven to be reckless, shortsighted, and overly optimistic that democracy along could transform the Middle East. Within Iraq itself, the inability of the neoconservatives to understand postwar realities, both during the time prewar planning period and in the post-Saddam phase, these efforts laid the foundation for a chaotic postwar Iraq that provided the environment that would allow the Sunni-led insurgency to flourish. The neoconservative misjudgments, their over reliance on Chalabi, eclipsed any gains made during the military operation to remove the regime.

Similarly, the neoconservatives were delighted to discuss their success in transforming US-Iraq policy, but a larger issue concerns the willingness of these individuals to accept responsibilities for their overt failings. A few examples are instructive. The neoconservatives have been silent with respect to their inept postwar planning and its consequences, namely the growing deaths of US military personnel, not to mention the horrific death toll among Iraqi civilians. Similarly, the neoconservatives are no where to be found when the debate erupted over the absence of credible a stable security environment for Iraq, the absence of which instilled confidence among Sunni-led insurgents that they could operate with impunity within postwar Iraq. Third, the neoconservatives have not challenged the statements made by General Zinni, who called their war planning criminal and inept. Equally significant the neoconservatives have sought cover when they were called upon to answer the loss of US moral authority in the war on terror as a result of an invasion that lacked international support, or how US policy in Iraq has affected relations with a host of countries (France, Germany, and Canada) that were formally major American allies.

Collectively, these realities according to Francis Fukuyama indicate that the "neoconservative moment"[126] is over, and their influence with the president has itself declined considerably. With the exit of notable neoconservatives, such as Wolfowitz and Fieth, combined with the situation on the ground in Iraq and the overt change in administration rhetoric, are other indicators that the twilight of the neoconservatives is upon us. Finally, the critique of the failings of the neoconservative ideology of war involves the illusion that Iraq could be "done on the cheap." That is the neoconservative assertion which argued that Iraq's oil industry would ensure a quick transformation of the Iraqi economy and thus the countries oil reserves would help

---

126   See Francis Fukuyama, (2004) "The Neoconservative Moment," *National Interest*, (76): 57–68, http://www.keepmedia.com/jsp/artricle_detail_print.jsp. Retrieved on 29 October 2005.

defray the costs of postwar reconstruction. Two indices demonstrate the folly of this logic. First, overt statements by administration officials touting the importance of Iraq's oil reserves galvanized the insurgency in this regard to attack weak points in the oil pipeline throughout Iraq. Worse the administration is concerns the fact that the coalition forces have had been unable to preclude such attacks. Second, the recent General Accounting Office (GAO) report that the price tag for the war will exceed $200 billion is evidence enough the neoconservative appraisal was woefully incompetent.

Finally, the neoconservative ideology has had a profound impact on US policy in Iraq and international relations in general. No matter what one may think of this ideology, one can not dismiss the fact those individuals that have carried the burden have themselves left an indelible impression on the US domestic and foreign policy. These realities aside, the war ideology has two tremendous burdens that will forever haunt any triumphs attributable to the neoconservatives: first there failings in Iraq will forever affect the short term and long term future of Iraq, and second, the outcome of Iraq will define the legacy of a US president.

Chapter 3

Legislative-Executive Relations and US Policy Toward Iraq

Louis Fisher[1]

Congressional Research Service

Introduction

Iraq has preoccupied the last three Presidents. In response to Iraq's invasion of Kuwait President George H.W. Bush in August of 1990 assembled a multinational coalition and forced Saddam Hussein back to his borders. President Bill Clinton regularly used military force against Iraq without congressional authorization. President George W. Bush asked Congress for legislation to authorize war against Iraq, insisting that the statute be enacted before the November 2002 mid-term elections. To build pressure for prompt legislative action, executive officials called attention to a number of imminent threats, especially the existence of Iraqi weapons of mass destruction. Members of Congress and their committees did a poor job of analyzing speculative, tenuous, and erroneous statements from the administration. The media later conceded that it functioned less as an independent check on executive assertions than as a conveyor belt for administration policy. A series of miscalculations and false statements from the administration led to a costly occupation of Iraq, rather than the rapid liberation and reconstruction of a democratic society that was so confidently predicted by executive officials.

The First Iraq War

In response to Iraq's invasion of Kuwait on 2 August 1990, President Bush sent one hundred thousand troops to Saudi Arabia and the Middle East. The strategy at that point was to deter further Iraqi aggression, but Bush's decision in November to double the size of US forces gave him the capacity to wage offensive war. Instead of seeking authority from Congress, the administration created a multinational alliance and encouraged the UN Security Council to "authorize" the use of military force. The coalition was willing to cover most of the costs of military action. On 29 November 1990, the Security Council passed Resolution 678 to authorize military force against Iraq.

---

1   The views expressed in this chapter are those of the author.

Secretary of Defense Dick Cheney testified before the Senate Armed Services Committee on 3 December telling lawmakers that Bush did not require "any additional authorization from Congress" before attacking Iraq.[2] The phrase "additional authorization" seemed to imply that Security Council approval was sufficient. The Justice Department argued in court that Bush could order offensive actions in Iraq without seeking advance authority from Congress. A district court held that the case was not ripe for judicial determination, but also rejected many of the sweeping interpretations of presidential power advanced by the administration. The judge pointed out that if the President "had the sole power to determine that any particular offensive military operation, no matter how vast, does not constitute war-making but only an offensive military attack, the congressional power to declare war will be at the mercy of a semantic decision by the Executive. Such an 'interpretation' would evade the plain language of the Constitution, and it cannot stand."[3]

Either because of the court's decision or other factors, on 8 January 1991, Bush asked Congress to pass legislation authorizing military action. When asked by reporters the next day whether he needed a resolution from Congress, he replied: "I don't think I need it. ... I feel that I have the authority to fully implement the United Nations resolutions."[4] On 12 January Congress authorized Bush to take offensive actions against Iraq. In signing the legislation, he indicated that he could have acted without congressional authority. He said his request for congressional support "did not, and my signing this resolution does not, constitute any change in the long-standing positions of the executive branch on either the President's constitutional authority to use the Armed Forces to defend vital US interests or the constitutionality of the War Powers Resolution."[5] Bush's signing statement did not alter the fact that the resolution passed by Congress specifically authorized him to act. What counts is language in the public law, not what the President says in signing it.

After a rapid victory, Bush decided to pull out of Iraq rather than continuing on to Baghdad. He was later criticized by those who believed he should have removed Saddam Hussein from power. However, he later gave several explanations why he chose to withdraw US forces:

> I firmly believed that we should not march into Baghdad. Our stated mission, as codified in UN resolutions, was a simple one—end the aggression, knock Iraq's forces out of Kuwait, and restore Kuwait's leaders. To occupy Iraq would instantly shatter our coalition, turning the whole Arab world against us, and make a broken tyrant into a latter-day Arab hero. It would have taken us way beyond the imprimatur of international law bestowed by the resolutions of the Security Council, assigning young soldiers to a fruitless hunt for a securely entrenched dictator and condemning them to fight in what would be an

---

2   "Crisis in the Persian Gulf Region: U.S. Policy Options and Implications," hearingsbefore the Senate Committee on Armed Forces, 101st Cong., 2d Sess. (1990), 701.

3   Dellums v. Bush, 752 F.Supp. 1141, 1145 (D.D.C. 1990).

4   Public Papers of the Presidents, 1991, I, 20

5   Ibid., 40.

unwinnable urban guerrilla war. It could only plunge that part of the world into greater instability and destroy the credibility we were working so hard to reestablish.[6]

Bush's position would be revisited by his son in 2003. After losing support from many nations, including France, Germany, and Russia, President George W. Bush chose to do what the critics of his father had wanted all along: go north to Baghdad, oust Saddam Hussein, and engage in nation-building.

Clinton's Actions

During the 1992 presidential campaign, then Governor Bill Clinton repeatedly expressed a willingness to use military force against other nations. His first opportunity came on 26 June 1993, when he ordered a cruise missile attack aimed at destroying an Iraqi intelligence facility. His address to the nation reviewed an attempted assassination of former President Bush during a visit to Kuwait, concluding that there was "compelling evidence" that the plot was directed and pursued by the Iraqi intelligence service. He called the attempted assassination "an attack against our country and against all Americans."[7] In a message to Congress, he said that he ordered the attack "in the exercise of our inherent right of self-defense as recognized in Article 51 of the UN Charter and pursuant to my constitutional authority with respect to the conduct of foreign relations and as Commander in Chief."[8]

On this occasion, in later military actions against Iraq and Haiti, and in the use of force in Bosnia and Kosovo, Clinton never sought Congressional authorization. Although he went to the UN Security Council or NATO for "authority," he concluded that he could act constitutionally as Commander in Chief. When lawmakers debated restrictive language, he announced his opposition to legislative amendments that "improperly limit my ability to perform my constitutional duties as Commander-in-Chief."[9]

In justifying the sending of 23 cruise missiles into Baghdad, Clinton explained that it was "essential to protect our sovereignty, to send a message to those who engage in state-sponsored terrorism, to deter further violence against our people, and to affirm the expectation of civilized behavior among nations." He underscored the message being sent to Iraq and other nations: "We will combat terrorism. We will deter aggression. We will protect our people."[10] That argument was not convincing. If the United States had evidence of terrorist activities by Syria, it would not have launched cruise missiles into Damascus. Other responses, with less military force, would have been used.

---

6   George Bush and Brent Scowcroft, *A World Transformed* (New York: Knopf, 1998), 464.

7   Public Papers of the Presidents, 1993, I, 938.

8   Ibid., 940.

9   Public Papers of the Presidents, 1993, II, 1770.

10   Public Papers of the Presidents, 1993, I, 938–9.

Clinton turned to military force against Iraq several more times. In September 1996, he ordered the launching of cruise missiles against Iraq in response to an attack by Iraqi forces against the Kurdish-controlled city of Irbil in northern Iraq. Cruise missiles also hit air defense systems in southern Iraq. Clinton explained the purpose of the strikes. The missiles "sent the following message to Saddam Hussein: When you abuse your own people or threaten your neighbors, you must pay a price."[11] This explanation stretched credulity. The United States is in no position to use military force against other nations, including Russia and China that abuse their people or threaten their neighbors.

Toward the end of January 1998, Clinton threatened once again to bomb Iraq, this time because Saddam Hussein had refused to give UN inspectors full access to examine Iraqi sites for possible nuclear, chemical, and biological weapons. Military action was delayed to give UN Secretary General Kofi Annan an opportunity to negotiate a settlement with Iraq, but in December Clinton ordered four days of heavy bombing. This military action commenced as the House of Representatives was engaged in voting on Clinton's impeachment.

Also in 1998, Congress passed the Iraq Liberation Act. The statute begins by itemizing a number of congressional findings about Iraq: the invasion of Iran and Kuwait, the killing of Kurds, the use of chemical weapons against civilians, and other offenses. It supported, as a legally nonbinding "sense of Congress," efforts to remove Saddam Hussein from power and replace him with a democratic government. The law states that none of its provisions "shall be construed to authorize or otherwise speak to the use of United States Armed Forces (except as provided in section 4(a)(2)) in carrying out this Act."[12] That section authorized up to $97 million in military supplies to Iraqi opposition groups as part of the transition to democracy in Iraq. By its explicit terms, the statute did not authorize war.

Drafting Plans for War

Neoconservatives, strategically located in the White House and executive departments during the Bush I administration, began drafting ambitious plans for military action against Iraq and converting its government to a liberal democracy. They would continue their work under Bush II. Prominent neocons in the defense establishment include Paul Wolfowitz, Douglas Feith, Abram Shulsky, I. Lewis (Scooter) Libby, William Kristol, Carnes Lord, Gary Schmitt, Richard Perle, Elliott Abrams, John Bolton, and Zalmay Khalilzad.[13]

---

11   Public Papers of the Presidents, 1996, II, 1469.

12   112 Stat. 3181, § 8 (1998).

13   Anne Norton, *Leo Strauss and the Politics of American Empire* (New Haven: Yale University Press, 2004), 6–18; John Micklethwait and Adrian Wooldridge, *The Right Nation: Conservative Power in America* (New York: Penguin Press, 2004), 200–207; James Mann, *Rise of the Vulcans: The History of Bush's War Cabinet* (New York: Viking, 2004), 22–9;

In 1992, Wolfowitz, Libby, and Khalilzad teamed up to produce a Pentagon document called the Defense Planning Guidance. A draft copy, leaked to the press, envisioned the United States as the world's only superpower, capable of using its military might to advance and protect US interests. After running into strong criticism, the draft was rewritten and toned down.[14] This strong military edge, set aside in 1992, would reappear in subsequent documents prepared by neocons.

Writing in 1996, William Kristol and Robert Kagan urged a hefty increase in military spending, "greater moral clarity," and a need to champion "American exceptionalism."[15] Here is the key phrase used to justify America's preeminent military role in the post-Cold War world: "Benevolent global hegemony." For those who considered such language as "either hubristic or morally suspect," Kristol and Kagan explain that a hegemon "is nothing more or less than a leader with preponderant influence and authority over all others in its domain." To those who object to the United States glorifying the notion of dominance, Kristol and Lawrence Kaplan reply: "Well, what is wrong with dominance, in the service of sound principles and high ideals?"[16]

Neocons offered many reasons to overthrow Saddam Hussein. Writing in 1999, David Wurmser devoted much of his analysis to Hussein's "pernicious, extortionist character" and his "brutal use" of force against Iraqi citizens and neighboring countries.[17] Hussein's bloody record was one way to build public support for military action, but Wurmser pointed to more strategic goals. Iraq occupied a "resource-laden territory" that marks a key transportation route "rich in both geographic endowments and human talent." Wurmser noted that Iraq "has large, proven oil reserves, water, and other important resources."[18]

In a book edited in 2000, Kristol and Kagan objected that Bush I failed to see the mission in Iraq "through to its proper conclusion: the removal of Saddam from power in Baghdad."[19] Also in 2000, the Project for the New American Century issued a report entitled "Rebuilding America's Defenses: Strategy, Forces and Resources For a New Century." The Project, established in 1997, is chaired by William Kristol. The back page, identifying 27 participants, includes the names of Wolfowitz, Libby, and Shulsky. The report explains that the Project builds "upon the defense

---

Elizabeth Drew, "The Neocons in Power," *New York Review of Books*, 12 June 2003, 20–22.

14   Mann, *Rise of the Vulcans*, 208–15.

15   William Kristol and Robert Kagan, "Toward a Neo-Reaganite Foreign Policy," *Foreign Affairs*, vol. 75, 18, 19 (1996).

16   Lawrence F. Kaplan and William Kristol, *The War Over Iraq: Saddam's Tyranny and America's Mission* (San Francisco: Encounter Books, 2003), 112.

17   David Wurmser, *Tyranny's Ally: America's Failure to Defeat Saddam Hussein* (Washington, D.C.: AEI Press, 1999), 116.

18   Ibid., 117.

19   Robert Kagan and William Kristol, eds., *Present Dangers: Crisis and Opportunity in American Foreign and Defense Policy* (San Francisco: Encounter Books, 2000), 6.

strategy outlined by the Cheney Defense Department in the waning days of the Bush Administration."

Making the Case for War After 9/11

When the Bush administration first began talking about war against Iraq, the White House repeatedly cautioned that President Bush was not rushing into war. At a news conference on 21 August 2002, Bush called himself a "patient man," prepared to look at "all technologies available to us and diplomacy and intelligence."[20] Toward the end of that month, however, Vice President Dick Cheney delivered a public speech that made it clear the administration had settled on a single option: going to war. He warned that Saddam Hussein would "fairly soon" have nuclear weapons and that it would be useless to seek a Security Council resolution requiring Iraq to submit to weapons inspectors.[21] Newspaper editorials interpreted Cheney's remarks as leaving "little room for measures short of the destruction of Saddam Hussein's regime through preemptive military action."[22]

In the midst of this talk of "regime change," President Bush agreed to address the United Nations on 12 September. After cataloguing Iraq's failure to comply with previous Security Council resolutions, Bush laid down five conditions for a peaceful resolution. If Iraq wanted to avoid war it would have to immediately and unconditionally pledge to remove or destroy all weapons of mass destruction, end all support for terrorism, cease persecution of its civilian population, release or account for all Gulf War personnel, and immediately end all illicit trade outside the oil-for-food program.[23] If Iraq complied with those conditions, Saddam Hussein could stay in power. The policy of regime change seemed to be set aside. Four days later Iraq agreed to unconditional inspections.

On 7 October, President Bush gave a major address in Cincinnati, calculated to convince the public and Congress that the nation faced a "grave threat" from Iraq. The speech was delivered just days before Congress was to vote on legislation authorizing war. Bush stated that Iraq "possesses and produces chemical and biological weapons," had a "growing fleet of manned and unmanned aerial vehicles" to disperse those weapons, was reconstituting its nuclear weapons program by purchasing aluminum tubes to enrich uranium for nuclear weapons, and claimed that Iraq and al Qaeda "have had high-level contacts that go back a decade." Moreover, Iraq had developed "mobile weapons facilities" to prevent inspectors from discovering its weapons of mass destruction.[24]

---

20   Weekly Compilation of Presidential Documents, vol. 38, 1393–4.
21   Elizabeth Bumiller and James Dao, "Cheney Says Peril of a Nuclear Iraq Justifies Attack," *New York Times*, 27 August 2002, A1.
22   Mr. Cheney on Iraq" (Editorial), *Washington Post*, 27 August 2002, A14.
23   Weekly Compilation of Presidential Documents, vol. 38, 1532.
24   Weekly Compilation of Presidential Documents, vol. 38, 1716–20.

Those statements and others were sharply contested at the time, both within the government and by the press. Before the war began in March 2003, UN inspectors searched for corroborating evidence to support the claim that Iraq had WMDs. They found nothing. Their efforts were derided by the administration, but when US inspectors later entered the country they found no evidence either. Finally, in January 2005, the press learned that the administration a month earlier had terminated the search for weapons of mass destruction in Iraq. The top US weapons inspector, Charles A. Duelfer, issued a comprehensive report that disclosed that Iraq had destroyed its chemical and biological weapons in the early 1990s.[25]

All of the claims made by the Bush administration concerning Iraq's WMDs and its alleged ties with al Qaeda were seriously challenged in 2002 before Congress voted on the Iraq Resolution. The assertions were disputed again when Secretary of State Colin Powell presented the administration's case to the United Nations on 5 February 2003, a month before the war began. Yet Congress passed the statute and the United States went to war on evidence that was unsubstantiated from the beginning and eventually found to be non-existent. The intelligence agencies were later faulted for their role in relying excessively on Iraqi exiles, but the errors of judgment and miscalculation covered a much wider community, including the White House, the Pentagon, the National Security Council, Congress, and the press.

The first issue was whether there was a link between Iraq and al Qaeda. Immediately following the 9/11 terrorist attacks, Congress passed legislation to authorize President Bush to use "all necessary and appropriate force against those nations, organizations, or persons he determines planned, authorized, committed, or aided" the attacks.[26] At a minimum, the statute authorized military action against the Taliban regime and al Qaeda camps in Afghanistan. If the Bush administration could establish a connection between Iraq and al Qaeda, it could justify war against Iraq on both moral and statutory grounds.

On 25 September 2002, President Bush claimed that Saddam Hussein and al Qaeda "work in concert."[27] A day later he stated that the Iraqi regime "has longstanding and continuing ties to terrorist organizations, and there are [al Qaeda] terrorists inside Iraq."[28] Yet members of Congress who attended classified briefings said that credible evidence of a link between Iraq and al Qaeda had not been presented.[29] There was some evidence of possible al Qaeda activity in the northeastern part of Iraq—the community of Ansar al-Islam—but that was Kurdish territory made semiautonomous by American and British flights over the no-fly zones. Saddam Hussein was not in a

---

25   Dafna Linzer, "Search for Banned Arms in Iraq Ended Last Month," *Washington Post*, 12 January 2005, A1; "Search for Illicit Weapons in Iraq Ends," *New York Times*,12 January 2005, A10.

26   115 Stat. 224 (2001).

27   Weekly Compilation of Presidential Documents, vol. 39, 1619.

28   Ibid., 1625.

29   Karen De Young, "Unwanted Debate on Iraq-Al Qaeda Links Revived," *Washington Post*, 27 September 2002, A19.

position to do anything about Ansar. Moreover, al Qaeda groups operated in some 60 countries. Presence alone could not justify military force.

After Congress voted to support the Iraq Resolution, the administration promoted a story about Mohamed Atta, the principal hijacker of the 9/11 attacks, meeting with an Iraqi intelligence officer in Prague in April 2001. Czech President Vaclav Havel and the Czech intelligence service denied that there was any evidence of such a meeting. CIA Director George Tenet told Congress that his agency had no information that could confirm the meeting.[30] Additional research disclosed that at the time Atta was supposedly in Prague, the FBI had evidence he was in Florida.[31]

On 11 February 2003, shortly before military operations began in Iraq, Secretary Powell referred to an audiotape, believed to be by Osama bin Laden, to show that he was "in partnership with Iraq."[32] The tape contains no evidence of a partnership. Bin Laden specifically criticized "pagan regimes" and the "apostacy" practiced by socialist governments in the Middle East, including Iraq. In a military confrontation between the United States and Iraq, the tape certainly supported Iraq, but that was not evidence of a partnership. It merely meant that as much as al Qaeda detests Iraq, it detests the United States even more.

The administration said that the activities of a Jordanian terrorist, Abu Musab Zarqawi, revealed a relationship between Iraq and al Qaeda. However, CIA Director Tenet told Congress that Zarqawi was not under the control of Saddam Hussein and that Zarqawi and his network were "independent" of al Qaeda.[33] Vice President Cheney remained convinced of a connection between Iraq and al Qaeda and that Iraq was somehow tied to the 9/11 attacks,[34] but a few days later President Bush said he had seen no evidence that Saddam Hussein was involved in 9/11.[35]

The staff of the 9/11 Commission denied that a "collaborative relationship" existed between Saddam Hussein and al Qaeda. Their investigation found that he had rebuffed requests from al Qaeda leaders in the 1990s for assistance and that there was "no credible evidence that Iraq and al Qaeda cooperated on attacks against the United States." The staff concluded that the alleged meeting between Atta and

---

30   James Risen, "Prague Discounts An Iraqi Meeting," *New York Times*, 21 October 2002, A1; James Risen, "How Politics and Rivalries Fed Suspicions of a Meeting," *New York Times*, 21 October 2002, A9; Peter S. Green, "Havel Denies Telephoning US on Iraq Meeting," *New York Times*, 23 October 2002, A11.

31   James Risen, "No Evidence of Meeting With Iraqi," *New York Times*, 17 June 2004, A14.

32   Dan Eggen and Susan Schmidt, "Bin Laden Calls Iraqis to Arms," *Washington Post*, 12 February 2003, A1 and A14; David Johnston, "Top U.S. Officials Press CaseLinking Iraq to Al Qaeda," *New York Times*, 12 February 2003, A1 and A16.

33   Dana Priest and Walter Pincus, "Bin Laden-Hussein Link Hazy," *Washington Post*, 13 February 2003, A20.

34   Dana Priest and Glenn Kessler, "Iraq, 9/11 Still Linked By Cheney," *Washington Post*, 29 September 2003, A1 and A15.

35   "Hussein 9/11 Role Doubted," *Washington Post*, 17 September 2003, A28.

an Iraqi intelligence official in Prague never occurred.[36] The 9/11 Commission reviewed the available evidence on Atta and concluded that he did not meet with an Iraqi official in Prague in April 2001.[37]

At about the same time that the commission staff released its study, the Senate Select Committee on Intelligence issued a report on prewar intelligence assessments on Iraq. It found "no credible information that Baghdad had foreknowledge of the 11 September attacks or any other al Qaeda strike."[38] It agreed with the CIA's conclusion that "there were likely several instances of contacts between Iraq and al Qaeda throughout the 1990s, but that these contacts did not add up to an established formal relationship."[39]

In October 2004, Defense Secretary Donald Rumsfeld said that even though there had been interactions between the Iraqi government and al Qaeda operatives, he had not seen "strong, hard evidence" linking Saddam Hussein and al Qaeda. Moreover, he doubted that Zarqawi had a formal allegiance to bin Laden.[40] A new CIA report also raised doubts that Iraq had harbored members of Zarqawi's group.[41] After the United States intervened militarily the relationship between Zarqawi and al Qaeda seemed to be closer, but that activity was after the war, not before.[42]

In the Cincinnati speech, President Bush offered other reasons for going to war against Iraq. He referred to Iraqi efforts to purchase aluminum tubes that could be used to enrich uranium as part of the process for making nuclear weapons. Appearing on CNN the previous month, on 8 September, National Security Adviser Condoleezza Rice spoke confidently about the relationship between the tubes and an Iraqi program for making nuclear weapons: "We do know that there have been shipments ... into Iraq, for instance, of aluminum tubes that are only ... for nuclear weapons programs, centrifuge programs."[43]

However, almost a year earlier her staff had been told that the government's foremost nuclear experts doubted that the tubes were part of a nuclear weapons program. They believed that the tubes were most likely intended for small artillery

---

36   Philip Shenon and Christopher Marquis, "Challenges Bush: A Chilling Chronology Rewrites the History of the Attacks," *New York Times*, 17 June 2004, A1 and A15; Walter Pincus and Dana Milbank, "Al Qaeda-Hussein Link Is Dismissed," *Washington Post*, 17 June 2004, A1.

37   *The 9/11 Commission Report* (New York: W. W. Norton, 2004), 228–9.

38   "U.S. Intelligence Community's Prewar Intelligence Assessments on Iraq," Report of the Senate Committee on Intelligence, S. Report 108-301, 108th Cong., 2d Sess. (2004), 322 (hereafter "Senate Intelligence Report").

39   Ibid., 346.

40   Thom Shanker, "Rumsfeld Sees Lack of Proof For Qaeda-Hussein Link," *New York Times*, 5 October 2004, A10.

41   Douglas Jehl, "A New CIA Report Casts Doubt on a Key Terrorist's Tie to Iraq," *New York Times*, 6 October 2004, A12.

42   Walter Pincus, "Zarqawi Is Said to Swear Allegiance to Bin Laden," *Washington Post*, 19 October 2004, A16.

43   *New York Times*, 3 October 2004, 17.

rockets.[44] In October 2002, when the CIA issued its National Intelligence Estimate (NIE) on Iraq's weapons of mass destruction, the intelligence agencies were divided. The CIA and the Defense Intelligence Agency (DIA) concluded that the aluminum tubes were part of an Iraqi nuclear weapons program. The Department of Energy's Office of Intelligence and the State Department's Bureau of Intelligence and Research (INR) believed that the tubes were intended for a conventional rocket program.[45]

Specialists from UN inspection teams determined that the specifications of the tubes were consistent with tubes used for rockets. There was no evidence that Iraq had purchased materials needed for centrifuges, including motors, metal caps, and special magnets.[46] Dr. Mohamed El Baradei, head of the International Atomic Energy Agency (IAEA), briefed the UN Security Council on 9 January 2003 and again on 27 January, concluding both times that the tubes were consistent for use as rockets.[47]

A day later, on 28 January, in delivering his State of the Union address to Congress, President Bush announced that US intelligence sources "tell us that [Saddam Hussein] had attempted to purchase high-strength aluminum tubes suitable for nuclear weapons production."[48] He did not explain, in this brief reference to the tubes, that the US intelligence community was divided on the issue, that the tubes could have a legitimate use as ordinary artillery shells, and that IAEA inspectors had reached that conclusion.

On 5 February 2003, in his presentation to the Security Council, Secretary Powell challenged ElBaradei's findings and laid out the case for war. He charged that Iraq was trying to reconstitute a nuclear weapons program by attempting to "acquire high-specification aluminum tubes from 11 different countries, even after inspections resumed." He acknowledged that experts were divided on how the tubes would be used,[49] but depended heavily on work done by a CIA analyst who argued that the tubes were so "overspecified" that Iraq would not waste money by using a costly alloy on a conventional rocket.[50] After the start of military operations in March 2003, mounting evidence supported the use of the tubes for rockets.[51] The July 2004 report by the Senate Intelligence Committee concluded that "the information available to

---

44   "How White House Embraced Suspect Iraq Arms Intelligence," *New York Times*, 3 October 2004, 1,

45   Senate Intelligence Report, 95.

46   Michael R. Gordon, "Agency Challenges Evidence Against Iraq Cited by Bush," *New York Times*, 10 January 2003, A10; Joby Warrick, "U.S. Claim on Iraqi Nuclear Program is Called Into Question," *Washington Post*, 24 January 2003, A1.

47   "Report on Nuclear Quest: 'Clarification' Is Needed," *New York Times*, 10 January 2003, A10; "Nuclear Inspection Chief Reports Finding No New Weapons," *New York Times*, 28 January 2003, A11.

48   Weekly Compilation of Presidential Documents, vol. 39, 115.

49   "Powell's Address, Presenting 'Deeply Troubling' Evidence on Iraq," *New York Times*, 6 February 2003, A15–16.

50   Senate Intelligence Report, 88–90.

51   Barton Gellman and Walter Pincus, "Depiction of Threat Outgrew Supporting Evidence," *Washington Post*, 10 August 2003, A1.

the Intelligence Community indicated that these tubes were intended to be used for an Iraqi conventional rocket program and not a nuclear program."[52]

On 3 October 2004, Condoleezza Rice was asked about her comments two years earlier that the tubes were suitable "only" for a nuclear weapons program. She said at the time she was aware of the debate within the administration about the tubes: "I knew that there was a dispute. I actually didn't really know the nature of the dispute."[53] If she knew only of the debate in general and not the specific details, why go on record on 8 September 2002—a month before Congress voted on the Iraq Resolution—and pretend to speak with such assurance and finality on one side of a contested, unsettled issue?

The administration offered another reason why Iraq was trying to restart its nuclear weapons program: An attempt to purchase uranium oxide (yellowcake) from a country in Africa. Reports of that nature circulated in the press in October 2002, just before the congressional vote on the Iraq Resolution.[54] In response to a UN Security Council resolution after Congress passed the statute, Iraq produced a lengthy "declaration" on 7 December on its WMDs. On 19 December, the State Department released a "Fact Sheet" (prepared jointly with the CIA) that gave examples of "omissions in the Declaration." According to the department, the declaration "ignores efforts to procure uranium from Niger. *Why is the Iraqi regime hiding their uranium procurement?*"[55] In an op-ed piece for the *New York Times* on 23 January 2003, Condoleezza Rice called the Iraqi document a "12,200-page lie." In support of that condemnation, she said that the declaration "fails to account for or explain Iraq's efforts to get uranium from abroad."[56]

It turned out that the lie was not by Iraq but by the Bush administration. The State Department's "fact" sheet was false in many respects. The department's own intelligence agency, INR, had substantial doubts that Iraq had tried to buy uranium ore from Niger, and so did many CIA analysts. To place disputed material in a "fact sheet" and release it to the public seemed more like partisan propaganda than professional analysis. When the department issued the fact sheet, one executive official recalled: "People winced and thought, 'Why are you repeating this trash?'"[57]

---

52   Senate Intelligence Report, 131.

53   Glenn Kessler, "Rice: Iraqi Nuclear Plans Unclear," *Washington Post*, 4 October 2004, A18. See also Jeff Gerth, "Rice Defends Going to War Despite Dispute About Iraqi Weapons," *New York Times*, 4 October 2004, A10.

54   Walter Pincus, "For Iraq Inspectors, 'Yellow Cake' and Other Quarries," *Washington Post*, 10 October 2002, A17.

55   U.S. Department of State, "Illustrative Examples of Omissions From the Iraqi Declaration to the United Nations Security Council," *Fact Sheet*, 19 December 2002 (emphasis in original).

56   Condoleezza Rice, "Why We Know Iraq Is Lying," *New York Times*, 23 January 2003, A27.

57   Dana Priest and Karen De Young, "CIA Questioned Documents Linking Iraq, Uranium Ore," *Washington Post*, 22 March 2003, A30.

In his State of the Union Address in January 2003, President Bush told Congress and the nation that the "British Government has learned that Saddam Hussein recently sought significant quantities of uranium from Africa."[58] Why did Bush rely on British intelligence instead of American intelligence? The previous October, when Bush prepared to give his address in Cincinnati, CIA Director Tenet personally intervened to ask that the reference to uranium ore be removed from the speech. The White House took it out.[59] When the claim reappeared in the draft State of the Union address, why didn't Tenet insist once again that it be stricken? In a letter to a member of Congress on 29 April 2003, the State Department disclosed that its 19 December fact sheet had been developed jointly with the CIA.[60] Had the CIA uncovered new evidence between October and December to justify this entry on the fact sheet? Apparently not. Tenet would later publicly apologize for allowing the Niger claim to appear in the State of the Union address.

The assertions by Rice and Bush were discredited on 7 March 2003, when ElBaradei told the Security Council that the key piece of evidence on Iraq seeking uranium ore from Africa was a fake. Someone had fabricated the documents.[61] A US official, after reviewing the documents, remarked: "We fell for it."[62] However, the mistake was not merely an unfortunate error that occurs in any human activity. Instead, it reflected the willingness and eagerness of the administration to go public with information that was tenuous and suspect, had been flagged by the CIA as unreliable, and depended on British rather than American intelligence.

During an appearance on *NBC*'s "Meet the Press" on Sunday, 8 June 2003, Condoleezza Rice said she was unaware that there were doubts about Iraq's attempt to buy uranium from Niger: "Maybe somebody knew down in the bowels of the agency, but no one in our circles knew that there were doubts and suspicions that this might be a forgery."[63] Her explanation did not put the matter to rest. On 7 July, the administration conceded that Bush should not have included in the State of the Union address the claim that Iraq tried to buy uranium in Africa.[64]

---

58   Dana Priest and Karen De Young, "CIA Questioned Documents Linking Iraq, Uranium Ore," *Washington Post*, 22 March 2003, A30.

59   Weekly Compilation of Presidential Documents, vol. 39, 115.

60   David E. Sanger and James Risen, "CIA Chief Takes Blame in Assertion on Iraqi Uranium" *New York Times*, 12 July 2003, A1, A5; Walter Pincus and Mike Allen, "CIA Got Uranium Reference Cut in Oct.," July 13, 2003, p. A1. For details on CIA's involvement with various drafts of the Cincinnati speech, see Senate Intelligence Report, 55–7.

61   Letter from Paul V. Kelly, Assistant Secretary of Legislative Affairs, U.S. Department of State, to Representative Henry A. Waxman, 29 April 2003, 1.

62   Transcript of ElBaradei's remarks appears in the *New York Times*, 8 March 2003, A8.

63   Joby Warrick, "Some Evidence on Iraq Called Fake," *New York Times*, 8 March 2003, A1, A18.

64   Walter Pincus, "CIA Says It Cabled Key Data to White House," *Washington Post*, 13 June 2003, A16.

On 11 July, Tenet took personal responsibility for the assertion being placed in the State of the Union address. He explained that agency officials, in approving the President's address, "concurred that the text in the speech was factually correct— i.e., that the British government report said that Iraq sought uranium from Africa." However, he said it was a mistake to clear a presidential address on that ground: "This did not rise to the level of certainty which should be required for presidential speeches, and CIA should have ensured that it was removed."[65]

The next question: Who drafted the speech and what role did the National Security Council play in reviewing it? The press learned that Tenet had personally spoken to Stephen J. Hadley, the deputy national security adviser, in early October 2002 and warned against Bush claiming in his Cincinnati speech that Iraq tried to buy uranium ore from Niger.[66] Instead of the intelligence wallowing in the bowels of the CIA or some other agency, as Rice suggested, it had reached her deputy. In an effort to quell the controversy, the White House released a declassified version of the National Intelligence Estimate on Iraq's WMDs. A reporter asked a "senior administration official" how Rice and other members of the National Security Council could be unaware that some agencies in the US intelligence community objected to the yellowcake claim. The official explained that they "did not read footnotes in a 90-page document." The reporters, looking at the NIE on their lap, could see that the disagreement within the Intelligence Community was not buried in footnotes. The reservations of the State Department were flagged in the very first paragraph of the opening section on key judgments.[67] A flurry of apologies were soon on their way from Hadley and Rice.[68]

In its report of 9 July 2004, the Senate Intelligence Committee said that the language in the October 2002 NIE that Iraq tried "vigorously" to purchase uranium ore was inappropriate because it "overstated" what the Intelligence Community knew about Iraq's procurement efforts. Moreover, even after obtaining the documents and being alerted by the State Department about problems, CIA and DIA analysts "did not examine them carefully enough to see the obvious problems with the documents." Finally, Tenet "should have taken the time to read the State of the Union [draft] speech and fact check it himself."[69]

---

65   Walter Pincus, "White House Backs Off Claim on Iraqi Buy," 8 July 2003, A1; David E. Sanger, "Bush Claim on Iraq Had Flawed Origin, White House Says," *New York Times*, 8 July 2003, A1.

66   David E. Sanger and James Risen, "CIA Chief Takes Blame in Assertion on Iraqi Uranium," *New York Times*, 12 July 2003, A1, A5.

67   Richard W. Stevenson, "Bush Declares His Faith in Tenet and CIA," *New York Times*, 13 July 2003, 1.

68   "Senior Administration Official Holds Background Briefing on Weapons of Mass Destruction in Iraq, as Released by the White House," 18 July 2003, 10, 12, 16; www.fas. org/irp/news/2003/07/wh071803.html. See also www.fas.org/irp/cia/product/iraqwmd.html.

69   Dana Milbank and Walter Pincus, "Bush Aides Disclose Warnings From CIA," *Washington Post*, 23 July 2003, A1; Richard W. Stevenson, "President Denies He Oversold Case for War with Iraq," *New York Times*, 31 July 2003, A11.

Other administration claims about Iraqi WMDs were scrutinized and found wanting. In his Cincinnati speech, President Bush said that Iraq "possesses and produces chemical and biological weapons." That flat assertion relied on a CIA report of October 2002. On the first page of the report, under "Key Judgments," appears this sentence: "Baghdad has chemical and biological weapons as well as missiles with ranges in excess of UN restrictions."[70] The CIA document appeared at a critical time, just as members of Congress were scheduled to vote on the Iraq Resolution.

The claim that Baghdad had chemical and biological weapons was highly misleading and did not accurately reflect the cautious and qualified statements in the analytical section of the CIA report. It stated that Iraq had the "ability" to produce chemical warfare (CW) agents, it "probably" had concealed equipment to continue its CW effort, it continued to expand a "dual-use infrastructure" that could be diverted to CW production, and had the "capability" of converting legitimate vaccine and biopesticide plants to pursue biological warfare (BW).[71] All of those statements pointed to the potential, but not actual existence, of chemical and biological weapons. The reference to "dual-use infrastructure" was revealing. Again and again the administration would analyze something that had two possible uses, as with aluminum tubes, and interpret the evidence to fit only one use: weapons of mass destruction.

The Senate Intelligence Committee analyzed the process used by the CIA to produce the October 2002 NIE, and concluded that some of the errors resulted from the compressed time period available to write it. But even the lack of time could not explain fundamental analytical flaws.[72] Three days after publication of the classified NIE, the CIA produced an unclassified version called a "white paper" on Iraqis WMDs. Many of the caveats and references to alternative agency views contained in the classified version were stripped from the white paper. Qualified statements about "we judge" and "we assess" became, in the publicly available document, statements of fact rather than assessment.[73] The blunt claim that Baghdad "has" chemical and biological weapons, the committee said, overstated what was known and relied on a source (called "Curve Ball") who had a drinking problem and was an Iraqi design engineer without any expertise in biological weapons or life sciences. Information about the biological weapons program also came from an Iraqi exile that some of the intelligence analysts regarded as unreliable and a fabricator.[74]

Secretary Powell told the UN Security Council that his statement was based on "sources, solid sources. These are not assertions. What we've giving you are facts and

---

70   Senate Committee Report, 72, 75, 77, 81.
71   Central Intelligence Agency, "Iraq's Weapons of Mass Destruction Programs," October 2002, 1.
72   Ibid., 8, 10, 13.
73   Senate Intelligence Report, 300–302.
74   Ibid., 286, 295.

conclusions based on solid intelligence."[75] What Powell presented were not facts but assertions, and the assertions were not grounded on solid intelligence. The sources turned out to be Iraqi exiles who offered inaccurate and unreliable information.[76]

The Bush administration also faulted Iraq for failing to disclose mobile labs used to make biological agents. The State Department "Fact Sheet" of 19 December 2002 asked: "*What is the Iraqi regime trying to hide about their mobile biological weapon facilities?*" In his State of the Union address of 28 January 2003, President Bush stated: "From three Iraqi defectors we know that Iraq, in the late 1990s, had several mobile biological weapons labs. They are designed to produce germ warfare agents and can be moved from place to a place to evade inspectors. Saddam has not disclosed these facilities. He's given no evidence that he has destroyed them."

Powell spent considerable time discussing these mobile labs in his presentation to the UN on 5 February 2003. "One of the most worrisome things," he said, "that emerges from the thick intelligence file we have on Iraq's biological weapons is the existence of mobile production facilities used to make biological agents." He claimed to have "firsthand descriptions" of biological weapons factories that moved on wheels or rails. He said one Iraqi chemical engineer was at the site when an accident occurred in 1998, killing twelve technicians from exposure to biological agents. He spoke of other sources who were "in a position to know" about the program.[77] Hans Blix, appearing before the Security Council on 3 March 2003, reported that his inspectors had found no evidence that Iraq had mobile labs that made biological weapons.[78]

In May 2003, the United States announced the discovery of a suspected mobile biological weapons lab in northern Iraq. The CIA and the DIA quickly prepared a report stating that coalition forces "have uncovered the strongest evidence to date that Iraq was hiding a biological weapons program." Strong evidence? The dramatic first sentence was not supported by the body of evidence that followed. The report conceded that some of the features of the labs "are consistent with both bioproduction [of BW agents] and hydrogen production" for artillery weather balloons.[79]

The report thus highlighted the familiar "dual-use" issue, but President Bush nonetheless took the occasion to announce from Poland, on May 30: "We found the weapons of mass destruction. We found biological laboratories."[80] He was mistaken. Closer examination of the mobile labs reached the conclusion that they were used to produce hydrogen for weather balloons.[81] The report by the Iraqi exile concerning

---

75   Ibid., 154–6, 160–61, 188, 211.
76   Transcript as printed in the *New York Times*, 6 February 2003, A14.
77   Douglas Jehl and David E. Sanger, "Powell's Case, a Year Later: Gaps in Picture of Iraq Arms," *New York Times*, 1 February 2004, 1; Glenn Kessler and Walter Pincus, "A Flawed Argument In the Case for War," *Washington Post*, 1 February 2004, A1.
78   Transcript printed in the *New York Times*, 6 February 2003, A15.
79   Transcript printed in the *New York Times*, 8 March 2003, A8.
80   Center Intelligence Agency and Defense Intelligence Agency, "Iraqi Mobile Biological Warfare Agent Production Plants," 28 May 2003, 1, 5.
81   Weekly Compilation of Presidential Documents, vol. 39, 690.

an explosion that killed twelve technicians probably referred to what happens when a spark encounters hydrogen. Powell, eventually conceding that the trailers were not mobile biological labs, rebuked the CIA for his misconception and their reliance on faulty sources.[82] In October 2004, US inspector Charles Duelfer said that the trailers could not have been used for a biological weapons program, and that the manufacturers of the trailers "almost certainly designed and built the equipment for the generation of hydrogen."[83]

The last claim of Iraqi weapons of mass destruction concerned the availability of unmanned aerial vehicles (UAVs, or drones) to disperse chemical and biological agents. The NIE of October 2002 discussed Iraqi efforts after the Gulf War of 1991 to convert a MIG-21 into a UAV to carry spray tanks capable of dispensing chemical or biological agents.[84] President Bush's Cincinnati speech warned that Iraq "has a growing fleet of manned and unmanned aerial vehicles that could be used to disperse chemical or biological weapons across broad areas." He expressed concern that Iraq was exploring ways of using these UAVs "for missions targeting the United States."[85]

Two months later the State Department "Fact Sheet" posed this question: "*Why has the Iraqi regime acquired the range and auto-flight capabilities to spray biological weapons?*" At his 5 February 2003 appearance before the UN Security Council, Secretary Powell charged that Iraq had developed UAVs as "an ideal method for launching a terrorist attack using biological weapons." Hans Blix and his inspectors were aware of the drones but did not regard them as a likely method of dispersing biological agents.[86]

On 12 March 2003, about a week before the start of the war, the press had an opportunity to see one of the drones. Reporters thought it looked "more like something out of the Rube Goldberg museum of aeronautical design than anything that could threaten Iraq's foes." The plane's two engines, each about the size of a whiskey bottle, were attached to tiny wooden propellers, "looking about powerful enough to drive a Weed Whacker." Its wings and twinned tail fins were made of wood and stretched fabric. In early test flights, the vehicle ventured no further than two miles from the airfield. Iraqi officers said that the craft had been designed for reconnaissance, jamming, and aerial photography.[87]

---

82   Douglas Jehl, "Iraqi Trailers Said to Make Hydrogen, Not Biological Arms," *New York Times*, 9 August 2003, A1.

83   Glenn Kessler, "Powell Expresses Doubts About Basis for Iraqi Weapons Claim," *Washington Post*, 3 April 2004, A19; Christopher Marquis, "Powell Blames CIA for Error on Iraq Mobile Labs," *New York Times*, 3 April 2004, A5.

84   Douglas Jehl, "U.S. Report Finds Iraqis Eliminated Illicit Arms in 90's," *New York Times*, 7 October 2004, A22.

85   Central Intelligence Agency, "Iraq's Weapons of Mass Destruction Programs," October 2002, 22.

86   Weekly Compilation of Presidential Documents, vol. 38, 1717.

87   Steven R. Weisman, "U.S. Says Blix Played Down Details of Banned Weapons," *New York Times*, 11 March 2003, A10; Walter Pincus, "Iraq Drone Scrapped After U.N.

In September 2004, the UN's chief weapons inspector concluded that there was no evidence that Iraq ever developed UAVs capable of dispersing chemical and biological agents. The UN report was consistent with earlier findings by US Air Force intelligence analysts and the Pentagon's Missile Defense Agency that the drones were being developed for reconnaissance, not as part of a WMD program.[88] In its report of 9 July 2004, the Senate Intelligence Committee concluded that the assessment by the Intelligence Community in the key judgments section of the NIE, that Iraq was developing a UAV "probably" intended to deliver biological warfare agents, "overstated both what was known about the mission of Iraq's small UAVs and what intelligence analysts judged about the likely mission of Iraq's small UAVs."[89]

Congress Prepares to Act

In the midst of these conflicting claims about Iraqi WMDs, early in September 2002 the administration began pushing Congress to pass legislation authorizing military action. It wanted Congress to complete action before the November elections. On 3 September Senate Minority Leader Trent Lott (R-Miss.) was asked by reporters about the need for rapid legislative action. Acknowledging the disarray within the administration, he said: "I do think that we're going to have to get a more coherent message together."[90] Asked whether he was comfortable with the White House's presentation of the case for war against Iraq, he responded gamely: "I'd like to have a couple more days before I respond to that."[91]

In building the case for war, Bush and other top officials invited members of Congress to sessions where they would receive confidential information about the threat from Iraq. The lawmakers who attended said they heard little that was new. After one of the briefings, Senator Bob Graham (D-Fla.) remarked: "I did not receive any new information."[92] House Minority Whip Nancy Pilose (D-Cal.), who also served as ranking Democrat on the House Intelligence Committee, announced that she knew of "no information that the threat is so imminent from Iraq" that Congress could not wait until January to vote on an authorizing resolution.[93] After a

---

Inspection," *Washington Post*, 11 March 2003, A16.

88   John F. Burns, "Iraq Shows One of Its Drones, Recalling Wright Brothers," *New York Times*, 13 March 2003, A12; Rajiv Chandrasekaran, "Iraqi Officials Proudly Exhibit a Disputed, Dinged-Up Drone," *Washington Post*, 13 March 2003, A12.

89   Colum Lynch, "U.N.: Iraqi Drones Were No Threat," *Washington Post*, 5 September 2004, A28.

90   Senate Intelligence Report, 235.

91   Alison Mitchell and David E. Sanger, "Bush to Put Case for Action in Iraq to Key Lawmakers," *New York Times*, 4 September 2002, A1.

92   Helen Dewar and Mike Allen, "Senators Wary About Action Against Iraq," *Washington Post*, 4 September 2002, A16.

93   Mike Allen and Karen De Young, "Bush to Seek Hill Approval on Iraq War," *Washington Post*, 5 September 2002, A1.

"top secret" briefing by Defense Secretary Rumsfeld in a secure room in the Capitol, Senator John McCain (R-Ariz.) soon rose and walked out, saying "It was a joke."[94]

Senator Robert C. Byrd (D-W.Va.) objected to the demand for urgent action. He deplored "the war fervor, the drums of war, the bugles of war, the clouds of war—this war hysteria has blown in like a hurricane."[95] Bush could not rely on the precedents established by his father. In 1990, after Iraq had invaded Kuwait, the administration did not ask Congress for authorizing legislation before the November elections. Instead, it went first to the Security Council to request a resolution authorizing military operations. Only in January 1991, after lawmakers had returned from the mid-term elections, did they debate and pass legislation to authorize war against Iraq. But now, in 2002, Congress was under pressure to act before the elections.

The administration offered a variety of reasons for war, often going beyond concerns about WMDs. Senator Paul Sarbanes (D-Md.) questioned the claims by Secretary Powell that Iraq, to avoid military action, would have to comply with a number of UN resolutions, including one directed against prohibited trade. Sarbanes asked: "Are we prepared to go to war to make sure they comply with U.N. resolutions on illicit trade outside the oil for food program? Will we take military action or go to war in order to make them release or account for all Gulf War personnel whose fate is still unknown? Would we do that?"[96] No answer was forthcoming.

The administration seemed unwilling or unprepared to distinguish between fundamental reasons and less consequential considerations. Senator Richard Lugar (R-Ind.) criticized the undifferentiated laundry list of charges against Saddam Hussein, such as brutality toward his own people. In conversations with top officials of the administration, Lugar was satisfied that they recognized that such conduct could not justify a US war.[97] Senator Chuck Hagel (R-Neb.) reacted to the repeated instances of executive officials rushing forth with "bulletproof" evidence of a link between Iraq and al Qaeda, only to find, when pushed by lawmakers and the press, that the evidence amounted to cloudy assertions and speculation. He told Secretary Powell: "To Say, 'Yes, I know there is evidence there, but I don't want to tell you any more about it,' that does not encourage any of us. Nor does it give the American public a heck of a lot of faith that, in fact, what anyone is saying is true."[98]

There was little doubt that almost all of the Republicans in Congress would support the Iraq Resolution. The question turned on what the Democrats, in control of the Senate, would do. Unable to devise a coherent and comfortable counterstrategy, the Democrats appeared to favor prompt action on the resolution as a way of getting

---

94   Jim VandeHei and Juliet Eilperin, "Democrats Unconvinced on Iraq War," *Washington Post*, 11 September 2002, A1.

95   Jim VandeHei, "Iraq Briefings: Don't Ask, Don't Tell," *Washington Post*, 15 September 2002, A4.

96   Congressional Record, vol. 138, S8966 (daily ed. 20 September 2002).

97   Todd S. Purdum, "The U.S. Case Against Iraq, Counting Up the Reasons," *New York Times*, 1 October 2002, A14.

98   David E. Sanger and Carl Hulse, "Bush Appears to Soften Tone on Iraq Action." *New York Times*, 2 October 2002, A13.

the issue "off the table." Senate Majority Leader Tom Daschle hoped to expedite action on the legislation "to focus on his party's core message highlighting economic distress before the November midterm elections."[99] Senator John Edwards (D-N.C.) counseled quick action: "In a short period of time, Congress will have dealt with Iraq and we'll be on to other issues."[100]

This approach offended some Democrats on both moral and practical grounds. How could Democrats credibly authorize a war merely to shift attention to their domestic agenda? As noted by Senator Mark Dayton (D-Minn.), trying to gain "political advantage in a midterm election is a shameful reason to hurry decisions of this magnitude."[101] Second, voting on the Iraq Resolution could never erase the White House's advantage in controlling the headlines, if not through the Iraq Resolution then through ongoing, cliff-hanging negotiations with the UN Security Council. Third, although these Democrats said they wanted to put the issue of war behind them, it would always be in front.

Many Democrats did not seem to know how to express their opposition to military action against Iraq without appearing to be "irresolute" on the war on terrorism. Republican nominees in congressional contests learned how to fashion a political weapon out of Iraq, comparing their "strong stand" to "weak" positions by Democratic campaigners. Some of the key races in the nation seemed to turn on what candidates were saying about Iraq.[102] Partisanship hit a high level on 23 September when President Bush, in a speech in Trenton, New Jersey, accused the Democratic Senate of being "more interested in special interests in Washington and not interested in the security of the American people."[103] The administration quickly explained that his remark was delivered in the context of the legislative delay in creating a Department of Homeland Security, but Democrats faulted Bush for using the war for partisan advantage in the House and Senate races.[104]

After the Trenton speech, Democrats could have announced that Bush had so politicized and poisoned the debate on the Iraq Resolution that it could not be considered with the care and seriousness it deserved. They could have criticized the many inconsistent and unsubstantiated charges issued by the administration about Iraqi WMDs. They could have pointed to the 1990–91 precedent, when the first President Bush asked for legislation after the midterm elections, not before. The clear leverage was in the Senate, which the Democrats controlled. In the end, Daschle not only allowed legislative action on the Iraq Resolution but voted for it.

---

99   Eric Schmitt, "Rumsfeld Says U.S. Has 'Bulletproof' Evidence of Iraq's Links to Al Qaeda," *New York Times*, 28 September 2002, A8.

100   David Firestone, "Liberals Object to Bush Policy on Iraq Attack.," *New York Times*, 28 September 2002, A1.

101   Dana Milbank, "In President's Speeches, Iraq Dominates, Economy Fades," *Washington Post*, 25 September 2002, A6.

102   Mark Dayton, "Go Slow on Iraq," *Washington Post*, 28 September 2002, A23.

103   Jim VandeHei, "GOP Nominees Make Iraq a Political Weapon," *Washington Post*, 18 September 2002, A1.

104   Weekly Compilation of Presidential Documents, vol. 38, 1598.

Several Senate Democrats criticized him for working too closely with Bush and getting nothing in return. Bush's comments at Trenton, they said, made it look like Daschle was being "played for a fool."[105]

In the House of Representatives, the question was whether Bush could attract a substantial number of Democrats. That prospect brightened when House Minority Leader Dick Gephardt (D-Mo.) broke ranks with many in his party to announce support for a slightly redrafted Iraq Resolution. He explained: "We had to go through this, putting politics aside, so we have a chance to get a consensus that will lead the country in the right direction."[106] Yet politics could not be put aside. Gephardt's interest in running for the presidency was well known, as was Daschle's and several other members of Congress. Gephardt had voted against the Iraq Resolution in 1991. A vote in favor in 2002 would arguably bolster his credentials on national security. Democratic Senators John Edwards and Joseph Lieberman, both interested in a 2004 bid for the presidency, voted for the 2002 resolution. Senator John Kerry, about to announce his bid for the presidency, initially expressed doubts about the wisdom of war against Iraq but voted for the resolution.[107] One Democratic lawmaker concluded that Gephardt, by supporting Bush, had "inoculated Democrats against the charge that they are antiwar and obstructionist."[108]

Why this sensitivity? The Democrats had already supported the war against Afghanistan. Was it necessary to support every military adventure, with or without merit, to demonstrate patriotism and a manly spirit? Why were Democrats so anxious about being seen as antiwar? There was no evidence that the public in any broad sense supported immediate war against Iraq. A substantial majority preferred to wait.[109] A *Washington Post* story on October 8 described the public's enthusiasm for war against Iraq as "tepid and declining."[110]

There were other reasons why politics could not be "put aside" by voting on the Iraq Resolution. Action on the legislation was quintessentially a political decision, probably the most important congressional vote of the year. Inescapably and legitimately it called for a political judgment. Lawmakers would be voting on whether to commit as much as $100 billion or $200 billion to a war stretching over a period of years. Their actions would stabilize or destabilize the Middle East, strengthen or weaken the war against terrorism, enhance or debase the nation's prestige.

105   Carl Hulse and Todd S. Purdum, "Daschle Defends Democrats' Stand on Security of U.S.," *New York Times*, 26 September 2002, A1.

106   Jim VandeHei, "Daschle Angered by Bush Statement," *Washington Post*, 26 September 2002, A6.

107   "For Gephardt, Risks and a Crucial Role," *Washington Post*, October 3, 2002, p. A15.

108   Dan Balz and Jim VandeHei, "Democratic Hopefuls Back Bush on Iraq," *Washington Post*, 14 September 2002, A4.

109   David E. Rosenbaum, "United Voice on Iraq Eludes Majority Leader," *New York Times*, 4 October 2002, A12.

110   Adam Nagourney and Janet Elder, "Public Says Bush Needs to Pay Heed to Weak Economy," *New York Times*, 7 October 2002, A1 and A14.

The House International Relations Committee reported the resolution, supporting it 31 to 11. A key section of the report expressed the hope that military force could be avoided. The committee calculated that "providing the President with the authority he needs to use force is the best way to avoid its use. A signal of our Nation's seriousness of purpose and its willingness to use force may yet persuade Iraq to meet its international obligations, and is the best way to persuade members of the Security Council and others in the international community to join us in bringing pressure on Iraq or, if required, in using armed force against it."[111] In this manner, the committee both authorized military force and hoped it would not be necessary. In either case, it left the decision to go to war with the President, not with Congress, where the Constitution puts it.

This kind of straddling with the Iraq Resolution reminds one of the Tonkin Gulf Resolution of August 1964, which President Lyndon B. Johnson presented to Congress. Lawmakers typically voted for the resolution (which passed unanimously in the House, with only two votes against it in the Senate) not as an endorsement of war but as a signal to North Vietnam to alter its conduct or face military action.[112] The reasoning: Joint action by Congress and the President, with strong bipartisan support, would convince the enemy to back down and thus avert a war. The Tonkin Gulf Resolution did not prevent war and neither did the Iraq Resolution. In both cases lawmakers transferred to the President the sole decision to go to war and determine its scope and duration. They chose to trust in the President instead of in themselves and in republican government.

After the House passed the Iraq Resolution, 296 to 133, Senator Daschle announced his support. He insisted that "we have got to support this effort. We have got to do it in an enthusiastic and bipartisan way."[113] No member of Congress has an obligation to vote enthusiastically on anything unless it merits support. Placing trust in the President or in bipartisanship are not proper substitutes for deciding whether it is necessary to go to war. Senator Kerry, who had earlier raised substantive arguments against going to war, now accepted presidential superiority over Congress: "We are affirming a president's right and responsibility to keep the American people safe, and the president must take that grant of responsibility seriously."[114] The President has no right to go to war unless lawmakers decide it is in the nation's interest. Daschle argued that "it is important for America to speak with one voice at this critical moment."[115] When lawmakers urge the nation to speak with one voice they mean the voice of the President. If the system of checks and balances and the deliberative

---

111   Dana Milbank, "With Congress Aboard, Bush Targets a Doubtful Public," *Washington Post*, 8 October 2002, A21.

112   H. Rept. No. 107-721, 107th Cong. 2d Sess. (2002), 4–5.

113   Louis Fisher, *Presidential War Power* (Lawrence: University Press of Kansas, 2d ed., 2004), 129–32, 227–8.

114   John H. Cushman, Jr., "Daschle Predicts Broad Support for Military Action Against Iraq," *New York Times*, 7 October 2002, A10.

115   Helen Dewar and Juliet Eilperin, "Iraq Resolution Passes Test, Gains Support," *Washington Post*, 10 October 2002, A16.

process are to have any vitality, members of Congress must vote in accordance with their individual conscience and personal judgment. They take an oath to support and defend the Constitution, not the President.

Role of the Media

Newspaper reporters, television correspondents, and other media outlets have done much to promote presidential wars. The attention is largely on battle plans, movement of troops, victories, and setbacks. Almost no consideration is given to the President's source of *authority* and how the expansion of executive power threatens representative government, civil liberties, and the constitutional system of checks and balances. There are important exceptions to this pattern, including the aggressive investigative reporting of Seymour Hersh.[116]

Through a combination of government manipulation and voluntary self-censorship, the media generally furthers the agenda of the executive branch. Under the banner of "objectivity," reporters convey administration statements that lack credibility and substance. William Greider of the *Washington Post* explained that the press, through this practice, serves as "more conduit than critic of the government." An "ingrown quality of deference" makes the press unwilling to challenge presidential announcements. Reporters print "reams and reams of rhetoric they themselves know to be wrong."[117]

During the Reagan years, the State Department released a report called "Communist Interference in El Salvador." Nineteen documents (in Spanish) were attached, but most reporters chose to rely on an eight-page summary that the department conveniently provided. The result was a "fantastic public relations coup for the State Department as reporters in effect reduced themselves to human transmission belts, disseminating propaganda that would later be revealed to be false."[118] Reporters would not show the same gullibility by printing summaries prepared by congressional committees or a lawmaker's personal office.

Reporters did a fairly good job in scrutinizing claims issued in 2002 by the Bush administration that Iraq possessed weapons of mass destruction. Again and again the press examined assertions about the use of aluminum tubes for nuclear weapons, pilotless aircraft carrying chemical or biological agents, efforts to obtain uranium ore from a country in Africa, and supposed ties between Iraq and al Qaeda. On a regular basis the press found executive statements to be either baseless or strained.[119]

---

116 Jim VandeHei and Juliet Eilperin, "House Passes Iraq War Resolution," *Washington Post*, 11 October 2002, A6.

117 For example, Seymour M. Hersh, *Chain of Command: The Road From 9/11 to Abu Ghraib* (New York: HarperCollins Publishers, 2004).

118 Mark Hertsgaard, *On Bended Knee: The Press and the Reagan Presidency* (New York: Farrar Straus Giroux, 1988), 67.

119 Ibid., 110.

A year after the Bush administration had gone to war with Iraq and after inspections throughout the country had failed to uncover any weapons of mass destruction, several newspapers and magazines expressed regret for the manner in which they had performed their First Amendment duties. On 26 May 2004, the *New York Times* prepared a statement that took pride in much of its coverage, but noted a number of instances where reporting "was not as rigorous as it should have been." The *Times* found special fault with its dependence on information "from a circle of Iraqi informants, defectors and exiles bent on 'regime change.'" Subsequent reports found much of the information from the exiles unreliable and false. Here is an interesting passage: "Complicating matters for journalists, the accounts of these exiles were often eagerly confirmed by United States officials convinced of the need to intervene in Iraq. Administration officials now acknowledge that they sometimes fell for misinformation from these exile sources. So did many news organizations–in particular, this one."

Why did that "complicate" matters for journalists? The first mistake was the media's reliance on exiles who not only had a political agenda (to get rid of Saddam Hussein) but who often had been out of the country for two or three decades and were arms-length from reliable information. The press should have been on guard and skeptical about their claims. The fact that executive officials "eagerly confirmed" the accounts of exiles should not have tipped the decision toward publication. It should have been seen as one red flag followed by another. The *Times* offered a more candid explanation:

> Editors at several levels who should have been challenging reporters and pressing for more skepticism were perhaps too intent on rushing scoops into the paper. Accounts of Iraqi defectors were not always weighed against their strong desire to have Saddam Hussein ousted. Articles based on dire claims about Iraq tended to get prominent display, while follow-up articles that called the original ones into question were sometimes buried. In some cases, there was no follow-up at all.[120]

On 28 June 2004, the *New Republic* offered its regrets for supporting the war in Iraq and accepting the administration's claims that Saddam Hussein was hiding WMDs. By early 2003, before the United States unleashed military power against Iraq, the magazine said "it was becoming clear that at least two pieces of evidence the administration cited as proof of Saddam Hussein's nuclear program—his supposed purchase of uranium from Niger and his acquisition of aluminum tubes

---

120   See Louis Fisher, "Justifying War Against Iraq," in James A. Thurber, ed., *Rivals for Power: Presidential-Congressional Relations* (Lanham, Md.: Rowman & Littlefield, 3d ed. 2005); James P. Pfiffner, "Did President Bush Mislead the Country in His Arguments for War with Iraq?," *Presidential Studies Quarterly*, vol. 34 (2004), 25; Louis Fisher, "Deciding on War Against Iraq: Institutional Failures," *Political Science Quarterly*, (2003).vol. 118, 389.

for a supposed nuclear centrifuge—were highly dubious. … In retrospect, we should have paid more attention to these warning signs."[121]

Additional soul-searching came from the *Washington Post*. The executive editor and other top editors said that the newspaper had made a mistake before the war began by not giving front-page prominence to articles that cast doubt on the administration's argument about WMDs in Iraq. Articles that questioned the administration's rationale appeared far back in the paper, on pages A18 or A24. In contrast, from August 2002 to the start of military operations on19 March 2003, the *Post* ran more than 140 front-page stories that highlighted administration rhetoric justifying war. Some of the headlines: "Cheney Says Iraqi Strike Is Justified"; "War Cabinet Argues for Iraq Attack"; "Bush Tells United Nations It Must Stand Up to Hussein or US Will"; "Bush Cites Urgent Iraqi Threat"; "Bush Tells Troops: Prepare for War." This drumbeat for war pushed aside stories that questioned the administration's facts and statements.[122]

Why Trust the Administration?

It is remarkable that after so many decades of executive lies and deceits that Congress and the media would ever take at face value anything said by a President or administration official. Those who serve in the executive branch, especially experts in national security, have little difficulty in lying to Congress, the public, and the international community. They believe they have access to superior information and have formulated a policy that is uniquely and intrinsically sound. With such a hold on the truth, they reason, the next logical step is to resort to whatever lies and deceptions will promote the policy. Sissela Bok, who teaches ethics at Harvard Medical School, explained that individuals who are convinced they know the truth can easily justify lies: "They may perpetuate so-called pious frauds to convert the unbelieving or strengthen the conviction of the faithful. They see nothing wrong in telling untruths for what they regard as a much 'higher' truth."[123]

Why single out lies only from the executive branch? The spotlight certainly needs to shine also on Congress and the judiciary. As with any policymaker, legislators and judges have the potential and the opportunity for lies and deception. However, the way their institutions are organized and function poses less of a danger, particularly with the war power. The structure of Congress, with its two chambers, multiple committees and subcommittees, and competing parties, is so decentralized and so riven with internal checks that a coordinated plan of lying is difficult to carry

121   "The Times and Iraq," *New York Times*, 26 May 2004, A10.

122   "Were We Wrong?," *The New Republic*, June 28, 2004, 8; see Howard Kurtz, "New Republic Editors 'Regret' Their Support of Iraq War," *Washington Post*, 19 June 2004, C1.

123   Howard Kurtz, "The Post on WMDs: An Inside Story," *Washington Post*, 12 August 2004, A1, A20; "Washington Post Rethinks Its Coverage of War Debate," *New York Times*, 13 August 2004, A14.

out. Individual lawmakers who resort to criminal activities can be, and have been, prosecuted and sent to prison.

Lies and deceits occur within the judicial arena, but those actions are at least subject to adversaries squaring off in a courtroom, the opportunity for appeals, and multi-member panels that make up the appellate courts and the US Supreme Court. Individual judges who step over the line can be, and have been, impeached and removed from office. They are also subject to prosecution for non-judicial acts that violate the criminal code. A number of lawmakers and judges have gone to prison. Not many examples can be found among top executive officials. Is that because they are more ethical or because the Justice Department pulls its punches when investigating them?

Few checks exist within the presidential system. Just as "unity" within the White House is considered a virtue for assuring coherent planning and execution, so does it provide an opportunity for deliberate, calculated, and coordinated lying.[124] The last administration to pay a heavy price for official corruption was Nixon's. Attorney General John Mitchell and other high-ranking officials went to prison. In the years since Watergate, punishment has been meted out only to mid-level members of the executive branch. During Iran-Contra, those who paid a price were people like Oliver North, John Poindexter, Robert McFarlane, and some CIA operatives, but often their convictions were overturned either on appeal (not for innocence but for newly created doctrines of immunity) or through a presidential pardon. Unlike John Dean in the Watergate years, no one in the White House or upper reaches of the executive departments breaks ranks to disclose illegal or unethical acts. For the last four decades the White House has run a tight ship.

The centralized structure of the White House, combined with an emphasis on personal loyalty and one-party discipline, enables executive officials to present false and misleading information to Congress with impunity. In 1969, the Nixon administration wanted Congress to authorize and fund the supersonic transport plane (the SST). The administration received a report from a panel of scientists commissioned to study the plane. Although the report had been written with appropriated funds, the White House refused to release it to Congress or the public. Denied full information, Congress initially provided funds. Close votes in 1971 eventually killed the project. After these votes, litigation forced the administration to release the report and it became public. It cited numerous reasons why Congress should deny funds for the aircraft.[125]

A more recent example of White House deceit is the prescription drug program, enacted in 2004. Members of Congress were told by the administration that the bill would cost $395 billion over a ten-year period. Republicans warned that if the

---

124   Sissela Bok, *Lying: Moral Choice in Public and Private Life* (New York: Pantheon Books, 1978), 7.

125   Bruce Ladd, *Crisis in Credibility* (New York: The New American Library, 1968); John M. Orman, *Presidential Secrecy and Deception: Beyond the Power to Persuade* (Westport, Conn.: Greenwood Press, 1980).

estimate topped $400 billion they would withhold their support. What was withheld, instead, were calculations by administration experts that the likely cost would be $500 billion or higher. The Chief Actuary of the Department of Health and Human Services, responsible for these cost projections, was ordered not to share the higher figure with Congress. It had been the understanding of Congress for decades that the Chief Actuary had a duty to share cost estimates with lawmakers to assist them with their legislative duties. The administration took the position that it could order the Chief Actuary to withhold the information as part of the President's constitutional duty to supervise and control the executive branch. According to this legal analysis, the administration is empowered to prevent the Chief Actuary from communicating accurate information, compiled with taxpayer funds, to Congress.[126] As a result, lawmakers voted on the prescription drug program with inaccurate and misleading cost estimates. The administration knew the facts, but not Congress (or the public). Will the Justice Department act against anyone in the administration for withholding this information? Not a chance.

Executive deception in the field of national security has a special history, full of various self-serving justifications. One advantage of the executive branch is its relative monopoly over information. Over classification and a penchant for secrecy narrowed the circle of policymakers. Those who are privileged to read classified documents, even if the documents are false and unreliable, regard those "not in the know" as uninformed and therefore unqualified and ineligible to participate in the formulation of policy. This climate encourages the Elite to justify misleading and deceptive statements to Congress, the courts, the public, and the international community

At times, lying about national security can be necessary and appropriate. If a President, acting as Commander in Chief, indicates to an enemy that US forces are likely to mount an attack from the North, when the planned attack all along is from the South, no one would question both the morality and appropriateness of the deception. This type of feint is common practice by both sides in time of war. During the 1960 presidential campaign, Senator John Kennedy raised the issue whether the Eisenhower administration was planning to use military force against Cuba. Vice President Richard Nixon, knowing that a covert operation had indeed been prepared, decided to dismiss Kennedy's suggestion in order not to put Fidel Castro on guard.[127] A country may decide to allow the enemy to bomb a city, even if it knows of the attack in advance, rather than reveal to the enemy that it has broken its secret code. Cruel choices of that nature are part of war.

---

126   Paul N. McCloskey, Jr., *Truth and Untruth: Political Deceit in America* (New York: Simon and Schuster, 1972), 75–84.

127   Christopher Lee, "Ex-Medicare Chief's Pay Illegal, GAO Says," *Washington Post*, 8 September 2004, A21; Robert Pear, "Inquiry Proposes Penalties For Hiding Medicare Data," *New York Times*, 8 September 2004, A16; letter from Jack L. Goldsmith III, Assistant Attorney General, Office of Legal Counsel, U.S. Department of Justice, to Alex M. Azar, II, General Counsel, Department of Health and Human Services, 21 May 2004.

Lying to an enemy is easily justified. What about lies to Congress, the Supreme Court, and the American public? Executive lies to the judiciary are sometimes dealt with through a writ of coram nobis (fraud against the court), leading to a reversal of judgment against a defendant. Examples include false statements made by executive officials to the courts about the treatment of Japanese-Americans during World War II and atomic testing in Nevada.[128] Although defendants in these extraordinary cases eventually gain justice, the individuals in the executive branch who engaged in the lies go unpunished. Executive officials who lie to Congress may face contempt citations and prosecutions for perjury. In extreme cases, presidential lies (and obstruction of justice) can result in impeachment and removal from office.

For the most part, executive lies and deception inflict severe and long-lasting damage to the nation. David Wise has written: "The excuse for secrecy and deception most frequently given by those in power is that the American people must sometimes be misled in order to mislead the enemy. This justification is unacceptable on moral and philosophic grounds, and often it simply isn't true. Frequently the 'enemy' knows what is going on, but the American public does not."[129] Certainly that is true for the covert budget of the Intelligence Community, estimated to be about $40 billion. The public isn't allowed to know how taxpayer funds are spent, but almost certainly the "enemy" knows. When the US government waged a "secret war" in Laos, American citizens were kept in the dark but surely not the Laotians. During the Vietnam War, the Johnson administration entered into secret commitments to provide funds to the Philippines, Thailand, and South Korea for their support. The allocation of those funds was kept from Congress and the public but not from the allies.[130]

A recent book by Eric Alterman offers what seems to be a largely benign view of presidential honesty. "Before the 1960s," he says, "few could even imagine that a president would deliberately mislead them on matters so fundamental as war and peace."[131] However, Alterman is aware of earlier transgressions. One of his four case studies is devoted to Franklin D. Roosevelt's public statements about the agreement struck at the Yalta Conference, falsely implying that the pact would put an end to a Soviet spheres of influence.[132] Those who participated at the conference understood that the Soviet Union was unlikely to relax its grip on Poland and Eastern Europe.

Alterman also refers briefly to the "deliberate dishonesty" of the Monroe administration regarding a set of Central American treaties, President Polk's misleading explanation for the triggering event for the war against Mexico, and

---

128   James P. Pfiffner, *The Character Factor: How We Judge America's Presidents* (College Station: Texas A&M University Press, 2004), 22–3.

129   *Korematsu v. United States*, 584 F.Supp. 1406 (N.D. Cal. 1984); Hirabayashi v. United States, 828 F.2d 591 (9th Cir. 1987); Howard Ball, *Justice Downwind: America's Atomic Testing Program in the 1950s* (New York: Oxford University Press, 1986).

130   David Wise, *The Politics of Lying: Government Deception, Secrecy, and Power* (New York: Random House, 1973), 344.

131   Fisher, *Presidential War Power*, 135–7.

132   Eric Alterman, *When Presidents Lie: A History of Official Deception and Its Consequences* (New York: Viking, 2004), 294.

President McKinley's provocative public statements about Spain's conduct in Cuba that helped propel the country to war in 1898.[133] Alterman characterizes FDR's steps toward World War II as "stealth and deception" and "deliberately disingenuous."[134] During the 1940 presidential campaign, Roosevelt assured the public that American sons would not be sent to fight in "foreign wars."[135]

Presidential deception, Alterman concludes, is the "rule rather than the exception." Presidents end up "not only in fooling the nation but also in fooling themselves." Heavy costs pile up against the President, his party, and the nation. Although public officials and some academics will explicitly or implicitly condone stealth and deception by Presidents, Alterman views presidential dishonesty as "ultimately and invariably self-destructive."[136]

Presidential lies to the American people are checked in part through elections. If a presidential war becomes unpopular, as with Korea and Vietnam, voters take it out on the President and his party. In the case of President Bush's war against Iraq in 2003, his reelection a year later underscores that the price for lying is not immediate. If the lies and deception lead to an ineffectual and costly occupation of Iraq, the price will come, both to Bush and his party. Sissela Bok notes: "Trust and integrity are precious resources, easily squandered, hard to regain. They can thrive only on a foundation of respect for veracity."[137]

Conclusion

The neocons who championed the second Iraq War are quite comfortable in using military power. America's commitment of armed force abroad is unlikely to be abusive, they argue, because "American foreign policy is infused with an unusually high degree of morality."[138] What if it isn't? What happens when a policy intended to be benevolent turns destructive or even evil? Why do conservatives, traditionally distrustful of human nature and, in the past, supportive of limited government and the need for checks and balances, find such a comfort level with unwavering dependence on the national government, military force, nation-building, and presidential power? The conservative hat fits awkwardly on the neocons.

Exactly why the Bush administration went to war against Iraq is anyone's guess. A half dozen or more "explanations" are available. Noah Feldman puts it well by saying that the American invasion "was the product of several disparate, mutually conflicting strands of thought, some benightedly idealistic, others brutally realist, and almost all based on some misunderstanding of the likely consequences of the

---

133   *The Public Papers and Addresses of Franklin D. Roosevelt, 1944-45* Volume (New York: Harper & Brothers, 1950), 541.
134   Ackerman, *When Presidents Lie*, 16.
135   Ibid.
136   Ibid., 17.
137   Ibid., 22.
138   Bok, *Lying*, 249.

invasion in Iraq itself."[139] Those who supported the removal of Saddam Hussein wondered if the Bush administration had the skills and ability to carry out the task in an effective manner.

There are two fundamental reasons for distrusting presidential power. One is constitutional: the pattern of executives (known to the framers) to use military power for personal or partisan objectives, not for the national interest. The second reason: the limited competence within the executive branch to plan and execute a successful war. Major strategic and tactical errors accompanied the Korean and Vietnam Wars. Miscalculations, errors of intelligence, and false statements have haunted the second war against Iraq. The mistakes came not from the military but from civilian leadership, especially at the level of the White House and within the Pentagon.

Whatever skills and talents are demanded of military officers in time of war, once the President obtains authority from Congress for offensive operations it is the President's duty to clarify overall goals. He must crystallize the objectives. In a book intended for business leaders, Larry Bossidy and Ram Charan explain the primary factors that yield success. Their advice translates quite nicely to the presidency. To execute a plan well, it must be based on reality, not fantasy.[140] Repeatedly the Bush administration relied on Iraqi exiles who predicted that US soldiers would be greeted as liberators, not occupiers. Based on an expectation that was misguided and misinformed, and relying on exiles who had their own agenda, the Bush war plan invited failure.

Bossidy and Charan explain what leaders need to do to discover reality: "You need a robust dialogue to surface the realities of the business."[141] Leaders "are actively curious, and encourage debate to bring up opposite views."[142] In formulating a plan, there must be openness and candor. A robust dialogue "starts when people go in with open minds."[143] The debate on assumptions "is one of the most critical parts of any operating review." Leaders cannot set realistic goals "until you've debated the assumptions behind them."[144] The essential standard: "See things as they are, not the way you want them to be."[145] The public record indicates that President Bush and his top advisers went to war in Iraq with a set of untested, shaky assumptions that were never subjected to rigorous review.

During a news conference on 13 April 2004, President Bush was asked if he would have to add more troops in Iraq. He responded: "Well, I—first of all, that's up to General Abizaid, and he's clearly indicating that he may want more troops. It's coming up through the chain of command. If that's what he wants, that's what

---

139   Kagan and Kristol, *Present Dangers*, 22.

140   Noah Feldman, *What We Owe Iraq* (Princeton: Princeton University Press, 2004), 19.

141   Larry Bossidy and Ram Charan, *Execution: The Discipline of Getting Things Done* (New York: Crown Business, 2002), 22 and 67.

142   Ibid., 23.

143   Ibid., 82.

144   Ibid., 102.

145   Ibid., 236.

he gets. … I'm constantly asking him, does he have what he needs, whether it be in troop strength or in equipment.".[146] In preparing for war, it was Bush's nondelegable duty to tell his civilian and military advisers: "Suppose the Iraqis do not view us as liberators? Suppose something goes wrong with our military actions, creating much more destruction than we intended? Iraqis might then regard us as occupiers, create an insurgency, and mount a strong guerrilla movement. Terrorists from Saudi Arabia, Egypt, and other countries might enter to lend their support to the insurgents. I need sufficient troops to make the country secure, prevent looting and violence, safeguard the existing Iraqi stockpiles of weapons in the country, and create a safe climate that will allow for reconstruction." Only after the President identifies his objectives can military leaders tell him how many troops are needed. Presidential questions come first. To be an effective leader, the President cannot sit by the phone, waiting for military commanders to call him and recommend an increase in troop strength.

U.S political institutions failed in their constitutional duties when they authorized war against Iraq. The Bush administration never presented sufficient, credible, or honest information to justify statutory action in October 2002 and military operations in March 2003. Members of Congress failed to insist on reliable arguments and evidence before passing the Iraq Resolution. There was no need for Congress to act when it did. Instead of passing legislation to authorize war, lawmakers agreed to compromise language that left the decisive judgment with the President. Placing the power to initiate war in the hands of one person was precisely what the framers hoped to avoid when they drafted the Constitution.

---

146   Weekly Compilation of Presidential Documents (2004), vol. 40, 583.

Chapter 4

Infighting in Washington: The Impact of Bureaucratic Politics on US Iraq Policy

Howard University

Introduction

Long before the commencement of *Operation Iraqi Freedom*, and most certainly in its aftermath, critics of the American intervention have incessantly critiqued the omnipresence of bureaucratic infighting that governed the prewar and post-reconstruction phases.[1] As a result of this discourse there is sufficient evidence to support the contention that the administration of George W. Bush's policy in Iraq is a by-product of bureaucratic politics. The focus of this study is to illustrate that bureaucratic politics was also a feature of the policies of the administrations of George H.W. Bush and Bill Clinton. The essence of this study is to delineate the degree and at what levels did bureaucratic infighting play in the evolution of US foreign policy in Iraq.

Divided into three sections, this study explores the fragmentation that polarized three administrations and ultimately impacted US strategy toward Iraq. Within the administration of the elder Bush, for example, infighting developed on several levels: the direction of US post-invasion policy, intelligence, over the appropriate military strategy (airpower versus ground troops), the use of Special Operations Forces to kill Saddam Hussein, or the use of bunker busters weapons to take out the Iraqi leader, and third, a debate emerged over when to conclude the war and whether this represented a sound strategy.

During the administration of President Bill Clinton, three issues divided the national security bureaucracy: to end or revise sanctions, comprehensive containment or pursuit of a policy rollback, and finally, an internal debate commenced over whether to employ covert or direct military intervention to unseat Saddam Hussein.

---

1   See the following, Glenn Kessler and Walter Pincus, "Bush Team Infighting Could Hurt War Plan," *Washington Post*, 1 April 2003; Dan Morgan, "Deciding Who Rebuilds Iraq Is Fraught With Infighting," *Washington Post*, May 4, 2003; and James Drummond in Baghdad and James Harding and Guy Dinmore, "US Infighting Blames For Iraq Failures," *Financial Times–UK*, 12 November 2003.

Third, this study asserts that several issues polarized the second Bush administration: the struggle over war plans, multilateral or unilateral approach during the prewar phase, control over postwar reconstruction, and which faction (State or Defense) should control US policy toward Iraq. These are the collective issues that will be addressed in this study.

Bush I: Prewar Squabbles, Infighting over Strategy and When to End the War

In the wake of the Iraqi invasion of Kuwait a series of internal disputes erupted over the course and direction of US policy. The dispute concerned how the administration should respond to Saddam's aggression in the Gulf. Second, another debate arose over Secretary of State James Baker's plan to consider Soviet participation in the coalition. On another level, with respect to military strategy, there were a plethora of factional debates on the use of air power; there were a host of polemics concerning the conclusion of the ground campaign, whether the US should oust the regime in Iraq, and finally there were politics surrounding the Safwan Treaty. The point of this section is to provide an account of the role of bureaucratic politics governing these issues and the subsequent impact on US strategy in the gulf.

In the administration of George H.W. Bush bureaucratic infighting over US policy toward Iraq commenced during the prewar period (Pre-*Desert Storm*). Much of the early debate centered on the president's belief that he could modify Iraqi behavior. That is the president argued the Reagan initiative in US-Iraqi relations represented an important first step but acknowledged there is considerable room to further improve the relationship. This position set the stage for the approval of National Security Directive 26 (NSD-26) in October of 1990. Through the directive the administration had hoped to pursue normal relations with Iraq believing this course would "serve our long-term interests and promote stability in the region."[2] The best way to convince Iraq of the US intentions according to Bush was to propose the utilization of a combination of economic and political incentives to modify Saddam's behavior while simultaneously increasing American influence in the region.[3] In short, the new president accepted that the United States should "engage Saddam to try to turn him into an ally."[4]

At senior levels of the administration there was general of acceptance of this approach and within the bureaucracy there was general agreement on the viability of the policy. However, there were factions within the Pentagon and elsewhere that argued administration policy should have been tougher. There were those such as Paul Wolfowitz in the Pentagon, along with a number of CIA analysts, including Kenneth

---

2   See text of National Security Directive 26 (NSD-26), The White House, Washington, DC, 2 October 1989.

3   See Bruce Jentleson, *With Friends Like These: Reagan, Bush and Saddam.* NY: WW Norton, 1994.

4   Kenneth Pollack, *The Threatening Storm-The United States and Iraq: The Crisis, The Strategy and The Prospects After Saddam* (New York: Random House, 2003), 28.

Pollack, along with his division chief, Winton Wiley, and his deputy, Bruce Riedel, who argued the administration policy of engagement with Iraq seemed oblivious to Saddam's burgeoning appetite for Weapons of Mass Destruction (WMDS) and his pursuit of regional ambitions.[5] Similarly, according to Pollack, he, along with Wiley and Riedel, "fought constant battles with other intelligence agencies to sound more ominous warnings" about Iraq's WMD programs, particularly the nuclear program.[6] This debate continued until Saddam invaded Kuwait and it is clear that those supporting the president's assessment that Iraq represented a force for stability in the region had been proven wrong.

Iraq's invasion touched off a major internal debate: the intelligence that warned of coming incursion into Kuwait and how the administration should respond. The CIA's perspective on the unfolding events in the gulf was mixed. Pollack, then a junior analyst, recognized that he was confident that Iraq's troop developments were indicators that Saddam was positioning for an invasion, but he admitted that he "had difficulty convincing my colleagues or getting my analysis out to the policy making community."[7]

The National Intelligence Officer (NIO) for Warning, Charles Allen, examined the available satellite intelligence on Iraqi forces on 1 August 1990 and had been confident that Iraq was prepared to invade Kuwait. Allen however had a series of dilemmas. First, he was not a senior advisor and second, he had been wrong in March 1990 about his view that intelligence indicated that Soviet Special Forces would intervene in Lithuania.[8] Even under these circumstances Allen decided it was too important and proceeded to pass the information up the chain of command. This information was provided to a senior aid to Powell, Lee Butler; the same information was then presented to Richard Clark, the director of military affairs in the State Department. Eventually, the information reached Brent Scowcroft.[9]

The DIA had similar dilemmas. The National Intelligence Officer for the Middle East and South Asia, Pat Lang examined the agencies intelligence and reached a similar conclusion as Allen: Iraq was preparing to invade.[10] Powell received the analysis on his desk but had been skeptical noting that a number of critical signatures of an invading force were not present. The general was addressing the absence of four critical indices: communications networks, the stockpiling of artillery shells, other required munitions, and a "sufficient logistical" trail.

In a subsequent meeting that consisted of Secretary of Defense Dick Cheney, Chair of Joint Chiefs of Staff Colin Powell and CENTCOM Commander Norman Schwarzkopf, ostensibly to examine evidence that Iraq was massing to attack

---

5   Ibid., 29.

6   Ibid.

7   Ibid., 34.

8   Michael R. Gordon and General Bernard E. Trainor, *The Generals War: The Inside of the Story of the Conflict in the Gulf* (Boston: Little Brown & Company, 1995), 4–5.

9   Gordon and Trainor, *The Generals War*, 4–5.

10   Bob Woodward, *The Commanders* (New York: Touchstone, 2002), 205.

Kuwait, the secretary of defense wanted to know the opinion of what should be done in the event of such an attack? The commander of CENTCOM bluntly stated "not a damn thing. The world will not care. It will be a fait accompli."[11] Even with this statement another source indicated that the Powell wanted Schwarzkopf to begin contingency planning.[12]

Unfortunately, Allen and Lang's warnings concerning the prewar intelligence about Iraq's intensions in Kuwait, though correct, had not been taken seriously by the White House, Defense, and over at State. Additionally, with the intelligence community (both the CIA and DIA) no consensus emerged on the significance of the intelligence. In fact the analytical work by Allen and Lang had been ignored. According to Gordon and Trainor, to do otherwise, those in know would have had to admit that administration "policy toward Baghdad has been an utter failure."[13] This perception was finally accepted following the invasion of Kuwait.

President Bush's reaction to Iraq's aggression against a sovereign state was as followed: "This will not stand." The problem for the president is that his rhetoric was way ahead of his war council that had yet to provide any contingencies for possible American action. The reason for the absence of any options is that within the administration there was a major rift among his senior advisors. In one side there was there those ready for a military response to remove Saddam forces from Kuwait. The problem for the civilians is that the military urged caution. This divide is symbolized in the first national security meeting. Secretary of Defense Richard Cheney argued, "We need an objective." By this the secretary spoke of removing Iraq from Kuwait and even toyed with the idea of removing Saddam from Iraq. Speaking in opposition to war with Iraq over their invasion of Kuwait, Chairman Powell bluntly asserted the American people do not want young American's dying for $1.50 gallon oil and his recommendation was that "we must communicate to Saddam Hussein that Saudi Arabia is the line."[14] The lines were drawn and the once cordial relationship between the civilian leader and military chief had been drastically altered forever. Powell's message was clear, the administration failed to make the case that Kuwait represented a country significant enough to defend, but this time the president could not repeat the same mistake with Saudi Arabia.

Third, on the role of Soviets in the coalition, Secretary of State James Baker thought that Moscow's participation would enhance, not detract from the alliance to eject Iraq from Kuwait. Baker's perception of the Soviet role involved his view that the Soviets should not a be shut out of Middle East Peace and that after the US-Soviet joint statement condemning Iraqi aggression it seemed naïve to construct

---

11   Gordon and Trainor, *The Generals War*, 26.

12   According to Woodward, Powell ordered Schwarzkopf to "draft a two-tiered plan for possible US responses to any Iraqi move against Kuwait … The first tier was what US forces could do to retaliate against Iraq; the second was what the United States might do to defensively to stop any Iraqi move." See Woodward, *The Commanders*, 209.

13   Ibid., 6.

14   Gordon and Trainor, *The Generals War*, 33.

a multilateral coalition without Soviet involvement. The initiative was a hard sell; notably, the state department bureaucracy opposed the idea of inviting the Soviets to participate in "US-sanctioned military presence" in the region "ran counter to forty years of American diplomacy" which endeavored to preclude Soviet mischief in the region.[15] The plan ran into additional opposition. Initially, the President, Secretary Cheney, Chairman Powell, and National Security Advisor Scowcroft all expressed their discontent. In the case of Powell, according to Baker, the general worried about providing Moscow with a voice in any possible military attack on Iraq.[16] According to Baker a consensus emerged to support the initiative but after an extended telephone conversation between the secretary and his Soviet counterpart, Eduard Shevardnadze on 8 August 1990, the foreign minister explicated that it was the view of the Soviet government not to support participation in the coalition but he noted that the Soviets would support the US in the security council.[17]

Fourth, the debate over strategy produced one of the more divisive debates within the administration. It was clear from the outset that the statement that the US war plan was based on "unity of command" did not represent the reality within the military services. Rather, irrespective of the Goldwater-Nichols Act, Joint Chiefs of Staff Publication 26 (JCS Pub 26), and the Joint Force Air Component Commander (JFACC), which endeavored to ensure US military campaigns were "run by a single functional commander,"[18] in reality most decisions were indeed made by the CENTCOM Commander but most of the decisions were governed and developed as a result of bureaucratic infighting.

In the wake of the Iraqi invasion of the Kuwait, Schwarzkopf had reviewed a number of CENTCOMs "possible retaliatory" contingencies but the general was not pleased with any of them.[19] Schwarzkopf had an additional set of dilemmas to wrestle with: his senior staff was devoid of strategists and should the President Bush make a statement that if necessary the US would remove Saddam from Kuwait, the general recognized that in absence of war plan the presidents credibility would have taken a hit.

Ironically, the military plan—dubbed *Instant Thunder*—emerged not from CENTCOM but from within the bowels of the Pentagon. Lt. Col. John Warden III was tasked to develop plans for a strategic air war campaign. Warden's air plan

15   James A. Baker, *The Politics of Diplomacy: Revolution, War and Peace, 1989–1992* (New York: Putnam's Sons, 1995), 282–3.

16   Ibid, 283.

17   Ibid.

18   See essay by Lt. Col. Richard P. King, "Where You Stand Depends Upon What (Or Whether) You Fly: Bureaucratic Politics and the Gulf War Air Campaign," National War College, National Defense University, 1995, 1.

19   Many of these plans involved the extensive use of cruise missiles but this weapon had never been utilized in a war before which explains the general's unhappiness with strategies involving these weapons; and in the early planning of the "ground invasion" of Iraq they were not, at that time, considered a viable option. For more on this point, see Gordon and Trainor, *The Generals War*, 75.

called for deep strike missions over a six day period inside Iraq but the plan did not envision the need to target Iraq's forces in Kuwait. After considerable planning within the confines of CHECKMATE (the name of the plan) in Pentagon,[20] Warden sold the plan to Powell. Thereafter on 17 August 1990 Powell instructed Warden to travel with members of his staff to meet with CENTCOM officials.

It was at this time that polemics commenced. Schwarzkopf was approving of the plan but warned the plan was problematic in that the UN Security Council would eventually intervene and put a halt to air operations; additionally, the general launched an inquiry into the massive six-day air campaign. What would happen if Saddam refused to capitulate after six days? Warden had no answer because his view was that the operation would be over before the six-day period but recognized the plan had no contingencies for unforeseen realities on the ground.

After meeting Schwarzkopf, Warden had a series of heated discussions with Lt. General Charles Horner, the head of Central Commands Air Force component (CENTAF). After listening to Warden's presentation, Horner expressed his displeasure warning that the plan mirrored much of the failures associated with the Vietnam War. Horner's point was that official's in Washington "picked the targets" during that ill-fatted war. Horner explicated that Goldwater-Nichols Act and JCS Pub 26 were created to prevent such tactics and his thinking was that Warden's plans had undermined the Congressional and Pentagon efforts that were put in place. To make his point clear the general offered this refrain to Warden: "If Folks from Washington want to fight this war, tell them to come to the theater."[21] Horner became more circumspect after receiving word the plan received additional credibility following Air Force Chief of Staff General Michael Dugan's glowing assessment.

To insure that things would meet with those realities, Warden was displaced and Brigadier Buster Glosson was tasked to complete the plan. This was an astute bureaucratic move in that Glosson had an affinity for Schwarzkopf and Horner and less supportive of interference in the planning of the war from Washington.

Glosson's arrival was timely for soon after he was given the authority to run the Special Planning Group, or the Black Hole, he had to report to Horner. The Black Hole evolved into the strategic planning center for the air assault during *Operation Desert Storm*. Though Glosson was tasked by Horner to start from scratch his new plan "embodied the same plans" associated with Warden's Instant Thunder. Even though they endeavored to keep Washington at bay, in time however Horner and Glosson had to confront a number of "internal fissures." The first came from the Tactical Air Command in Langley Virginia that opposed Warden's concept and was no less indifferent to the new version that emanated from CENTCOM. The second dispute came from the Navy. The Navy representative of the Black Hole Donald McSwain referred to the plan as "Distant Blunder" in recognition that the plan had been drafted in Washington and "because of its emphasis on attacking Baghdad at

---

20   Gordon and Trainor, *The Generals War*, 79.
21   Gordon and Trainor, *The Generals War,* 93.

the outset of the campaign."[22] The Navy had other objections most notably the plan as envisioned did not take into account the protection of the fleet. The Navy found itself handcuffed and outflanked owing to three dilemmas: first its senior component commander was aboard ship and not a direct participant in CENTCOM debates, and when he did participate in CENTCOM meetings in Riyadh he found himself outranked.[23] And second the Air Force wielded another important bureaucratic tool, the Air Tasking Order (ATO), which was responsible for day-to-day planning of all air sorties, which meant that they would control which services flew when and where. Additionally, JFACC had another comparative advantage: all air refueling could not take place without Air Force tankers. This dispute was resolved when the ATO allowed the Navy control over sorties to protect the fleet in the Gulf.

The Marines were equally cautious about the air plan. Initially, the Commandant of the Marines had accepted the authority of the JFACC that translated that all sorties to protect their in-theater forces would be under the control of the ATO. The Ominbus Agreement was utilized as a tool by Marine senior military officials. It was this agreement that allowed the Marines to withhold "at least half" of the air sorties for use by the Marine Air-Ground Task Force (MAGTF) unit.[24] The Marines had skillfully used a bureaucratic move and "quickly forced through the joint process an ambiguous compromise (Omnibus Agreement) in Washington that protected their position in-theater operations. Finally, there was yet another dispute: this one coming from the Army and the CENTCOM Commanding General Schwarzkopf who made two major requests: first that B-52 Bombers target Iraqi Republican Guard positions at the start of the war and that the air plan target Iraqi units in the Kuwaiti Theater of Operations (KTO), and second, the general wanted the plan changed to allow (the JFACC would not have control over them) for Army helicopters for use in the eventual ground assault.[25]

In the end the plan looked very different from its original version, but in the final analysis, despite the constant bureaucratic squabbles, it developed into one acceptable to all services. Similarly, even though the in-theater commander had hoped to exclude Washington from the process, the plan still evolved with the assistance of CHECKMATE back in the Pentagon.[26]

---

22   Ibid., 97.

23   King, "Where You Stand Depends Upon What (Or Whether) You Fly: Bureaucratic Politics and the Gulf War Air Campaign," 5–6.

24   Lt. Col. Stephen J. McNamara, *Air Power's Gordian Knot: Centralized Versus Organic Control* (Maxwell, AL: Air University Press, 1994).

25   King, "Where You Stand Depends Upon What (Or Whether) You Fly: Bureaucratic Politics and the Gulf War Air Campaign," 7.

26   Lt. Col. Kathleen M. Conley, USAF, "Campaign for Change: Organizational Processes, Governmental Politics, and the Revolution in Military Affairs," *Aerospace Power Journal*, Fall 1998. http//www.airpower.au.af.mil/airchronicales/apj/apj98/fal98/conleytxt. htm. Retrieved on 7 March 2005.

Postwar Controversies

Another set of polemics in Washington illustrated the war within a war revolved around the politics of war termination. This version of politics is critical to comprehending how the end of the Operation Desert Storm impacted the legacies of the Bush I, Powell, and Schwarzkopf, and how the resulting negative impressions of the wars' conclusion forced subsequent presidents (Clinton and Bush II) to contend with Saddam's survival.

The bureaucratic politics that erupted at the close of the war were a result of a fundamental flaw within administration strategic planning, an issue that again surfaced under the second Bush administration. In the words of Schwarzkopf's chief foreign policy advisor much of what occurred with respect to the postwar period concerned the fact that "we never did have a plan to terminate the war."[27] Gordon and Trainor offer this additional statement that symbolizes the administrations missed opportunities in this area:

> The untidy end to the conflict showed that it is not enough to plan a war. Civilian and military officials must also plan for the peace that follows. Civilian policy makers also had not given much thought to the possibility that Iraq might break apart, let alone the prospect that Saddam Hussein's foes might call on the allies for protection. Their failure to anticipate the upheaval in Iraq, their ignorance of the Shiites, and the White House's ambivalence about committing itself to toppling Saddam Hussein reflected the administrations absence of a clear political strategy for postwar Iraq—all of which was reflected in the negotiations at Safwan.[28]

In fact the resulting failures—failure to destroy the vaunted Republican Guard, complete other key military objectives in Iraq, failed intelligence, and other matters— occurred as a result of political considerations made in the White House and the Pentagon which produced subsequent infighting in Washington that invariably touched off disputes among the commanding generals in the field.

The central reason why the ground war was concluded in 100 hours had much to do with White House and Pentagon reaction to the events associated with the "Highway of death" at Mutlah Ridge. In brief, as Iraqi troops were fleeing Kuwait, a long column of military vehicles remained visible from the air. American aircraft bombed the convoy repeatedly and the media incessantly replayed the images of the vehicle carnage on the nightly news.[29] President Bush and his war council had a major public relations issue to manage. US intelligence indicated that over 1400 Iraqi vehicles were destroyed, and the exaggerated press reports of the "scene of

---

27   Gordon and Trainor, *The Generals War*, 461.

28   Ibid., 476.

29   For more on this point see, Rick Atkinson, *Crusade: The Untold Story of the Persian Gulf War*. Boston: Houghton Mifflin Co, 1993), 466 and William Claiborne, and Caryle Murphy, "Retreat Down Highway of Doom: U.S. Warplanes Turned Iraqis' Escape Route into Deathtrap," *Washington Post*, 2 March 1991.

wholesale destruction later emerged as a major factor" in deciding to end the war.[30] The event induced a perception that the once successful demonstration of US military prowess might appear "un-American and unchivalrous" should the military continue the fighting.[31] Richard Haass lamented that "If the war ended on a sour note, this could complicate postwar politics. For these reasons the President was now inclined to conclude the war."[32] Thus the decision to end the war was based not on "politico-military considerations but on public relations concerns."[33] On the events on the ground, with a clear sense the war was over, President Bush replied "We do not want to lose anything now with charges of brutalization."[34]

This statement occurred on 27 February 1991 in a meeting of the president's war council. Those in attendance were Vice President Dan Qualye, Secretary's Baker and Cheney, Chairman Powell, and National Security Advisor Scowcroft (British Foreign Minister Douglas Hurd was also in attendance). The point of the meeting had been clear too all: war termination. In response to a query from the president concerning bringing the war to a close, Powell responded that "We are in the home stretch Norm and I would like to finish tomorrow, a five-day war."[35]

Among those gathered this decision produced no second guessing due in part to the burgeoning negative worldview of events on the highway of the death. It was not until the matter of war termination was transmitted from Washington to the generals in the field that the polemics, both in Washington and among the generals in the field, began to take hold.

The rapid pace of events therefore caught CENTCOM unprepared not just in meeting its final military objectives but for preparing the peace (This is a failure of the US government in general). Following Powell's conversation with Schwarzkopf, the general had agreed with Powell that the war should end in five days. The most telling part of this conversation was Powell's query "what are your plans for tomorrow?" This question relates both to the final military objectives and invariably to war termination. As it turned out Schwarzkopf was not prepared for either.[36]

On the matter of strategy, the commanders in the field were concerned that Washington's pretensions with public relations blinded them to the situation on the ground. Many commanders spoke up and challenged Schwarzkopf's contention that the "gate was closed." On this point, a reference to Schwarzkopf's famous end of the battle briefing, General Glosson remarked that it "was one of the most dishonest

---

30   Gordon and Trainor, *The Generals War*, 370.

31   Col. Mark Garrard, USAF, "War Termination in the Persian Gulf-Problems and Prospects," *Aerospace Power Journal*, Fall 2001.

32   See Robert R. Soucy II, Kevin A. Shwedo, and John S. Haven II, "War Termination and Joint Planning," *Joint Force Quarterly*, Summer 1995, 97.

33   Mackubin Thomas Owens, "With Eyes Wide Open-A Strategy for War With Iraq," *National Review Online*, www.nationalreview.com/owens/owens08402.asp. Downloaded on 3 April 2005.

34   Gordon and Trainor, *The Generals War*, x.

35   Ibid.

36   Ibid., 417.

presentations."[37] Further the call for a cease-fire infuriated many other generals. Two examples are instructive. On the first, General Waller, Schwarzkopf's deputy, using expletives, the general thought it awkward that the war was being concluded. He had mentioned pointedly that until the "gate was closed" blocking any Republican Guard escape route, then the war should continue. In response to Waller's concerns, Schwarzkopf exclaimed: "Then you go argue with them,"[38] a reference to the national command authority in Washington. In the second instance, it is clear the war appeared different in Washington then on the critical front in theater. As Gordon and Trainor explicate "neither McCaffrey nor his key commanders" thought Saddam's elite forces were destroyed but "the commanders who knew the most about the battlefield were not asked their views."[39] The perception from most commanders is that if the war had been prosecuted at the rate of the previous day the objective of destroying the Republican Guard would have been achieved.[40] The point here is that strategic military objectives were supplanted by political objectives dictated in Washington without much debate from the senior military officers in the field.

The debate assumed greater importance once it was clear the VII Corps, led by General Fredrick Franks, whose zone of responsibility within Iraq concerned the destruction of retreating Republican Guard divisions. For Schwarzkopf his view was that long before the war Franks was too cautious, yet the CENTCOM commander allowed him to stay in place, leading a critical battle. In the end, the administration paid a heavy price for this decision.

The aforementioned resurfaced at the location of the cease-fire talks in Safwan. Another issue surfaced in Washington: the issue concerned whether the administration should establish a demilitarized zone in Southern Iraq under the auspices of United States. In another ad hoc example to secure the peace, Baker carried a plan developed by Robert Kimmit and US Ambassador to the United Nations Thomas Pickering. This plan contained military and political responsibilities. It was viewed this way: "Militarily, any Iraqi intrusion into zone would provide Kuwait and Saudi Arabia with substantial warning in case the Iraqis ever again tried to threaten the Gulf States."[41] On the political dimensions, the zone would decrease Iraq's authority over the South, which included the critical Rumaila oil field and control over the highway "from Amman to Baghdad, allowing the allies to crack down on sanctions busting from Jordan."[42] Baker believed it important to obtained coalition support. At another level, Pickering remained confident that the plan had UN Security Council support. There were two additional hurdles, the requirement of interagency support and the blessings of Schwarzkopf.

---

37   Ibid., 423.
38   Ibid.
39   Ibid., 425.
40   Ibid.
41   Ibid., 451.
42   Ibid.

After two days of debate within the bureaucracy, the plan looked as though it would proceed. In the administration, however, the plan began to loose support. In one example, Wolfowitz, who formerly supported the initiative, had now withdrawn his support. Second, within the State Department there was little support for the Shiites despite the efforts of Baker to the contrary. Third, in his meeting with Schwarzkopf, Baker attempted to gain the generals approval. Schwarzkopf however was indifferent and the planned security zone collapsed.[43]

As was the case with all of the issues discussed in this section, initiatives and disputes emerged in Washington leading to subsequent debates in the field among senior military leaders. The result of this fragmentation produced disharmony resulting in ad hoc war termination efforts which detracted from the battlefield successes. The greatest tragedy associated with the infighting is this: the administration missed and opportunity to achieve its most significant political-military objective. This is a reference to the failure to destroy the Republican Guard, which say experts, would have precipitated Saddam's demise; the failure to achieve this objective produced a feeling of a "triumph without victory." On this point Brian Bond offers this statement: "The ironic result of the Gulf War seems to be either Saddam Hussein will be left in power to build up his forces for renewed aggression or, by some means short of another great coalition war, he will have to be deposed. There can rarely have been a case in history where the chasm between a decisive military victory and an unsatisfactory political outcome has been so wide."[44] It was indeed a triumph without victory.

In the final analysis, President Bush and senior military leaders made a number of telling statements that illustrate the importance of the need to plan for war termination. President Bush made two telling declarations. On the first, in at statement on the consequences of his decision to terminate the war, Bush explicated: "You know, to be honest with you, I haven't yet felt this wonderfully euphoric feeling . . . but I think it's that I want to see an end. You mentioned World War II—there was a definite end to that conflict. And now we have Saddam Hussein still there—a man that wreaked this havoc upon his neighbors."[45] The president's most telling remarks were these: "let the civilians and the president do the diplomacy, do the politics, wrestle with the press, and when the war is over, bear responsibility for the terms of surrender. But at the outset, once the lead-up to the fighting has begun, let the politicians get out of the way and let the military fight the war, and let them fight to win."[46] The problem with this statement is that it is clear the president made the fundamental mistake of "divorcing war and politics." Sadly, for the United States concerns the fact that his son, George W. Bush, would repeat the same mistake which resulted in far greater consequences.

---

43   Ibid., 450–52.
44   Brian Bond, *The Pursuit of Victory – From Napoleon to Saddam Hussein* (New York: Oxford University Press, 1996), 197.
45   Garrard, "War Termination in the Persian Gulf-Problems and Prospects," 7
46   Ibid., 4.

On the inadequacy of US war termination, Schwarzkopf made two important statements that symbolized the American failure in this venue. First, he noted that it never occurred to him that he would have to sit down with his Iraqi counterpart and lay down the terms of a settlement; second, in an after-action report Schwarzkopf said the following: The rapid success of the ground campaign and our subsequent occupation were not fully anticipated" and therefore some of the "necessary follow-on actions were not ready."[47]

Finally, the bureaucratic politics that engulfed the administration and the polemics regarding war termination were lessons for subsequent presidents. The great irony, at least in the case of George W. Bush concerned two issues: the failure to learn from these lessons, and second, as a by-product of the first, "W" suffered in ways that were far more pronounced than that of the elder Bush.

Clinton: Infighting and the Search for a Policy

The bureaucratic politics that occurred within the administration of Bill Clinton never reached the level of that of the previous administration. There are two reasons for this conclusion. First, the Clinton administration never formerly intervened (with the use of ground forces) in Iraq and second, the White House worked to prevent Iraq from becoming a major issue which, in the view of some observers would have hindered the administrations domestic agenda. Thus the parameters of the infighting were far different from the polemics that consumed the first Bush I administration.

That said the level of bureaucratic politics did unfold in a way that hampered administration policy toward Iraq, a point consistent with the previous administration. This section focuses on the debate concerning the "tough choices over how much priority and how many resources—political, diplomatic, and military—should be devoted to dealing with Saddam."[48] Second, this section examines the burgeoning undercurrent that endeavored to shift administration policy to one of confrontation with Saddam and to one that sought accommodation. On the former, the author will explore the covert efforts of regime change and the resulting internal infighting. Consistent with the above, this chapter concerns three sets of bureaucratic politics that impacted administration policy decisions in Iraq: (1) the schools of thought surrounding the strategy that should govern administration policy; (2) the polemics over the ill-fated covert mission to unseat Saddam, and (3) the decision to launch *Operation Desert Fox*.

In the early months of the Clinton administration two factions—the proponents of roll back (or regime change) and a second faction that supported a long-term comprehensive containment—were locked in a struggle to influence the new president. The prize for each faction: control of the direction of US policy toward Iraq.

---

47   Ibid.
48   Pollack, *The Threatening Storm – The United States and Iraq*, 56.

The roll back faction included the likes of Vice President Al Gore, UN Ambassador Madeline Albright, Martin Indyk, the special assistant to the president for the Near East and South Asia, along with Bruce Riedel (then director of Persian Gulf Affairs), and Mark Parris, the deputy assistant secretary of state for the Near East. Collectively, this group warned that Saddam Hussein would eventually outlast US and coalition efforts to contain him. Thus the view of this hawkish group was that Saddam's removal is the only satisfactory action to preserve US interests and to remove the single greatest threat to regional stability. Interestingly, this group acknowledged (through statements made by the vice president and others) that the core tenets of the administration's policy were consistent with that of the previous administration.[49]

The second group consisted of a powerful troika that included Secretary of State Warren Christopher, National Security Advisor Anthony Lake, and Deputy Secretary of State Strobe Talbott. According to Pollack, this group "recognized that the containment policy that their predecessors had stumbled onto remained effective and offered an opportunity to pursue a different agenda."[50] In short, the containment of Iraq allowed the administration to advance a different vision of New World Order, where the president would advance "global economic development, cooperative security, and "the use of force to aid the oppressed and defeat aggression."

The two factions served the interests of domestic and international vestiges. The proponents of regime change had a number of allies within the US foreign policy establishment (and a minority of states within the coalition) that held the additional view that President Bush failed to "finish the job" in Iraq. The "dovish factions" position on Iraq is based upon recognition of a series of realities: preserve the coalition, enforce UN Security Council resolutions; a clear understanding that the international community and domestic public opinion was not supportive of roll back, and lastly, the administration, as stated earlier, recognized that the containment of Iraq offered the means to promote a new era of liberal internationalism. Thus the resulting internal dispute over the direction of US-Iraq policy produced a policy that was "ambiguous."

Perhaps more dangerous is that this bureaucratic incident induced a far significant problem for the administration (one which would greatly impact the decision making in second Bush administration) concerned a compromise: regime change. The results of this debate had two consequences. First, the administration launched a covert operation designed to unseat the regime in Iraq. This decision produced unforeseen polemics, resulting in substantial infighting to the point that administration officials were willing to scapegoat one of the countries foremost Middle Eastern spies— Robert Bear then America's eye's and ears to the opposition groups operating inside

49   Robert Litwak, *Rogue States and US Foreign Policy: Containment After the Cold War* (Washington, DC: Woodrow Wilson Center Press, 2000), 127 and Pollack, *The Threatening Storm – The United States and Iraq*, 66.

50   Pollack, *The Threatening Storm – The United States and Iraq*, 65.

Iraq—to protect President Clinton from any potential damage associated with the coup attempt in Iraq.

The debate and evolving polemics surrounded a covert mission involving the CIA and their trained contacts that consisted of Chalabi's INC, the Kurdish Democratic Party (KDP), and the Patriotic Union of Kurdistan (PUK), groups that operated inside Northern Iraq. The essence of the plan called for the destruction of one of Saddam's weakest military units, the 38th Infantry Division. This unit received few supplies, and soldiers had not been paid or fed for months. It was thus the view of the planners that a quick and decisive defeat of this unit could force a domino effect whereby other Iraqi units would join in the operation to end Saddam's regime.

There were a number of problems associated with the CIA plan. First on the eve of the attack on the 38th Infantry division, Washington backed out of the plan; second, the KDP withdrew its support for the operation leaving the PUK and the INC to devise a strategy to implement the operation. In Washington, then national security advisor Anthony Lake blasted the CIA operation and later cabled Baer with the following words that should thereafter be delivered to opposition leaders: "A. The action you have planned for this weekend has been totally compromised. B. We believe there is a high risk of failure. Any decision to proceed will be on your own."[51] The operation went ahead as planned. Though the operation succeeded in its initial objective (the defeat the 38th Infantry division), Saddam's Special Republican Guard Units launched a counterattack that smashed the revolt and killed untold numbers of PUK and INC forces.

In the aftermath of the operation, the FBI summoned CIA agent Baer and queried him on whether he had deliberately violated the Executive Order prohibiting foreign assassinations. The FBI investigation infuriated the CIA, which charged that their agent merely followed orders. The point here is that the agency would not allow one its own to be used as a scapegoat when it was clear that the administration had gotten cold feet, unwilling to provide air cover for the operation. In the end the episode dissipated with the bureau clearing Baer of all charges and later honored for his efforts in Iraq.

Second, the administration was facing increasing pressure from the republicans in congress to act decisively in Iraq. In response to this pressure, in order to justify the administrations new position, the president later sought legislation from the Congress that resulted in the passage of the Iraq Liberation Act of 1998. This act provided funds to the Iraqi National Congress and other anti-Saddam opposition groups, whose goal was to covertly unseat the regime. The problem with the decision is that it touched off several rounds of bureaucratic enmity that encompassed bureaucratic entities throughout the national security bureaucracy, and worse regional command structures were dragged along for the ride, which only exacerbated the situation for the administration both for its goal (regime change) and for its image.

---

51   See Robert Baer, *See No Evil: The True Story of a Ground Soldier in the CIA's War on Terrorism* (New York: Crown Books, 2003) and Evans Thomas and Christopher Dickey, "Bay of Pigs Redux," *Newsweek*, 23 March 1998.

Within the White House, the presidents political advisors exclaimed that Clinton acquiesced to the neo-conservatives that clamored for war, going so far as to write a letter detailing the affect of not unseating Saddam (and administration that was timid). Second, perhaps just as significant, these same advisors noted that by accepting this initiative, the appearance was obvious: that the republicans in and out of office had consistently pushed Clinton to remove Saddam, thereby completing the task of former President Bush. To this group of domestic advisors the implications were salient: the president was adopting an agenda not of his making, but one borne of pressure from the republicans. For Clinton, in his mind, the fact that the efforts were covert and not an overt invasion, provided credibility that the plan was his and therefore would be implemented by the executive and not the legislative branch.

The discourse concerning regime change induced disagreement from the within the bureaucracy. Both the State Department and CIA were onboard to the degree that they wanted to rid Iraq of Saddam, but both entities remained incredulous with respect to trusting the opposition forces, particularly the INC. In short, there were so many historical problems among the various groups that State and CIA experts felt it not only impractical that for them to cooperate but equally important, impossible. There was another issue, Ahmed Chalabi. For State and CIA experts he could not be trusted, and worse he had not accounted for funds already allocated to him. Worse, within the structures of State and CIA each was confident that Chalabi represented a tool of the neoconservatives, and thus he would be doing the bidding in support of their aims and not those of the president.

CENTCOM Commander General Anthony Zinni was drawn into this dispute, and offered little support for the covert operation.[52] Worse, Zinni was an outspoken critic of the notion of regime change in Iraq, which touched off a firestorm within the administration. First, the general, in a testimony before the Senate Armed Services Committee, explicated "I don't see an opposition group that has the viability to overthrow Saddam at this point." In short, the plan was doomed to fail. This criticism in and of itself was damaging to the president, but the following statement represented open opposition to the president's policy toward Iraq. In a direct challenge to the Iraq Liberation Act, and thus administration policy, according to Litwak, Zinni's critique "represented the continuing tension within American policy: rollback or comprehensive containment? This tension continues to engender confusion and a potential drift toward what President Clinton himself warned of as 'an ambiguous third route.'"[53]

---

52   The role of the US military went as follows: "The Pentagon [in the form of CENTCOM] or the CIA will train 300 former Iraqi military officers to use anti-tank weapons, encryption and communications gear. The men will train an additional 1, 000. The rebels will infiltrate by land, sea or air. They will capture an air base that will become a magnet for disaffected Iraqi soldiers. The Americans will provide air cover. Soon, they will set up a provisional government." For more on the plan, see Dana Priest and David B. Ottaway, "Congress's Candidate to Overthrow Saddam Hussein," *Washington Post*, 21 April 1999.

53   As quoted in Litwak, *Rogue States and US Foreign Policy*, 149.

Additionally, Zinni argued that Iran, with its support of terrorist groups within the region along with their WMD programs represented a greater threat than Saddam; the general clearly indicated his opposition and displeasure with administration policy.[54] Within the White House and elsewhere, there were those who felt that the general was out of line, noting that the military implemented rather then set public policy.

During the second term President Clinton's policy underwent a transformation. First, the president made a number of critical changes among his senior advisors. Former UN Ambassador Albright was named Secretary of State; Richard Cohen was tapped as the Secretary of Defense, Sandy Berger, the former deputy national security advisor, was promoted and became the president's new national security advisor. Second, these and other changes were indicators that the administration's aversion to the use of force seemed to have ended.

Irrespective of these changes, the administration had a major issue to confront: the sanctions regime within the UN was unraveling. Similarly, the Russians, Chinese and the French were openly opposed to the use of force against Iraq. Thus, if and when the administration proposed harsher sanctions (as in the case of UNSC resolution 1134) against Saddam, the aforementioned troika, instead of voting for such measures, would abstain (an indicator of opposition). Additionally, as Saddam's defiance against UNSCOM weapons inspectors increased, the United States and Britain commenced a military build-up that would be used as a diplomatic means to force Saddam's compliance with UNSC resolutions. This build-up had another unintended consequence: the Saudis and other regional and European allies distanced themselves from the threats of the use of force against the regime.[55]

This division among the coalition subsided after Iraq forced UN inspectors to vacate the country. Oddly, this action forced cohesion in the coalition that had not been witnessed since the *Operation Desert Storm*. Thereafter, the administration utilized a UN report as a justification to launch an air strike, with the desire to force the return of UN inspectors and Iraq's compliance with UNSC resolutions. Following a series of national security meetings the administration listed five demands that could prevent an American-led air campaign against Iraq:

> Resolution of all outstanding issues raised by UNSCOM and the IAEA: Unfettered access for inspectors with no restrictions, consistent with the February 23 memorandum signed by Iraq; Turnover by Iraq of all relevant documents; Acceptance by Iraq of all U.N. resolutions related to mass destructions weapons, [and,] No interference with the independence or professional expertise of weapons inspectors.[56]

With US forces in the region prepared to launch missile strikes in support of *Operation Thunder* on "November 14 the Clinton Administration delayed them upon learning that Iraq had agreed to resume cooperation with UNSCOM" and "after

---

54   Ibid.

55   Pollack, 88.

56   Alfred B. Prados and Kenneth Katzman, "Iraq-U.S. Confrontation," *CRS Report*, 27 February 2001. Accessed on line on 23 June 2005.

further negotiations, Iraq agreed in a letter to the Security Council on November 15 to provide unconditional cooperation to UNSCOM and rescind its ban on UNSCOM activities."[57] Subsequent to this reality the president was forced to cancel the planned strikes one hour before the commencement of operations.

Ironically, in the aftermath of the aborted strike bureaucratic rumblings resurfaced among the presidents senior advisors. There were those, including Cohen, Albright, and Chairman of Joint Chiefs of Staff, General Hugh Shelton wanted to "go ahead with the attack despite initial reports of an Iraqi offer to US and United Nations demands."[58] Those in agreement with the president's position included Gore and Berger. This spilt exposed two salient realities. Internationally, according to one administration official, "things were not going to line up any better for a military strike than they were."[59] Second, reports surfaced that Clinton feared that some 10,000 Iraqi's might die as a result of the strike of the president's aversion to force still remained.

In the midst of debate on the Lewinsky Scandal in the House of Representatives on 16 December 1998, the president finally unleashed the long awaited attack against Iraq (following a report by the UN inspectors to the Security Council). Owing to the fact that there was little internal debate on the matter—thus preventing any bureaucratic wrangling—*Operation Desert Fox*, which involved some 30 plus naval vessels and nearly 350 aircraft, resulted in the devastation of key installations in Iraq.[60] The absence of a serious debate within the foreign policy establishment produced skepticism that the action occurred to deflect attention away from the domestic scandal.

With the administrations time in office coming to a rapid conclusion a number of themes registered in defining administration infighting. First, the inability to settle on a definitive policy produced ad hoc decisions whereby a series of costly military build-ups and operations (see Table 4.1) became the substitute for a policy. Second, the infighting within the administration left several significant issues unresolved: determining a policy or doctrine that would govern administration decision making regarding how to approach the myriad problems posed by Iraq's Saddam Hussein. Third, the ad hoc nature of administration policy induced discourse that the administration remained adrift and at worst adopted a position of limited escalation. Fourth, the internal debates left a lasting reality that the Bush II administration used to their advantage. That is, the prevailing view that conflict with Iraq was inevitable became a rallying theme for invasion in the new administration, about which the

---

57   Ibid.

58   Bradley Graham, "Senior Officials Split on Aborting Airstrikes," 18 November 1998.

59   Ibid.

60   According to Iraq analyst, Kenneth Pollack, the administration struck several sites that were dubbed "key components of Saddam's police state." Those installations included: "eighteen command-and-control facilities, eight Republican Guard barracks, six airfields, and nineteen sites related to the concealment mechanism—which actually consisted of Special Republican Guard garrisons." For more on this point, see Pollack, 93.

decision to invade emerged following a long dangerous and divisive round of bureaucratic polemics.

Table 4.1   Costs of Persian Gulf Operations (in US $ millions)

Operation	FY1998	FY1999	FY2000	FY2001*
Southern Watch	1,497.2	954.8	755.4	678.0
Northern Watch	136.0	156.4	143.6	138.7
Desert Spring (Kuwait training)**	5.6	13.8	239.8	241.8
Desert Thunder (Nov. 1998 build-up)	n/a	43.5	n/a	n/a
Desert Fox (Dec. 1998 air strikes)	n/a	92.9	n/a	n/a
Totals	1,638.8	1,261.4	1,138.8	1,058.5

*   Estimate
**   Known as Intrinsic Action until FY2000
Source: Department of Defense, Comptroller.[61]

Bush II: The War Behind Closed Doors

The parameters of the infighting under "W" were, among the three presidents in this study, by far the most pronounced. Of the three American presidents only President George W. Bush would formally and incessantly declare the need to overtly unseat the regime. Indeed, the bureaucratic politics that so characterized the current white house occupant had its roots in the administration of the senior Bush. This section opens with a discussion of the critical features of the pre-President George W. Bush infighting and indicates how such infighting affected the prewar period and the formation of the anti-Powell faction in the administration. The second part of this study examines the Powell faction and the secretary of states battle to hold the line during the formation of administration Iraq policy. The third part of this study illustrates the intensity of the engagement during the post-9/11 period (prewar and war periods). The fourth part of this study addresses the polemics during the turbulent postwar reconstruction period. These are the topics of discussion for this section.

The Emergence of the Anti-Powell Faction

To place the infighting within the administration of George W. Bush in perspective, the reader should understand that the critical bureaucratic battles which ultimately set the stage for the showdown over Iraq policy from September 2001–August 2004, evolved after three decisions that occurred during the senior Bush administration.

---

61   As quoted in Prados and Katzman, "Iraq-U.S. Confrontation."

The first decision involved the debate to end the first gulf war. The pivotal question came from the senior Bush on the afternoon of 27 February 1991 who wanted to ascertain when the war should come to an end? This question, in a room filled with his war cabinet, was addressed to chairman of Joint Chiefs of Staff, General Colin Powell.[62] Powell's response called for ending the war within twenty four hours, a decision that received support from General Norman Schwarzkopf. The decisions by Powell and Schwarzkopf touched off a new round of infighting. For his rivals, principally Secretary Defense Cheney and Under Secretary of Defense Wolfowitz, they were furious at Powell's matter of fact response, which as it turned out, produced no substantive debate and even worse for these individuals and others President Bush did not seek or request their advice on the issue.

The second decision, the signing of the Safwan agreement which formally concluded the war, would again unnerve and frustrate those opposed to ending the war without the unseating of Saddam Hussein. The anti-Powell faction was concerned because the president supported a war-ending negotiated process led by Powell and Schwarzkopf that permitted Iraq's military to utilize its inventory of helicopter gun-ships to killed thousands of Shiites, in many instances in the view of US forces. Once again, this group made it clear that they were in disagreement with the decisions at Safwan and the subsequent non-US actions in the face of what they concluded was Iraqi defiance. They wanted to punish the regime but the president based his decision on the advice of Powell and others who noted that the war had concluded, US forces were in the process of withdrawing, and therefore it made little sense to fight a second war.

The third decision was consistent with the former, the president, relying on the counsel of senior military advisors failed to punish the regime for the mistreatment of the Kurds in northern Iraq. The response from the anti-Powell faction was the same: had the administration unseated the regime these and other postwar problems would not have occurred. Viewed collectively, the anti-Powell faction was born, its target and objective clear: in serving future republican presidents if the neoconservative objectives were to reach fruition Powell's influence over US Iraq policy must be held in check.

This view would serve as the impetus and a call to arms for the neoconservatives in the second Bush administration. The anti-Powell faction emerged from exile with its objective intact: regime change in Iraq. There were many lessons learned from the service to two previous presidents (Bush and Clinton). The most important were these: increase the number of neoconservatives within the new administration, ensure that those serving "W" had access, for access meant power, and finally, with these numbers overwhelm the foreign policy process and therefore as a by-product reduce Powell's potential to dominate administration Iraq policy.

The anti-Powell faction had additional advantages. The first concerned the role of Vice President Cheney. Cheney's relationship with Powell remained contentious since the pivotal decisions that concluded the Gulf War. In defeat Cheney recognized

---

62   Gordan and Trainor, *The General's War*, vii.

that in a second Bush administration Powell's influence had to be contained. To thwart this influence Cheney was in a remarkable position: he headed the transition team and therefore had played a major role in the hiring of senior and middle level administration appointments. Thus Powell's perceived isolation within administration "was reinforced from the start by the fact that the people named to the number two and three spots in the national security bureaucracy dismissed his pragmatic approach" and more important "were close to Cheney, Rumsfeld or both."[63]

Of those officials that would serve the younger Bush many held to the neoconservative philosophy. Thus when Rumsfeld took over the stewardship of the Pentagon, with the assistance of Wolfowitz and Douglas Feith, the trio, with Cheney protecting their flank in white house crisis meetings, held the belief that they would be principal architects of US policy toward Iraq. To achieve this objective this faction returned to a privately held goal of minimizing Powell's influence. This point is instructive. According to Daadler and Lindsay, "when asked why he agreed to become deputy secretary of defense for the younger Bush, he reportedly gave a one-word answer: Powell."[64]

Second, Cheney through his own office (Office of the Vice President) hired additional individuals that strengthened the influence of this faction. Similarly, the vice president developed an infrastructure within Office of the President (OVP) that was consistent with a mini-State Department.[65] Through this bureaucratic entity Cheney was in position to represent the faction's position, most notably in Iraq, on key administration policies.

Consistent with his influence, Cheney worked with National Security Advisor Condoleezza Rice to ensure that additional elements of this faction filled positions within the National Security Council Staff, among them were Elliott Abrams who held the portfolio of the Near East. The end result meant that the faction insulated themselves from Powell's bureaucratic skills. To put it succinctly, the quantity associated with the anti-Powell faction combined with the influence of Cheney and Rice collectively ensured, at least on paper, this faction's control of administration policy toward Iraq. Interestingly, 43 did not learn a critical lesson from 41: limit the influence of the neoconservatives.

Powell Strikes Back: Prewar Battle Over US-Iraq Policy

One of the great fascinations about the internal infighting among combatants in the Bush administration is that Powell was perceived as the "odd man out,"[66] a perception that the general had been "isolated" or that he was simply not a player when it came to Iraq policy. The realities say otherwise. Though on paper it appeared that Powell

---

63   Ivo H. Daadler and James M. Lindsay, *America Unbound: The Bush Revolution in Foreign Policy* (Washington, DC: Brookings, 2003), 58.

64   Daadler and Lindsay, *America Unbound*, 46.

65   Ibid., 58.

66   Johanna McGeary, "Odd Man Out," *Time*, 10 September 2001.

had little chance to influence administration policy toward Iraq, especially in view of the prominence and bureaucratic skills and positioning of anti-Powell faction. That said, one should remember that the faction was erected with Powell's bureaucratic skills in mind. Many of these skills were honed as senior military aide to former Secretary of Defense Casper Weinberger (ironically it is during this same period that the contentious Powell-Wolfowitz relationship began) under President Reagan. Those skills were further developed when Powell served as national security advisor. In this capacity Powell had to remake the structure of the national security staff after Colonel Oliver North conducted secret operations that produced the Iran-Contra scandal. Though he had a presidential mandate for such changes elements within the bureaucracy fought many of Powell's proposed changes, requiring the general to confront such individuals.

The first test of those skills emerged under the second Bush administration during the debate over the review of US policy toward Iraq. The policy positions of both factions were rudimentary.[67] In the intense interagency meetings from February 2001 through August of 2001 both sides had staked out positions: the anti-Powell faction argued that containment of Iraq had proved expensive and hand not achieved tangle results; the Powell faction (which consisted of George Tenet at CIA and elements within the military over at the DoD, or Powell's backchannel) had incessantly called for smart sanctions, an effort to seriously limit Saddam's efforts "to acquire the technology and equipment to produce weapons of mass destruction."[68]

The interagency meetings, dubbed the deputies meetings, were chaired by deputy national security advisor Stephen Hadley. Within these series of meetings (four in total) the infighting became more intense. Richard Armitage, Powell's deputy at State, made the case for smart sanctions, while Wolfowitz, Rumsfeld's deputy, made the case for regime change. Armitage argued strenuously against the notion of unseating the regime without a provocation. Wolfowitz remained insistent on any plan that would end the regime in Iraq, but preferred one that included the Iraqi opposition, led by the Iraqi National Congress (INC), due in part because Ahmed Chalabi was his ally. In the end the process yielded no clear victor although both factions were in agreement to "increase pressure on Saddam, to try to create fissures and disagreements within the regime."[69] The issues concerning how and when and utilizing what type of pressure (sanctions, covert operations, or direct US military intervention) ultimately produced stalemate.

Thereafter with no solution on a clear discernable policy regarding how the administration would deal with Saddam Hussein upon which all the bureaucratic entities could agree, the infighting shifting to the senior members of the administration, or the principals. It is at this level that Powell reaffirmed the need for smart sanctions.

---

67   Pollack, op, cit., 105.

68   Anthony Cordesman, Iraq and Smart Sanctions, Reshaping US Policy in the Gulf, *Center of Strategic and International Studies*, Washington DC, 19 April 2001. http://www. csis.org//burke/iragsmartsanctions.pdf. Retrieved on 27 August 2005.

69   Bob Woodward, *Plan of Attack* (New York: Simon & Schuster, 2004), 20.

However, the anti-Powell faction was unceasing and offered a series of "draft plans"[70] each of which forced Powell to defend his position while simultaneously defeating each of these plans that were variants of strategies for regime change.

Unable to defeat Powell in direct bureaucratic debates, the anti-Powell faction attempted to use an incident in the no fly zone on 10 August 2001 as a means by which to influence administration policy. After coalition aircraft were fired upon the US and British aircraft launched the largest response to date against the Iraq threat, one that involved over one-hundred aircraft to demonstrate that things would be different under the Bush administration (a not-so thinly veiled reference to the Clinton administration's weak response to similar provocations). The tactic failed to yield any tangle results in the support of regime change. By mid-August the results were in: another stalemate. For Powell a small victory had been won: the administration would not pursue regime change but instead continued Clinton's policy of dual containment until the events of 11 September. There were two other consequences. First, after seven months of infighting the interagency process yielded no policy recommendation on Iraq but instead produced an ad hoc policy. Second, the anti-Powell faction had to confront a new and dangerous verity that even with a numerical advantage of forces on deputies and later a series of meetings of the principals they were unable to defeat Powell and his forces in the first serious confrontations over Iraq policy. For the anti-Powell faction they were studying the lessons learned for what they believed would be become a renewed set of confrontations with Powell. This time the stakes were higher.

Open Warfare: Post-11 September and the Struggle for Control over Iraq Policy

The tragedy of 9/11 produced a new round of intense acrimony over Iraq policy within the Bush administration. The anti-Powell faction was adamant that the focus should be on Saddam Hussein and not the Osama Bin Laden-led al Qaeda transnational empire in Afghanistan. In the subsequent post-11 September war councils, Cheney, Rumsfeld, and Wolfowitz asserted the first phase of the war on terror should include states, and argued that Afghanistan presented too few strategic targets. The Powell faction, that expanded to include Richard Clarke and Hugh Shelton, then the chairman of the Joint Chiefs of Staff, and chief of staff to the president Andre Card, responded that the first campaign should focus exclusively on bin Laden and not Saddam Hussein, particularly since there was no conclusive evidence of Iraqi complicity in the attack. Moreover, Powell and Armitage made a convincing case to the president that the coalition would only support a large scale operation in Afghanistan and not Iraq. As the debate unfolded the Powell faction won this round with the vote tally yielding the following numbers: 4 to 0 with Rumsfeld

---

70   Ibid., 22.

abstaining.[71] Accordingly, Clarke celebrated the opening victory, only to be warned by Powell that the debate on Iraq had not ended.[72]

There were several reasons why the debate about attacking Iraq did not dissipate: the first is that the president did not reject regime change "out of hand" and the second is that the anti-Powell faction remained relentless in their pursuit of this goal. Third, even worse it was clear that both sides were prepared for a protracted debate on the future course of US-Iraq policy.

The anti-Powell faction may have lost a new round of debate on Iraq policy, but they received an unusual if not purposeful reward: on 17 September 2001 a secret presidential directive was signed authorizing the Pentagon to begin planning for military operations against Iraq. On the 19 and 20 September in a meeting of the Defense Policy Board, those in attendance (including Rumsfeld) were "animatedly" discussing "the importance of ousting Hussein."[73] The Pentagon utilized an earlier creation, the Office of Special Plans (OSP), to its advantage in providing civilians at the Pentagon with its own intelligence outside the purview of the CIA. Similarly, the OVP was now heavily involved in the collection of intelligence, and worst still, particularly for Powell (and later for the agency itself), the CIA, which should have objected to the bureaucratic power grabs, by the OSP and OVP, had by now had involved itself in "stovepiping,"[74] the politicalization of intelligence on Iraq.

The Powell faction had not at this time introduced any new bureaucratic instrument, but continued its efforts to keep the war on terror focused on al Qaeda. This was done successfully by Powell and those loyal to the faction, via public pronouncements, leaks to press, and direct statements by Powell in press conferences to repudiate the views of the anti-Powell faction. In one notable example, following a query from a reporter during a Pentagon briefing, Wolfowitz responded, "I think… [about] removing the sanctuaries, removing the support systems, ending states who sponsor terrorism. And that's why it has to be a broad and sustained campaign."[75] According to Dan Balz, a reporter for the *Washington Post*, this statement alarmed Powell and senior members of the State Department, which "again felt it was inflaming the situation, taking their eye off the real ball, which was to go after al Qaeda and Afghanistan."[76] In a subsequent press conference, Powell used the occasion to respond to Wolfowitz, with these words:

---

71   Ibid., 25.

72   Richard Clarke, *Against All Enemies: Inside America's War on Terror* (New York: Free Press, 2004), 31.

73   Glenn Kessler, "US Decision on Iraq Has Puzzling Past," *Washington Post*, 12 January 2003. Retrieved on-line on 27 August 2005; http//www.commondreams.org/cgi-bin/print.cgi?file=/headlines03/0112-08.htm.

74   Seymour Hersh, "The Stovepipe: How Conflicts Between the Bush Administration and the Intelligence Community Marred the Reporting on Iraq's Weapon's," *The New Yorker*, 27 October 2003. Retrieved on 27 August 2005.

75   See "The War Behind Closed Doors" *Frontline*, 20 February 2003. Transcript viewed on line at http//www.pbs.org/wgbh/pages/frontline/shows/iraq/

76   Ibid.

We're after ending terrorism, and if there are states and regimes, nations that support terrorism, we hope to persuade them that it is in their interests to stop doing that..But I think ending terrorism is where I would like to leave it, and let—let Mr. Wolfowitz speak for himself.[77]

These actions defined the post-11 September debate on Iraq but for the American people and the international community these were fissures in a much larger debate that came to both dominate and symbolize the course and direction of the war on terror.

The turning point in the debate came not from the position of the anti-Powell faction or their numbers but instead as a result of a presidential request. Accordingly, on 21 November 2001 President Bush had formerly decided it was time to "turn back to Iraq." And the fact the president requested hard data on the specific military plans represented an unmistakable indicator that a key moment in the Iraq debate had developed. For Rumsfeld the fact this request occurred outside the war council deliberations signaled to him that his faction now had the upper hand. On the very same day Rumsfeld spoke to General Tommy Franks, the CENTCOM Commander, that he wanted "a commander's estimate on the Iraq war plan."[78]

Finally, in a related move, and on his "own initiative" without presidential or DoD guidance, former general Wayne Downing, and former head of counterterrorism unit in the Bush white house, single-handedly began drawing up war plans for Iraq. Though Downing informed his immediate superiors, the very fact that another bureaucratic entity was strategizing about war plans without informing Powell and others at state, illustrated the depth of bureaucratic politics and the struggle for control over Iraq policy.[79] Viewed collectively, these bureaucratic moves set the stage for open warfare over administration Iraq policy.

In the run-up to the president's state of the union address in 28 January 2002, the subsequent use for the phrase "axis of evil" sealed Powell's fate. Powell offered objections to the use of such verbiage (knowing that it would likely cause alarm in Europe), he recognized that though his enemies were behind this language, and it was equally clear that this language appealed to Bush.

During the same period, the president "secretly signed and intelligence order" authorizing the CIA to begin preparations for covert operations to unseat the Iraqi leader.[80] Thus while Tenet may have joined Powell in opposition to funding the INC, with the need to rid the Middle East of rogue regimes, and the subsequent power and closeness to the president that this authority granted, Tenet easily joined in the bureaucratic fray.

Even worse this new reality further undercut Powell and set the stage for even more isolation of the secretary state. Later in a subsequent meeting between Rice and Richard Haass, the director of policy planning at state, represented the final nail in

---

77   Ibid.

78   Woodward, *Plan of Attack*, 31–2.

79   Kessler, "US Decision on Iraq Has Puzzling Past," *Washington Post*.

80   Ibid.

the coffin. In this meeting Rice acknowledged that it made little sense at this point in the debate over Iraq policy; the president, she lamented had made up his mind.[81] Interestingly, a Powell fought to prohibit a potential conflict between India and Pakistan, along with his subsequent efforts to refine the coalition, the anti-Powell utilized this period to sure up their positioning and hold over Iraq policy.

Thereafter, beginning in July of 2002 a new and more contentious round of infighting emerged over the issue of tactics; that is, should the administration utilize the multilateral option (UN legitimacy) which was favored by the Powell faction or would the anti-Powell faction have its way, which called for unilateral intervention. In the early days of August of 2002 it appeared that Powell, with the assistance of outside allies, would win this round. Aided by assistance from British Prime Minister Tony Blair, who also felt that it was essential to seek UN legitimacy, and after a subsequent meeting between Bush and Powell on the importance of utilizing the UN, the secretary of state appeared to have again out witted his foes. However, in recognition of this move by the opposition faction both Cheney and Rice reentered the fray. In a speech to the Veterans of Foreign Wars in Nashville, TN on 26 August 2002 the vice president asserted that there was little doubt that Iraq maintained a WMD capacity, and that even if the inspectors were to regain access to Iraq, Cheney acknowledged that the Iraqi minders would again thwart any real search. Not long thereafter, Rice in an interview with the *BBC* discussed the realities of a unilateral attack. [82]

Powell would win this round of the infighting as Bush formally declared he would use the fall UN General Assembly Plenary Session as the forum to make the multilateral case for Saddam's removal. Predictably it was at this time the anti-Powell snipping resumed. To protect Powell's flank, the senior Bush[83] and former national security advisor Brent Scowcroft[84] openly proclaimed that Powell's pragmatic position was the correct route. These actions quieted the Powell barbs but the infighting continued apace. Indeed, the struggle over tactics actually did not conclude until the day when Bush was to formally address the UN. Thereafter in November of 2002 Powell would again celebrate victory following the unanimous passage of UNSCR 1441.[85]

This reality temporarily caught the anti-Powell faction off guard, but they quickly re-group. Beginning in December of 2002 and January of 2003 this faction began to finalize military plans, and with General Franks making repeated trips to white house, it had become obvious that the road to war, at least in terms of military preparations, was all but finalized. Beginning in December some 52, 000 US military

---

81   Ibid.

82   Ibid.

83   Glenn Kessler, "Bush Team Infighting Could Hurt War Plan," *Washington Post*, 1 April 2003. Retrieved on online at http://www.detnews.com/2003/nation/0304/01/a01-125187.htm

84   Ibid.

85   See Nicholas Lemann, "How It Came to War. When Did Bush Decide that he Had to Fight Saddam?" *The New Yorker*, 31 March 2003.

personnel were sent to Kuwait. By February 2003 that number increased to over 100, 000. In late January a turning point in the infighting took place: in a private meeting with the president, Rumsfeld formally requested and subsequently received control over postwar reconstruction. This was the first of many moves that solidified the anti-Powell factions control over Iraq policy. To provide a structure to secure their new authority, the Office of the Reconstruction and Humanitarian Assistance (ORHA) was created following the signing of a national security directive. This structure ended states' hold over postwar planning. This was important because in recognized that the road to war was around the corner, Powell began work on the Future of Iraq Project, which would have granted State's traditional responsibility over reconstruction in Iraq, but the two year effort had been bypassed following the creation of ORHA. This structure, headed by Douglas Feith, a long time critic of Powell, was dominated by individuals that opposed the Powell faction, and the fact that too few Iraq experts were not attached to the apparatus clearly did not sit well with Powell. Thus in the final analysis, the prewar debate had finally yielded a victor, the anti-Powell faction would have their war.

While the anti-Powell faction was on course for war, they encountered one final round of infighting over the war plan. In a meeting between the presidents and members of the war council, Powell bluntly asserted that the war plan, dubbed "rolling start," was flawed and took unnecessary risks. *Newsweek* recounts the meeting with the following details:

> Powell emerged from his diplomatic foxhole at the State Department to question sharply the first war plans presented by General Tommy Franks, and of US forces in the Gulf, and General Myers, chairman of the Joint Chiefs of Staff. In particular, Powell challenged the early plans favored by Rumsfeld for a relatively small-scale force to surgically destroy strongholds of Saddam's regime. "I was a former chairman [of the Joint Chiefs] and I was in the gulf war," Powell says. "So I think I have made useful contributions, appropriate to my experience but also appropriate to my current position."[86]

Members of the anti-Powell faction were shocked at Powell's arrogance. To them the issue was fundamental: how could a sitting secretary of state question Pentagon war planning?[87] After this small but important victory this was the last of the major bureaucratic disputes leading up to the war.

Postwar Wrangling

After the internal disputes over war plans subsided, *Operation Iraqi Freedom* deposed of the regime of Saddam Hussein in twenty-one days. No modern military had travel so far and so fast. Unfortunately, the swift victory quickly yielded to criticism of

---

86   Richard Wolffe and Tamara Lipper, "Powell in the Bunker," *Newsweek*, 24 March 2003.
87   Ibid.

postwar planning and a new round of bureaucratic infighting that threatened to destroy the administrations military gains that occurred during the war.

Perhaps the number one issue for the administration concerned the inability of the Iraq Survey Group to locate any WMD in Iraq. For members of the anti-Powell faction this represented a troubling reality, after all Iraq's possession of WMD and the likelihood they would pass them along to terrorists was the major reason for unseating the regime. Without such weapons the administration was beside itself, an open to criticism that it had lied to the American people and the international community. In short, the war in Iraq threatened the all important "moral underpinnings" of the war on terror. Indeed, there was talk of "distraction" and "the loss of momentum" words which forced the administration to go into crisis mode.[88]

In the wake of this criticism the administration erected the White House Iraq Group or the WHIG. The WHIG, chaired by the chief of staff, Andrew Card, with the assistance of "Karl Rove, the president's senior political adviser; communications strategists Karen Hughes, Mary Matalin and James R. Wilkinson; legislative liaison Nicholas E. Calio; and policy advisers led by Rice and her deputy, Stephen J. Hadley, along with I. Lewis Libby."[89] The mandate of this group, which met weekly in the Situation Room in White House, was to formulate a strategy to the sell the war in Iraq to the American people. This micromanagement drew the ire of outsiders who asserted that such activity was a reminder of the overzealous white house involvement of the Johnson administration during the Vietnam War.

President Bush and the anti-Powell faction had another problem: the whispers that in the absence of WMD in Iraq there was a growing chorus of critics that suggested the administration "cooked intelligence" so as to justify the war in Iraq. Even more alarming is the fact that a senior official in the administration was himself openly asserting this position. According to David Kay, former UN Inspector and head of the Iraq Survey Group, responsibility for the problems in the postwar Iraq lay at the feet of the anti-Powell faction, with Rice the leading culprit. As recounted in the book *Losing Iraq: Inside the Postwar Reconstruction Fiasco*, the author David Phillips notes that Kay "accused Rice of botching the intelligence management of Iraq's WMD and [for] turning a blind eye as hawks on the principals committee cherry-picked intelligence to justify policy decisions that had already been made."[90]

Internally the snipping continued. General Franks, General Jake Garner and Lt. General Michael DeLong, Franks' deputy at CENTCOM, were dumbfounded with the anti-Powell factions position that the military in Iraq had to be disbanded, what was dubbed de-Baathification. Such a move they, along with the Powell faction, thought would lead to chaos and assist in the growth of the insurgency. The person responsible for much of this criticism was of course Feith, but the press went further,

---

88   John Davis, *The Global War on Terrorism: Assessing the American Response* (New York, Nova, 2004), Chapter 12.

89   See *Washington Post*, 10 August 2003.

90   See David Phillips, *Losing Iraq: Inside the Postwar Reconstruction Fiasco* (Westview Press, 2005), 64.

criticizing the president, the vice president, Rumsfeld and his second in command, Wolfowitz. For the Powell faction, they had escaped this criticism altogether. Many were privately gloating over the demise of the anti-Powell faction, others, particularly Powell and Armitage were concerned that the war on terror would invariably suffer unless Iraq was back on track.

It was at this time that Powell would again float the idea of multilateralism, enlarging the coalition of states that had troops on the ground, allowing the UN to play a more direct role in postwar Iraq, and finally, this faction thought it prudent to rebuild the UNSC, whose credibility itself to a major hit as the war unfolded. In the war councils beginning in late May, Powell, over the objections of Cheney, Rumsfeld and Wolfowitz, succeeded in convincing the president that to turn the tide in Iraq, and thus preventing the issue from dominating his presidency (an important point with the 2004 presidential election around the corner [Iraq still remained a feature among campaign]), multilateralism had to assume a greater share of administration postwar policy in Iraq. Powell succeeded eventually working with the Pentagon to enlist the support of other countries to provide a troop presence in Iraq and second the secretary then sponsored a host of postwar UNSC resolutions that passed unanimously (these include 1483 and 1511, to name a few). These efforts were in affect the first sign of Powell's revival both from the disastrous UN presentation that severely damaged his credibility and his defeats in the prewar period.

Powell ascendancy received a setback following Bush's decision to establish the Iraq Stabilization Group (ISG). With the burgeoning criticism of the Pentagon's mismanagement of postwar Iraq, along with the increasing threat of the insurgency, the president's confidence in the Pentagon declined considerably. As such this group, which was under the control of Rice, acknowledge that the "White House has ordered a major reorganization of American efforts to quell violence in Iraq... and to speed reconstruction."[91] The group was divided into four components: counterterrorism would be under the direction of Frances F. Townsend; another compartment with the task of economic development directed by Gary R. Edson; a specialized organization to handle the political transition and headed by Robert D. Blackwill, and the final component, pubic relations, was headed by Anna M. Perez.[92] Collectively, this new organization stripped Rumsfeld of much of the day to day running of postwar Iraq, and the new entity temporarily marginalized Powell and the state department which remained amazed at the assorted efforts to preclude Powell from direct control over administration Iraq policy.

While Powell found himself still marginalized, an area that showed his increased influence over administration concerned the venue of reconstruction aid. Much of the assistance though mandated by congress for distribution by State Department was very much under the control of the Pentagon and the anti-Powell faction. With perhaps another use of a secondary back channel (some assert that Powell informed

---

91   Dana Milbank, "Stabilization Is Its Middle Name," *Washington Post*, May 2004, A 17.

92   Ibid.

his allies in the congress on both sides of the isle recognized that reconstruction was improperly distributed), the state department was now controlling a significant portion of the reconstruction aid. In short order the congress openly argued, and the president shared the prevailing sentiment, that postwar funding should be controlled by state and not defense.

As August concluded, and the presidential election nearing the pivotal fall season, the infighting dissipated. With Bush's re-election bid hanging in the balance, it was hardly advantageous for either faction to publicly reprove of the other. Moreover, a second reality had been clear. Within each faction dramatic changes would take place in the event of Bush second term. In the anti-Powell faction, with the multiple mistakes during the post-reconstruction phase, it had become clear with growing congressional pressure and criticism from the president's own party, Wolfowitz and Feith would have to go. Over at State, noting that he would serve for one term only, Powell resigned following the President Bush's re-election and Armitage followed his boss out of the door. With Rice moving to State, at this point there was no talk of factionalism, primarily because with Powell's exit there was now intellectual harmony and policy symmetry, a reference to administration dominated by hawks. Ironically, even with this symmetry the administrations policy toward Iraq remains in state of flux. While the elections in Iraq proved successful for example, the post-election problems with the selection of new government provided a period of uncertainty that allowed the insurgents to regroup. As a result the period of January of 2005 through September 2005 became a period of insurgent offensive that has produced a dramatic increase in violence throughout Iraq.

Conclusion

The research effort has illustrated that infighting represented a critical feature in the evolution of US policy toward Iraq covering three presidential administrations. Most interesting, regardless of the administration, but most importantly, for Bush I (41) and Bush II (43), infighting impacted the period of review of policy, the prewar, war and postwar periods of each administration. With respect to Clinton (42) infighting covered all phases of administration policy accept in the case of postwar planning (with no efforts of direct regime change—the use of US ground forces—the administration had no realistic hope of unseating Saddam Hussein, and thus no need for postwar planning). Perhaps the most obvious feature that emerged as a result of the infighting is this: each administrations policy decisions were a by-product of bureaucratic wrangling. Such infighting produced periods of incoherence. This was often the case because each faction, covering all administrations, routinely made policy pronouncements that very opposed to the other. Moreover, the all-to-numerous voices in the policy process left often the issues of who was in charge or what was the direction of US policy. Even worse, during the war on terror under 43, critics repeatedly charged the "airing of dirty laundry" inhibited efforts to present a united front among allies and thus impacted Atlantic relations as well as destroyed the carefully crafted coalition within the Security Council.

Second, the infighting prohibited lessons learned. In a critical example, post-*Desert Storm* infighting inhibited the preparation for the all-important preparation for reconstruction. This produced a policy that illustrated wartime success but produced a feeling of success on the battlefield without a triumphant postwar peace. The result of this failure produced a postwar period characterized by chaos. Ironically, the anti-Powell faction which incessantly spoke of completing the unfinished business of the senior Bush missed this most important lesson: preparing for post-reconstruction represents the critical phase of policy evolution. In the triumphalism that accompanied the historic battlefield achievements that defined *Operation Iraqi Freedom*, the ongoing discourse focused attention on the successes on the battlefield rather than on the administration's feeble postwar plans. Thus like 41, 43, with respect to their legacies, each will receive negative commentary for failing to secure the peace after the war.

Third, each of the presidents—41, 42, & 43—is characterized by another common link: they failed to halt the infighting; even worse the management styles of the presidents assisted in creating an atmosphere that allowed the bureaucratic wrangling to flourish. The senior Bush's pragmatic realism failed to yield a strategic policy that was acceptable to all the services, and worse, this same dilemma produced open warfare following the decision to conclude the war without achieving the prescribed military objectives. In the case of Clinton, with an ad hoc policy, and one too driven by concerns for polls, along with the president's legendary indecisiveness, produced a national security apparatus replete with infighting. With respect to the younger Bush, he boasted to the press that he wanted strong independent advisors willing to present their views on policy during the meetings of principal advisors. In the case of Iraq policy, this decision approach produced no discernable policy toward Iraq after the conclusion of first phase of the war on terror. Sadly, it was during this very period that the level of intensity of infighting increased to a level not present under the two previous administrations. The net result produced a policy that destroyed the cohesiveness that was exhibited during *Operation Enduring Freedom* and a national security bureaucracy that had been split among competing factional interests.

Finally, rarely are there cases in US foreign policy where multiple presidents have an opportunity to define a countries policy toward a given a country. In the case of Iraq, each president, failing to learn from the other, eventually left the same legacy: a policy characterized by unfinished business and one that their successors would have to contend with. For the next American president, two things are certain. The first is that the international community awaits a policy not hatched in fit of bureaucratic fury; and second, the next president, if victory is to be won, will have to devise a policy that brings victory to 43's Iraq policy. It is clear that one road may produce a policy of disengagement which will surely anger elements of the bureaucracy or a completely new strategy that will finally produce the peace that satisfies the people of Iraq, there neighbors, and the executive foreign policy departments within the

United States. The reality of this process is that regardless of the policy decision one thing is certain: a new round of infighting will most assuredly commence.

PART II
The Diplomatic Perspective

Chapter 5

Personal Diplomacy and US Policy Toward Iraq

Robert Pauly, Jr.

University of Southern Mississippi, Gulf Coast

Introduction

Interactions between states—whether economic, military or political in character—are central to the conduct of international relations. That has been the case throughout recorded history, during which myriad states have fought wars against and built bilateral and multilateral coalitions with their governmental and institutional counterparts. On a daily basis, events unfold that involve and are influenced to varying degrees by leaders and their advisors, and the states they serve. That is indisputable. However, the reasons why states—and the individuals in control of the governments of those entities—behave in a particular manner serve as perpetual sources of debate among scholars of international relations, who base their observations and analyses on a variety of historical and political scientific approaches.

One of the most contentious issues with respect to inter-state relations is the extent to which individuals possess the ability to drive the course of human events. In short, there are two basic schools of thought on this issue, those rooted in the academic disciplines of history and political science. Historians emphasize the unpredictable nature of world affairs and the importance of individual behavior in conditioning international interactions, suggesting that one leader—whether a politician, diplomat or general—may react to a given situation in a different manner from another under similar, if not identical, circumstances. Most political scientists, by contrast, give credence to the primacy of the structure of the international system, and the institutions within that construct in determining the actions of states.

Contemporary political scientists are split primarily between two theoretical schools—neo-realism and neo-liberal institutionalism. Seminal neo-realist thinker Kenneth Waltz promulgated the fundamental precepts of this paradigm in the 1979 work, *Theory of International Politics*. Put simply, Waltz assumes the structure of the international system—unipolar, bipolar or multipolar—determines the behavior of the states interacting therein. Irrespective of historical time frame and contextual characteristics, he describes the nature of that system as anarchic, in that it lacks an effective government, a uniform set of laws above states, a credible police force to enforce any such strictures, or a common sense of community. Additionally, he discounts the relevance of the internal characteristics of states—political and economic ideology, ethnicity, language, culture and religion—in the ordering of the system.[1]

Neo-liberals and other critics of neo-realism acknowledge the existence of anarchy but contend that institutions have the potential to facilitate cooperation rather than conflict among states in the global system. They are also less averse than Waltz and his adherents to the notion that individuals are influential players regarding interactions among both states and institutions. P. Terrence Hopmann and David Dessler, for instance, are critical of Waltz's parsimony regarding the exclusivity of the international system as a motivator of state behavior. Hopmann asserts that a comprehensive model of negotiating processes and the roles of individuals therein is essential in order to enable diplomats to cope with an increasingly interdependent world.[2] Dessler proposes a transformational paradigm based on a hybrid of neo-realist and neo-liberal precepts. He links states and the systemic constructs within which they act and interact in the following manner. First, the structure of a system both enables and constrains actions. Second, states' actions can alter the underlying structure of the system.[3]

The principle weakness of neo-realist theory is its rigidity and resultant inability to explain or forecast accurately alterations in the international system and the management of crises therein. Historians and political scientists critical of neo-realism focus more on the roles of individuals, states and institutions in given scenarios, whether unfolding events involve politics, economics, military conflict, diplomacy or an admixture of those elements. While neo-realism was generally effective in explaining events during the Cold War, it failed to anticipate either the conclusion of that global struggle in 1989–90 or the increasing complexity of the international system in the 1990s and 2000s.

Since the end of the Cold War, the United States has engaged in two major inter-state military conflicts—the 1990–91 Persian Gulf War and 2003 Second Iraq War—both of which entailed the development and leadership of a coalition of states to confront Iraqi President Saddam Hussein. With the preceding theoretical discussion as a useful point of departure, this chapter considers the role of personal diplomacy in the conduct of U.S. policy toward Iraq by the administrations of Presidents George H.W. Bush, William J. Clinton and George W. Bush. In particular, it addresses the following five research questions. First, to what extent has personal diplomacy proven indispensable to the development and implementation of American policies toward the Persian Gulf generally and Iraq specifically since 1989? Second, which general presidential policymaking models did the Bush I, Clinton and Bush II administrations, respectively, employ in dealing with Saddam and why? Third, what

---

1   Kenneth Waltz, *Theory of International Politics* (Reading, MA: Addison-Wesley, 1979).

2   P. Terrence Hopmann, *The Negotiation Process and the Resolution of International Conflicts* (Columbia: University of South Carolina Press, 1996), 28.

3   David Dessler, "What's at Stake in the Agent-Structure Debate?" *International Organization* 43-1 (1989), 452.

were those administrations' most significant relative strengths and weaknesses in their use of personal diplomacy to minimize if not preclude the threats posed by Saddam's regime to U.S. interests at home and abroad? Fifth, given those strengths and weaknesses, what type of policymaking approach is likely to prove most effective in future American dealings with states across the Greater Middle East?

With respect to the research questions, the chapter presents and evaluates two theses. First, the George H.W. Bush and George W. Bush administrations formulated and implemented their foreign and security policies toward Iraq through the use of a one-plus-a-few model, in the context of which the president and a small circle of his advisors determined the most prudent course of action to take in order to safeguard U.S. interests against threats posed by Saddam's regime. The Clinton administration, on the other hand, employed a one-plus-many framework with the president relying upon a wider—and often less manageable—array of domestic and foreign policy aides in deciding how best to deal with Iraq. As a result, the two Bush administrations were able to develop and implement clearer—and, with respect to threat reduction, more effective—policies toward Baghdad than was true of the Clinton administration. Second, as opposed to the Clinton administration, both Bush administrations delivered unambiguous warnings to Saddam and backed those ultimatums with the robust use of military force. In the process, George H.W. Bush, his son and their respective inner circles employed personal diplomacy in as multilateral a fashion as feasible in building military coalitions, which were then deployed to achieve clearly stated objectives—Iraq's expulsion from Kuwait in February 1991 and the elimination of Baghdad's weapons of mass destruction (WMD) programs via Saddam's removal from power in April 2003. Each of these examples stands in stark contrast to the Clinton administration's diplomatic ambiguity and reliance on the limited use of military force against Iraq, a course of action that did little to discourage Saddam from continuing to defy both the United States and the broader international community by refusing to comply with a series of United Nations (UN) Security Council Resolutions between 1993 and 2001.

In order to assess the research questions and theses both logically and incisively, the balance of the chapter unfolds in the contexts of four related sections. The first section examines the George H.W. Bush administration's policy toward Iraq from 1989–93. The second section examines the Clinton administration's policy toward Iraq from 1993–2001. The third section examines the George W. Bush administration's policy toward Iraq from 2001–2003. And the fourth section assesses the relative strengths and weaknesses of Bush I, Clinton and Bush II administrations' approaches to dealing with Iraq as a means to determine which of the three is likely to prove most effective in the future.

Examination of Bush I Administration's Policy Toward Iraq

The George H.W. Bush administration possessed two fundamental strengths that enabled it to develop and implement foreign policies and take critical decisions effectively. First, Bush and the members of the inner circle of his foreign policy team had lengthy records of public service at the federal level. Men such as Bush, Secretary of State James Baker, National Security Advisor Brent Scowcroft, Secretary of Defense Richard Cheney and Chairman of the Joint Chiefs of Staff Colin Powell had served under President Ronald Reagan during the 1980s. Second, in working together in the past, they developed a rapport and resultant ability to avoid the types of intra-administration disputes that have the potential to complicate policymaking during international crises. The combination of these assets served the Bush administration well during the 1990–91 Persian Gulf imbroglio.

Bush's accession to the presidency was the culmination of a distinguished career of federal government service spanning nearly two decades. Born into a politically connected family the head of which was Republican Senator Prescott Bush, he served as a naval aviator in World War II and earned an undergraduate degree from Yale in 1948. In addition to his 1981–89 stint as vice president under Reagan, George H.W. Bush served as ambassador to the UN from 1971–73 and Director of Central Intelligence (DCI) from 1976–77. Bush gained valuable experience in each of these capacities, particularly at the global level, where he developed a rapport with a range of world leaders and a practical understanding of the workings of international politics.

In order to ensure the development of a cohesive policy-making framework, Bush constructed a close-knit circle of advisors with whom he had worked closely and established cordial relationships in the past. His choice of Scowcroft as head of the National Security Council (NSC) and Baker as secretary of state exemplified this approach. Scowcroft and Bush served together in the administration of President Gerald Ford, the former in the same capacity as in the Bush administration and the latter as DCI. Scowcroft was knowledgeable on foreign policy matters and familiar with the workings of the executive branch. He also shared Bush's prudence in formulating policy initiatives, preferring to err on the side of caution. After his initial choice for secretary of defense, John Tower, failed to clear the Senate confirmation process, the President turned instead to Cheney, an old Washington hand then serving in the Congress as a ranking member on the House Select Committee on Intelligence. As was true of Baker and Scowcroft, Cheney had previous experience in the executive branch, having acted as chief of staff under Ford. These attributes made for an effective mix in a position that would involve considerable interaction between the White House and Congress.[4]

Bush's selection of Powell as chairman of the JCS following the retirement of Admiral William Crowe from that position in September 1989 was historic in two respects. At age 53, Powell became the youngest officer and the first African American to serve in the position. A career military officer, Powell fought in the Vietnam War and also served in the Carter and Reagan administrations. In the latter

---

4   George Bush and Brent Scowcroft, *A World Transformed: The Collapse of the Soviet Empire; the Unification of Germany; the Gulf War* (New York: Alfred A. Knopf, 1998), 16–18.

administration, he assumed the post of National Security Advisor in 1987, shortly after the Iran-Contra affair rocked the Reagan White House. Essentially, he possessed attributes equally suitable for the distinctive structures of the executive branch of the government and those of the armed forces. He served as an excellent bridge between those entities.[5]

Assembling a team composed of members with both the intellectual and inter-personal skills to develop and implement prudent policies under fire was Bush's first step in developing the capacity to respond effectively to international crises. Next, the administration had to construct a framework within which cabinet members and their staffs could interpret events and deliver the requisite policy advise to enable Bush to take informed decisions that served American interests constructively at a given juncture. The Bush administrative devised a decision-making approach that, as political scientist Steve Yetiv notes, involved four interrelated levels of interaction during the Persian Gulf crisis. The first level consisted of bilateral discussions between Bush and his closest colleagues, most notably Scowcroft and Baker. The second level featured policy-making interactions within an inner circle of administration officials known as the "Gang of Eight." This group included Bush, Baker, Scowcroft, Cheney and Powell, as well as Vice President Dan Quayle and White House Chief of Staff John Sununu. The third layer was composed of the chief aides of the individuals in the Gang of Eight and thus known as the deputies committee. The fourth layer consisted of a smaller group drawn from the deputies committee, including officials from the Departments of State and Defense, the Central Intelligence Agency (CIA), the JCS and NSC staffer Richard Haas, who drafted most of the entity's position papers.[6] The deputies committee handled day-to-day matters in managing crises, while the fourth-layer group concentrated on the conception of overarching policy initiatives, which it then sent up the pipeline for consideration at the two upper levels of interaction.[7]

Iraq's invasion of Kuwait on 1 August 1990 afforded the Bush administration an opportunity to use its one-plus-a-few policymaking formula in cobbling together a coalition to ensure that Saddam's aggression did not go unchallenged. It achieved that objective by way of a three-stage process, which featured, in turn, (a) direct rhetorical warnings from Bush to Saddam that the United States would not allow Baghdad's invasion to stand, (b) the marshalling of UN support in the form of a series of resolutions demanding that Iraq withdraw its troops from Kuwait or face military action to compel it to do so and (c) Baker's diplomatic overtures to gain support for, if not direct participation in, a military coalition to force Iraqi compliance. Ultimately, this process led to the multilateral conduct of the Persian Gulf War, which resulted in Iraq's military defeat and subsequent withdrawal from Kuwait in February 1991.

---

5   Ibid., 22–4.
6   Steve A. Yetiv, *The Persian Gulf Crisis* (Westport, Conn.: Greenwood Press, 1997), 61–2.
7   Ibid.

Following the Iraqi invasion, Bush phoned American Ambassador to UN Thomas Pickering in New York with instructions to attempt to convene an emergency meeting of the Security Council and push for a resolution condemning Iraq's invasion. From the outset of the crisis, Bush was determined to exhibit firm Washington-based leadership, but he also acknowledged that the United States required UN support to legitimize its actions, the attainment of which demanded cooperation from the Soviet Union. As he recalls, "I was keenly aware that this would be the first post-Cold War test of the Security Council in crisis. I knew what had happened in the 1930s when a weak and leaderless League of Nations had failed to stand up to Japanese, Italian and German aggression. The result had been to encourage the ambition of those regimes."[8]

In Washington, Bush took a firm but prudent approach in responding to Iraq's aggression. On the morning of 2 August, he signed an executive order to freeze all Iraqi and Kuwaiti assets in the United States both to ensure that Saddam recognized the seriousness of the situation and would not benefit financially prior to the imposition of UN sanctions. In addition, he expressed support for Iraq's Arab neighbors in the region, most notably offering to dispatch a squadron of F-15s to Saudi Arabia, which was potentially Saddam's next victim. Concurrently, Pickering achieved the desired result in New York in the form of UN Security Council Resolution 660, which on 2 August condemned Saddam's aggression and demanded that Iraq "withdraw immediately and unconditionally all its forces to the positions in which they were located on 1 August 1990."[9]

Following an evening flight back to Washington Bush convened a second NSC meeting on the crisis on the morning of 3 August. As opposed to the gathering of the same group twenty-four hours earlier the tone of the meeting was more one of confrontation than accommodation vis-à-vis Saddam.[10] The initial UN resolution against Iraq and the shifting tone among Group of Eight members served to strengthen Bush's commitment to take firm action against Iraq. That shift was reflected in an impromptu statement by Bush to the press on the South Lawn of the White House on 5 August: "[t]his will not stand, this aggression against Kuwait."[11]

Once Bush had expressed his stance on the need for American intervention publicly, the administration was free to construct fully an international coalition to confront Saddam and—if necessary—forcibly expel Iraqi forces from Kuwait. Initially, Bush and his aides consulted with Middle Eastern leaders—primarily Saudi Arabian King Fahd, Egyptian President Hosni Mubarak, Jordanian King Hussein and Syrian President Hafez Assad—in order to facilitate a buildup of American military ground and air forces in Saudi Arabia through Operation Desert Shield. Second, the administration solidified support for the coalition and UN resolutions it

---

8   Bush and Scowcroft, *A World Transformed*, 303–304.
9   Congressional Quarterly, *The Middle East*, 7th ed. (Washington, DC: U.S. Government Printing Office, 1991). Reference made in Yetiv, *Persian Gulf Crisis*.
10   Bush and Scowcroft, *A World Transformed*, 323.
11   Ibid., 332–3.

sought to implement through consultations with Middle Eastern, Western European, Soviet and Asian leaders. This included a mission by Baker to extract financial contributions from those states with the requisite resources to reduce the economic burden on the United States and coalition partners unable to afford the revenue strains the sanctions brought about. Third, Bush and Baker worked to ratchet up the pressure on Saddam through a UN-mandated use-of-force resolution against Iraq. After setting clear political objectives requiring military means to achieve, Bush worked the phones and Baker undertook a three-week diplomatic tour in order to secure support from Security Council members within and without the coalition for the resolution.

Bush employed a two-part approach to convince Fahd of the need for American forces in Saudi Arabia and the administration's commitment to maintain a military presence until the present situation vis-à-vis Iraq had been redressed fully. First, Bush requested that Saudi Ambassador Prince Bandar bin Sultan meet with Scowcroft at the White House, where the former expressed concerns over Washington's propensity to back out on commitments in the Middle East under fire in the past. Scowcroft responded by assuring Bandar that the United States would not back down and sending him to the Pentagon for a full briefing on American plans for a force buildup in Saudi Arabia. Second, concurrent with the administration's efforts to obtain Fahd's support for the dispatch of American troops to Saudi Arabia, Bush pressed other world leaders in the Middle East and Europe to support a UN resolution imposing economic sanctions on Iraq. On August 3, for example, Bush spoke first with Turkish President Turgut Ozal and later with French President François Mitterrand, and West German Chancellor Helmut Kohl.[12]

Bush's 8 August address to the American people—and essentially the international community as well—was effective primarily because of the manner in which he spelled out the ends he sought to achieve through military deployment in the Persian Gulf. He alluded to "[f]our simple principles" guiding the administration's policy. First, the United States sought the "immediate, unconditional, and complete withdrawal of all Iraqi forces from Kuwait. Second, "Kuwait's legitimate government must be restored to replace the puppet regime" Saddam had installed in advance of the annexation of that entity to Iraq the day of the address. Third, the administration was "committed to the security and stability of the Gulf." Fourth, Bush was "determined to protect the lives of American citizens abroad." He concluded his remarks with a reference to the role of the United States in bringing the Cold War to its conclusion, noting that "[w]e succeeded in our struggle for freedom in Europe because we and our allies remain[ed] stalwart. Keeping the peace in the Middle East will require no less …. [I]f history teaches us anything, it is that we must resist aggression or it will destroy our freedom."[13]

The administration had additional issues to redress, the most pressing of which involved burden sharing among coalition members—whether military or financial—

---

12   Ibid., 325–30.
13   Ibid., 341.

concurrent with the buildup in Saudi Arabia. As a means to achieve that end, Bush dispatched Baker on a September tour of coalition states with one clear task in mind. Put simply, Baker was to approach those members of the coalition with the economic capacity to help fund the buildup and compensate those states without similar resources at their disposal. In the process, he would reassure all coalition members of the administration's firm commitment to the eviction of Iraq from Kuwait and attempt to take on an additional partner in Syria. A subsequent month-long American diplomatic effort proved effective, resulting in the 29 November passage of UN Security Council Resolution 678, which authorized the coalition to use "all necessary means" to eject Iraq from Kuwait if Saddam had not removed his forces by 15 January 1991.[14] Three days later, the U.S. Congress approved the use of American military forces to liberate Kuwait—the House voting 250-183 and the Senate 52-47—leaving it to Bush to make the final decision. Predictably, the 15 January deadline passed without Iraqi compliance and Bush ordered the prosecution of Operation Desert Storm, which commenced with air raids and cruise missile strikes on 17 January.

Examination of Clinton Administration's Policy Toward Iraq

As opposed to George H.W. Bush, Clinton failed to develop a clear foreign policy blueprint during his eight years in office. Rather than prioritize American interests consistently on the basis of the clear emphasis on a particular region or issue area, the Clinton administration launched and pursued a wide variety of initiatives, ranging from military intervention in the Balkans to often overbearing mediation in the context of the Israeli-Palestinian peace process, few of which it followed through to completion. As Haass, who now serves as head of the policy planning staff in Powell's Department of State in the George W. Bush administration, explains, "Clinton inherited a world of unprecedented American advantage and opportunity and did little with it .... A foreign policy legacy can result either from achieving something great on the ground (defeating major rivals or building major institutions, for example) or from changing the way people at home or abroad think about international relations. Clinton did neither."[15]

There were two causes for the Clinton administration's lack of strategic vision, neither of which had been entirely was the president's fault. First, Clinton's longevity in the White House detracted from his ability to maintain a foreign policy team whose members shared the same viewpoints throughout his tenure. He had two National Security Advisors (Anthony Lake and Samuel Berger), three Secretaries of Defense (Les Aspin, William Cohen and William Cohen) and two Secretaries of State (Warren Christopher and Madeleine Albright) in eight years, most of whom had at least subtly different ideas of how to define and pursue U.S. interests. Albright

---

14   Congressional Quarterly, *The Middle East*.
15   Richard N. Haass, "The Squandered Presidency: Demanding More from the Commander-in-Chief," *Foreign Affairs* (May/June 2000).

and Berger, for instance, tended to have a greater affinity for the use of military force than either Lake or Christopher. Second, Clinton assumed office in the immediate aftermath of the Cold War, a period during which the American public had no appetite for the expression of grand strategic visions or the expenditure of tax dollars abroad given that the threats previously presented by the either the Soviet behemoth or Saddam Hussein were at least perceived to have been diminished. Clinton's personal interest in domestic as opposed to foreign policy—and the primacy he often ceded to the former at the expense of the latter—only complicated matters further.

And once Clinton did decide to focus on foreign and security policy—in the context of his second term in particular—he and his advisors elected to try to do everything rather than concentrate on one or two initiatives. Consider, for instance, Berger's characterization of the President's legacy in January 2001: "Today … America is by any measure the world's unchallenged military, economic and political power. The world counts on us to be a catalyst of coalitions, a broker of peace [and] a guarantor of global financial stability."[16] Berger's overarching statement is also reflected in the Clinton administration's National Security Strategy (NSS) of December 1999. That document promulgated three overarching objectives. First, "to enhance America's security." Second, "to bolster America's economic prosperity. And third, "to promote democracy and human rights abroad."[17]

By contrast, the George W. Bush administration's initial NSS, which it issued just over one year to the day of the 11 September 2001 terrorist attacks carried out by al Qaeda against the World Trade Center in New York and the Pentagon on the outskirts of Washington, D.C., articulated three indispensable national interests—the defense, preservation and extension of the peace by way of collaboration with the world's great powers at the expense of its terrorists and tyrants—on behalf of which Bush promised to utilize America's unparalleled economic, military and political assets. However, it cleverly framed those interest-based objectives in principled rhetoric, noting that the United States would endeavor to promote a "balance of power that favors … political and economic freedom, peaceful relations with other states and respect for human dignity."[18]

As Yale University historian John Lewis Gaddis, perhaps the most authoritative scholar of American national security policy over the past half-century has pointed out, the differences between the Bush NSS and the 1999 Clinton NSS "are revealing. The Bush objectives speak of defending, preserving, and extending the peace; the Clinton statement seems simply to assume peace …. Even in these first few lines,

---

16   Samuel R. Berger, "A Foreign Policy for the Global Age," Remarks to the United States Institute of Peace (17 January 2001).

17   William Clinton, "A National Security Strategy for a New Century," *White House Office of the Press Secretary*, December 1999, iii.

18   Ibid.

then, the Bush NSS comes across as more forceful, more carefully crafted, and—unexpectedly—more multilateral than its immediate predecessor."[19]

The contrast between the use of containment and preemption as strategic means to reduce, if not eliminate, the threats to American interests posed by Iraq is striking. Choosing the former strategy, for example, the Clinton administration sought to mitigate Saddam Hussein's potential to develop and proliferate WMD by relying upon the UN to dispatch weapons inspectors to Iraq and oversee Baghdad's use of proceeds from the sale of its petroleum resources for selected items such as food and medicine. It also employed limited military strikes against Iraq on several occasions from 1993–98, the most robust of which came in response to Saddam's expulsion of the inspectors in December 1998. According to Kenneth Pollack, the point man on Iraq in Berger's NSC, "Bill Clinton was certainly not looking to make Iraq the centerpiece of his foreign policy. And when the president found himself in domestic political turmoil as a result of the Monica Lewinsky affair, avoiding foreign policy crises became an even higher priority."[20] Consequently, Clinton attempted to contain the threats posed by Iraq on the cheap in terms of both economic and political capital domestically as well as internationally. As Lawrence Kaplan and William Kristol assert, the Clinton "administration embraced a kind of wishful liberalism that, in the case of Iraq, meant following the lead of the United Nations, employing American power fitfully and apologetically, often ignoring Saddam's challenges, and eventually presiding over the erosion of sanctions and weapons inspections."[21]

Yet, notwithstanding Clinton's inability to respond to Saddam's infractions of UN Security Council Resolutions as effectively as George H.W. Bush managed the Persian Gulf crisis, the outcomes in each of those contexts were not related exclusively to styles of policymaking and diplomacy. The interests of the actors differed in each case, which speaks to the unpredictable nature of international affairs. The states that joined the coalition against Saddam in 1990–91 felt Iraq threatened their national interests. Many of those states held different judgments when Clinton was in office than was the case in the early 1990s, whether because of the desires to reap profits through the development of Iraqi oil resources and quell potential unrest among growing domestic Muslim communities (France), to boost the fortunes of a governmental facing a stiff reelection challenge (Germany) or a desire to retain influence as a regional and global player (Russia). Those disparate interests proved perhaps even more complicating in the context of the second Bush administration's campaign to remove Saddam from power.

---

19   John Lewis Gaddis, "A Grand Strategy of Transformation," *Foreign Policy* (November/December 2002): 50–51.

20   Kenneth M. Pollack, *The Threatening Storm: The Case for Invading Iraq* (New York: Random House, 2002), 86–7.

21   Lawrence F. Kaplan and William Kristol, *The War Over Iraq: Saddam's Tyranny and America's Mission* (San Francisco: Encounter Books, 2003).

Assessment of Bush II Administration's Policy Toward Iraq

As was true of the George H.W. Bush administration, the George W. Bush administration has employed a one-plus-a-few approach to foreign policymaking in general and confronting and then rebuilding Iraq in particular over the past three years. Similar to Clinton, Bush opened his tenure in the White House as a neophyte with respect to international politics. However, he assembled a team of advisors whose collective federal governmental experience bridged several decades, administrations and crises. Three of the four most influential members of the Bush foreign policy team—Vice President Cheney, Secretary of State Powell and National Security Advisor Condoleezza Rice—served in prominent positions in the administration of the President's father. A fourth, Secretary of Defense Donald Rumsfeld, had served under Republican Presidents Richard Nixon and Gerald Ford, and in a range of advisory positions in the 1980s and 1990s. Notwithstanding their limited personal and policy differences—most notably those between the relatively dovish Powell and hawkish Rumsfeld on the use of force to deal with Saddam—the members of Bush's inner circle proved adept in handling both the events of 9/11 and the run-up to the Second Iraq War, the details of which are discussed in detail in the balance of this section.

At the conclusion of the 1990–91 Persian Gulf War, the United States and its allies negotiated a United Nations (UN) sponsored cease-fire with Iraq. Most significantly, that settlement stipulated that Saddam discontinue the acquisition and production of weapons of mass destruction (WMD) and the requisite medium and long-range missile systems to use such munitions to attack his adversaries.[22] Between 1991 and 2003, Saddam consistently violated the terms of that cease-fire and a series of subsequent UN resolutions designed to eliminate his nuclear, chemical and biological WMD and missile development programs and sponsorship of regional and global terrorist organizations.

Ultimately, Iraq's record of defiance prompted President George W. Bush to issue a firm set of dictates to Saddam in an address before the UN General Assembly in New York on 12 September 2002. In the context of that address, which was delivered symbolically just over one year to the day of the 9/11 attacks, Bush made three unequivocal points. First, he demanded that Iraq comply immediately with all of the promises it made to the international community at the end of the Persian Gulf War, noting that Saddam has ignored 16 separate UN Security Council resolutions in the past decade.[23] In particular, the President emphasized that because it continues to

---

22   Steve A. Yetiv, *The Persian Gulf Crisis* (Westport, CT: Greenwood Press, 1997), 184–5. These requirements are set forth explicitly in United Nations (UN) Security Council Resolution 687, which was approved on 3 April 1991.

23   George W. Bush, "Remarks at the United Nations General Assembly," *White House Office of the Press Secretary*, 12 September 2002; National Security Council (NSC), "A Decade of Deception and Defiance: Saddam Hussein's Defiance of the United Nations," Background Paper for President Bush's UN Address, *White House Office of the Press Secretary*, 12 September 2002: 4–7.

pursue the acquisition and production of WMD and long-range missile systems, Iraq remains "a grave and gathering danger" to international security.[24] Second, Bush challenged the UN to carry out its responsibilities by impressing upon Saddam the need to disarm in an internationally-verifiable manner, asking members of that body's General Assembly: "Will the United Nations serve the purpose of its founding, or will it be irrelevant?"[25] Third, he pledged that the United States would indeed take action to eliminate the threats Iraq poses to American interests—with the UN's help if possible, but also unilaterally if necessary—noting that "we cannot stand by and do nothing while dangers gather."[26]

Bush's address to the UN General Assembly and his subsequent release of the aforementioned NSS set the stage for concurrent—and equally vigorous—domestic and international debates over the need to disarm Iraq, which led to the passage of two measures: a U.S. Congressional resolution authorizing the use of force against Iraq[27] and a UN Security Council resolution demanding that Saddam readmit and grant unrestricted investigative access to UN inspectors charged with determining the extent to which his regime has disarmed.[28] These measures and the diplomacy that led to their passage provide a useful contextual foundation for a more detailed examination of the Bush administration's policy toward Iraq and its consequences.

In the contexts of UN Security Council Resolution 687 and 16 subsequent Security Council resolutions since 1991—the last of which (Resolution 4112) was passed unanimously on 8 November 2002—the UN demanded that Iraq make a range of behavioral modifications to ensure its re-acceptance as a productive member of the international community.[29] Saddam's regime failed to comply fully with each one of these resolutions. In particular, Iraq defied UN mandates by declining to: (a) eliminate its biological, chemical and nuclear WMD development programs in a verifiable manner; (b) cease its attempts to acquire ballistic missiles with ranges greater than 150 kilometers; (c) renounce all terrorist organizations and refuse to harbor any members of such groups within its borders; (d) return all foreign prisoners seized during its 1990 invasion of Kuwait and subsequent Persian Gulf War; and (e) refrain from repressing its domestic population.[30]

Ultimately, the Bush administration applied a variety of economic, diplomatic and politico-military tools in the context of a four-stage approach to the disarmament of Iraq and liquidation of Saddam's regime. The first stage was rhetorical in nature. It commenced with Bush's address to the UN General Assembly in September 2002

---

24   Bush, "Remarks at the UN."

25   Ibid.

26   Ibid.

27   United States Congress, "Joint Resolution Granting Authorization for the Use of Military Force Against Iraq," *United States Congress*, 10 October 2002.

28   UN Security Council, "UN Security Council Resolution 1441," *United Nations Press Office*, 8 November 2002.

29   NSC, "A Decade of Deception and Defiance," 4–7; UN Security Council, "Resolution 4112."

30   NSC, "A Decade of Deception and Defiance," 4–7.

and continued with his nationally televised speech to the American people from Cincinnati a month later.[31] In each case, the President issued stern demands for Iraq to disarm in order to impress upon Saddam and the international community how seriously Washington viewed the matter. However, Bush was also careful to express his willingness to afford the UN an opportunity to achieve that objective peacefully before the United States would consider either the multilateral or unilateral use of military force against Iraq. Furthermore, key members of the administration's national security team—most notably Rice, Rumsfeld and Powell—and also British Prime Minister Tony Blair struck similar tones in reiterating the administration's demands between September 2002 and March 2003.

The political stage focused on the development of American and international legal measures to justify diplomatic and military action against Iraq. Domestically, Bush worked diligently to secure Congressional authorization of the use of force to disarm Iraq should such action become necessary, which he achieved through the resounding passage of a joint resolution to that end by the House and Senate in October 2002.[32] Internationally, Powell collaborated with his British, French, Russian and Chinese counterparts on the Security Council to fashion Resolution 4112, which called for Saddam to readmit and cooperate unconditionally with weapons inspectors under the auspices of the UN Monitoring, Verification and Inspection Commission (UNMOVIC) or face "serious consequences."[33] The resolution passed by a 15-0 vote in the Security Council on 8 November 2002 and was agreed to by Iraq six days later.

Put simply, the Bush administration used its policy toward Iraq as a test case for the practical implementation of the NSS. It did so through a three-part strategy that has unfolded between September 2002 and the present. First, Bush attempted to use diplomatic measures to ensure Iraqi disarmament, most notably by securing the return of UN weapons inspectors to Iraq under the auspices of Security Council Resolution 4112.[34] Second, when Saddam refused to comply fully with the weapons inspectors, the United States collaborated with the United Kingdom—and, to a lesser degree, a range of other allies including Australia and several Eastern and Central European states—to forcibly remove the Iraqi regime from power in orchestrating a campaign that lasted just over one month between mid-March and mid-April 2003. Third, the Americans and British are currently leading a coalition of the willing to build a democratic system in Iraq over the long term.

During the initial stage of the above process, French President Jacques Chirac was the most vociferous of several foreign leaders to express their unambiguous opposition to the use of military force to disarm Iraq and employed all diplomatic

---

31   Bush, "Remarks on Iraq at Cincinnati Museum Center"; Bush, "Remarks at UN General Assembly."

32   The House approved the resolution by a 296-133 vote on 10 October 2002; the Senate approved it by a 77-23 vote on 11 October 2002.

33   UN Security Council, "UN Security Council Resolution 1441."

34   "The Cold Calculation of War," *Economist* (3 April 2003).

measures at his disposal to block that course of action. For example, although France voted for Resolution 4112, it did so only because that measure did not explicitly sanction the use of force against Iraq. Ultimately, when the United States, the United Kingdom and Spain indicated they would seek a second resolution condoning military action to disarm Saddam's regime, Chirac responded that "whatever the circumstances, France will vote no," ensuring that the campaign for any such resolution was stillborn.[35]

Chirac's behavior raised one overarching question: Why was he so insistent that the United States not remove Saddam from power? In short, there were three reasons, each of which included both domestic and international components. First, France had close public and private economic ties with Saddam's regime, which it was understandably eager to preserve. Second, France plays host to a growing Muslim population, one whose members were unequivocally opposed to U.S. military action against Iraq and by no means averse to expressing their opposition in violent—and thus socially destabilizing—ways. Third, Chirac perceived the Iraq crisis as an opportunity to revitalize flagging French prestige—both within and outside of Europe—in opposition to American predominance in the post-Cold War international system.

In the process of opposing the use of force to remove Saddam from power, Chirac sparked divisions within both NATO and the European Union (EU). Most significantly, Germany elected to join France in obstructing U.S. attempts to forge consensus within NATO on Washington's policy toward Iraq, resulting in a de facto division of the European continent into wings favoring and opposed to the Bush administration's doctrine of preemption. These divisions, in turn, had spillover effects in the context of the EU. With respect to transatlantic community broadly defined, France, Germany—and a number of less influential states including Belgium and Luxembourg—entrenched themselves on one side of the debate over Iraq, while the United Kingdom, Spain, Italy, Portugal and the vast majority of prospective EU and NATO members from Eastern and Central Europe aligned themselves with the United States on the other side. Put bluntly, such divisions pose an inopportune— and unnecessary—complication to the scheduled enlargement of NATO and the EU to include several Central and Eastern European states that have staked out positions in opposition to two of the three most politically influential states in Europe.

Ultimately, the United States, France—and, albeit to a lesser degree, Germany— are each at least partially responsible for the predicament in which the transatlantic community finds itself on the eve of the dual enlargement processes slated to move forward in 2004. Bush, for example, could have done a better job accommodating Western European concerns over issues ranging from global warming to the imposition of American steel tariffs in 2001. Chirac, on the other hand, could have been more understanding of U.S. worries over Iraq's development of WMD and sponsorship of terrorist groups, particularly in light of the tragic events of 9/11.

---

35   "It's Not Easy Being French," *Economist* (3 April 2003).

Conclusions

American presidents have employed a variety of means in conducting foreign policy over the past two and one-quarter centuries. The particulars of their approaches were in the past and are at present conditioned by the contemporary circumstances and events—both at home and abroad—to which they have had to respond. However, irrespective of the historical context, three rules are indispensable to effective policymaking. It is essential first to define a state's national interests, second to prioritize those interests and third to take policy decisions accordingly. More pointedly, policies are the product of an admixture of three elements—interests, commitments and capabilities. States develop interests on the basis of geography, history, economics, individual leadership, politics, security and the unpredictability of unfolding events. Those interests then serve to define commitments that are conditioned by capabilities, the employment of which demand explanations rooted in ideological principles.

The final stage of the Cold War in 1989–90 altered the structure of the international system from one of bipolar confrontation to one in which the United States stood alone as the predominant superpower. The Bush administration demonstrated its aptitude in adapting to this geopolitical alteration through its management of the collapse of the Soviet empire in Central and Eastern Europe and orchestration of the German unification process. In each instance, Bush and Baker displayed the requisite political leadership and diplomatic acumen to achieve Washington's principle objectives—most significantly the inclusion of a unified Germany in NATO—without alienating the Soviets. In responding to these events, individuals within the administration deepened their relationships with European and Soviet leaders and gained valuable experience in dealing with a wide range of state leaders and governments from the East and West during a period of unprecedented continental and global transformation. Both assets proved valuable in meeting the challenges of the subsequent crisis in the Persian Gulf.

As was the case during the unification process, Bush responded to Iraq's invasion of Kuwait with a mixture of resolve and prudence. From the outset of the crisis, he was determined not to allow Saddam's aggression to stand. However, Bush also recognized the need to avoid unilateral American action in a region generally averse to Western culture and influence. In order to achieve that end, he set about the construction of a broad coalition of Western, Eastern and Middle Eastern states that would act only under the auspices of the UN and thus mitigate if not preclude fully the perception that the United States was acting solely in its own interest. Through the personal and professional relationships Bush and Cabinet members such as Baker, Cheney, Powell and Scowcroft had established with world leaders in the past and contemporary contexts, the administration mobilized international support against Iraq more rapidly than would likely have been the case had a set of individuals lacking those attributes been in power at the time.

Throughout the crisis, the administration focused on the use of personal diplomacy—whether over the telephone or through frequent airplane shuttles from

Washington to European, Persian Gulf and Middle Eastern state capitals—in order to maintain cohesion within the coalition by ensuring that each of its members' needs were met sufficiently. Baker's September trip to procure financial contributions from coalition partners both to offset the costs of the military buildup and offer aid to states making significant sacrifices to enforce the economic sanctions against Iraq, and his November mission to mobilize support for the passage of the UN use-of-force resolution are two cases in point. These consultations were effective primarily because they demonstrated Bush's personal commitment to the coalition and the objectives that entity sought to achieve.

The crisis served as an ideal context within which the administration skillfully cobbled together a coalition based on a confluence of the myriad interests listed above. However, Bush recognized that the coalition would remain united only so long as its members deemed its existence beneficial. As a result, he set limited objectives, all of which were codified explicitly in UN resolutions. Bush understood that once the coalition had achieved its principal goals—the ejection of Saddam's forces from Kuwait and restoration of the Emir's regime—that entity would lose its principal source of legitimacy. Thus, he did not press for a removal of Saddam from power through a military offensive in Iraq. The administration managed the crisis masterfully given the existential circumstances during the coalition's existence; Bush and his advisors also displayed the requisite geopolitical prudence to retire that diplomatic creation before it collapsed under its own weight.

The administrations of Clinton and George W. Bush took starkly different approaches to the threats Saddam posed to U.S. interests, which were conditioned both by unfolding world events and their own personal preferences. In short, the Clinton and Bush administrations fashioned policies toward Iraq that, relative to the actions of the George H.W. Bush administration in that context, are perhaps best described as Bush I light and Bush I heavy, respectively. The Clinton administration responded to the complexities of the post-Cold War world by focusing on a range of different issues, but did little to mitigate the emerging threats to American interests presented by transnational terrorist networks (most notably al Qaeda) and those states suspecting of sponsoring such groups (Iraq in particular). Those half measures Clinton did choose to take—the aforementioned December 1998 air strikes—only emboldened Saddam and allowed al Qaeda to continue planning the 9/11 attacks that George W. Bush would have to deal with.

Bush's leadership in the immediate aftermath of the events of 9/11 was laudable and his administration's conduct of the subsequent war against al Qaeda and Taliban forces within and beyond Afghanistan from October to December 2001 and maintenance of cohesion in a variety of bilateral and multilateral coalitions therein was equally masterful. Bush's NSS was a logical continuation of his response to the 9/11 attacks, one that acknowledged the need to preempt—rather than simply react after the fact—to future attacks on American interests at home and abroad by confronting terrorist organizations and their state sponsors. Put simply, the rational for the administration's security strategy was both sound and innovative, and its legal basis—that of self-defense—clearly legitimate under established principles of international behavior. Thus the failure to take action while threats to the security of the United States proliferate would have been indefensible.

George W. Bush's willingness to confront Iraq directly in a more robust manner than that of George H.W. Bush and the resolve the latter's administration demonstrated in refusing to allow Saddam to remain in power were both essential under the altered conditions of the post-9/11 era. However, the personal diplomacy the latter Bush and his advisors employed was of a selectively rather than unambiguously multilateral nature. As a result, the United States has had trouble mobilizing the requisite broad-based international support to avoid shouldering the burden for the reconstruction of Iraq alone. Now that the threats posed by Saddam's regime have been eliminated, it would be prudent for the second Bush administration to demonstrate similar diplomatic flexibility the first Bush administration displayed in pursuing its policies toward the Persian Gulf generally and Iraq specifically in the future.

Chapter 6

Coalition Diplomacy and Iraq

Tom Lansford

University of Southern Mississippi, Gulf Coast

Introduction

Central to any exploration of US security policy toward Iraq is an examination of the role of coalition diplomacy. Indeed, the success of US policy during the first confrontation with Iraq was based principally on the broad and inclusive nature of the alliance that the administration of George H. W. Bush was able to array against Saddam Hussein. From the first Gulf War onward, successive administrations in Washington endeavored to develop broad-based coalitions of potential military partners and diplomatic supporters. Consequently, the administrations of Bill Clinton and George W. Bush loosely reflected the actions of the first Bush administration. However, neither president was able to match the success of the original anti-Saddam coalition as changing global circumstances and recalculations of national security priorities lessened the impetus for multilateral action and reinforced unilateral tendencies within both administrations.

This chapter analyzes the policies of the three administrations in regards to the multiple coalitions and alliances that were formed to contain, and later, overthrow the regime of Saddam Hussein. The chapter begins with an exploration of coalitions and US preferences for coalition warfare, including the transition from broad, multilateral coalitions to "coalitions of the willing" from the 1990s through the first years of the new century. Specifically, the chapter examines the shifting presidential priorities of the three US leaders in the context of broader trends in international relations. Included in the chapter are three main case studies: 1) George Bush's initial "grand" coalition; 2) Clinton's attempts to maintain the anti-Saddam coalition within the UN Security Council in regards to the sanctions regime and Operation Desert Fox; and 3) George W. Bush's efforts which resulted in UNSCR 1441 and the subsequent breakdown within the United Nations. Finally, the chapter summarizes the second Bush administration's efforts to assemble a broad-based coalition during the reconstruction phase in the aftermath of the fall of the Saddam regime.

Coalitions and Coalition Warfare

Throughout history, a common component of international relations has been the rise and fall of coalitions and alliances as actors have banded together to counter hegemonic, or potential hegemonic, powers. The coalition and the more formal security alliance share many common traits and may be conceptualized as "a formal or informal arrangement for security cooperation between two or more sovereign states."[1] The key difference between an alliance and a coalition is the degree of formality. Alliances tend to be highly rigid and lasting structures, based on formal treaties, while coalitions are usually ad hoc or temporary reactions to specific threats.[2] As such, coalitions are frequently based on informal agreements with broad or ill-defined objectives.[3] NATO is an example of an alliance while the collection of nations which opposed Iraq during the Persian Gulf War is an example of a coalition.

Both types of security arrangements emerged in response to external security threats. Such threats serve as the impetus for cooperation and provide cohesion. The totality of resources or capabilities of a potential enemy is the "threat quotient."[4] While an alliance is long-lasting, the strength and longevity of a coalition is directly proportional to the threat quotient arrayed against it. With stronger adversaries, it is more likely that a coalition will remain unified and act resolutely. If a coalition faces a weak threat quotient, the allies are more likely over time to develop internal rivalries for primacy and an overall decline in commitment to the purpose or goals of the coalition. Even broad-based coalitions confronted with a weak opponent often dissolve quickly or lack coherence.[5]

Coalitions form when governments seek to maximize their national security. They may develop among states trying to "*balance* [italics in original] (ally in opposition to the principal source of danger) or *bandwagon* [italics in original] (ally with the state that poses the major threat)."[6] Balancing often occurs as states join the weaker side in order to prevent a country or group of countries from dominating the international order, while bandwagoning results when states are comfortable with the current international system and seek to preserve it.[7] Bandwagoning is

---

1   Stephan M. Walt, *The Origins of Alliances* (Ithaca: Cornell University Press, 1987), 12.

2   For a more comprehensive examination of the differences between alliances and coalitions, see Glenn H. Snyder, "Alliance Theory: A Neorealist First Cut," *International Affairs* 44 (Spring 1990): 103–24.

3   See Wayne A. Skillet, "Alliance and Coalition Warfare," *Parameters* 23 (Summer 1993), 74–85.

4   Michael W. Doyle, "Balancing Power Classically: An Alternative to Collective Security?" in George Downs, ed., *Collective Security Beyond the Cold War* (Ann Arbor: University of Michigan, 1994), 158.

5   For recent examples of this trend, see Keith Neilson and Roy A. Prete, eds. *Coalition Warfare: An Uneasy Accord* (Waterloo, Ont.: Wilfrid Laurier University Press, 1983); or Jehuda Wallach, *Uneasy Coalition: The Entente Experience in World War I* (Westport: Greenwood Press, 1993).

6   Stephan M. Walt, "Alliance Formation and the Balance of Power," *International Security* 9/4 (Spring 1985), 4.

7   The seminal work on balance of power systems is Kenneth Waltz, *Theory of International Politics* (Reading, Mass.: Addison-Wesley, 1979), especially chapter 6.

more likely if states share similar values or interests with the major power. States may even accept hegemony if it protects or preserves their own core interests.[8] As John Ikenberry and Charles Kupchan note: "rightful rule emerges if the hegemon is able to induce smaller powers to buy into its vision of international order and to accept as their own—in short, to internalize and embrace –the principles and norms espoused by the hegemon." David Lake concurs and writes that the success of any security system dominated by one state is the ability of that primary power to "build loyalty and compliance by credibly committing not to exploit their subordinates."[9] Meanwhile, coalitions also serve as tools of the great powers. Such arrangements can augment the power and resources of a hegemonic state through burdensharing and cooperation.[10]

Many scholars note that in the twentieth century, the United States has been particularly adroit at using international organizations, alliances and coalitions to maintain its security primacy and lessen the cost of superpower status. John Gerard Ruggie asserts that the growth of multinational institutions, including the United Nations, NATO and the World Trade Organization, was the result of very specific American preferences for the post-World War II "world order."[11] These preferences helped institutionalize habits of formal and informal cooperation and collaboration, even as the military threat posed by the Soviet Union declined.[12] By the time of the first Bush administration, transatlantic security cooperation had become a security priority on both sides of the Atlantic as opposed to being perceived as a means to secure larger policy goals.[13]

American Preferences and Coalitions

In the post-World War II era, US security policy has consistently revolved around the use of military alliances and coalitions. The noted Cold War historian John Lewis Gaddis asserts that early during the Cold War, the Truman and Eisenhower administrations understood that US capabilities might not be enough to counter the Soviet Union and that instead, "the United States would also need the manpower

---

8   Robert L. Rothstein, *Alliances and Small Powers* (New York: Columbia University, 1968), 178.

9   David A. Lake, "Beyond Anarchy: The Importance of Security Institutions," *International Security* 26/1 (Summer 2001), 140.

10   For a more thorough discussion, see Robert O. Keohane and Joseph S. Nye, *Power and Interdependence*, 2nd ed., (New York: HaperCollins, 1989).

11   See John Gerard Ruggie, "Third Try at World Order? America and Multilateralism After the Cold War," *Political Science Quarterly* 109 (Fall 1994): 553–70.

12   For an expansion of these preferences, see Robert J. Lieber, "No Transatlantic Divorce in the Offing," *Orbis* 44, no. 4 (Fall 2000): 571–85.

13   Gunther Hellmann and Reinhard Wolf, "Neorealism, Neoliberal Institutionalism, andthe Future of NATO," *Security Studies* 3, no. 1 (Autumn 1993), 20.

reserves and economic resources of the major industrialized non-communist states."[14] Secretary of State John Foster Dulles stated that security arrangements had greater importance than nuclear deterrence and such that alliances remain the "cornerstone of security for the free nations."[15]

In the post-World War II era, the majority of military coalitions deployed by successive US administrations were "coalitions of the willing." Instead of negotiating in order to gain the full range of capabilities and resources available through formal military alliances, American presidents often deliberately chose to develop informal coalitions of those nations willing to bandwagon on a particular issue. This strategy was designed to minimize possible leadership issues or problems of mission scope. Such coalitions of the willing generally increased the effectiveness of the US-led arrangements, although not all problems were eliminated.[16]

Key to the success of coalitions of the willing is the role and importance of leadership by the major powers.[17] As G. John Ikenberry points out, leadership in the international arena is really about "power": "To exercise leadership is to get others to do things that they would not otherwise do."[18] Throughout the Cold War period, the US exercised considerable hard and soft power.[19]

A core issue of leadership is the potential for free-riders undermining the cohesion of the coalition. Within any coalition there is the potential that certain members will not do their share (they become free-riders). Since states always seek to maximize their interests, so they often seek methods to "cheat" in terms of burdensharing.[20] It is therefore incumbent on the coalition leadership to provide disincentives to cheat or "undercontribute."[21] One way to do this is through the "shadow of the future." If states perceive that they will have to cooperate again in the future, even if on

---

14   John Lewis Gaddis, *Strategies of Containment: A Critical Appraisal of Postwar American National Security Policy* (New York: Oxford University Press, 1982), 152.

15   John Foster Dulles, "Policy for Security and Peace," *Foreign Affairs* 32 (April 1954), 355–7.

16   Mark Schissler *Coalition Warfare: More Power or More Problems?* (Newport: US Naval War College, 1993).

17   For an examination of theories on international leadership, see David P. Rapkin, ed., *World Leadership and Hegemony* (Boulder: Lynne Rienner, 1990).

18   G. John Ikenberry, "The Future of International Leadership," *Political Science Quarterly* 111, no. 3 (Fall 1996), 388.

19   Hard power is "a country's economic and military ability to buy and coerce" while soft power is "the ability to attract through cultural and ideological appeal"; Joseph S. Nye, Jr., "Redefining the National Interest," *Foreign Affairs* 78, no. 4 (July/August 1999), 24. Nye notes that in the post Cold War "information age soft power is becoming more compelling than ever before;" ibid., 25.

20   Michael Hechter, " Karl Polanyi's Social Theory: A Critique," *Politics and Society* 10, no. 4 (Winter 1981), 403.

21   Charles Lipson, "Is the Future of Collective Security Like the Past?" in Downs, *Collective Security*, 115.

different issues, they are much less likely to cheat.[22] Recalcitrant states may also find themselves shut-out of decision-making procedures in the current coalition or alliance or have their influence curtailed in other ways.[23]

With the end of the superpower conflict, US leadership increasingly faces challenges from other states and from international organizations seeking to balance against US primacy. This reflects the nature of the international system which is neither unipolar nor multipolar, but instead a "uni-multipolar" configuration in which there is one superpower and a number of major powers.[24] Because the United States lacks clear hegemony, it must rely on coalitions with some combination of the major powers.[25] The post-Cold War began with the formation of one of the largest and most successful coalitions in history as the first Bush administration was able to bring together a range of former and contemporary adversaries to oppose the regime of Saddam Hussein.

The Gulf War: The Bush Administration

The coalition developed by the United States during the Persian Gulf War is frequently used by scholars and policymakers as a benchmark by which subsequent multilateral military operations are judged.[26] The administration of George H.W. Bush developed a broad-based, informal coalition which included a range of individual states and

---

22   Arthur A. Stein argues that groups of states and international organizations "may be required again in the future, and destroying them because of short-term changes may be very costly in the long run. Institutional maintenance is not, then, a function of a waiving calculation; it becomes a factor in the decision calculus that keeps short-term calculations from becoming decisive;" Arthur A. Stein, *Why Nations Cooperate: Circumstance and Choice in International Relations* (London: Cornell University, 1990), 52.

23   France's withdrawal from NATO's integrated military command in 1966 provides an example of how sanctions are applied. After the French withdrawal, Paris found itself prevented from influencing many of the major military decisions of the Alliance. For a more thorough examination of the incident, see Michael M. Harrison and Mark G. McDonough, *Negotiations on the French Withdrawal From NATO: FPI Case Studies, No. 5* (Washington, D.C.: Johns Hopkins, 1987).

24   Samuel Huntington, "The Lonely Superpower," *Foreign Affairs* 78, no. 2 (March/April 1999), 36.

25   Huntington describes the regional powers of the contemporary international system as: "the French-German condominium in Europe, Russia in Eurasia, China and potentially Japan in East Asia, India in South Asia, Iran in Southwest Asia, Brazil in Latin America, and South Africa and Nigeria in Africa;" ibid. He argued that these regional powers "are preeminent in areas of the world without being able to extend their interests and capabilities as globally as the United States;" ibid.

26   See Mashhud H. Choudhry, *Coalition Warfare: Can the Gulf War-91 Be the Model for Future?* (Carlisle Barracks: US Army War College, 1992); or James P. Dunnigan, and Austin Bay, *From Shield to Storm: High-Tech Weapons, Military Strategy, and Coalition Warfare in the Persian Gulf* (New York: Morrow, 1992).

multilateral organizations. Colin Powell, who was Chairman of the Joint Chiefs of Staff at the time, pointed out that there was an unprecedented degree of cooperation between the world's major powers. For instance, Powell notes that the Soviet Union did not treat the "crisis as another East-West confrontation, with the Soviet Union willy-nilly lining up behind its onetime friend Saddam."[27] Instead, the United States and the Soviet Union would be on the same side during a major military conflict for the first time since the Second World War. In addition, the US gained the support of the United Nations. Following the invasion, the UN Security Council, in UNSCR 660, voted 14-0 to condemn the Iraqi invasion. It also ordered an immediate Iraqi withdrawal from Kuwait.[28] Before it attempted to initiate military action, the Bush administration specifically sought a Security Council Resolution which would authorize the use of force. In response, on 29 November 1990, the council voted 12-2 in UNSCR 678 to authorize the removal of Iraqi forces by "all necessary means to uphold and implement resolution 660."[29] The importance of the resolution to the US was underscored by the lengths to which the Bush administration took in order to gain the UN's approval. For instance, the Bush administration even altered its original draft in response to concerns by members of the Security Council and Secretary of State James Baker had the resolution changed to specifically include the phrase "the use of force" and to include one last chance for Saddam to withdraw.[30]

The Grand Coalition

The formation of the anti-Saddam coalition was facilitated by the high threat quotient posed by the Iraqi dictator. Saddam's invasion threatened regional stability and the post-Cold War international order. As a result of the perceived Iraqi threat, states which supported the international status quo, and therefore US global leadership, bandwagoned with the United States. The coalition was also strengthened by a series of extraordinary measures undertaken by the Bush administration. These steps were designed to enhance the coalition and augment US leadership. Beginning in August 1990, the administration initiated an international campaign to solicit contributions from its main allies and the major powers of the world. Senior administration figures, such as Deputy Secretary of State Lawrence Eagleburger and Treasury Secretary Nicholas Brady, were repeatedly sent to bolster the coalition through personal shuttle

---

27   Colin Powell, with Joseph E. Persico, *My American Journey* (New York: Random House, 1995), 463.

28   In the resolution, the Security Council declared that it "demands that Iraq withdraw immediately and unconditionally all of its forces to the positions in which they were located on 1 August 1990;" UN, Security Council Resolution 660, S/RES/660 (2 August 1990).

29   UN, Security Council Resolution 678, S/RES/678 (29 November 1990). Yemen and Cuba voted against the resolution, while China abstained.

30   The UN Security Council resolution declared that "Iraq comply fully with resolution 660 (1990) and all subsequent relevant resolutions, and decides, while maintaining all its decisions, to allow Iraq one final opportunity, as a pause of goodwill, to do so;" and it mandated that Iraq had until 15 January 1991 to meet its demands; ibid.

diplomacy.[31] At one point, Secretary Baker even traveled to 12 different countries in 18 days.[32] These administrative figures not only endeavored to garner direct support for the coalition, they also sought to secure support for coalition members from other coalition partners. For instance, Great Britain contributed a substantial number of troops and the Bush administration helped secure funds from Germany and Japan to cover part of the costs of the British forces.[33] During the major combat operations of the campaign, Germany and Japan provided the British with an average of $55 million each day.[34] The administration also provided its own financial incentives for coalition participation. One example of this strategy was the decision announced on 1 September 1990 that the US would forgive Egypt's $7 billion debt to the US[35]

The administration's efforts to use financial enticements to bolster the coalition are demonstrative of the broad nature of the anti-Saddam group. The administration sought to gain support from as many states as possible and, therefore, Bush and his senior advisors did not seek only military contributions. To provide itself the time to build a grand coalition, the administration developed its timetable based on diplomatic imperatives and not military considerations. One military historian notes that "as the diplomatic process wore on, the sailors, airmen and ground troops did their best to keep sharp, but it wasn't easy in the morale-sapping heat" and that "there were doubts [among the military] not only about it being worth assembling such a large coalition ... but also whether or not it could be efficiently knitted together."[36] Throughout this period, the administration proceeded along two tracks: first, it sought to gain diplomatic pledges of support from as wide an array of states as possible; and second, it endeavored to gain military support from a much smaller group of states who could provide either assets needed to bolster American forces or soldiers whose presence would enhance the credibility of the coalition.[37]

The result was a coalition of willing states that could be broadly divided into an "inner" and "outer" band of nations. The "inner" band consisted of those core nations

---

31   See Alan Riding, "US Officials Begin Tour to Seek Financial Backing for Gulf Force," *The New York Times* (5 September 1990); and Patrick Tyler and David Hoffmann, "US Asking Allies to Share the Costs," *Washington Post* (30 August 1990).

32   Tom Lansford, *The Lords of Foggy Bottom: The American Secretaries of State and the World They Shaped* (Baldwin Place, NY: Encyclopedia Society, 2001), 48.

33   The British deployment was the largest that the country had undertaken since World War II.

34   "Making 'Em Pay," *The Economist* (26 January 1991), 18.

35   The decision was made public on 1 September 1990, and approved by Congress two months later; Patrick E. Tyler, "Bush to Forgive $7.1 Billion Egypt Owes for Military Aid," *Washington Post* (1 September 1990); and William Claiborne, "Mubarak Sets Summit, Seeks All Arab Force," *Washington Post* (9 August 1990).

36   Iain Ballantyne, *Strike From the Sea: The Royal Navy and US Navy at War in the Middle East, 1949–2003* (Annapolis: Naval Institute Press, 2004), 83.

37   For a more thorough examination of the Bush administration's attempts to promote burdensharing, see Andrew Bennet, Joseph Lepgold and Danny Unger, "Burden-sharing in the Persian Gulf War," *International Organization* 48, no. 1 (Winter 1994): 39–75.

which contributed military resources to the coalition. This "inner" band can be further divided into two categories. First, there were those states that offered major military assets. The states formed the "inner core band." The maintenance of these states within the coalition was considered critical as their withdrawal could have created major fiscal or manpower problems. The interests and preferences of these states were carefully considered and taken into account. Second, the "outer core band" concerns those states that contributed to the military effort, but whose contributions actually created problems or strains on the coalition. Some states provided very small military units which were difficult to integrate within the force structure. Other states came to be known as "fire alarm" states (these states consistently threatened to withdraw from the coalition if they perceived the US led allies were violating some principle or norm which they perceived formed the basis of the consensus).[38] These states often created significant constraints on the coalition's range of options.[39]

The "outer" band of states was made-up of those states which provided financial, diplomatic or material support, but not troops, to the coalition. Japan and Germany were among the states that provided significant financial support.[40] Many of these states had internal, often constitutional constraints, on the deployment of troops. However, their ability to offer financial backing for the coalition actually proved more beneficial than troops. The small number of states or actors in the region, such as Jordan or the Palestine Liberation Organization, which did not bandwagon with the US, in either the inner or outer band, suffered a loss of both prestige and diplomatic clout.

The resultant coalition of the willing was the "largest and most capable international military coalition in a generation."[41] The naval blockade included ships from 60 different nations and coalition states provided some 200,000 troops, sailors and airmen. The coalition's inner band of states included 26 states. In addition, to troops from traditional NATO allies, Arab states such as Syria and Egypt provided some 50,000 troops to the US-led coalition. Even states such as Bangladesh, Senegal and Zaire provided small numbers of forces as members of the outer band. The military campaign lasted less than 100 days and resulted in the complete rout of the Iraqi forces. In order to maintain the coalition and to prevent the emergence of a power vacuum in the region, the decision was made to not invade Iraq or endeavor to

---

38   Lake, 152.

39   One example of such constraints involved the decision to limit airstrikes on the retreating Iraqi forces; Jeffrey Record, *Dark Victory: America's Second War Against Iraq* (Annapolis: Naval Institute Press, 2004), 8–9.

40   Japan provided some $13 billion for the coalition, while Germany contributed $12 billion; John M. Goshko, "Germany to Complete Contribution Toward Gulf War Costs Thursday," *Washington Post* (27 March 1991). Both nations also dispatched naval minor naval forces after the end of the war to assist in the ongoing naval blockade; Steven R. Weisman, "Breaking Tradition, Japan Sends Flotilla to Gulf," *The New York Times* (25 April 1991).

41   Gary G. Sick and Lawrence G. Potter, "Introduction," in Gary G. Sick and Lawrence G. Potter, eds., *The Persian Gulf at the Millennium: Essays in Politics, Economy, Security, and Religion* (New York: St. Martin's, 1997) 1.

force Saddam's removal.[42] After the liberation of Kuwait, formal hostilities end the Gulf War ceased on 27 February 1991. On the next day, Saddam officially accepted all of the UN conditions.

Coalition Lessons

The first Bush administration's grand coalition was successful for several reasons. First, Bush was able was to secure domestic support for his foreign policy agenda. As Richard Rose writes, to "take charge in an international crisis, a president must do three things more or less simultaneously: act effectively in the international arena, mobilize public opinion [in the US], and maintain support in Washington."[43] Second, Bush expended considerable time and energy in personal or "Rolodex diplomacy" to ensure foreign support. This included 35 calls to foreign leaders and summits with leaders of a range of countries, including the Soviet Union, Canada, Jordan and Great Britain.[44] Third, Bush offered considerable incentives for states to join the coalition. For instance, the US softened its stance toward China in the aftermath of the Tiananmen Square massacre and lobbied nominal US enemy Syria to join the coalition. Fourth, because Bush was able to convince both his domestic audience and foreign leaders that the Iraqi invasion was a substantial threat to world stability, the coalition had a high degree of cohesion and solidarity. Bush made several compromises, including the scope and goals of the military, in order to maintain that cohesion. Finally, Bush took advantage of the fact that most of the major powers perceived it to be in their interest to bandwagon with the US. Thus the shadow of the future seemed to hold the promise of continued cooperation under the auspices of benign American primacy. Many states that were formerly enemies of, or at least antagonistic toward, the US participated in the coalition in the hope that US leadership would help ensure regional and global stability through continued engagement with multilateral organizations such as the UN.

As testament to the success of the original coalition, Bush was able to maintain the core elements of the anti-Saddam alliance beyond its original impetus (the invasion of Kuwait). Even after Saddam accepted the truce, Bush was able to implement a containment strategy toward Iraq with broad international support. The main elements of this strategy were international economic sanctions, UN weapons

---

42   Lawrence Freedman and Efraim Karsh, *The Gulf Conflict 1990–1991: Diplomacy and War in the New World Order* (Princeton: Princeton University Press, 1993).

43   Richard Rose, *The Postmodern President* (Chatham, NJ: Chatham House, 1991), 333.

44   Bush also traveled to the Middle East and had leading figures in the administration also engage in personal diplomacy; see Colin Campbell and S.J. and Bert A. Rockman, *The Bush Presidency: First Appraisals* (Chatham, NJ: Chatham House, 1991) or Rose. On Rolodex or telephone diplomacy, see Brigitte Lebens Nacos, "Presidential Leadership During the Persian Gulf Conflict,' *Presidential Studies Quarterly* 24, no. 3 (Summer 1994): 543–62.

inspections, the imposition of a UN protectorate over the Kurdish regions of northern Iraq and the establishment of no-fly zones over northern and southern Iraq.[45]

While the diplomatic success of the grand coalition was widely recognized and accepted, the military operations demonstrated potential problems inherent in coalition warfare. Instead of a unified and coherent command and control structure, the nature of a military coalition lends itself to a more diffuse arrangement. During the Gulf War, several coalition partners resisted US attempts to streamline decision-making procedures and simplify command structures. For instance, France and Italy consistently strove to develop a separate role for the European forces as part of a broader policy to enhance the autonomy of European security structures such as the West European Union. At one point, a British naval officer declared that "political games were going on which had less to do with efficient execution of the [naval] blockade and rather more to do with eroding American domination of NATO and the newly formed Coalition."[46] Such problems led American military planners to increasingly devalue the utility of coalitions, a sentiment that future multilateral military actions in the 1990s would reinforce.[47]

The Clinton Administration and Coalition Diplomacy

Throughout the Clinton administration, the president endeavored to maintain the core elements of the Bush containment strategy toward Iraq. Although Clinton did send mixed signals about his Iraq policy before he took the oath of office[48], however, after he received significant negative press about his waffling, the president came into office determined to maintain the core policy elements of the first Bush administration,

---

45   For more on US containment strategy toward Iraq, see Alexander George and William E. Simmons, eds., *The Limits of Coercive Diplomacy* (Boulder: Westview Press, 1994): Zalmay Khalilzad, "The United States and the Persian Gulf: Preventing Regional Hegemony," *Survival* 37, no. 2 (Summer 1995): 95–120; and Richard Haas, ed., *Economic Sanctions and American Diplomacy* (New York: Council on Foreign Relations, 1998).

46   Theodore Craig, *Call for Fire: Sea Combat in the Falklands and the Gulf War* (London: John Murray, 1995), 168.

47   See, for instance, Stephen D. Wrage, ed., *Immaculate Warfare: Participants Reflect on the Air Campaigns Over Kosovo and Afghanistan* (Westport: Praeger, 2003) or Tom Lansford, *A Bitter Harvest: US Foreign Policy and Afghanistan* (Aldershot: Ashgate Publishing Limited, 2003).

48   In an interview Clinton stated: "I am a Baptist. I believe in death-bed conversions. If he Saddam] wants a different relationship with the United States and the United Nations, all he has to do is change his behavior;" "Clinton Backs Raid but Muses About a New Start," *The New York Times* (14 January 1993). Clinton immediately faced a barrage of criticism from domestic politicians and media sources and reaffirmed that the Bush would continue in his administration: "There is no difference between my policy and the policy of the present administration [the first Bush administration] ... I have no intention of normalizing relations with him [Saddam];" "Clinton Affirms US Policy on Iraq," *The New York Times* (15 January 1993).

including the extensive use of coalition diplomacy to contain Saddam Hussein. Soon after entering office, Clinton continued the State of Emergency With Respect to Iraq that Bush had put in place through a series of executive orders.[49] Clinton's containment strategy would evolve into the "dual containment" policy toward Iraq and Iran that guided US policy in the Persian Gulf throughout his presidency.[50]

This erosion of the original Grand Coalition slowly proceeded as key European allies of the first grouping, especially France, sought to reopen economic ties with Iraq. In addition, the domestic emphasis of the Clinton administration undermined the needed US leadership as foreign perceptions were that Washington's Iraq policy was mainly reactive. This encouraged under contributions to the continuing efforts to contain the Iraqi regime. Throughout the 1990s, the US accepted an ever-increasing share of the costs of containment with only the UK providing significant resources and assets. Furthermore, the administration was unable to maintain the support of key Arab states as the threat of Iraq continued to be diminished as a result of the degradation of Iraqi security forces following the original conflict. The Arab neighbors of Iraq simply perceived that the Saddam regime was not the threat it had been prior to the 1991 war. One result of these trends was an increasingly unwillingness by former coalition partners to contribute to US initiatives later in the decade.

Questions would also arise about Clinton's foreign policy actions in the midst of his impeachment. Clinton also generally enjoyed widespread domestic support for his Iraq policies. As Daniel Byman and Matthew Waxman point out in a Rand Institute study on US foreign policy and Iraq:

> In general, both the Bush [George H. W. Bush] and Clinton administrations enjoyed considerable support in Congress and among the US public for their efforts to punish Iraqi aggression and end Iraq's NBC [Nuclear, Biological and Chemical] programs. In addition to supporting a large US military presence in the region, the American people strongly supported US policymakers' calls to combat proliferation among rogue regimes. If anything, the American people and US Congress are often more hawkish than the US leadership. As a result, President Clinton at times was criticized for not threatening or using enough force.[51]

Although Clinton endeavored to maintain the central elements of the grand coalition, the domestic focus of his administration and difficulties faced in maintaining the original grand coalition quickly led to fissures among the allied states. US international

---

49   For instance, Executive Order No. 12722 froze Iraqi assets in the US, while No. 12724 aligned US sanctions with UN Security Council Resolution (UNSCR) 661 and No. 12817 implemented UNSCR 778; William J. Clinton, "Message to the Congress on the National Emergency With Respect to Iraq," Office of the White House (16 February 1993).

50   Martin Indyk, National Security Advisor on the Middle East, codified the dual containment strategy in a speech in May 1993; Martin Indyk, "Address to the Washington Institute for the Near East" (18 May 1993).

51   Daniel Byman and Matthew Waxman, *Confronting Iraq: US Policy and the Use of Force Since the Gulf War* (Santa Monica: Rand 2000), 38–9.

prestige was seriously undermined by Somali episode. In addition, Saddam grew increasingly adept at exploiting divergences among the coalition members and in brinksmanship with his US counterpart. The weapons inspections and the no-fly zones also significantly lowered the perceptions of Saddam's threat potential to regional stability. Furthermore, differences between the US and its major Gulf War allies on a range of international issues spilled-over into Iraq policy. The result was the aforementioned decline in US leadership potential and a corresponding erosion of the cohesion of the alliance.

Initial Coalition Tests

The cohesion of the coalition was tested many times during the Clinton presidency. For instance, in June 1993, Clinton gained international support for air strikes on Iraq after Iraqi intelligence units attempted to assassinate former President Bush in Kuwait in April of that year.[52] The first significant challenge to the coalition during the Clinton administration occurred in 1994 when Saddam deployed two Republican guard divisions along the border with Kuwait. In response, Clinton launched *Operation Vigilant Warrior*. The operation replicated the main successes of the Bush coalition. The UN Security Council passed Resolution 949 which called on Saddam to withdraw his forces and a variety of states, including Great Britain and France, deployed additional forces centered around a US carrier battle group. Saddam withdrew his forces and the swift US-led response reaffirmed the power of the coalition.

During the remainder of Clinton's tenure, Saddam engaged in a strategy designed to consistently test and undermine the coalition. The Iraqi regime repeatedly undertook provocative actions, including threatening Kuwait and engaging in aggressive action toward allied aircraft patrolling the UN-sanctioned no-fly zones. Saddam's actions were designed to strengthen his domestic control and improve his popularity in the Middle East all the while degrading international support for the US containment policy. His tactics proved successful as the cohesion of the coalition weakened over time and the US enjoyed less and less "freedom of action" in its efforts to contain the Iraqi regime.[53]

One main cause of the weakening of the coalition was the increasing sentiment that the US sought to expand the role and function of the anti-Saddam alliance beyond its original mandate. For instance, in 1996, when the Clinton administration launched 44 cruise missiles in *Operation Desert Strike* against the regime after Iraqi military units made incursions into the Kurdish regions, both regional and major international partners opposed, and they even openly criticized, the strikes. Both

---

52   See David von Drehle and R. Jeffrey Smith, "US Strikes Iraq for Plot to Kill Bush," *Washington Post* (27 June 1993); Stewart M. Powell, "Ending Iraqi Threat is Personal for Bush," *Times Union* (10 November 2002).

53   Michael Eisenstadt, "Target Iraq's Republican Guard," *The Middle East Quarterly*, 3/4 (December 1996), online at http://www.meforum.org/article/415.

Saudi Arabia and Turkey denied the US permission to use their bases to launch the attacks while Russia vetoed a British-sponsored UN Security Council resolution to condemn the Iraqi attacks on the Kurds.[54] Even the European allies, with the exception of the British, only gave the strikes lukewarm support. For instance, Spain did not allow the US to use its air bases, while France refused to support the attacks and a variety of leading European dailies asserted that the attacks were simply a ploy to bolster Clinton's reelection campaign.[55] In the aftermath of the attacks, there was a clear perception in both the US and other nations that Saddam was "the clear winner" as the episode demonstrated deep cracks in the coalition and strengthened Saddam's standing in the region.[56]

Operation Desert Fox

Saddam's efforts to weaken the coalition also extended to the ongoing UN weapons inspections regime. From 1997–98, Saddam embarked on a series of actions designed to end the UNSCOM inspections. While the Iraqi regime had consistently interfered with and harassed inspectors, from 1997 onward, Saddam was "emboldened" by the refusal of the Security Council to endorse US and British efforts to increase pressure in order to ensure compliance.[57] The result was a strategy of "cheat and retreat" in which the Iraqi leader seemed to go to the brink of war and then back down.

In 1997, Saddam announced that Iraq intended to expel US members of UNSCOM. UN Secretary General Kofi Annan endeavored to defuse the crisis and it initially seemed as if Saddam had gone too far as his defiance seemed to re-energize the coalition.[58] However, Russia and China signaled strong opposition to potential military strikes[59] while the Clinton administration faced growing domestic criticism over its perceived weakness in the face of Iraqi aggression. Many foreign

---

54   Russia and China also publicly condemned the attacks, "Moscow 'Working With Iraq', Urging Restraint," *Interfax* (14 September 1996).

55   Spain did publicly support the attacks; M. Gonzales and I. Cembrero, "More on Refusal to Allow US to Use Base," *El Pais* (14 September 1996). France did support a warning to Saddam to not violate the no-fly zone, but the government opposed the strikes and joined in criticism of the strikes at the UN; Charles Miller, "Britain, France US Send 'Clear Warning' to Saddam," *Press Association* (16 September 1996). On the European press reaction to the attacks, see Herbert Kremp, "Europe is Sinking Under the Horizon of US Policy," *Welt am Sonntag* (29 September 1996).

56   Andrew Phillips and William Lowther, "Why Saddam Won," *McLean's* (16 September 1996), 24–5.

57   Byman and Waxman, 64.

58   For instance, the major Gulf allies signaled support for stronger action against Saddam; "Barbara Crossette," US Welcomes Arab Statement on Iraq," *The New York Times* (13 November 1998).

59   Russian President Boris Yeltsin even suggested that military action could lead to a US-Russian confrontation; David Wurmser, *Tyranny's Ally* (Washington, D.C.: AEI Press, 1999), 4.

and domestic supporters of a hardline policy against Iraq suggested that Clinton, in the words of Daniel Schorr, "gave up the best chance he may ever have to attack Iraq with the international community behind him in return for yet another promise to comply with weapons inspections."[60] Both domestic and international leaders also decried the inability of the Clinton administration to develop a long term Iraq policy beyond containment. Commenting at the time, political scientist Ruhi Ramazani stated that "we have nothing left except economic sanctions and that's it, and a lot of people have very serious doubts that those kinds of sanctions can be effective."[61] The administration's policies further undermined the coalition as key states such as France and Russia signaled increasing frustration over UN sanctions and the subsequent loss of economic opportunities—an issue that Saddam was well aware and endeavored to exploit.[62]

On 15 December 1998 the UN Security Council received a report from UNSCOM that stated Iraq was not in compliance with pledges made by the Saddam regime to defuse the earlier crisis. The next day, UN weapons inspectors were withdrawn from Iraq and the Security Council went into emergency session. That afternoon, the US and Great Britain launched *Operation Desert Fox* against Iraq. The attack included cruise missile and aircraft sorties against a range of Iraqi targets, including security sites and a number of facilities, such as presidential palaces that were directly connected to Saddam's power base. Although the operation was larger than any previous attack since the Gulf War, the 400 cruise missiles fired and 600 aircraft sorties made the four-day campaign very "limited" in nature.[63] On 19 December, Clinton gave a national address that evening in which he declared that "Saddam's days of cheat and retreat were over."[64] That same day, the House of Representatives voted 228-206 and 221-212 to impeach Clinton on two articles.

The president's domestic problems undercut his credibility and support both at home and abroad. As he initiated military action, Clinton lacked the broad-based bipartisan support that Bush had enjoyed in the first Gulf action. Clinton's advisors were concerned that the strikes might be interpreted as an attempted divergence from his domestic problems (the House of Representatives did delay impeachment proceedings until the combat phase of *Operation Desert Fox* had ended).[65]

---

60   Daniel Schorr, "To the Brink to See Who Blinks," *The Christian Science Monitor* (20 November 1998), 11.

61   Jonathon Landay, "Weapons Showdown Goes Beyond Iraq," *The Christian Science Monitor* (21 September 1998), 4.

62   Jonathon Landay, "Can Clinton Trust Saddam?" *The Christian Science Monitor* (24 February 1998), 1.

63   Byman and Waxman, 68.

64   Bill Clinton, "Statement on the End of Strikes," (19 December 1998).

65   As Byman and Waxman point out, "the timing of the attack led many foreign governments to question whether the attacks were launched to influence the imminent US presidential impeachment vote rather than because of Iraq's actions," Byman and Waxman, 70.

Concurrently, the administration did not endeavor to gain the same degree of international support that had been characteristic of earlier campaigns. Secretaries of State Warren Christopher and Madeleine Albright were unable to develop the same personal connections that Baker had been able to achieve, and Clinton failed to engage in the same personal diplomacy that had characterized George H.W. Bush's efforts. Consequently, the leadership necessary for coalition success was not employed. For instance, Russian President Boris Yeltsin was not even informed of the strikes by American officials and instead had to learn about the operation from French President Jacques Chirac after the attack began.[66] This reinforced the impression that the attacks were mainly for domestic consumption in the United States and undermined any efforts to gain broad international support.

In response to the attacks, Russia recalled its ambassadors from Washington and London (the first time such an action had been taken since 1971).[67] Meanwhile, both China and France officially protested the strikes. US allies in the Gulf also voiced official displeasure at the missions and previously reliable coalition partners such as Saudi Arabia limited the ability of American forces to launch attacks from bases on their territory and denied overflight rights.[68] Regionally, when the strikes ended, there was a perception that Saddam had won the contest. Because of the limited nature of the attacks, the former commander of British military forces in the Gulf noted that the most likely outcome of the strikes would be "to strengthen Saddam in his position," while a diplomat in Baghdad proclaimed that "anytime Saddam Hussein is still alive or in power, he is a winner."[69] Significantly, the attacks did not accomplish their ostensible aim of forcing Saddam to comply with UN Security Council resolutions and allow the unfettered return of the UNSCOM inspectors.

Coalition Lessons

In the aftermath of the operation, the Clinton administration endeavored to develop a more comprehensive containment policy and sought to undermine the Saddam regime through increased support for Iraqi opposition groups.[70] However, the administration's policy choices were increasingly narrow as the cohesiveness of the coalition unraveled. The Iraqi regime was seen as less and less of a threat and there was broad unease with US leadership, particularly among key states such as France, Russia and China, as well as many of the Gulf allies.

---

66   "Russian MPS Brand Clinton 'Sex manic'," *BBC* (18 December 1998).

67   Ibid.

68   Douglas Jehl, "US Fighters in Saudi Arabia Grounded," *The New York Times* (19 December 1998).

69   Scott Peterson, "Iraq Hurt by Bombs, But Can US Topple Saddam?" *The Christian Science Monitor* (21 December 1998), 1.

70   For a detailed examination of the potential for US-supported Iraqi groups to overthrow Saddam in the late 1990s, see Daniel Byman, Kenneth Pollack and Gideon Rose, "The Rollback Fantasy," *Foreign Affairs*, 78, 1 (January 1999): 24–41.

Throughout the Clinton years, US policy toward Iraq became increasingly unilateral in nature, albeit with continued military support from Great Britain. Concurrent military actions in the Balkans seemed to confirm the utility of the administration going it alone, or with only a few trusted allies. For instance, during the military actions in Bosnia and Kosovo, US military officials faced a range of problems as they sought to plan missions and decide on targets.[71] Specifically, US officers asserted that their European allies frequently let political considerations overcome military issues during the day-to-day operations.[72] A National Defense University symposium concluded that "National (parochial) decisions constrained Allied Operations" and that "the constraints imposed on the planning process were the inhibitions of those nations doing the planning."[73]

The Balkan operations and the limited military strikes against Iraq also highlighted the growing gap in military capabilities between the US and its European allies. The former leader of the British Conservative Party, Iain Duncan Smith, stated that the "Kosovo conflict underlined the considerable gap in capability between the European and United States' forces."[74] Meanwhile, a Defense Science Board report pointed out, "US and allied military commanders and other officials have expressed concern that with the USA's unmatched ability to invest in next-generation military technologies, it runs the risk of outpacing NATO and other allies to the point where they are incapable of operating effectively with US forces on future battlefields."[75] The result was that by the time the administration of George W. Bush came into office, within both the diplomatic and military wings of the national security apparatus, there were increasing doubts about the utility of military coalitions and a marked preference for only involving a limited number of allies, namely Great Britain, in future combat missions.

The Bush Coalition Against International Terrorism

In response to the terrorist attacks of 11 September 2001, the administration of George W. Bush endeavored to form a broad coalition of the willing. In this effort, the administration was successful and this success set the stage for later American strategy in regards to Iraq. Bush's policy choices over Iraq were shaped by the

---

71   Suzanne Daley, "NATO Quickly Gives the US All the Help That It Asked," *The New York Times* (5 October 2001).

72   See Wesley Clark, *Waging Modern War: Bosnia, Kosovo, and the Future of Combat* (Washington, D.C.: Public Affairs, 2001).

73   Institute for Strategic Studies, "After Kosovo: Implications for US and Coalition Warfare—Executive Summary" (Fort McNair: NDU, 1999).

74   Iain Duncan Smith, "European Common Foreign, Security and Defense Policies— Implications for the United States and the Atlantic Alliance," *Congressional Testimony Before the House Committee on International Relations, 105th Congress,* (10 November 1999).

75   As reported by Bryan Bender, "US Worried by Coalition 'Technology-Gap'," *Jane's Defence Weekly* (29 July 1998): 8.

administration's experiences in Afghanistan and the broader war on terror. They were also influenced by the unilateral trends that were increasingly evident during the latter years of the Clinton administration.

Deputy Secretary of State Richard Armitage characterized the Bush administration's first coalition of the willing that would serve as the model for the Iraq coalition, noting that "in this coalition building there is a continuum from, on the one hand, rhetorical or political support for activities… and at the far end of the continuum is the possibility of some military activity either together or unilaterally."[76] Hence, just as the original anti-Saddam grand coalition included a range of states with different levels of participation, the second Bush administration also sought a broad, multifaceted coalition.

One significant difference emerged between the two coalitions. While the second Bush administration also endeavored to build robust diplomatic support, it purposely formed a narrow, limited military arrangement. The administration gained endorsements and support from all of the major international organizations, including the UN, NATO, Organization of American States (OAS) and the EU. However, this was not done to fashion a large, multilateral coalition. Instead, the broad levels of support allowed the Bush administration to, as Armitage noted, "pick and choose among its allies, fashioning the moral authority of an international coalition without having to deal with the problems of the whole alliance."[77]

In the end, the Bush administration pursued policies designed to produce a global counterterrorism coalition which "would assign different tasks to different countries, with many of the players involved in intelligence-gathering, police work, and bushwacking on money trails – but perhaps few actually joining in the military phase."[78] National Security Advisor Condoleezza Rice described the effort in the following manner: "This is a broad coalition in which people are contributing on very different and very many fronts. The key to the broad coalition is to remember that, while everybody understandably wants to focus on military contributions, this is not the Gulf War."[79] The nature of the coalition encouraged many states to bandwagon with the US since the terrorist threat was potentially quite high and the Bush administration offered a number of inducements for states to cooperate.[80]

---

76   NATO, "Press Availability: US Deputy Secretary of State Armitage and NATO Secretary General Lord Robertson," Brussels (20 September 2001).

77   Ibid.

78   Howard LaFranchi, "Despite Talk of Coalition, US Mostly Goes it Alone, *The Christian Science Monitor* (29 October 2001).

79   Condoleezza Rice, Press Briefing, Washington, D.C. (8 November 2001).

80   For example, Bush issued Presidential Determination 2001-28 which ended arms sanctions on Pakistan and India "in the interest of the national security of the United States;" US, White House, "Presidential Determination 2001-28," (22 September 2001). In addition, Pakistan received a $1 billion non-military aid package (this made Pakistan the second largest recipient of foreign aid after Israel); Rory McCarthy, "US to Reward Pakistan With Billions in Aid," *The Guardian* (20 September 2001).

It was not until after the military phase of *Operation Enduring Freedom* that the Bush administration made its major requests for troop assistance. As Philip Gordon summarized, the US saw multilateral support as politically useful but not particularly significant militarily. In this case it was reinforced by what many Americans saw as a key 'lesson' of Kosovo. Whereas many in Europe saw the Kosovo air campaign as excessively dominated by the United States and American generals, most Americans —particularly within the military—saw just the opposite: excessive European meddling, with French politicians and European lawyers interfering with efficient targeting and bombing runs, and compromising operational security. This time, the Bush team determined, would be different.[81]

The use of precision weaponry during the campaign reinforced the exclusivity of the military operation. For instance, more than 70 percent of the aerial ordnance used in the Afghan campaign was precision-guided. In contrast, 30 percent of the munitions used in Kosovo were precision-guided while only 10 percent of the ordinance in the Gulf War was precision-guided.[82]

Although the coalition only provided minimal troops for the Afghan campaign, the allies provided the bulk of the peace-keeping troops after the fall of the Taliban. Furthermore, the UN forces would actually be under the operational command of the US. Thus the British government, which initially commanded the UN mission, stated that the UN operations would be conducted "in cooperation with the Americans, they are the big brother."[83] Other nations were less pleased. Berlin protested the arrangement and called for autonomous command.[84] Meanwhile Paris objected to having to "clean-up" after the Americans. French policymakers claimed that Washington seemed to say "We'll do the cooking and prepare what people are going to eat then you will wash the dirty dishes."[85]

Bush's Coalition-Building and Operation Iraqi Freedom

In his State of the Union address on 29 January 2002, Bush identified Iran, North Korea and Iraq as members of an "axis of evil." The administration concurrently began to lay the groundwork to mark Iraq as the next target in the US-led war on

---

81   Philip H. Gordon, "NATO After 11 September," *Survival* 43, no. 4 (Winter 2001–2002), 4.

82   Joseph Fitchett, "High-Tech Weapons Change the Dynamics and the Scope of Battle," *International Herald Tribune* (28 December 2001).

83   James Meek, Richard Norton-Taylor and Michael White, "No. 10 Retreats on Plan to Send More Troops," *The Guardian* (20 November 2001).

84   Carola Hoyos and Gwen Robinson, "Multinational Peacekeeping Force Approved," *Financial Times* (21 December 2001); and Carola Hoyos, Andrew Parker and Hugh Williamson, "Anti-terrorist Coalition Threatened With Split," *Financial Times* (20 December 2001).

85   Joseph Fitchett, "US Allies Chafe at 'Cleanup' Role," *International Herald Tribune* (26 November 2001).

terror. Bush also stated that he would take preemptive military action.[86] This doctrine of preemption would later be codified in the National Security Strategy.[87] In concrete terms, Bush authorized increases in covert aid to anti-Saddam elements while his national security team worked through the late summer of 2002 to develop specific policy options. Secretary of State Colin Powell emerged as the foremost advocate for building a strong coalition, while Vice President Dick Cheney and Secretary of Defense Donald Rumsfeld argued for immediate action, even if it meant unilateral military strikes. Powell was able to sway the President who used a 12 September 2002 UN speech to launch the diplomatic effort.[88]

Throughout the fall of 2002, US coalition-building efforts were directed on a variety of fronts. First, American diplomats sought to gain UN resolutions which would authorize the use of force. Successful passage of a strong UN Security Council Resolution was seen as a precondition for the participation of several major allies, including France, Germany and Canada. Second, US officials worked to gain bilateral support from a number of states by offering military and economic inducements. Third, and finally, Bush sought to shore-up domestic support within the United States.

Negotiations over a UN resolution initially moved slowly, however, on 10 October 2002, Congress overwhelmingly passed a resolution which authorized the President not only to use force against Iraq, but to take unilateral and preemptive action, if he deemed it necessary. The threat of unilateral action on the part of the US spurred the Security Council into unanimously adopting Resolution 1441 on 8 November. The resolution imposed a new inspection regime and threatened "serious consequences" should Iraq not comply and fully embrace disarmament. UN inspectors were dispatched to Iraq on 27 November. The following month, Iraq produced a 12,000-page declaration on its WMD programs which claimed that it did

---

86   Bush stated that "I will not wait on events, while dangers gather. I will not stand by, as peril draws closer and closer. The United States of America will not permit the world's most dangerous regimes to threaten us with the world's most destructive weapons;" George W. Bush, "The President's State of the Union Address," (29 January 2002), online at http://www.whitehouse.gov/news/releases/2002/01/20020129-11.html.

87   The policy document notes that "While the United States will constantly strive to enlist the support of the international community, we will not hesitate to act alone, if necessary, to exercise our right of selfdefense by acting preemptively against such terrorists, to prevent them from doing harm against our people and our country;" US, National Security Council, *The National Security Strategy of the United States* (17 September 2002), online at http://www.whitehouse.gov/nsc/nss.html.

88   Powell met with Rice and Bush on 5 August and was able to convince the President of the importance of a coalition effort. Rice even noted that she felt the "headline" from the meeting should have been "Powell Makes Case for Coalition as Only Way to Assure Success," Bob Woodward, *Bush At War* (New York: Simon and Schuster, 2002), 334. On 14 August, Powell met with other members of the national security council (though not the President) and argued to make the September speech about Iraq. The others, including Rice, Cheney and Rumsfeld, agreed; ibid., 335.

not possess any banned weapons and that it was not engaged in any illicit weapons programs.

A key difference between the original grand anti-Saddam coalition and the one formed in 2002–2003, was the perceived threat posed by the Iraqi leader. Unlike 1990, many pivotal states did not perceive Saddam to be an immediate threat to regional peace and security. Indeed, Saddam had worked diligently to rehabilitate his regime during the late 1990s. One strategy was a "return to Islam" in which the Iraqi leader began to champion Arab causes, including the Palestinian intifada.[89] One sign of his improved status among Arab states was that in October 2002, after being banned from 1991 onward, Iraq participated in the annual meeting of the Arab League. In addition, states such as Syria restored full diplomatic relations with Iraq. Concurrently, several major powers were gaining clear economic benefits under the sanctions regime and the US containment policy. In 2001, Iraq's major trade partners were France, Russia, China and Egypt – all key states in the formation of any renewed coalition.[90]

Hardline officials within the Bush administration, namely Cheney and Rumsfeld, questioned the interests and resolve of these states even as domestic sentiment within Western states such as France and Germany became increasingly anti-war. The result was increased tensions on both sides of the Atlantic.[91] Former US Secretary of State Madeleine Albright described the situation as "European unease with American pretensions, coupled with American doubts about European resolve" and noted that the diplomatic conflict "created the potential for a long-term and dangerous rift."[92] When the Bush administration attempted to secure a second UN resolution which would specifically authorize the use of force, the diplomatic initiative was stymied. The US was unable to exercise its leadership potential as diplomatic concerns were overtaken by military interests. To the Bush administration, *Operation Enduring Freedom* confirmed the utility of a military-centric strategy. One of the main lessons touted was that "a military hub-and-spoke command operation has worked far better for Washington than the consensus decision-making on which it had to rely during the NATO air campaign over Kosovo and Serbia in 1999, which left many in the

---

89   For instance, Saddam began paying the families of Palestinian suicide bombers a $10,000 bounty and pledged $881 million for the Palestinian Authority; Jerrold M. Post and Amatzia Baram, "Saddam is Iraq: Iraq is Saddam," *Counterproliferation Papers: Future Warfare Series*, no. 17 (November 2002), 57.

90   In August of 2002, Iraq and Russia even signed a $40 billion economic package; Ibid., 45.

91   The Iraqi crisis created the greatest strain in German-American relations since World War II. Explaining the breakdown in relations, German Chancellor Gerhard Schröder referred to a speech by Cheney and asserted that "it just isn't good enough to learn from the American press about a speech which clearly states 'we are going to do it, no matter what the world or our allies think';" quoted in James P. Rubin, "Stumbling Into War," *Foreign Affairs* 82/5 (September/October 2003), 49.

92   Madeleine Albright, "Bridges, Bombs, or Bluster?" *Foreign Affairs* 82/5 (September/October 2003), 7.

US Defense Department deeply frustrated."[93] Hence, Washington sought broad diplomatic support, but only limited military contributions. Far more important to officials in the Bush administration than large military contributions was the ability to utilize bases and confirm overflight rights for the planned attack which would be carried-out mainly by US forces.

US military deployments continued throughout December of 2002 and then into the following year. The only other countries to contribute significant forces were the British and Australians (Poland would later contribute forces as well). While this satisfied Pentagon planners it undercut the ability of the Bush administration to build a broader coalition. A series of reports from UN inspectors complicated matters for the administration since they both criticized Iraqi compliance and noted progress in the inspections. Among many members of the UN Security Council there was a sense that the inspections should be allowed to continued into the summer.

This timetable posed concrete military problems for the US and the administration ultimately allowed military considerations to overcome diplomatic concerns. This further undermined the credibility of coalition-building attempts. Former Assistant Secretary of State James Rubin noted that on the eve of war, most European leaders perceived that for the US "force had become an object in itself, and that Washington was using diplomacy simply to smooth the way for an invasion."[94] Critics of the administration argued that a key manifestation of this trend was the proposed Security Council resolution submitted in February by the US, Great Britain and Spain which authorized the use of force based on Iraqi non-compliance with Resolution 1441. The resolution was introduced to enhance British Prime Minister Tony Blair's domestic credibility and to entice more coalition partners. However, when it became clear that the other members of the Security Council sought more time and would not authorize the resolution as it stood, the proposal was withdrawn. French and Russian officials noted that they would have been satisfied with a concrete deadline in the range of nine months, while "swing votes" on the security council, including Angola, Cameroon, Chile, Guinea, Mexico and Pakistan, wanted as little as four months.[95] The diplomatic wrangling became even more complicated as France, Germany and Russia began to actively campaign against the American coalition to prevent support for a second resolution and impede states from joining the coalition.[96] The most striking example of this involved French President Jacques Chirac publicly berating East European states that supported the US.[97]

---

93   David M. Malone, "When America Banged the Table and the Others Fell Silent," *International Herald Tribune* (11 December 2001).

94   Rubin, 49.

95   Ibid., 53.

96   For example, Germany sought to diplomatically "isolate" the US within the UN, Melissa Eddy, "Report: Germany Aimed to Block US on War," *Associated Press* (16 March 2003).

97   At an EU forum, Chirac called the pro-American stance of the East European states "dangerous" and "reckless" and declared that their policy positions could "only reinforce an attitude of hostility" in a not-so-subtle threat over future EU membership by these states;

The pace of the military preparations also caused a serious breach with Turkey. While the US did not seek Turkish forces because of the history of conflict between the Turks and the Kurds, it did seek permission to use Turkey as a base of operations for a second front against Iraq. In return, the US offered Turkey some $5 billion in economic assistance. However, the Bush administration misread the Ankara government and on 1 March 2003, Parliament voted not to allow US forces to launch their second front in a move that "bewildered Americans who had seen Turkey as the most reliable of allies."[98] At the core of the Turkish legislature's action was an acknowledgment of domestic opposition to the war and the sense that the US could be pressured into providing more incentives. The US also had to realign bases in the Persian Gulf as key regional allies such as Saudi Arabia limited the ability of US forces to utilize bases and have overflight rights.

Coalition Lessons

When the Iraq war began, the anti-Saddam coalition was a shadow of its former size and scope. The coalition forces which took part in the military campaign were predominately US and the diplomatic coalition lacked the backing of major powers such as France, Russia, China and Germany. During the major combat operations, there were approximately 45,000 British personnel, 2,000 Australians and about 200 Poles in addition to the 235,000 American forces.[99] Nonetheless, the Bush administration did gain significant military concessions from a number of countries. For instance, even those European states opposed to war gave the US overflight rights and allowed the use of bases on their territory.[100] Even Jordan, which did not join the original coalition, allowed several thousand allied troops to be deployed from its territory. In military terms, the US-led effort was highly successful and the lightening-quick campaign easily overran the Iraqi forces.

Bush also enjoyed considerable domestic support for the war. While his counterparts in Europe faced widespread protests and even political infighting within their own political parties, US political and public approval for the war remained high and only began to significantly waver as the toll from insurgency campaign mounted. As such, Bush was spared many of the domestic pressures faced by Clinton. The loss of public support in the aftermath of the cessation of major

---

"John Vinocur, "Chirac's Outburst Exposes Contradiction Within EU," *International Herald Tribune* (18 February 2003).

98   Alan Cowell, "Turkey's Stand Against the War in Iraq Costs It Influence in Region," *International Herald Tribune* (19 April 2003).

99   Several countries, including South Korea, sent non-combat personnel, such as medical staff or engineers, to support the coalition in Iraq while other states, including the Czech Republic, Ukraine, Romania, Slovakia and even Germany, deployed support troops to Kuwait.

100   States provided a variety of indirect support. For example, German troops provided base security for US bases in Germany which freed-up US forces for deployment to Iraq. In addition, Canada and other countries deployed naval forces to the Persian Gulf.

combat will, however, constrain the ability of the US to form future coalitions as it is likely that considerable leadership will be necessary to gain the support of the public and opposition political leaders.

On the diplomatic level, the results were mixed. Former US Ambassador to NATO, Robert Hunter, described the alignment of states as a "coalition of the convinced, the concerned and the co-opted."[101] More significantly, the Bush administration's hopes for an international peacekeeping force in post-war Iraq with troops from the major powers failed to materialize. Although on 22 May 2003, the administration successfully arranged a UN Security Council passed a resolution lifting sanctions and recognizing the US and Britain as occupying powers, France, Germany and Russia all declined to commit forces to the reconstruction effort. The administration also failed to convince states such as India, Brazil and Pakistan to contribute troops. Instead, the administration developed an occupying coalition of mostly minor states. By August 2003, the US had military contributions from 27 countries, for a total of 21,700 non-US troops in Iraq.[102] This number far exceeds the troop contributions to the NATO-led stabilization force in Afghanistan, but is short of the administration's expectations.

The Bush administration sought a narrow military coalition and broad diplomatic support to develop a coalition of coalitions similar in nature to that fashioned for the Afghan conflict. The administration was successful in its narrow military goals, but failed in its attempt to gain international support. This hindered the ability of the coalition to attract new members for the reconstruction phase, a task made more difficult by the ongoing insurgency campaign. Nonetheless, even those governments opposed to the war acknowledged that it is in their interests for the US to succeed. Furthermore, the US has been more successful in securing international funds for reconstruction than most officials expected.[103] Although the $33 billion pledged at an international donors conference falls short of the estimated $55 billion needed to rebuild Iraq, political and development officials note that the "promised aid for one country over four or five years dwarfs what other impoverished or war-torn countries have received in the modern history of aid projects."[104]

---

101   Barbara Slaven, "US Builds War Coalition with Favors–and Money," *USA Today* (25 February 2003).

102   These countries include Albania, Azerbaijan, Bulgaria, the Czech Republic, Denmark, the Dominican Republic, Georgia, El Salvador, Estonia, Honduras, Hungary, Italy, Kazakhstan, Latvia, Lithuania, Macedonia, Mongolia, the Netherlands, Nicaragua, Norway, Poland, Romania, Slovakia, South Korea, Spain, Ukraine, and the United Kingdom. Four countries, Moldova, the Philippines, Portugal, and Thailand have pledged troops, while 15 countries are considering future deployments.

103   David Chance and Monica Megalli, "Donors Pledge $33 Billion, Smashing Expectations," *Reuters* (24 October 2003).

104   Steven R. Weisman, "Over $13 Billion in Aid is Pledged to Rebuild Iraq," *The New York Times* (25 October 2003).

Conclusion

While the administration of George W. Bush accomplished its short-term goals in regards to the overthrow of the Saddam regime, the manner in which the coalition was formed created future problems for both contemporary policy and future US diplomacy. Combined with unilateralist trends during the Clinton administration, the original grand coalition of the first Bush administration is unlikely to be replicated in the near future. The increasing reluctance to allow allies significant political or military influence within coalitions will limit the incentives for states to bandwagon with the US. Consequently only a broad and significant threat to the international order is likely to compel states to accept US coalition leadership.

While the US often utilized coalitions to counter security threats, the experiences of the two Bush administrations and the Clinton administration offer reinforcing lessons on coalition development. The high degree of personal diplomacy and national leadership employed by the administration of George H. W. Bush was not replicated by successor administrations. Instead, unilateralist trends, which emerged in the Clinton administration, were continued by the administration of George W. Bush. Further complicating US efforts in the 1990s and 2000s was the diminishing threat posed by the Iraqi regime. This undermined coalition cohesiveness and accelerated the free rider problem as former coalition partners developed rational strategies to maximize their own relative gains in light of the willingness of Washington to accept a greater share of the costs of regional security in the Middle East and Persian Gulf areas. As a result, the US was increasingly unable to ensure a reasonable degree of burdensharing among the remaining coalition members.

Resistance to an expansion of the war on terror is one manifestation of this trend. Furthermore, long-held sentiments about the benign nature of US primacy have been eroded and mid-level states increasingly seek means to check US power. The current president Bush is internationally perceived as the most unilateralist chief of state since the inter-war years. Concurrently, the prestige of international bodies, mainly the UN, has been diminished—a trend which suits neither the interests of the US nor those of the states that seek to use the world body as a means to counter US primacy.

In the end, and in spite of the potential negative consequences, the multi-layered form of coalitions of the willing, or the coalition of coalitions, will remain the preferred organization for future US-led multinational security missions. This type of arrangement continues to offer a variety of benefits to US officials, including maximum control and direction of operations. It also ensures the primacy of US interests. For America's allies, coalitions of the willing provide national governments the means with which to carefully pick and choose missions and resources and thereby balance domestic interests with international or coalition obligations. For these loosely-bound arrangements to attract partners, however, it remains incumbent on the US to exercise the necessary leadership and to engage in coalition diplomacy on par with that of the first Bush presidency.

Chapter 7

Post-Gulf War, Post-Desert Fox, and the Post-Saddam Phase: US Policy Against Iraq and its Impact in the Middle East

Mohamed A. El-Khawas
University of the District of Columbia

Introduction

Saddam Hussein's invasion of Kuwait in August 1990 presented a major challenge to the US, which had hoped that the end of the Cold War would bring an era of peace. This new conflict in the Middle East not only shattered that hope but also presented a test for the US leadership as the only superpower. US administrations—Republicans and Democrats alike—had always considered the oil resources of the Persian Gulf as a vital interest. They had always tried to keep conservative, pro-Western Arab governments in power and had not hesitated to intervene to maintain the status quo. They have been ready to deploy American troops and use force, if necessary, to prevent the emergence of any hostile power that threatened the region's oil supplies. President George H.W. Bush was not the first president to favor the use of military force against Iraq to save the oil-rich Kuwait. This had also happened in 1958, when a military coup overthrew the pro-West monarchy in Baghdad. Although it turned out to be a false alarm, President Dwight Eisenhower sent a Marine division to the Persian Gulf "to guard against a possible Iraqi move into Kuwait."[1]

The 1991 Gulf war was the first major US military intervention in the region. It has had a lasting impact on US foreign policy because it propelled the Middle East to the top of the US agenda. Following this intervention, US presidents have subsequently had to deal with further challenges, including Iraq's Saddam Hussein, the long-standing conflict between the Israelis and Palestinians, and, recently, al-Qaeda's terrorism.

This chapter looks at the Gulf War and its aftermath, which set the stage for further conflict in the region. The harsh US stance toward Iraq that emerged with

---

1   Micah L. Sifry, "US Intervention in the Middle East: A Case Study," in *The Gulf War Reader, History, Documents, Opinions*, edited by Micah L. Sifry and Christopher Cerf (New York: Random House, 1991), 30.

the Gulf war has provoked criticism time and again, most recently with the 2003 invasion of Iraq. The contrast in US behavior toward Iraq and toward Israel has undermined efforts to ease the Israeli-Palestinian conflict, which has become the core of US policy in the Middle East.

Every US administration since 1990, including George H.W. Bush, Bill Clinton, and George W. Bush, has faced a dilemma in the Middle East because of the contradictions in US policies toward Iraq and Israel. While President George H.W. Bush and his successors insisted on Saddam Hussein's total compliance with UN Security Council resolutions, they refused to demand that Israel do so. Arab governments have been critical of Washington's double standard, not out of love for Saddam Hussein but out of concern for the Palestinians. In their view, none of the US presidents has gone to the same length to force Israel to comply with UN Security Council resolutions.

Partly in response to such criticism, each US administration since the Gulf War has tried to address the Israeli-Palestinian conflict. Yet, their "soft" stance toward Israel has only complicated matters. This double standard, and the resentments it generated, has made it hard for Washington to maintain good relations with Arab states. It also helped spur the birth of al-Qaeda and the rise in anti-Americanism across the region, both of which pose deep new threats to American security. The following sections examine the policies of the three successive presidents—George H.W. Bush, Bill Clinton, and George W. Bush—as each tried to settle the Israeli-Palestinian conflict once and for all. Each was unsuccessful in reconciling the contradictions in how the US treated Iraq and Israel.

Shift in Policy: From War to Containment

Iraq's 1991 invasion of Kuwait sent shock waves around the world. The US President, George H.W. Bush, reacted immediately without waiting for a signal from Arab leaders. He ordered warships to move to the Persian Gulf and dispatched the US Air Force to the area.[2] The Bush administration considered Saddam Hussein's action a threat because they believed the Iraqi leader's goal was to control Kuwait's vast oil resources. American officials also suspected that a quick victory in Kuwait might tempt Hussein to move against Saudi Arabia—a major oil producer and a key ally of the US. The presence of Iraqi troops within ten miles of the Saudi border was seen as hostile because it threatened ARAMCO oilfields as well as the huge American military and communication base in Dhahran.

Bush decided he must stop Saddam Hussein from dominating Middle Eastern oil and from becoming a hegemonic power that might threaten US strategic and economic interests in the Gulf. He first tried diplomacy by rallying the international community against Saddam Hussein and by getting the UN Security Council to impose sanctions against Iraq. When the Iraqi leader did not budge, Secretary of

---

2   George Bush and Brent Scowcroft, *A World Transformed* (New York: Alfred A. Knopf, 1998), 314.

State James Baker convinced Turkey, which relied heavily on Iraqi oil, to enforce the UN embargo against Iraq. Furthermore, the US Navy patrolled the Persian Gulf to enforce the UN sanctions.

To increase the pressure, Bush prepared for war. He put a coalition together and secured Saudi permission to station American troops there. He made sure that other Arab and Muslim countries, including Saudi Arabia, Egypt, and even Syria, joined the coalition. Their involvement was seen as essential to prevent an outbreak of anti-Americanism in the region. After six months of preparation, the war began on 17 January 1991, with US air strikes. It ended on 27 February with the defeat of Iraq and the restoration of the Kuwait government (Al-Sabah family) to power. In March 1991, Bush reported on this success to a joint session of Congress and also announced that "our commitment to peace in the Middle East does not end with the liberation of Kuwait."[3]

After the war, Bush had to confront the problem that Saddam Hussein remained in power and continued to defy the US. The US and Britain established no-fly zones to protect the Kurds in the north and Shiite Muslims in the south, and the US re-enforced its position by maintaining a huge military presence in the Gulf area to safeguard American interests. They wanted to preserve stability in the strategic region, to continue to protect oil resources, and to combat terrorism.

The tiny Gulf States, who considered Saddam Hussein a threat to their security, favored US military presence in the area to protect their countries and to deter Saddam Hussein from embarking on new ventures. In March 1991, they endorsed Bush's plan for an increased US naval presence in the Gulf region and American participation in joint air and ground exercises. A few days later, the headquarters of the US Central Command was transferred to the area.[4]

The next president, Bill Clinton, also pursued a policy of containment to prevent Saddam Hussein from threatening his neighbors or American interests. He utilized a two-prong approach designed to depose the Iraqi leader without using American troops. The first step was to destabilize Hussein's regime by stirring up ethnic and religious violence. Clinton spent millions of dollars to strengthen opposition groups that could bring about a regime change in Baghdad,[5] and the CIA provided funds and training to the Kurds in the north and encouraged the Shiites in the south to revolt. However, when these groups rose against Saddam Hussein, they were left on their own and, as a result, their uprisings were crushed.

The second part of Clinton's approach was to tighten the screws on Saddam Hussein by enforcing UN sanctions and by using US air power to hit Iraq's military

---

3   William B. Quandt, *"Peace Process: American Diplomacy and the Arab-Israeli Conflict Since 1967* (Washington, D.C.: Brookings Institutions, 1993), 495.

4   Lorenza Rossi, Who Shall Guard the Guardians Themselves? An Analysis of US Strategy in the Middle East Since 1945 (Bern, Switzerland, Peter Lang, 1998), 182.

5   Robert O. Freedman, "US Policy Toward the Middle East in Clinton's Second Term," *MERIA* (*Middle East Review of International Affairs*), vol. 3, no. 1 (March 1999), 12–13.

installations and intelligence headquarters whenever American planes were challenged in the no-fly zones. The objective was to humiliate Iraq's military so they might stage a coup. This did not happen, however, because Saddam Hussein always put trusted loyalists in charge of the military, police and intelligence. Clinton's officials consequently settled for containment, ensuring that Saddam Hussein did not violate the no-fly zones and that he did not interfere with UNSCOM inspections of Iraq's weapons programs.[6] Clinton's tough stance on Saddam Hussein led Arab officials to criticize the lack of consistency in US policy toward Iraq and Israel. Several Arab analysts also questioned the close ties their governments had with Washington at a time when the US used the stick to bring about Iraq's compliance with UN Security Council resolutions but looked the other way when Israel refused to do the same. The following sections will examine US policies since 1990 on the Israeli-Palestinian problem, focusing on how the three presidents continued to have their efforts undermined by this policy inconsistency.

The Israeli-Palestinian Conflict: Mixed Signals from the US

The Gulf War triumph in 1991 gave George H.W. Bush confidence to try something his predecessor, Ronald Reagan, had never thought of doing. Bush felt that the time was ripe to end the Arab-Israeli conflict through diplomacy and to do so he should break away from the traditional American policy of outright support for Israel. Instead, he adopted an even-handed approach, advocating a land for peace settlement within the framework of the UN resolutions. He resisted pressures by the powerful Israeli lobby, the American Israel Public Affairs Committee (AIPAC), to follow Reagan's policy favoring Jewish settlements in the occupied territories, and he publicly stated that the Israelis should stop building new settlements in the occupied West Bank or in East Jerusalem.[7]

In his address to a joint session of Congress in March 1991, Bush advocated a comprehensive peace based on UN Security Council Resolutions 242 and 338. He favored a settlement that would take care of Israel's security concerns and at the same time recognize legitimate Palestinian political rights.[8] The president's stance changed the course of the debate on Israeli-Palestinian issues and influenced American foreign policy for years to come.

Bush thought the time was right to revive the peace process that had stalled during the Reagan presidency. First, both Israel and the Arab states had cooperated with the US during the Gulf war. Israel had stayed out of the fight even when it was hit by Iraqi missiles, while Egypt, Saudi Arabia, and Syria joined the war against Saddam Hussein. Second, radical Arab states, which opposed making peace with Israel, were weakened after the collapse of the Soviet Union, leaving them without

---

6   Ibid, 8–11.

7   Rossi, 183.

8   Quandt, 399, 496.

a superpower to back their defiance of the US. Lastly the end of the Cold War had ushered in a new era of cooperation between Moscow and Washington.

To revive the peace process, the Bush administration invited Russia to co-sponsor a regional conference on the Middle East conflict. Israel initially objected to Russian sponsorship of the conference but that obstacle was removed when Moscow recognized the Jewish state. US Secretary of State Baker then used shuttle diplomacy to promote a conference agenda based on Israeli withdrawal from the occupied territories in return for peace in accordance with UN Security Council Resolutions 242 and 338. His proposal called for an opening session to be followed by bilateral talks between Israel and its Arab neighbors. Both Syria, a member of the anti-Saddam coalition, and Jordan, which was searching for a way to get back in US graces after siding with Saddam Hussein, accepted the invitation, as did Lebanon.[9]

It took Baker eight trips to the Middle East to organize the conference. It was not easy for Baker to persuade Israel's Prime Minister, Yitzhak Shamir, who had several objections. As a strong advocate of "Greater Israel," he was opposed to the land for peace formula. He planned to incorporate the occupied territories, which he called Judea and Samaria, into Israel and argued that Jerusalem will always be part of Israel. He also needed to construct new settlements to accommodate the flow of Russian emigrants. In an attempt to scuttle the talks, Shamir announced a plan to double the number of settlements in the occupied territories. In response, Bush postponed congressional action on Israel's request of $10 billion in loan guarantees to help settle Russian Jews in Israel.[10] Shamir finally conceded to participate in the conference, but objected to Palestinian participation. Although he finally accepted Baker's proposal to include them as part of the Jordanian delegation, he did not intend to negotiate in good faith. His strategy was to drag the peace talks on for years while he built more settlements and settled a half a million Jews in the occupied territories.[11] In brief, his goal was to change the facts on the ground to make it impossible to separate the territories from Israel in the long run.

On 30 October 1991, the conference opened in Madrid, with George H.W. Bush and Mikhail Gorbachev in attendance. Bush had succeeded in bringing all parties together to restart the peace process. It was a historic and unprecedented attempt to try to reach a comprehensive peace within the parameters of UN resolutions. Another accomplishment was bringing the Palestinians to the table, which gave them legitimacy and got the Americans to view them in a different light. From now on, they had to be included in talks on the future of the occupied territories and US administrations would have to take their views into account.[12]

---

9   Peter Mansfield, *History of the Middle East* (New York: Penguin, 1991), 351–2; For the texts of the UN Security Council Resolutions 242 (1967) and 338 (1973), see Charles D. Smith, *Palestine and the Arab-Israeli Conflict* (Boston: Bedford/St. Martin, 2004), Documents 8.1 and 8.3, 331–2, 335.

10   Quandt, 402–403.

11   Mansfield, 352.

12   Kathleen Christison, *Perceptions of Palestine: Their Influence on US Middle East Policy* (Berkeley, CA: University of California Press, 1999), 270.

Bush did not follow up on the peace talks, however, and fell back to the non-intervention policy that had characterized his approach prior to the Gulf War. He needed to focus on domestic problems, especially the economy, which haunted his reelection campaign and eventually denied him a second term in office.

In June 1992, Israel changed directions. The Labor Party's Yitzhak Rabin won the Israeli election on pledges to reach an agreement with the Palestinians within a year and to freeze settlement construction. He removed the ban on contact with the Palestine Liberation Organization (PLO) and reached out to Palestinian leadership without relying on any US involvement. Rabin planned to take advantage of Arafat, who had been weakened by his isolation in Tunisia and unable to influence events in the occupied territories. Rabin thought that Arafat might be able to end the first *Intifada,* which the Israelis could not do militarily, and halt the growing popularity of Hamas in Gaza. In addition, Arafat's backing of Saddam Hussein during the Gulf War had resulted in the loss of his financial backing by the Gulf States.[13] Rabin hoped to give Arafat an opportunity to climb back to the center stage by reaching an agreement, but with minimal cost to Israel. This turned out to be impossible as their talks reached an impasse after ten rounds of secret meetings.

Meanwhile, another set of secret talks began in Oslo, Norway. In December 1992, two Israeli historians, Ron Pundak and Yair Hirschfeld, a PLO representative, Ahmed Queria, and a Norwegian researcher, Terje Rod Larsen, met to explore ways to narrow the gap between the Israelis and Palestinians.[14] Once again, the US was not involved and had no knowledge of these negotiations. During this time, the White House was changing hands and a new administration was being installed.

Clinton's Search for Peace

Like any new president, Bill Clinton wanted to develop his own policies and to put his own stamp on the peace process. In fact, he devoted more time than any other US president trying to end the Israeli-Palestinian conflict. He met with Israeli and Palestinian leaders separately and jointly on many occasions and spent countless hours trying to reconcile Israel's security concerns with Palestinian aspirations for a state. Over time, he became sympathetic to the Palestinian cause but not at the expense of Israel. Throughout, he remained a strong supporter of Israel.[15]

---

13   Mansfield, 352–4; Laura Zittrain Eisenberg and Neil Caplan, "The Israeli-Palestinian Peace Process in Historical Perspective," in *The Middle East Peace Process: Interdisciplinary Perspectives*, edited by Ilan Peleg (Albany: State University of New York Press, 1998), 10; Shimon Peres, *The New Middle East* (New York: Henry Holt and Company, 1993), 18–19.

14   Stephen Zuno, *Tinderbox: US Foreign Policy and the Roots of Terrorism* (Monroe, Maine: Common Courage Press, 2003), 114.

15   Augustus Richard Norton, "America's Middle East Peace Crisis," *Current History* (January 2001), 4.

In June 1993, Secretary of State Warren Christopher set the tone for the Clinton administration's policy. His "statement of principles" reversed the long-standing US position on settlements, which President Carter had called illegal. Christopher also did away with the concept of land for peace, and instead endorsed Israel's position that "the extent of Israeli withdrawals from occupied territories would not be subject to negotiations, but unilateral Israeli decisions."[16] This stance negated UN Resolution 242, which instructed Israel to withdraw from occupied Arab territories except for "minor border adjustments" in return for Arabs' recognition of Israel. By his new statement, Christopher denied the Palestinians the right to negotiate the final status of the occupied territories. In doing so, he legitimized the settlements and complicated efforts to solve the refugee issue and the future of Jerusalem.[17] This policy reversal raised serious questions about Clinton's ability to act as an honest broker between Israel and the Palestinians.

Despite this one-sided statement, Clinton hosted the signing of the Oslo I declaration by Rabin and Arafat on the White House lawn on 13 September 1993. It was not an agreement but a "Declaration of Principles," in which the PLO and Israel recognized each other. Israeli also agreed to withdraw from Gaza and Jericho within four months and to set out a framework for a phased Israeli withdrawal from the West Bank and Gaza. The declaration allowed for establishing a Palestinian Interim Authority with jurisdiction over local matters during a five-year period. At the beginning of the third year, talks would begin on a final agreement based on UN Security Council Resolutions 242 and 338, to be completed by the deadline of May 1999.[18] The declaration had two significant omissions, however. First, Rabin made no commitment that the talks would lead to establishing a sovereign and independent Palestinian state. Second, the most contentious issues like Jerusalem, settlements, and refugees were to be dealt with later.

The Oslo declaration led extremists on both sides to resort to violence in order to derail the peace process. Yet, despite the escalating violence, Israeli troops left Gaza and Jericho on 18 May 1994. PLO leaders, including Arafat, returned to their homeland to take charge of the Palestinian Authority.[19] With these arrangements in place, Jordan's King Hussein, who could no longer represent the West Bank, had no reason not to normalize relations with Israel. In October 1994, the two governments signed a peace treaty, with Clinton in attendance.[20]

---

16   Ibid.

17   Christison, 277–80.

18   Smith, Document 11.1, 476–80; Jewish Virtual Library, "Declaration of Principles (Oslo I) on Interim Self-Government Arrangements," 13 September 1993. http://www.us-israel.org/jsource/Peace/dop.html.

19   Amanda Roraback, *Israel in a Nutshell* (Santa Monica, CA: Eisen Publishing, 2004), 50.

20   Smith, 437.

On 28 September 1995, the Interim Agreement (Oslo II) was signed in Washington. This time Israel agreed to turn over the West Bank cities of Bethlehem, Jenin, Nablus, Qalqilya, Ramallah, and Tulkarm to the Palestinian Authority.[21]

Oslo II was criticized by Israel's Likud Party and by right-wing Israelis, who believed that Rabin was giving away land that belonged to Israel. A Jewish extremist, Yigal Amir, assassinated Rabin at a peace rally in Tel Aviv in November 1995. Meanwhile, the Palestinian militant group, Hamas, carried out a wave of attacks in Tel Aviv and Jerusalem, killing and injuring many Israeli civilians, in February and March 1966. This Palestinian violence angered many Israelis and turned them against the peace process. The Labor Party's Prime Minister Shimon Perez, who had promised to finish the work that Rabin had started, rapidly lost popular support.

In May 1996, the anti-peace candidate, Binyamin Netanyahu of the Likud Party was elected as the new prime minister. He refused to withdraw Israeli troops from the West Bank cities by January 1997, as had been specified by the Oslo II accord. Netanyahu also announced in February his decision to expand settlements in the West Bank and in Arab neighborhoods of East Jerusalem. This meant that Palestinian families would be evicted from their homes to make room for Jewish settlers. His actions froze the peace process for over a year and halted the normalizing of relations with Arab states, which had begun under the Labor government. It also led to a renewal of bomb attacks by Palestinian militants and, in return, retaliation by the Israelis.

Clinton did not pressure Netanyahu to stop settlement expansion and to revive the Oslo process because he did not want a confrontation with Israel's supporters in the US Congress. His wait and see strategy left Netanyahu in the driver's seat. Unlike Bush, Clinton did not use American aid as leverage to extract concessions from Netanyahu. On the contrary, the Clinton administration continued to side with Israel in the United Nations, vetoing a Security Council resolution that could have condemned the construction of settlements in Arab East Jerusalem.

In October 1998, Clinton met with Netanyahu, Arafat, and King Hussein at the Conference Center of the Wye River Plantation, Maryland. A memorandum was signed to implement the Oslo agreement after several days of talks. Netanyahu agreed to withdraw from 13 percent of the West Bank in three stages, to transfer an additional 14 percent of land that was jointly controlled to the Palestinian Authority, and to open a Palestinian airport in Gaza as well as two corridors of safe passage between Gaza and the West Bank and an industrial zone between Israel and Gaza. In return, Arafat agreed to eliminate any reference to Israel's destruction from the Palestinian National Charter, to suppress violence, to reduce the number of Palestinian police, to arrest 30 Palestinian suspects wanted by Israel, and to collect illegal weapons. All parties agreed to let the CIA monitor Palestinian efforts to curtail

---

21   Smith, Document 11.2, 481–6; Jewish Virtual Library, "The Israeli-Palestinian Interim Agreement on the West Bank and Gaza"(Oslo II), 28 September 1995. http://www.us-israel.org/jsource/Peace/interim.html. For criticism of the Oslo Accords, see Edward W. Said, *The End of the Peace Process: Oslo and After* (New York: Pantheon Books, 2000), 14–19.

violence and promised to meet again to discuss remaining issues. In December, Clinton went to Gaza and witnessed the vote to remove all references to Israel's destruction from the Palestinian National Charter. His visit increased the legitimacy of the Palestinian Authority in the eyes of the international community and also improved its relationship with the US, which was instrumental in raising $3 billion in international pledges to aid the beleaguered Palestinian economy.[22]

Although the Wye River Memorandum was modest in what it accomplished, it did revive the stalled peace process. It soon became evident that Netanyahu had balked at implementing it. In early 1999, the resignations of several Israeli ministers, including defense and finance ministers, forced him to call new elections, which he lost. In May, the Labor Party returned to power, which pleased the White House. The new Prime minister, Ehud Barak, had pledged to pursue peace during his campaign. After a meeting with Arafat, he came to Washington in July to talk with Clinton about his hope to achieve a comprehensive peace agreement within 15 months. However, he made it clear that he would not agree to the partition of Jerusalem ant the Palestinian right of return to Israel.[23] Clinton proposed to deal directly with Arafat, who was in a weak bargaining position. In a meeting at Sharm al-Sheikh in September 1999, both Barak and Arafat agreed to complete an agreement within a year, an unrealistic deadline in view of the many hurdles to cross. All Israeli politicians—doves and hawks alike—have held to similar views on three issues: Jewish settlements, which they call neighborhoods, must remain as part of Israel; Jerusalem will never be divided again; and Palestinian refugees will have no right of return.

When Clinton's next initiative—the Camp David talks—got underway in July 2000, these three issues were the most contentious. There was tough bargaining but, with US prodding, the parties managed to narrow some differences. Israel was willing to give up most of the West Bank and the Palestinian Authority was ready to allow Israel to keep some settlements in the West Bank.[24] A stalemate was reached because of sharp disagreement over the Palestinian right of return and Jerusalem. The sticking point was the Al-Aqsa Mosque/Temple Mount Temple area, holy sites to both Muslims and Jews. As a compromise, Barak had suggested that the Palestinians could be "custodian" of the mosque but insisted that Israel retain sovereignty. Clinton stated that Barak's offer was reasonable and that Arafat should agree. On his part, Arafat proposed that Israel keep the Jewish Quarter, the Western Wall and Jewish

---

22   Freedman, "US Policy," 5–6; Jewish Virtual Library, The Wye River Memorandum, 23 October 1998. http://www.us-israel.org/jsource/Peace/wye.html.

23   Remarks and Joint Press Conference by President Clinton and Prime Minister Barak, 15 July 1999. http://www.us-israel.org/jsource/US-Israel/barakclinton- 71599.html.

24   Joshua Ruebner, Clyde Mark, Kenneth Katzman, and Alfred Prados, "The Current Palestinian Uprising: Al-Aqsa Intifadah," in *Israel: Current Issues and Historical Background*, edited by Edgar S. Marshall (New York: Nova Science Publishers, 2002), 2. Jewish Virtual Library, Trilateral Statement on the Middle East Peace Summit at Camp David, 25 July 2000.

settlements in East Jerusalem—areas that had been under Arab control prior to the 1967 war. His proposal was rejected.[25]

At this point, Clinton pressured Arafat to accept the Israeli offer, failing to realize the depth of the religious feelings held by Muslims about Al-Aqsa. When the Palestinian leader did not budge, Clinton publicly blamed Arafat for the failure of the summit. He even threatened to move the US Embassy to Jerusalem if an agreement was not reached before he left office in January 2001. Consequently, relations between the Palestinians and the US worsened and Clinton was once again accused of taking the side of Israel.[26]

With his presidency about to expire and his legacy as a peacemaker slipping away, Clinton decided to try one last time. He summoned the Israelis and Palestinians to the White House on 23 December 2000 and outlined his ideas for a final agreement. He proposed the establishment of a Palestinian state in Gaza and in 95 percent of the West Bank and Palestinian sovereignty over East Jerusalem neighborhoods and the top of Al-Aqsa Mosque. Israel would keep 5 percent of the West Bank in exchange for a tract of land in Israel's Negev Desert. In return, the Palestinians would give up the right of return.[27]

Barak was willing to use Clinton's proposals as a basis for discussion but would not consent to the transfer of sovereignty of the Temple Mount. The Israeli military also expressed concerns about security and pointed out that the Knesset and the prime minister's office would be "within the range of Palestinian mortar fire."[28]

Arafat also had some questions. The Clinton plan was marginally better than the one Arafat rejected at Camp David in July 2000 but Arafat was not sure that Barak would be around to implement any agreement. The Likud's party candidate, Ariel Sharon, was far ahead in the polls for the February elections. Because Arafat was not agreeable, Clinton sought the help of Arab leaders to pressure the Palestinian leader. They argued, instead, that the proposed settlement was weighted too heavily in favor of Israel.[29]

In February 2001, Barak lost the elections and Likud's candidate Ariel Sharon became the new prime minister. He told the Israelis to forget about peace agreements

---

25   Shibley Telhami, "Camp David II: Assumptions and Consequences," *Current History* (January 2001), 10. For Israel's Prime Minister Barak's proposal on Jerusalem, see Jewish Virtual Library, "The Proposed Division of Jerusalem, July 2000." http://www.us-israel.org/jsource/Peace/jerdivid.html.

26   Telhami, 10.

27   Douglas Waller, "A Bridge to Peace," *Time*, 8 January 2001, 42; Associated Press, "Clinton Gives Barak, Arafat Deadline on Plan," *Washington Post*, 26 December 2000. For more information, see David Makovsky and Eran Benedek, "The 5 Percent Solution," *Foreign Affairs* (September/October 2003), 26–7.

28   Waller, 42.

29   Ben Barber, "Sharon: No Peace Talks While Violence Continues," *Washington Times*, 25 January 2001; Lee Hockstader, "Sharon Set to Govern a Fearful Populace," *Washington Post*, 7 March 2001.

with the Palestinians.[30] He wanted to prolong Israeli occupation of the West Bank and Gaza, which would give Israel the upper hand in any negotiations. The Camp David talks had therefore collapsed. The second *intifada*, which was triggered by Sharon's visit to al-Aqsa Mosque in Jerusalem in September 2000 during his campaign, turned more violent after the talks ended. This was the situation when the new administration took office.

George W. Bush: Disengagement, then Advocacy

Upon gaining the US presidency, George W. Bush (the son of the former president, George H.W. Bush) had to decide whether to keep Clinton's momentum or, instead, to come up with a new approach. His administration was reluctant to play an active role in negotiations, fearing a repeat of Clinton's failure after eight years of talks. Arafat had already rejected Bush's recommendation, made after winning the 2000 elections, that Arafat accept Barak's proposed settlement.

At the same time Sharon, by then the Israeli Prime Minister, also turned his back on the peace process. He had never supported the process even when his party was in power. He had objected to the Camp David Accords, which swapped Sinai for peace with Egypt (1978), and to the Madrid Conference (1991). Once in office, Sharon reiterated that he would not abide by any concessions Barak had made and would not use Clinton's proposals as a framework for future talks—a position that was endorsed by Bush.[31] Sharon quickly abandoned his predecessor's policy of restraint and initiated a more aggressive military campaign to squash the Palestinian resistance to Israel's occupation.[32] His return to military tactics backfired, however, because it caused the Palestinians to respond in kind in order to raise the cost to Israel.[33] They escalated their own tactics, from throwing stones to launching mortar attacks on settlements, and eventually to suicide bombings inside Israel.

The Bush administration was divided on the best way to handle the problem. Secretary of State Colin Powell favored continued involvement and pressing Sharon to limit his military effort. On the other hand, Secretary of Defense Donald Rumsfeld and Vice President Richard Cheney wanted to back Sharon and to downgrade the

---

30   Ben Barber, "Sharon: No Peace Talks While Violence Continues," *Washington Times*, 25 January 2001; Lee Hockstader, "Sharon Set to Govern a Fearful Populace," *Washington Post*, 7 March 2001.

31   An interview with Israel's Prime Minister Ariel Sharon by Lally Weymouth, "A New Leader Makes New Directions," *Washington Post*, 11 March 2001; Robert O. Freeman, "The Bush Administration and the Arab-Israeli Conflict: the Record of Its First Four Years," *MERIA (Middle East Review of International Affairs)*, vol. 9, no. 1 (Spring 2005), 2.

32   Editorial, "Mideast Escalation," *Washington Post*, 19 April 2001; Daniel Williams, "Old Tactics, Get New Life Under Sharon," *Washington Post*, 21 April 2001.

33   "Sharon's Israel," *Economist*, 10 February 2001, 20.

peace process to give more attention to Saddam Hussein.[34] Bush chose the latter, and his administration began a retreat from mediating the Israeli-Palestinian conflict. In March 2001, it terminated the CIA's security role in the occupied territories, which had defused tension and fostered cooperation between the Israelis and Palestinians. This decision was made despite Arafat's personal appeal to Powell the month before. Bush also was in no hurry to assemble his team of experts on the Middle East, including a replacement for US special envoy, Dennis B. Ross, who resigned in January 2001. Nor did he commit his administration to a full implementation of the Mitchell Report to end the violence and restart the peace process.[35] This hands-off US approach gave Sharon a great deal of latitude and allowed him to reoccupy areas controlled by the Palestinian authority and to build up new settlements in the occupied territories.

Bush's supportive treatment of Sharon sharply contrasted with his approach to Arafat. During Bush's first six months in office, he talked with Arafat only twice on the phone and refused to meet with him despite pleas from Arab governments. In contrast, he met with Sharon many times in the Oval Office and often talked by telephone. He closely coordinated his policy with Sharon and Israeli officials, and lobbyists had ready access to the White House. Bush even called Sharon a "man of peace" with complete disregard to his long history of violence against Palestinians.[36]

On 27 March 2001, the US voted against a UN Security Council resolution that would send UN observers to separate the two parties and stop the upsurge in violence in the occupied territories. The Bush administration sided with Israel and ignored pleas from the Palestinians and from Arab governments. The US also split with its European allies, who abstained on this vote. The resolution had the necessary nine votes for passage, but the US, as a permanent member, used its veto power.[37] The following day, Arab governments criticized the American veto and reiterated their support for the land for peace formula.[38]

The policy tilt was striking. Bush's policy became almost identical with Israel's. He endorsed Sharon's position that there be no negotiations as long as the violence

---

34   Richard Cohen, "The Undoing of Mideast Diplomacy," *Washington Post*, 19 April 2001.

35   Editorial, "The Middle East Vacuum," *Washington Post*, 3 March 2001, Alan Sipress and Vernon Leob, "Bush Ends CIA's Role as Middle East Broker," *Washington Post*, 22 March 2001. For Mitchell Report, see US Department of State, Office of International Information Programs, "Sharm El-Sheikh Fact-Finding Committee Final Report," 30 April 2001. http://www.usinfo.state.gov/regional/nea/mitchell.htm

36   Glenn Kessler, "Bush Sticks to the Broad Strokes," *Washington Post*, 3 June 2003; Glenn E. Robinson, "Israel and the Palestinians: The Bitter Fruits of Hegemonic Peace," *Current History* (January 2001) 17.

37   Edith M. Lederer, "US Vetoes UN Observer Force to Protect Palestinians," *Washington Post*, 28 March 2001.

38   Howard Schneider, "Arabs Pledge," *Washington Post*, 29 March 2001.

continued.[39] He also expected the Palestinian leadership to stop the violence or, if the violence continued, to be marginalized. Bush thus ignored the lessons of the first *Intifada* that such an uprising has a momentum of its own and feeds upon itself. Israel's military had not quelled the first uprising, despite high Palestinian casualties, until Oslo I was concluded in 1993. As Mohammed Dahlan, then chief of security of Gaza, pointed out, "No one can fully control the reactions of a mass of people who are angry."[40]

When the violence escalated, Arab leaders appealed to Washington to help end the hostilities. In early April, Egypt's President Hosni Mubarak and Jordan's King Abdullah met separately with Bush in the White House and urged him to get involved.[41] Egypt's Foreign Minister Amr Mousa was more specific, calling on Washington to draw "a road map" of security and economic measures that might lead to renewed peace talks. He stressed that the Israeli-Palestinian conflict "could not be resolved unless the United States played the role of honest broker."[42]

In response, Bush only agreed to facilitate talks but not to force a peace on the reluctant parties.[43] During the same month, the US Ambassador to Israel arranged several meetings between the Israelis and the Palestinians to renew cooperation on security. Additionally, the Bush administration urged Sharon to consider the Jordanian-Egyptian proposals, which called for an end to Palestinian violence, a halt in settlement building, withdrawal of Israeli troops, and lifting the blockade of Palestinian-ruled areas. Raanan Gissin, a spokesman for Israel's Prime Minister, called the proposals "a non-starter."[44] As a result, like other peace initiatives, nothing came out of it.

Bush's general strategy—to keep his distance from the Middle East conflict—continued. He let Powell urge the Israeli and Palestinian leaders to reduce violence, but left the details of the timing and scope of negotiations to them and their neighbors (i.e. Egypt and Jordan). This approach created a vacuum, however, and led the Arab League Summit to call on the European Union to play "a more active role."[45]

---

39   Jane Perlez, "Bush and Sharon Find Much in Common," *New York Times International*, 21 March 2001.

40   Deborah Sontag, "In Absence of Talks, Israeli-Palestinian Violence Speaks," *New York Times*, 4 April 2001.

41   An interview with Egypt's President Hosni Mubarak by Lally Weymouth, "Jerusalem Can Stop Everything," *Washington Post*, 1 April 2001; Marc Lacey, "Mubrak Urges Strong US Role on Mideast," *New York Times International*, 3 April 2001; Dana Millbank, "US Vows to Pursue Jordanian Trade Pact, Bush Won't Pledge Increased Mideast Role," *Washington Post*, 11 April 2001.

42   Dana Millbank and Alan Sipress, "Events Abroad Pus Bush Administration," *Washington Post*, 3 April 2001.

43   Ibid.

44   Daniel Williams, "Israel Balks at a Jordanian Peace Proposal," *Washington Post*, 17 April 2001.

45   Howard Schneider, "Jordanian Will Ask Bush to Expand Mideast Role," *Washington post*, 4 February 2001.

The terrorist attacks on the World Trade Center and the Pentagon, on 11 September 2001, had a major impact on American attitudes toward the Middle East. Several American groups — including Jewish organizations and evangelical Christians — also used the tragic events to pressure the White House to support Sharon's tough campaign against the Palestinians. In November, eighty-nine senators urged Bush to let Israel use "all [its] strength and might" to deal with Palestinian terrorism. The previous April, House Majority Leader Tom Delay (R-Texas) had told a Jewish group in Washington that Israel should keep Judea and Samaria, using the Likud Party's terms for the West Bank.[46]

11 September put the White House in a crisis mode and resulted in a significant reversal in US foreign policy. Bush greatly increased his attention to US security and solicited help from other nations for a war on terrorism. He adopted strident new language that divided the world into "good and evil," insisting that other nations are "either with us or against us." Israel, as America's most reliable ally, was naturally "with us." By the same logic the Palestinians were "against us." Bush accepted the new Israeli argument that America's war against al-Qaeda is no different than Israel's fight against Palestinian terror. He thus defended Sharon's crackdown on Palestinians on the ground that Israel has the right to defend itself. According to Stansfield Turner, a former CIA director, Bush "incorporated the Palestinian Intifada into the global war he declared on terrorism."[47]

The Bush administration also turned mute on Sharon's "security fence," which is being built along the length of the West Bank. Much like the Berlin Wall, it will encircle Palestinian areas, separate cities, and disrupt transportation. This fence, along with settlements and roads already in the West Bank, will make it impossible to create a viable Palestinian state.

Although Bush insisted that initiatives must come from the region, he was not helpful when, in April 2002, Saudi Arabia's Crown Prince Abdullah presented him a proposal for an international conference and a comprehensive peace based on trading land for peace and normalizing relations between Israel and its Arab neighbors. Like Clinton, he proposed the creation of a Palestinian state with Jerusalem serving as the capitals of the two states, with joint authority over religious areas and airspace, and a pledge not to wage military action against each other. Abdullah proposed that the refugee question be settled on the basis of UN Security Council Resolution 194, which called for repatriation, compensation, and rehabilitation.[48]

Sharon opposed the right-of-return, insisting that the Palestinian state be the home of all Palestinians just as Israel is the home to all Jews. He also was a staunch

---

46   Robert Kaiser, "Bush and Sharon Nearly Identical on Mideast Policy," *Washington Post*, 9 February 2003. http://www.washingtonpost.com/ac2/wp-dyn/A45652-2003feb8?lang auge=printer.

47   Stansfield Turner, "The Critical Nature of US Policy in the Middle East," *Mediterranean Quarterly*, vol. 14, no. 4 (Fall 2003), 53.

48   Anthony N. Celso, "The Death of the Oslo Accords: Israeli Security Options in the Post-Arafat Era," *Mediterranean Quarterly*, vol. 14, no. 1 (Winter 2003), 75.

advocate of building and expanding settlements in the occupied territories. During this first two years in office, seventy new settlements were erected in the West Bank and existing ones were substantially expanded.[49]

The Bush administration offered only muted criticism of Israeli actions, and Washington's calls for Sharon to stop his military offensives were routinely ignored without any consequence. A dramatic example occurred in April 2002, when Israel attacked Arafat's compound in Ramallah, which had been under the Palestinian Authority since 1995, and surrounded his headquarters with tanks and armored cars. Secretary Powell asked Sharon to "consider the consequences" of his actions and to limit civilian casualties but White House officials made it clear that there was no plan "to restrain or launch any initiative to halt the violence."[50] However, when the Bush administration realized that Arab support for the war on terrorism was waning, it supported the UN Security Council's call for Israeli withdrawal from Ramallah, and pressured Israel to end its siege of Arafat's headquarters and to pull its forces from key West Bank towns.[51] Even so, Bush still told Arafat and Arab leaders to "do a lot more" to stop Palestinian terror in response to criticism by the Israelis and their American supporters that he was getting soft on terrorism.[52]

In contrast, Bush actively joined Sharon's effort to isolate Arafat. They both accused Arafat of complicity with militant Palestinians and blamed him for not ending the violence, even though Israel's frequent military incursions had also failed to stamp it out. Arafat had been left with no means to fight or restrain militants. Israeli military operations had systematically decimated his security forces, weakened his administration, and destroyed the Palestinian economy.

On 24 June 2002, Bush delivered a major speech that emphasized steps that the Palestinians must take to revive the peace process. He called for a provisional Palestinian state, but made his backing conditional upon removing Arafat and electing a new leader who must renounce violence and reform Palestinian institutions. The implementation of his plan depended on a lessening of violence. Such developments would lead to a freeze on new settlements, withdrawal of Israeli troops to areas held prior to 28 September 2000 and removing restrictions on Palestinian movement.[53]

Bush envisioned a Palestinian state with a democratic government and a free-market economy. A new constitution should be drafted, to include separation of powers, an independent judiciary, and a new security system. Such reforms were laudable but hard to achieve while Palestinian cities and towns were under siege or

---

49   "It's the Settlement, Stupid," *Economist*, 17 May 2003, 10.

50   Romesh Ratnesar, "Season of Revenge, The Inside Story of How Israel Imprisoned Arafat—And Why the Rage Keeps Burning," *Time*, 8 April 2002, 31.

51   Celso, 75–6.

52   Ratnesar, 31.

53   Nicholas A. Veliotes, "The Bush 'Vision' for Palestine: Realistic or Apocalyptic?," *Mediterranean Quarterly*, vol. 13, no. 4 (Fall 2002), 11; "George Bush's Peace Plan," *Economist*, 29 June 2002, 11; "Bush Peace Plan on the Middle East, 24 June 2002. www. whitehouse.gov/news/releases/2002/06/20020624-3html.

military occupation.[54] Bush criticized the Palestinian violence but made no mention of Israel's crackdown on Palestinians, including demolition of homes, assassination of militant leaders, and killing of civilians. His speech showed no recognition that a major cause of violence was the occupation of the West Bank and Gaza and the failure to create a Palestinian state. In fact, the Israeli military has killed far more Palestinian civilians than the number of Israeli citizens killed by suicide bombers.

There was a strong reaction to Bush's June speech. It was widely interpreted as if Bush was advocating a coup against Arafat. Bush's interference spurred a backlash among Palestinians and renewed support for Arafat, who won election easily. Some analysts accused Bush of abandoning rather than advancing the peace process. He was seen as placing all burdens on the Palestinians and none on the Israelis to avoid any political risks at home. His speech was welcomed by the Israelis and their American supporters. It was a victory for the administration's hard-liners in the Pentagon. In December 2002 he appointed Elliott Abrams, an opponent of the peace process and a strong supporter of Israel, to handle the Middle East at the National Security Council. He thus joined other pro-Likud officials, including his mentor Richard Perle, chairman of the Pentagon's Defense Policy Board, Douglas J. Feith, Undersecretary of Defense, and David Wurmser, a special assistant to the Undersecretary for Arms Control. Three of these officials had participated in a 1996 study suggesting that Prime Minister Netanyahu reject the Oslo accords and the UN principle of trading land for peace. In their view, "Israel should insist on Arab recognition of its claim to the biblical land of Israel."[55] With these officials in key policy-making positions, James Zogby of the Arab-American Institute wondered whether the administration "is losing its ability to act as an honest broker in the Middle East."[56]

In 2003, Bush was preoccupied with Iraq and his plan to wage war against Saddam Hussein. Although he failed to persuade Arab governments to join his war efforts—as they had done in 1991—he still needed their support to contain anti-American demonstrations when the war broke out. As a way to convince reluctant leaders, he pledged to "dedicate himself to resolving the Israeli-Palestinian conflict" once the war was over.[57]

After a period of uncertainty, Arafat offered to comply with Bush's demands in his June speech if Israel would withdraw from reoccupied cities and towns. The US quickly rejected this offer. Arafat then came under pressure from Egypt and Saudi Arabia to agree to power sharing in order to revive the dormant peace process. He already faced criticism for his autocratic style and accusations of corruption within

---

54   International Crisis Group (ICG), "Middle East Endgame I: Getting to a Comprehensive Arab-Israeli Peace Settlement," *IGC Middle East Report*, no. 2 (16 July 2002), 2.

55   Kaiser.

56   Ibid.

57   Massimo Calabresi et al, "How Bush Got Religion," *Time*, 16 June 2003, 27 (Special Edition, Pearson/Prentice Hall, World Politics).

his administration. When some members of the Palestinian Legislative Council called for democratic reforms, Arafat had no choice. On April 29, Mahmoud Abbas, Secretary-General of the PLO Executive Committee, became the prime minister in charge of administering the Palestinian areas. Abbas was known to favor reform and had publicly spoken against violence.[58] His appointment paved the way for getting the peace process back on track.

During the same month Sharon, who once argued vehemently against permitting a Palestinian state, said that the US victory in Iraq had created an "opportunity for Middle East peacemaking which we mustn't let slip by." He was ready to make "painful concessions" for the sake of a lasting peace. He admitted, "some settlements would have to go to make way for a Palestinian state, which, realistically speaking would eventually come into being."[59]

With the Israelis on board and a new Palestinian leader in place, the British Prime Minister, Tony Blair, urged Bush to announce the peace initiative that had been drafted in December by the US, the European Union, Russia, and the United Nations. On 30 April 2003 with great rhetoric, Bush unfolded the "Road Map" to a two-state solution, which called upon Israelis and Palestinians to take parallel steps in three phases that would lead to the creation of an independent Palestinian state by 2005.

The first phase called on Palestinians to end violence and to resume Israeli-Palestinian cooperation on security. The rebuilding of Palestinian security forces would be overseen by the US and assisted by an oversight board that included Egypt and Jordan. Israel must undertake "no actions undermining trust, including deportations, attacks on civilians ... [or] destruction of Palestinian institutions or infrastructure,"[60] withdraw military forces from the West Bank and Gaza, dismantle settlement outposts erected since March 2001 (when Sharon became prime minister) and freeze all settlement construction activities, including the so-called natural growth of settlements.[61] The second phase called for the creation of "an independent Palestinian state with provisional borders and attributes of sovereignty" by the end of 2003.[62] During the third and last phase, negotiations would be completed and a full independent Palestinian state would be established by 2005.[63]

Bush now made the Road Map the cornerstone of his policy. Palestinians were the first to accept the plan, while Sharon initially declined because some members of his coalition opposed key provisions of the plan. Pro-settler factions—the National Union and the National Religious Party—threatened to resign from the cabinet and

---

58   "After You." "No After You," *Economist*, 12 April 2003, 43.

59   "A Moderate Spin," *Economist*, 19 April 2003, 41.

60   David Ignatius, "The Deadly Price of Resisting the Road Map," *Washington Post*, 20 May 2003.

61   "A Moderate Spin," 41.

62   "Dusting It Off, Perhaps," *Economist*, 22 March 2003, 23.

63   Molly Moore and John Ward Anderson, "Bombings in Israel Undercut Peace Talks," *Washington Post*, 19 May 2003.

bring down the government if Sharon accepted the peace plan.[64] As Israel's Foreign Minister Silvan Shalom argued, "the Palestinians must curb terrorism and stop all incitement. Only after a long period of quiet would Israel's obligations kick in, including the settlement freeze."[65]

The Israeli government had nearly 100 reservations about the plan. During the first two weeks of May, Sharon made several statements that revealed his intention to undermine the peace initiative. Substantive changes were proposed. First, he stated that the peace process should not move forward unless the Palestinians renounce the right of return. Second, he rejected any dismantling of settlements. As he put it, the building of new settlements and the expansion of the old ones are "a delicate issue that should come up in the final phase of negotiations. We should not have to deal with it now."[66] His critics accused him of using delaying tactics to gain time to further expand settlements. He also argued that Palestinians should go ahead to disarm militant groups, even while the Israelis continued their military re-occupation of Palestinian cities. By inserting a word here and a phrase there, he deleted any reference to parallel measures by Israel. As the Israeli opposition commented, Sharon's revisions "will mean no movement at all; beyond the moderate spin, the substance remains as unyielding as ever."[67]

In early May, US Secretary of State Powell went to the region to drum up support for the peace plan. He met with Sharon but was unable to get his endorsement of the Road Map. In his meeting with Abbas, Powell urged him to move against militant factions to end the violence.

On 17 May 2003 Abbas and Sharon met. It was the first high-ranking meeting in two years and was described as "constructive and serious." According to Raanan Gissin, Sharon's spokesman, the two leaders agreed that "stopping terrorism is essential to any kind of progress."[68] Abbas pointed out that "for Israel to get security," they had to cease the assassination of Palestinian leaders and invasions into Palestinian areas.[69] He also stressed that the implementation of security measures depended on Israel's acceptance of the Road Map.

Soon after the Abbas-Sharon meeting, a wave of suicide bombings struck Hebron, Jerusalem, Afula, and Kafr Darom, lasting two days and killing 12 Israelis. Sharon immediately canceled his scheduled May meeting with Bush and re-imposed a travel ban and curfews on the West Bank and Jordan Valley. Some cabinet members called for the expulsion of Arafat from the West Bank but Sharon did not support the idea

---

64   Ibid.

65   "After You," 43.

66   "A Moderate Spin," 41.

67   Ibid.

68   John Ward Anderson, "Jerusalem Suicide Bombing Kills 7, Sharon Cancels Planned Visit to Washington," *Washington Post*, 18 May 2003.

69   Ibid.

under pressure from the White House.[70] The Israeli government decided not to hold meetings with foreign visitors if they had met with Arafat.[71]

The suicide bombings shocked the US. The White House condemned the attacks and announced that terrorism would not deter American commitment to the peace process. Secretary of State Powell called on "the Palestinians to begin to take immediate and decisive action to eradicate the infrastructure of terrorism."[72]

Sharon was confident that Bush would continue his strong support for Israel. Israel's supporters, with their money and enormous influence in Washington, could press Israel's position, especially as elections approached. President Bush needed to raise millions of dollars for his reelection campaign and he also needed Jewish votes to secure a second term in the White House. In fact, Bush was under pressure from two key constituencies—Jewish groups and evangelical Christians—to forget about his peace plan because it "could lead to disaster." Gary Bauer, a conservative Christian leader, wrote to Bush that any attempt to be "evenhanded" between Israelis and Palestinians would be "morally reprehensible."[73] Republican Congressional leaders, worried about their own reelections, also criticized the Road Map, saying that it "is flawed and would undercut Israeli security with its call for parallel steps by Israel to ease its military occupation of Palestinian territory even as it demands that Palestinians move to end terrorist violence."[74]

American and Israeli officials argued that Palestinian militants were using suicide bombing to sabotage the peace process. Yet, by rejecting the Road Map, Sharon was also derailing the prospects for peace. With Israel's frequent military incursions in Gaza and in the West Bank, and with continuing damage to the Palestinian economy, no leader could end the *Intifada* without having a viable peace plan to show that there was a better alternative than violence. Abbas did not want to start his term facing a civil war at home, but he faced a constant challenge to deal with the consequences of Israel's lethal strikes against Palestinian civilians and property. For Abbas to be able to reform the Palestinian Authority, he needed an end to Palestinian violence but also to show progress on withdrawing Israeli troops from the West Bank and Gaza.

For several weeks, the peace process was in limbo. Britain and Russia, who were US partners in the peace initiative, urged Bush to use his leverage with Israel to rescue the Road Map from collapse. They believed that because Bush is a staunch supporter of Israel, he was the only leader who could persuade Sharon to give peace a chance. He had given Israel over $100 million to fight terrorism at home and had gotten rid of Saddam Hussein. Some observers believed that "if Bush prods

---

70   Moore and Anderson; Massimo Calabresi at al, "Facing Reality," *Time*, 22 September 2003, 23 (Special Edition, Pearson/Prentice Hall, *World Politics*).

71   Karen de Young, "Bush: Peace Bid Will Go Forward," *Washington Post*, 20 May 2003.

72   Moore and Anderson.

73   De Young.

74   Ibid.

hard enough," Sharon would accept the Road Map because "he cannot afford to jeopardize his ties with America."[75]

Sharon resisted the American effort to reschedule his meeting with Bush. To avoid pressure to accept the Road Map without major revision, he decided to stay home and bargain from a distance, allowing more time to consult with his coalition members. After lengthy, long-distance haggling, the US agreed to "fully and seriously" address Israeli concerns during the implementation stage. On 23 May 2003, with US assurances given, Sharon accepted "the steps set out in the Road Map" and two days later, Israel's cabinet endorsed it.[76]

Following Israel's conditional acceptance, American officials hurriedly arranged two summits in the Middle East. As the National Security Advisor Condoleezza Rice explained, "the Israelis and Palestinians will directly negotiate the details of an arrangement between themselves." Because Bush argued that "any lasting arrangement is going to need the support of the neighbors," he met with Abbas and the leaders of Egypt, Bahrain, Jordan, and Saudi Arabia on June 3, in Sharm El-Sheikh, to line up regional support for his peace plan. Bush gave assurances of his personal commitment to "establishing a Palestinian state that is free and at peace" and secured their pledge to cease supporting militant Palestinian groups. To address Arab skepticism, he stressed Israel's responsibility to deal with the settlements as outlined in the Road Map and that "Israel must make sure there is a continuous territory that the Palestinians call home." He avoided addressing other contentious issues, which had scuttled Clinton's peace initiative. As Secretary Powell put it, "we will get to each and every one of them in due time."[77]

The following day, Bush met with both Sharon and Abbas in Aqaba, Jordan. He urged them to end the cycle of violence, which had claimed the lives of more than 2,000 Palestinians and 780 Israelis over a thirty-two month period. He nudged both leaders to take steps to improve the climate for meaningful dialogue. Abbas promised to end violence, while Sharon pledged to ease Israeli control over Palestinian areas, to dismantle unauthorized outposts, and to negotiate in good faith on the creation of a Palestinian state. As the *Washington Post* put it, "each of the concessions was limited and carefully worded and did not fully satisfy the other side."[78]

At the summit, Sharon made no statement about implementing the Road Map. He showed no inclination to remove all the settlement outposts it required, nor did he agree to withdraw troops from the West Bank and Gaza. Furthermore, he made no commitment to the creation of a Palestinian state by 2005, as the Road Map had stipulated. He only endorsed the establishment of a Palestinian state, with its nature,

---

75   "After You," 43.

76   Harvey Morris and James Guy Dinmore, "Israel Set to Accept 'road map' for Peace," *Financial Times*, 24 May 2003; Joel Brinkley, "Tentatively, Israel Accepts Peace Plan," *Herald Tribune* (International), 24 May 2003.

77   Mike Allen and Glenn Kessler, "Five Arab Leaders Denounce Violence, Bush Vows to Pursue a Palestinian State," *Washington Post*, 4 June 2003, A18.

78   Mike Allen and Glenn Kessler, "Sharon and Abbas Vow Moves to End Violence," *Washington Post*, 5 June 2003.

size, and boundaries to be determined later. His spokesman Raanan Gissin commented that "a political solution is a long process; it does not happen in one generation."[79] If it were up to Sharon, a Palestinian state would look like a "Bantustan," a state with no sovereignty, no viable economy, and no territorial contiguity. As Sharon had put it in December 2002:

> This Palestinian state will be completely demilitarized. It will be allowed to maintain lightly armed police and interior forces to ensure civil order. Israel will continue to control all entries and exits to the Palestinian state, will command its airspace, and not allow it to form alliances with Israel's enemies.[80]

In June 2004, after meeting with Sharon in the White House, Bush backtracked on earlier pledges to Arab leaders, announcing that the Palestinian right of return is null and void based on the facts on the ground. In the end President Bush had come full circle to adopt his predecessor's stance on the issue, a shift made for political reasons in an election year and at a time when he faced a growing criticism of the Iraq war. His action was designed to line up support from evangelical Christians, who are diehard supporters of Israel's claim of biblical land, including the West Bank. It also sought to attract a larger share of Jewish votes than he received in the 2000 election. By the end of his first term, Bush had failed to push the Road Map forward and there was an almost complete absence of US involvement.

Recently, two events persuaded the Bush administration to revisit the Middle East problem. The first was the death of Arafat in November 2004, which accomplished Bush's demand for new Palestinian leadership. Arafat's departure paved the way for a democratic election to choose a new head of the Palestinian Authority. In January 2005, Abbas was elected by a comfortable margin in a competitive election. He also is acceptable to both Bush and Sharon because, as a former prime minister, he had demonstrated his commitment to both reform and the suppression of terrorism.[81]

The second event was Sharon's unilateral decision to withdraw Israeli troops from Gaza and some parts of the West Bank. It has been very costly for Israel to protect 7,000 settlers in Gaza. Sharon was able to weather a storm of opposition to this decision from the far right members of his coalition. With the support of the Labor Party, he gained the Knesset's endorsement but caused a split in his own party and angered supporters in both Israel and the US To appease his opponents, he announced a plan to expand the large Ma'ale Adumim settlement and to connect it to Jerusalem.[82] During his visit to the US in May 2005, he told American Jewish organizations that there will never be a right of return for Palestinians.

---

79   Glenn Kessler, "Carefully Drafted remarks Avoid Political Land Mines," *Washington Post*, 5 June 2003.

80   Allen and Kessler, "Sharon and Abbas."

81   "Exit Arafat," *Economist*, 13 November 2004, 11; "A New Man, a New Chance," *Economist*, 8 January 2005, 10.

82   "Another Shove," *Economist*, 9 April 2005, 11–12.

Bush welcomed Sharon's move as a sign of progress toward the Road Map. In February 2005, the new Secretary of State Condoleezza Rice, during her first visit to London, was urged to renew US involvement in the peace process. The following month, she attended a British-sponsored conference on the Palestinian situation. The Israelis, however, did not attend. In late May, Bush met with Abbas in the White House and promised to give $50 million directly to the Palestinian Authority for housing and infrastructure projects in Gaza. Bush, for the first time, stated that the final status of the West Bank, Gaza, and Jerusalem will be determined through negotiations. He called on Israel to refrain from taking any unilateral action that would undercut the prospects of a peaceful settlement.[83] However, he was not responsive to Abbas' plea to restart the peace process.

Conclusion

Since the early 1990s, every US administration has tried to deal with the Arab-Israeli conflict, but their efforts have been complicated by the stark contrast between the tough US approach toward Iraq and its "soft" policy toward Israel. With both countries, there were continuing issues over their compliance with UN Security Council resolutions. Yet, contradictions in how Washington treated their non-compliance has led to Washington being accused of a double standard. It also fueled the rise of anti-American sentiment across the region and the emergence of al-Qaeda's terror campaign against the US. The repercussions of the contradictory US policy have posed new threats to American security.

After the 1991 Gulf War, President George H.W. Bush attempted to address the disparity in treatment between Iraq and Israel. In recognition of Arab contributions to the Gulf War, he initiated an even-handed approach to the Israeli- Palestinian conflict. His shift, which was a temporary break from the traditional US policy of outright support to Israel, led to Palestinian participation in the Madrid Conference in 1991. Their inclusion gave the Palestinians legitimacy and made them a viable partner in the peace process.

Bush's successor, Bill Clinton, did not maintain this evenhandedness. Instead, he returned to a one-sided policy in favor of Israel. During his first six months in office, Clinton refused to meet with PLO representatives, while Congress continued to insist on excluding the PLO from peace talks. This happened at a time when Israelis and the PLO were secretly meeting in search of a formula to start the peace process. Their talks in Oslo, without US involvement, led to a major breakthrough, the signing of a "Declaration of Principles" in 1993. Later, despite good intentions and several efforts, Clinton could not get Prime Minister Netanyahu to implement the Wye Memorandum of October 1998. During his last six months in office, Clinton tried to reach a comprehensive peace agreement but could not bridge the gaps on such highly contentious issues as Jerusalem and the Palestinian right of return. Nor

---

83   Andrea Stone, "President Backs Palestinians, Warns Israel about Expansion," *USA Today*, 27 May 2005.

did he serve as an honest broker, advocating for both sides. Instead, as a senior State Department official put it, "what we ended up doing was advocating Israel's positions before, during, and after the [Camp David] summit."[84]

Thus Clinton, and after him, President George W. Bush, continued to use a double standard by not insisting that Israel abide by their obligations under the UN charter, especially to comply with UN Security Council resolutions regarding the occupied territories. US administrations have taken a pro-Israel policy and disregarded Palestinian rights to self-determination. Domestic politics have been a decisive factor. There are many constituencies for Israel in the US Most important are American conservative groups and far-right Christians, who have a hold on the Republican Party through campaign contributions and voting power, especially in close elections. The Republicans also have tried to lure Jewish voters away from the Democratic Party. In addition, the powerful Israeli lobby, the American Israel Public Affairs Committee (AIPAC), has strongly influenced US policy because of its access to both the executive and legislative branches of government.

In contrast to the treatment of Israel previous US presidents took a tough stance on Iraq's non-compliance with UN Security Council resolutions. Clinton actively pursued the ouster of Saddam Hussein, using non-military methods. The president fomented religious and ethnic tensions by providing funds and training to the Kurds in the north to help them rise against the regime in Baghdad, while millions of dollars were allocated to support Iraqi opposition groups, which might bring a change of regime in Iraq. In addition, Clinton enforced the no-fly zones set up by George H.W. Bush by hitting back when Iraqi planes entered these areas; he also used the US military to ensure that UN sanctions were forcefully implemented. George W. Bush, even before 9/11, had planned to use force to overthrow Saddam Hussein and had instructed the CIA and Pentagon officials to find evidence to justify a war on Iraq. After the 9/11 terrorist attacks, he tried to tie Saddam Hussein to al-Qaeda but, when this failed, Bush did not want to give more time to UN inspectors to find and destroy any weapons of mass destruction (WMD) in Iraq. When he could not receive the UN Security Council's approval, he put a coalition together and went to war. Arab governments did not support the invasion of Iraq and, in private, pointed out the discrepancy in the US dealings with Iraq and Israel. The dominant modus operandi has been for US administrations to closely coordinate their policies with Israeli governments, but also to be reluctant to pressure them to implement the agreements they signed. US presidents have avoided any confrontation with Israel's supporters on Capitol Hill or among Israel's key constituencies. For example, Netanyahu ignored Clinton's pressure to implement the Oslo Accords. His failure effectively froze the peace process for over a year. According to a Middle East scholar, Charles D. Smith, "Jerry Falwell's Moral Majority and Pat Robertson's Christian Coalition were staunch supporters of Israel's retention of the [occupied] territories and lobbied Congress on Netanyahu's behalf."[85]

---

84   Aaron David Miller, "Israel's Lawyer," *Washington Post*, 23 May 2005.

85   Smith, 458.

George W. Bush's initial strategy—making strong declarations followed by retreat—did not end the violence or advance the cause of peace between Israel and the Palestinians. His refusal to get personally involved and the limited US involvement served Sharon's agenda, which was to prolong the occupation as a way to allow for building a security fence and for settlement expansion in the West Bank and Gaza, thus creating new facts that will favor Israel in future negotiations. After the terrorist attacks on New York and Washington on 9/11, George W. Bush adopted a harsh approach to Iraq, insisting on quick actions, leading an invasion, and then occupying the country. His approach to Israel also changed after 9/11 but it with the administration selecting took a much softer style. Bush's policy became largely identical to Sharon's as he aligned the US more strongly with Israel. Bush agreed with Sharon that violence is violence, whether it is directed against the Americans or the Israelis. Bush turned a blind eye on Israel's crackdown on Palestinians and blamed Arafat for the violence. They both agreed that talks not be resumed until violence ended and Arafat was gone. Although Bush had promised Arab governments that he would get personally involved to work for peace in the Middle East after Saddam Hussein was removed, he failed to follow up on the Road Map, which had been drawn by the US, Britain, the EU, Russia, and the UN Arafat's sudden death and the election of Abbas in January 2005 as the head of the Palestinian authority provided a new opportunity to move the peace process forward, but neither Bush nor Sharon has been in a hurry to restart it.

The US effort will fail as long as the Palestinians are not treated as a full partner in the peace process. Unlike the Israelis, they are not consulted ahead of time. Nor do they participate in give and take sessions, such as those that are held between American and Israeli officials. These sessions often agree on a package behind closed doors that is later offered to the Palestinians as a fait accompli, with no room for negotiations.

At present, there is little prospect of a lasting peace in the Middle East. The peace process is at a standstill despite the progress made during the 1990s. Recent history indicates that the US is the only power that can bring the parties together, yet, the lack of a strong US push for peace is not helping to defuse tension and the Israelis and Palestinians are locked in a no-win situation. The current situation poses a real danger because the US influence is at its lowest point in the Arab world. Bush's support for Israel's policies has helped al-Qaeda to promote its radical ideology and find new recruits to spread terror and undermine American interests in a highly volatile, but strategic region.

It is not enough for Bush to lay out the Road Map he decided to intervene personally to promote a peaceful solution to the decades-long conflict that has caused death and suffering too many Israelis and Palestinians. Violence will not end unless the US acts as an honest broker, with a policy that is independent from Israel. Aaron David Miller, a US career diplomat who served as a Middle East negotiator, warned that the traditional US policy of "run[ning] everything by Israel first, stripped our policy of the independence and flexibility required for serious peacemaking." He also pointed out that "when we have used our diplomacy wisely and functioned as advocates and lawyers for both sides, we have succeeded."[86] President Carter used this approach in mediating the Camp David Accords (1978) between Egypt and Israel; Secretary of State Baker employed it to bring all the parties to the Madrid Conference (1991). The Bush administration has a real opportunity to conclude peace, but only if it will become advocate for both Israelis and Palestinians. This is a large order, considering that the Bush administration has so far been reluctant to pressure Israel to implement the Road Map.

---

86   Miller.

PART III
The Military Dimensions

Chapter 8

From Containment to the Bush Doctrine: The Road to War with Iraq

Cameron G. Thies,
Louisiana State University

Introduction

An uneasy peace emerged in the Middle East at the conclusion of *Operation Desert Storm* in February of 1991. The United States and its coalition partners had succeeded in driving Iraq's military from Kuwait. However, rather than continuing the war by marching on Baghdad to remove Saddam Hussein from power, President George H. W. Bush declared an end to this phase of the military campaign. The uprisings he had encouraged among the Kurds in the north and the Shiites in the south to accomplish regime change were ruthlessly crushed by Hussein. Containment of Hussein's Iraq emerged as official US policy, though the strategic details of its implementation would change under the Clinton administration, only to be replaced again by rollback during George W. Bush's presidency.

This study traces the history of US foreign policy toward Iraq between the First and Second Gulf Wars. It begins with a brief history of US foreign policy in the Persian Gulf region after the exodus of the British in 1971 through the first Gulf War. It proceeds to describe the policy of containment implemented by George H. W. Bush, followed by changes introduced during the Clinton administration that produced the "dual" containment policy. It also describes the debate in the foreign policy establishment that surrounded containment of Iraq prior to September 11, 2001. The study then analyzes the impact of those tragic events on the formulation and application of the foreign policy doctrine of George W. Bush. In hindsight, the change from containment to rollback does not seem quite as startling as it did when it was announced as part of the war on terrorism. The study concludes with some speculation on the impact of the Bush Doctrine on the future of the Persian Gulf region and the Israeli-Palestinian peace process.

Containing Iraq

As British power and influence declined in the Middle East, culminating with the withdrawal of all remaining forces in 1971, the United States emerged as the dominate external power responsible for regional security and order. US policy was premised on the notion of maintaining a regional balance of power that would prevent any one state from achieving regional hegemony. In particular, Iraq was seen as the main potential threat to the US engineered balance in the Cold War era, as it was viewed as potentially aligned with the Soviets through a 1972 Treaty of Friendship. The US supported friendly regimes in Iran and Saudi Arabia, with Iran playing the major role in checking Iraqi ambitions in the Gulf. However, US policy was forced to change with the overthrow of the Shah in 1979 followed by the emergence of an anti-American regime in Tehran. The Soviet invasion of Afghanistan heightened fears about US dominance of the region and the security of oil supplies. These two events, combined with the advent of the second oil shock in 1979, prompted the issuance of the Carter Doctrine. In his 1980 State of the Union Message to Congress, President Carter declared that "…any attempt by any outside force to gain control of the Persian Gulf region will be regarded as an assault on the vital interests of the United States of America, and such assault will be repelled by any means necessary, including military force." The Carter Doctrine recognized that the US had emerged as a Middle Eastern power with permanent security interests in the region.[1]

Later that year, Iraq launched a war against Iran in the attempt to take advantage of its post-revolutionary weakness. Iraq's poor performance in that endeavor provided US officials with an opportunity to replace their former reliance on Iran for a balance in the Persian Gulf with a "tilt" toward Iraq. The US began supplying arms and intelligence to Iraq and embargoing arms for Iran. This policy was undermined to some extent by the infamous Iran-Contra Affair during the Reagan administration, which channeled arms to Iran in exchange for cash to support the Nicaraguan contras and assistance in freeing US hostages in Lebanon. However, Reagan's policy continued to maintain the general tilt toward Iraq, culminating in world pressure on Iran to accept a cease-fire with Iraq in 1988. Though both countries were exhausted by the long war, Iraq emerged as the preeminent military power in the Gulf. The George H. W. Bush administration maintained the Reagan-era tilt toward Iraq during the two years prior to the Iraqi invasion of Kuwait in August of 1990.[2]

In response to that invasion, President Bush chose to dramatically increase US forces in the region, build a broad-based global coalition, and secure UN authority to drive Hussein's military from Kuwait. As Tucker and Hendrickson argued, Bush could have pursued a policy of "punitive containment" characterized by a security guarantee for US allies in the region and the maintenance of economic sanctions until Iraq withdrew from Kuwait.[3] Instead, the rollback option was chosen and the First Gulf War of January and February of 1991 succeeded in removing Iraqi forces

---

1   Cecil Van Crabb, *The Doctrines of American Foreign Policy: Their Meaning, Role and Future*, (Baton Rouge: Louisiana State University Press, 1982).

2   See Robert S. Litwak, "Iraq and Iran: From Dual to Differentiated Containment," in Robert J. Lieber, ed., *Eagle Rules? Foreign Policy and American Primacy in the Twenty-first Century*, (Upper Saddle River, NJ: Prentice Hall, 2002), 173–93.

3   Robert W. Tucker and David C. Hendrickson, *The Imperial Temptation: The New World Order and America's Purpose*, (New York: Council on Foreign Relations Press, 1992), 94–110.

from Kuwait. Coalition forces did not pursue a march on Baghdad, but hoped that an internal Baathist party coup might lead to Hussein's ouster. Instead of a military coup, the Kurds and Shiites began revolting at least in part because of the Bush administration's call for the people of Iraq to depose their leader. Although regime change might have been accomplished by supporting these uprisings, the Bush administration eventually chose not to support these groups for fear that dismantling the Iraqi state would dramatically enhance the power of Iran in the region. The brutal reprisals experienced by the Kurds and Shiites prompted the establishment of two "no-fly" zones in the North and South, and a "safe haven" in the North that also prohibited ground forces, which had the effect of alleviating the number of Kurds heading for the Turkish border. Thus, the containment of Iraq as a unitary state became the official US policy in order to guarantee regional stability and prevent Iranian dominance in the Gulf.

In April of 1991, the cease-fire agreement with Iraq was codified in United Nations Security Council Resolution (UNSCR) 687. Iraq was required to recognize its border with Kuwait and provide compensation for losses from the occupation. Iraq was also required to eliminate its existing weapons of mass destruction (WMD) and all programs designed for future production and research. UNSCR 699, adopted in June of 1991, implemented Section C of UNSCR 687 through the creation of the United Nations Special Commission (UNSCOM) charged with inspecting Iraqi weapons programs on behalf of the Security Council. Iraq had already been subject to economic sanctions, including a prohibition on oil exports since UNSCR 661, just four days after its invasion of Kuwait. Though these sanctions would be attenuated over the years, including the 1996 oil-for-food program (UNSCR 986), they undoubtedly had a severe effect on Iraqi civilians.[4]

While the first Bush administration had pursued a policy of containment—keeping Hussein "in his box," they also sought the long-term goal of removing him from power. The rhetorical underpinnings of this approach changed during the Clinton administration, though the substance remained largely the same. In March of 1993, Clinton administration officials deleted the call for regime change in a discussion of the continuance of economic sanctions. This move shored up support for continued sanctions among Security Council members like Russia and France that did not support overt calls for the removal of Hussein from power. Instead, the Clinton administration argued that sanctions should remain in place until Iraq was in compliance with all Security Council resolutions. US officials adopted the rhetorical shift with a firm belief that Iraq would not come into compliance while Hussein was in power.

Internal debate over US policy toward Iraq during the Clinton administration concerned two positions. The first was a policy of rollback, which called for the immediate removal of Hussein through covert action designed to support Iraqi

---

4   For an overview of Security Council action on Iraq, see Mark A. Drumbl, "Self-Defense and the Use of Force: Breaking the Rules, Making the Rules, or Both?," *International Studies Perspectives*, Vol. 4, No. 4, (November 2003), 409–431.

opposition groups. This approach was popular with many members of Congress, but obviously would rupture relations with many members of the Gulf War coalition. The second option was a more comprehensive form of containment. In May of 1993, Martin Indyk, a National Security Council expert on the Middle East, outlined the policy of "dual containment" in a speech given to the Washington Institute for Near East Policy.[5] Indyk stated that the US would no longer continue the policy of creating a balance of power in the region through building up Iran or Iraq to counter the other. Instead, the US would rely on its own strength and the cooperation of friendly regimes in the region, including Saudi Arabia, Egypt, Israel, Turkey and the Gulf Cooperation Council (GCC) states to contain both Iran and Iraq. Indyk further declared that "the current regime in Iraq is a criminal regime, beyond the pale of international society and, in our judgment, irredeemable." However, his speech did not explicitly advocate regime change in Iraq, rather it maintained the administration's stance that the US sought full compliance with UN Security Council Resolutions and the Hussein regime seemed an unlikely candidate to deliver such compliance. Litwak argued this constituted an "implicit" policy of rollback.[6] Of equal importance in his speech was the statement that the Clinton administration was not opposed to an Islamic government in Iran, only that it sought a change in the government's policies.

Anthony Lake, Clinton's National Security Advisor, further elaborated this option in a 1994 *Foreign Affairs* article.[7] Lake identified five "backlash" states: Cuba, North Korea, Iran, Iraq, and Libya, for which the United States as the sole superpower had a special responsibility. Of the backlash states, which would eventually be renamed "rogue states" and later "states of concern," Iraq and Iran were of special importance due to their geostrategic location in the oil producing Persian Gulf. Lake again rejected the traditional US policy of building up Iraq or Iran to balance the other, while accepting the goal of establishing a balance of power in the region favorable to US interests, including the free and unfettered flow of oil. Both Indyk and Lake were clear that a preoccupation with containing Iraq could allow Iranian power to grow unchecked. While suggesting that more normal relations with Iran were conceivable, Lake identified a number of Iranian policies as roadblocks to that end. These policies included Iranian support for international terrorism (including Hezbollah and Hamas), opposition to the Arab-Israeli peace process, and subversion of regional regimes favorably disposed to the US, its conventional military buildup, and its continued attempts to acquire WMD.

Criticism of the dual containment policy was widespread in the US foreign policy establishment. Gause argued that the policy would actually work to push Iraq and

---

    5   The Washington Institute for Near East Policy, "Special Report: Clinton Administration Policy toward the Middle East," *Policy Watch* (21 May 1993).
    6   Ibid, 177.
    7   Anthony Lake, "Confronting Backlash States," *Foreign Affairs*, Vol. 73, No. 2, (March/April 1994), 45–55.

Iran together, despite the longstanding hostility between the two.[8] Further, he argued that it was unlikely that the US would be able to "stage-manage" developments in the two countries to maintain the regional status quo. For example, if Hussein should fall and a power struggle ensued, Iran would have every interest and opportunity to intervene to install a friendly regime. Instead, Gause recommended a policy of constructive engagement with Iran about the future of a post-Saddam Iraq. This type of discussion would not be seen as a tilt toward Iran, but rather a type of engagement akin to Kissinger's initiation of opening to China in 1971. While there were several cultural exchanges during the Clinton administration little happened in the way of constructive engagement. In fact, the Clinton administration heavily criticized the European Union's policy of "critical dialogue" with Iran. In 1996, President Clinton signed into law the Iran-Libya Sanctions Act, which threatened to impose secondary sanctions on firms trading with those countries. This policy, in addition to the language of "rogue" states and its inconsistent application around the world, furthered a widening gulf between the US and its former coalition partners concerning the future of the Persian Gulf region. The effects of ongoing sanctions on the people of Iraq also drew strong criticism, despite the fact that they were continually renewed in the Security Council.[9]

In mid-1995, Iraq claimed to have met its obligations under UNSCR 687 and asked for UNSCOM to leave the country. France and Russia began to push for eliminating sanctions in the Security Council. US policymakers were on the defensive until Hussein's son-in-law defected to Jordan with evidence of noncompliance with UNSCR 687, including evidence of a secret biological weapons program. This prompted a series of denials from Iraq and a resumption of the status quo in terms of inspections and sanctions.

Zbigniew Brzezinski, Brent Scowcroft and Richard Murphy continued the intellectual assault on the Clinton policy of dual containment in their 1997 *Foreign Affairs* article, in which they called for a nuanced or "differentiated" containment for Iraq and Iran.[10] They argued for the continued military containment of Iraq for the duration of Hussein regime, even if it meant US unilateral action. However, they suggested that the US should be more flexible in the political and economic aspects of containment by pursuing a number of policies. First, the US should attempt to mitigate the effects of sanctions on the Iraqi people. Second, the US should commit itself to maintaining the territorial integrity of Iraq while looking forward to a post-Hussein regime. Third, the US should consult with Turkey regarding *Operation Northern Watch* and any policy that affected the Kurds. Fourth, the US should also indicate a willingness to work with a post-Hussein regime, whether it turned out

---

8   F. Gregory Gause III, "The Illogic of Dual Containment," *Foreign Affairs*, Vol. 73, No. 2, (March/April 1994), 56–66.

9   Eric Rouleau, "America's Unyielding Policy Toward Iraq," *Foreign Affairs*, Vol. 74, No. 1, (January 1995), 59–72.

10   Zbigniew Brzezinski, Brent Scowcroft, and Richard Murphy, "Differentiated Containment," *Foreign Affairs*, Vol. 76, No. 3, (May/June 1997), 20–30.

to be democratic or not. Finally, the US should resolve to punish Hussein's regime when it threatened other countries or faltered in dismantling its WMD programs.

In their view, Iran represented a more important geopolitical challenge than Iraq in the long term. As a result, they recommended that the US avoid demonizing Islam in a manner that might overcome existing ethnic and sectarian cleavages that divide the Islamic world. They advocated US efforts to prevent Iran from achieving nuclear weapons through existing nonproliferation mechanisms. Instead of simply punishing Iran with sanctions, the US should also explore more positive inducements to accept restrictions and inspections of its nuclear programs. Further, the unilateral US sanctions imposed on Iran in 1996 were deemed counterproductive in terms of US relationships with traditional allies and potentially friendly regimes in possession of gas and oil in Central Asia. Therefore, differentiation in treatment of these two regional threats would keep Hussein "in his box," but also allow for policy modifications to maintain the unity of the Gulf War coalition. It would further enable the flexibility to improve relations with Iran, while maintaining the overall goal of regional order and access to oil.

It should be clear from the discussion of this debate over containment that the US has pursued two objectives toward Iraq since the end of the first Gulf War.[11] The short-term goal has been to keep Hussein "in his box," essentially containment of some sort, while the long-term goal has been to work for his overthrow, essentially a policy of rollback. By January of 1998, the Clinton administration began to discuss the possibility of military action against Iraq, with or without the Security Council's authorization. The administration was struggling with how best to respond to Hussein's obstruction of UNSCOM inspections in the fall of 1997. Many Congressional Republicans began to voice support for the rollback option, including the possibility of airstrikes and other methods of supporting the Iraqi opposition in an effort to remove Hussein. UN Secretary General Annan narrowly prevented US air strikes in February of 1998 with a trip to Baghdad that produced renewed pledges of cooperation. However, Iraq's eventual failure to cooperate led to *Operation Desert Fox* in December of 1998, which was a punitive four-day series of air strikes. After the air campaign, the rules of engagement were expanded for British and American pilots in the no-fly zones, which resulted in near daily attacks on Iraqi military targets.

As Daniel Byman, Kenneth Pollack, and Gideon Rose noted, rollback was a hot concept in Washington during the 1997–98 crisis with Iraq, supported by Congressional leaders, former government officials (many of whom have high-ranking positions in the current Bush administration), and columnists and editors at a variety of the country's newspapers.[12] In October of 1998, the US Congress passed, and Clinton signed, the Iraq Liberation Act, designed to provide military assistance to the Iraqi opposition. A special coordinator for Iraq, Frank Ricciardone,

---

11   Ibid, 180.
12   Daniel Byman, Kenneth Pollack, and Gideon Rose, "The Rollback Fantasy," *Foreign Affairs*, Vol. 78, No. 1, (January/February 1999), 24–41.

was appointed by the administration to implement the act and assist Iraqi opposition groups. Both Ricciardone and Assistant Secretary of State for Near East Affairs Martin Indyk held meetings with such groups after the passage of the act.

Byman, Pollack and Rose outlined three possibilities for rollback: using air power to remove Hussein, assisting opposition groups to gain control over large parts of Iraq, and funding a guerilla war. They dismissed the viability of each of these options, yet agreed with those who argued that the containment regime was collapsing by 1998. They argued that there was no better alternative to containment, but additional steps must be taken to shore up the policy. One approach would have been to preserve containment in the current form along with sanctions, inspections, punishments, and continued isolation. This renewed commitment would have required considerable effort to sway international opinion in favor of such a US-led policy. A second approach would have shifted away from broad-based containment toward a narrower version of the policy. The US would end economic sanctions and the no-fly zones in return for another Security Council resolution banning Iraq from possessing WMD or new conventional weapons coupled with inspections and severe reprisals for noncompliance.

Mueller and Mueller similarly called for an end to sanctions and the implementation of some type of export control process that would prevent Iraq from importing goods that would assist with WMD or conventional rearmament.[13] After Iraq ceased cooperating with UNSCOM, Gause also suggested revising the sanctions in exchange for intrusive inspections of WMD facilities and programs.[14] UNSCOM was replaced with UNMOVIC (United Nations Monitoring, Verification and Inspection Commission) in December of 1999 according to UNSCR 1284. However, Iraq repeated its calls for lifting economic sanctions and refused to permit UNMOVIC inspections. By 2000, Bengio's statement that "the truth is that after a decade of containment, the United States and its allies still have no real vision for Iraq's future" seemed to summarize the general dissatisfaction with US policy in Iraq.[15] However, Bengio's prescription was much the same: combine a modified form of containment and help create the conditions that would produce a coup to topple Hussein. "Containment plus regime change" became the hallmark of the Clinton administration's policy toward Iraq.[16]

Litwak argued that the June 2000 decision by the State Department to drop the term "rogue state" in favor of the "states of concern" appellation signaled a shift from the dual containment policy to the differentiated containment approach

---

13   John Mueller and Karl Mueller, "Sanctions of Mass Destruction," *Foreign Affairs*, Vol. 78, No. 3, (May/June 1999), 43–53.

14   F. Gregory Gause III, "Getting it Backward on Iraq," *Foreign Affairs*, Vol. 78, No. 3, (May/June 1999), 54–65.

15   Ofra Bengio, "How Does Saddam Hold On?," *Foreign Affairs*, Vol. 79, No. 4, (July/August 2000), 90–103.

16   John Lancaster, "In Saddam's Future, A Harder US Line," *Washington Post* (3 June 2000).

advocated by Brzezinski, Scowcroft and Murphy.[17] Hardliners on Iraq in Congress and the press found the semantic change troubling, but in the end, the Clinton administration policy changed very little. Either way, high-level officials in the George W. Bush administration came to office with the belief that the Clinton years were wasted with regard to Iraq. As Litwak noted, the Bush administration felt that the Clinton administration's lack of resolve to hold Hussein strictly accountable to the UN resolutions made the possibility of rollback under their watch even more difficult to achieve, despite the longstanding preferences held by many officials for Hussein's removal. Notable hawks favoring rollback in Iraq in the new Bush administration included Vice President Cheney, Secretary of Defense Rumsfeld, and Deputy Secretary of Defense Wolfowitz.[18]

The Bush Doctrine and Rollback

George W. Bush assumed the presidency in January of 2001 with little expertise in foreign policy. He had criticized the Clinton administration for its use of force in Kosovo and its attempts at "nation building" around the world. Bush claimed that under his leadership the US would stop being the world's policeman. He advocated a reevaluation of US military deployments around the world and questioned the future need for NATO. Altogether, Bush seemed to suggest a retrenchment in US foreign policy, perhaps even a swing back to isolationism in some respects. However, the events of September 11, 2001 dramatically altered his actions, if not his fundamental beliefs about the US role in the world.

What would come to be known as the Bush Doctrine emerged in a series of press conferences, speeches, and ultimately was ensconced as official policy in *The National Security Strategy of the United States of America* in September of 2002.[19] Initially, Bush stated that the US would "hunt down and punish those responsible for these cowardly acts," seemingly implicating the terrorists behind the attacks on New York and Washington, D.C.[20] Just a few days later in his proclamation of a National Day of Prayer and Remembrance, Bush stated that "those who helped or harbored the terrorists" would be punished. On September 20, before a joint session of Congress, this logic was made clear: both Al Qaeda and the Taliban regime in

---

17   Ibid, 189.

18   Ibid, 191.

19   For analyses of the evolution of the Bush Doctrine, see Cameron G. Thies, "The Bush Doctrine: Redefining the US Role in World Politics for the Twenty-first Century?" in Tom Lansford and Robert P. Watson, eds., *George W. Bush: A Political and Ethical Assessment at Midterm* (Albany: SUNY Press, Forthcoming, 2004); Cameron G. Thies and Leigh A. Galatas, "Assessing the Foreign Policy Doctrine of George W. Bush," in John Davis, ed., *Assessing the War on Terrorism.* (Hauppauge, NY: Nova Science, Forthcoming, 2003); and Peter Dombrowski and Rodger A. Payne, "Global Debate and the Limits of the Bush Doctrine," *International Studies Perspectives*, Vol 4., No. 4, (November 2003), 395–408.

20   President Bush's remarks at Barksdale Air Force Base, (11 September 2001).

Afghanistan would be the targets of US action. The targets of the Bush Doctrine were further clarified in the 2002 State of the Union Address, in which Bush declared that the US would bring terrorists to justice, and prevent terrorists and regimes that seek WMD from threatening the world. In particular, he targeted Iran, Iraq, and North Korea as comprising an "axis of evil" that consorted with terrorists and sought to obtain WMD. The new language and redefinition of the targets of the "war on terror" caused a stir worldwide. It was clear that Iraq and Iran would no longer be differentiated, and soon it was clear that containment was no longer official policy either.

In *The National Security Strategy*, the Bush Doctrine appears in its final form. "Our immediate focus will be those terrorist organizations of global reach and any terrorist or state sponsor of terrorism which attempts to gain or use weapons of mass destruction (WMD) or their precursors."[21] Reverting to earlier Clinton administration language, "we must be prepared to stop rogue states and their terrorist clients before they are able to threaten or use weapons of mass destruction against the United States and our allies and friends."[22] Finally, the means of enacting the Bush Doctrine were also clarified:

> The United States has long maintained the option of preemptive actions to counter a sufficient threat to our national security. The greater the threat, the greater is the risk of inaction—and the more compelling the case for taking anticipatory action to defend ourselves, even if uncertainty remains as to the time and place of the enemy's attack. To forestall or prevent such hostile acts by our adversaries, the United States will, if necessary, act preemptively.[23]

Thus, the "cold war" doctrine of containment via deterrence was declared dead, with rollback via preemption heralded as the Bush administration's approach to the new and uncertain post-11 September world. The Bush Doctrine thus laid the rhetorical foundations for the second Gulf War with Iraq.

The Bush administration quickly moved to demonstrate that Iraq was reconstituting its WMD programs, that it was in violation of UN Security Council resolutions, and that it might have links to terrorist groups, including Al Qaeda.[24] Bush pursued these issues in the UN Security Council after it appeared that domestic public opinion and a majority in Congress would not consent to action against Iraq without UN consultation. However, that process turned out to be troublesome, as Russia and France were not convinced that Iraq was reconstituting its WMD programs, or that it was actively working with terrorists. Bush warned the Security Council that failure

---

21   *The National Security Strategy of the United States of America*, (September 2002), p. 6.

22   Ibid, 14.

23   Ibid, 15.

24   For a version of the path to war from a former Clinton administration official, see James P. Rubin, "Stumbling Into War," *Foreign Affairs*, Vol. 82, No. 5, (September/October 2003), 46–66.

to support his resolution would reduce the UN to a mere "debating society." The resolution that Bush sought provided for an automatic application of military force if Iraq failed to allow inspections. Instead, the Security Council demanded that Iraq allow weapons inspections to resume. The consequences of noncompliance were not spelled out in advance. Bush was clearly dissatisfied with the Security Council, and stated, "If you won't act, and if Saddam Hussein won't disarm, for the sake of peace, for the sake of a future for our children, we will lead a coalition of nations and disarm Saddam Hussein."[25] Bush therefore maintained the right to intervene in Iraq unilaterally if he deemed it necessary in keeping with the newly enunciated Bush Doctrine. The US Congress, facing midterm elections and a very popular president, went along with Bush's request for authorization to intervene in Iraq should it be necessary, particularly given that he did take the matter to the UN

In a surprise move, Saddam Hussein consented to having UN inspectors enter Iraq on 13 November 2002. According to the Bush administration, inspections would show evidence of a reconstitution of WMD programs. The inspection teams were given relatively unfettered access to sites, but they found nothing of consequence. The Bush administration still insisted that it had intelligence demonstrating the existence of WMD programs, and when Iraq failed to declare them according to the UN deadline, the US would demonstrate Iraq's deception to the world. However, Security Council members were unimpressed by the evidence supplied by Secretary Powell's much anticipated presentation. In fact, much of the intelligence used to make the administration's claims has turned out to be unreliable. It appears that the Bush administration dismantled many of the normal channels used to vet intelligence information, engaging in the process known as "stovepiping," whereby raw information is channeled directly to decision makers.[26] For example, the intelligence behind a purported Iraqi purchase of five hundred tons of uranium oxide from Niger was based on poorly forged documents.[27]

The attempt to secure a follow-up Security Council resolution authorizing the use of force against Iraq failed despite intense US and British diplomatic efforts. After an emergency summit in the Azores on the weekend of 15 March 2003, the US, Britain and Spain decided to abandon these efforts. Few Security Council members appeared to back such a resolution, while France promised to veto it. On 17 March 2003, Secretary of State Colin Powell declared that "the time for diplomacy has passed." Secretary General Kofi Annan ordered the UN weapons inspectors and others providing humanitarian assistance to leave Iraq that same day. President Bush addressed the nation that evening and gave Saddam Hussein and his two sons 48 hours to leave Iraq or face war. Bush maintained that Hussein possessed WMD, and that he had "aided, trained, and harbored terrorists," fulfilling all of the requirements for an application of the Bush Doctrine.

---

25   "US Recrafting Resolution on Iraq," *USA Today*, (1 November 2002).

26   Seymour M. Hersh, "The Stovepipe," *The New Yorker*, (27 October 2003), 77–87.

27   Seymour M. Hersh, "Who Lied to Whom?," *The New Yorker*, (31 March 2003).

Operation Iraqi Freedom began on 20 March 2003 with a precision cruise missile "decapitation" strike on a compound where Saddam Hussein was thought to be staying. Hussein is still thought to be alive somewhere in Iraq, but his sons were killed by US forces in a raid in Mosul in late July. By 27 March, US and British forces had succeeded in capturing the Iraqi port of Umm Qasr, securing the southern oil fields, surrounding Basra, and had pushed within 50 miles of Baghdad. The coalition forces faced more resistance than expected, leading to some problems with securing supply lines on the road to Baghdad. But by 9 April, Hussein's regime appeared to have collapsed in Baghdad, and most government officials had fled the city. By 14 April, US government officials were declaring that the major combat phase of the war was finished. Since that time the Bush administration has been faced with the task of rebuilding Iraqi infrastructure and reconstituting an Iraqi government, neither of which has proven a simple task. The "nation building" that candidate Bush scorned is now a central feature of President Bush's Iraq policy. The tension between containment and rollback that dominated during the Clinton administration was clearly resolved in favor of rollback.

How was that tension resolved? Rollback was discussed publicly in the Clinton administration, yet "containment plus regime change" remained official US policy throughout his term in office. Many prominent political realists continued to call for some type of containment of Iraq right up to the start of the war, rather than rollback.[28] As Fouad Ajami noted just prior to the second Gulf War, a US intervention resulting from a failure to impose UN inspections would be viewed by most Arabs as "an imperial reach into their world, a favor to Israel, or a way for the United States to secure control over Iraq's oil."[29] At the beginning of the Bush administration, "containment plus regime change" seemed to be the policy. Secretary Powell and others made public statements to that effect. The opportunity for those who favored rollback did not present itself until 11 September 2001. Again, Ajami notes that "it was September 11 and its shattering surprise, in turn, that tipped the balance on Iraq away from containment and toward regime change and 'rollback.'" When asked if new intelligence had come to light between the start of his administration and 11 September that indicated Iraq was an imminent threat to the US, President Bush said "no," that he had just "changed his mind." According to National Security Adviser Condoleezza Rice, an "earthquake" shook Bush's political priorities.[30] Following a January 2003 meeting with Prime Minister Blair, President Bush said, "My vision shifted dramatically after September the 11th, because I now realize the stakes. I realize the world has changed. My most important obligation is to protect the American people from further harm. And I will do that." Thus, the opportunity

---

28   John J. Mearsheimer and Stephen M. Walt, "An Unnecessary War," *Foreign Policy*, (January/February 2003), 50–59.

29   Fouad Ajami, "Iraq and the Arabs' Future," *Foreign Affairs*, Vol. 82, No. 1, (January/February 2003), 2–18.

30   Robin Wright and Doyle McManus, "The World Attacks Redefine Bush Foreign Policy," *Los Angeles Times*, (7 January 2002).

provided by 11 September met with the willingness of administration officials to implement a policy change to rollback.

The Middle East in the Aftermath of the Second Gulf War

In October of 2001, columnist Charles Krauthammer argued that the US should unilaterally intervene in countries whose regimes supported terrorism.[31] He suggested that the US start with Afghanistan, then proceed in order to Syria, Iran, and Iraq. While the decision to attack Al Qaeda and the Taliban regime in Afghanistan seemed a foregone conclusion in the days following September 11, the sequence Krauthammer suggested was probably more in keeping with a true "war on terrorism" for those predisposed to unilateral military intervention. The jump the Bush administration made to intervene in Iraq as part of the "war on terror" after Afghanistan seemed out of place if the concern really was terrorism, since little evidence existed of links between Hussein's regime and terrorists of any sort. However, Syria and Iran have not escaped US scrutiny. In fact, the imposition of US forces in Iraq has had the effect of putting both countries on edge.

Defense Secretary Rumsfeld has expressed a view common in the Bush administration; the Middle East is ripe for remaking into a region full of democracies. The Iraqi democracy currently in the planning stages would serve as a beacon to the region, perhaps resulting in the overthrow of authoritarian regimes unfriendly to the US[32] Iran, one of the remaining "axis of evil" states is now high on the list for regime change, as a known supporter of Hezbollah and Hamas, and opponent of the Israeli-Palestinian peace process. The US has been insistent in pressing for international inspections of Iranian nuclear programs, to which Iran is grudgingly acceding. Syria would also be a target after its suspected covert support of Saddam Hussein's regime during the current war in Iraq and its support of terrorist groups. In fact, on 14 April 2003 Secretary Powell called on Syria to "review their actions and their behavior, not only with respect to who gets haven in Syria and weapons of mass destruction, but especially the support of terrorist activity." Powell warned that Syria might be subject to "measures of a diplomatic, economic or other nature."

With the demise of dual containment or even differentiated containment, one wonders what US policy toward Iran will be in the coming years. Presumably, as long as US forces are in Iraq in large numbers, some form of containment would be relatively easy to implement. The US no longer need rely on partners in the region to maintain a favorable balance of power as it is preponderant in the Persian Gulf. However, given the relative ease with which regimes were toppled in Afghanistan and Iraq, is it feasible to believe the US would continue a policy of rollback vis-à-vis Iran or Syria? At this point in time such a policy does not seem plausible. The

---

31   Krauthammer, Charles, "Our First Move: Take Out the Taliban," *The Chicago Tribune*, (1 October 2001).

32   For an argument that this is unlikely to happen, see Thomas Carothers, "Why Dictators Aren't Dominoes," *Foreign Policy*, (July/August, 2003), 59–60.

US public and Congress are having a hard time grappling with the daily casualties appearing in the news and the increased demands for public funds to rebuild the country. The military is stretched relatively thin at this point, with approximately 325,000 troops deployed around the globe. The 130,000 troops in Iraq have had their tours of duty extended and more reservists are being called up. The level of violence shows no sign of diminishing as resistance groups even strike within the so-called "green zone" in Baghdad, supposedly the most secure enclave in the country. Deputy Secretary Wolfowitz was staying at the Al Rasheed hotel in the green zone when it was struck by rocket launched grenades on 26 October 2003. While President Bush stated that an escalating level of violence in Iraq indicated that the US is succeeding in its mission, critics like Senator John McCain argue the opposite. The realization of the enormity of the undertaking in Iraq probably will reign in any calls for future rollback(s) in the region.

Many have suggested that the focus of the Bush administration's efforts in the Middle East and as part of the war on terrorism should be to resolve the Israeli-Palestinian conflict. Doran suggests that the refrain "It's Palestine, stupid" resounded throughout the Middle East and Europe when Iraq became the focus on the Bush administration's attention after Afghanistan.[33] The attack on Iraq, while the US allowed Sharon's Israel free reign with the Palestinians, drove a wedge between the US and the Arab world according to this argument. The first Gulf War was framed by the Palestinian struggle, with Iraq's invasion of Kuwait coming on the heels of the first Intifada. The coalition building that led to the removal of Iraq from Kuwait also laid the ground for the Madrid Conference and eventually the Oslo peace process. Despite the fact that President Clinton was unable to secure a final agreement between Barak and Arafat at Camp David, many observers expected the peace process would continue during the Bush administration.

In fact, the opposite was true, with the Bush administration seeming to throw unequivocal support behind Sharon's policies of continued settlement expansion, military reprisals with large civilian casualties, and the construction of a wall designed to cut off Palestinian areas of the West Bank from contact with Israel. In fact, it was only with strong encouragement from Prime Minister Blair during the days leading up to the war that the Bush administration turned much attention at all to the peace process. It remains to be seen whether the so-called "road map" to peace will produce any positive developments. Doran questions whether a strong US tilt toward the Palestinians would even generate the kind of goodwill necessary to overcome the region's problems at this point. In combination with the Israeli-Palestinian road map, Perkovich argues that the US, Iran and Iraq will need a "navigational chart" to bring stability and security to the Persian Gulf in the aftermath of the second Gulf War.[34]

---

33   Michael Scott Doran, "Palestine, Iraq, and American Strategy," *Foreign Affairs*, Vol. 82, No. 1, (January/February 2003), 19–28.

34   George Perkovich, "Can Iran and the United States Bridge the Gulf?," *Foreign Policy*, (July/August 2003), 65.

Pollack offers three approaches to US foreign policy in the post-Hussein Persian Gulf.[35] The first would be a return of offshore balancing. In this approach, the US would dramatically reduce its military presence in the region. US power and cooperation with the GCC states would be enough to deter future aggression from Iran or a reconstituted (and potentially unfriendly) Iraq. A second approach would be the formation of a new regional defense alliance—a NATO of the Middle East, which would encompass the new government of Iraq and the GCC states. The third approach is a security condominium for the Persian Gulf based on the arms control experiences between NATO and the Warsaw Pact at the end of the Cold War. This approach would bring together the US, Iraq, Iran, and the GCC states to engage in confidence building measures that could ultimately lead to arms control agreements. Certainly, the Bush administration does not seem disposed to incorporate one of the remaining "axis of evil" states into such a condominium. It also seems unlikely that offshore balancing, with a massive reduction of US forces in the region would be acceptable. Pollack's second approach may be the default option for the Bush administration. However, the region's historical experience with the US dominated Central Treaty Organization of the early Cold War years may stand in the way of a formal alliance. Whatever policy the US chooses to follow, it is clear that access to oil will remain a high priority for future administrations, along with the establishment of a balance of power between Iran and Iraq that ensures such access.

Conclusion

While many foreign policy analysts were startled by the direction that US policy took toward Iraq under George W. Bush, in retrospect, it seems less surprising. Some version of containment of Iraq dominated the foreign policy agenda for the Persian Gulf since the end of the first Gulf War. Few analysts were satisfied by the form that containment took during the Clinton administration. The deadlock over weapons inspections, the humanitarian consequences of the sanctions regime, and the persistence of a brutal dictator with aggressive intentions toward his neighbors and US interests in the Gulf all prompted a variety of suggestions for improving the method of containment. Interestingly enough, few members of the foreign policy establishment seriously entertained the prospect of rollback. Clinton administration officials discussed this option, Congressional leaders often advocated the approach, and conservative columnists liked the idea, but it would be members of previous Republican administrations that would bring the idea to the forefront of discussion. However, this was only possible after the events of 11 September 2001.

The Bush administration initially continued the policy of containment plus regime change until the terrorist attacks in New York and Washington, D.C. The Bush Doctrine evolved over the course of the following year until it included terrorists of global reach, the regimes that supported them, and states that sought WMD. The

---

35   Kenneth Pollack, "Securing the Gulf," *Foreign Affairs*, Vol. 82, No. 4, (July/August 2003), 2–16.

2002 State of the Union Message made it clear that rogue states comprising the axis of evil—Iraq, Iran, and North Korea, met the criteria for the application of the new doctrine in the Bush administration's eyes. The *National Security Strategy* also clarified the Bush administration's new approach to foreign policy—unilateralist and preemptive when deemed necessary by the president. The shift from containment to rollback in Iraq was virtually sealed at that point. Domestic pressures forced the Bush administration to attempt to work through the UN, but no grand coalition was forthcoming for this Gulf War. However, in keeping with the Bush Doctrine, the policy of rollback was implemented in Iraq without much international support. The opportunity provided by September 11 and the willingness on the part of the Bush administration officials to enact their longstanding policy preferences in the context of a war on terrorism transformed US policy in Iraq with long-term consequences for the Persian Gulf and the world.

Chapter 9

The No-Fly Zones and Low Intensity Conflict with Iraq, 1991–2003

Douglas M. Brattebo
US Naval Academy

Introduction

This chapter examines the role that the no-fly zones, imposed by the Gulf War victors over northern Iraq in 1991 and southern Iraq in 1992, impacted US policy toward Iraq for more than a decade before the start of *Operation Iraqi Freedom* in March 2003. Designed to protect the Kurds in the north and the Shiites in the south, as well as to contain Saddam Hussein's ambitions and prevent him from threatening neighboring countries, the no-fly zones soon became the main venue for political provocations and military confrontations between allied and Iraqi military forces. Never officially sanctioned by the UN Security Council (UNSC), the no-fly zones by the end of the presidency of George H.W. Bush emerged as a source of tension among the Gulf War allies.

During President Bill Clinton's first term, Saddam often expressed his discontent with UN weapons inspections in his country by orchestrating flare-ups in the no-fly zones. Hoping to get out from under UN economic sanctions against Iraq, used his flaunting of the no-fly zones increased the already widening divisions among the Western powers. Clinton's response to Saddam's renewed aggression against the Kurds in the northern no-fly zone resulted in the expansion of the southern no-fly zone and target assets of value to Saddam in the south and center of Iraq. This approach encouraged criticism within the Republican controlled US Congress that Clinton was not taking an assertive enough stance toward the Iraqi dictator.

When Osama bin Laden issued his 1998 fatwa calling for the murder of Americans, "civilian and military," he cited two main grievances: the presence of US troops on Saudi Arabia's holy soil, and US bombing of Iraq in the name of enforcing the no-fly zones.[1] By December 1998, with Saddam at loggerheads with the world community over weapons inspections and Republicans in Congress demanding stronger medicine for Baghdad, President Clinton ordered *Operation Desert Fox*, the largest use of force against Iraq since the Gulf War. The President also gave up on reintroducing UN weapons inspectors into Iraq, opting instead to

---

1   Newspaper Editorial, "The 12-Year War," *Wall Street Journal*, 18 March 2003, A16.

use Saddam's defiance as justification for a perpetual low-level air war against Iraqi targets in the no-fly zones. The mounting toll taken on the Iraqi people by both the bombing and the UN economic sanctions soon prompted the opening of many cracks in the sanctions regime. By the end of the Clinton presidency, enforcement of the no-fly zones was almost exclusively a US-led effort, with measured but consistent assistance from Britain.

President George W. Bush continued the Clinton administration's hard line toward Saddam, but the increasing sophistication of Iraqi antiaircraft attacks on allied jets in the no-fly zones, combined with the watershed of 11 September 2001, moved his administration to seek regime change in Baghdad. The US now sought to restore UN weapons inspectors into Iraq, which the President named as a member of the tripartite "axis of evil" along with Iran and North Korea. Using confrontations in the no-fly zones as the ostensible reason, the US initiated an unacknowledged but unremitting and intensifying air campaign in the no-fly zones of Iraq. The administration also argued its case for unilateral war against Iraq, contending that Iraqi violations of the no-fly zones were a sufficient "material breach" of the November 2002 UN Security Council resolution to justify war. Although the international community did not accept the administration's rationale, the US and Britain were quietly ramping up their bombing campaign, which throughout the second half of 2002 and early 2003 was the de facto first phase of outright war with Iraq. By the time *Operation Iraqi Freedom* commenced on 19 March 2003, a path into southern Iraq for coalition forces had already been cleared. At the conclusion of *Operation Iraqi Freedom*, the long-lived and expensive no-fly zones ceased to exist, and the implications for US foreign policy were significant.

The Presidency of George H.W. Bush

Shortly after the Gulf War concluded in February 1991, the Kurds of northern Iraq rebelled against Saddam's regime and ejected his military forces from within parts of Kurdistan.[2] An Iraqi counterattack then forced an estimated 1.5 million Kurds to flee through mountain passes into Turkey and Iran.[3] The US and their allies, spurred by the domestic public reaction to the Kurds' cold and hungry trek, launched *Operation Provide Comfort* to alleviate the televised suffering.[4] The UN Security Council also kept in place a broad economic embargo on Iraq that it had imposed in 1990 after Saddam's invasion of Kuwait, cutting off the economic lifeblood of oil exports.[5] Soon, 21,000 allied troops were administering *Operation Provide Comfort* from a

---

2   Caryle Murphy and Thomas W. Lippman, "'It's Important Work': US Still Committed to Protecting Kurds," *Washington Post*, 15 April 1994, A1.

3   Ibid.

4   Ibid.

5   Ibid.

center just inside Iraq near the Turkish border.[6] Starting on 3 April 1991,[7] allied pilots enforced a no-fly zone over northern Iraq from Incirlik, Turkey, while *Operation Provide Comfort* repatriated the Kurds and gradually restored a semblance of normal life in the region.[8]

The George H.W. Bush administration maintained for some time that extending protection to the Shiite rebels in southern Iraq would provide an entrée for Iranian fundamentalism into Iraq and lead to the partition of the country.[9] In August 1992, however, the President changed his policy of ignoring the plight of the Shiite rebels who now had spent 18 terrible months resisting the regime from the marshes.[10] Administration officials said the turnabout in policy came after Shiite leaders provided assurances that they were committed to the territorial integrity of Iraq and appeared to be just one part of a diverse Iraqi opposition that included members from all quarters of Iraqi society.[11] The decision, then, was rooted more in the realist desire to contain and threaten Saddam's regime than in purely humanitarian motives.[12] Saddam's slightly rebuilt military was not in good enough condition to menace neighboring countries, even if it had managed to hide Scud missiles and other weapons from UN inspectors, but absent external pressures it was more than adequate to the task of keeping the dictator in power.[13]

On 24 August 1992 National Security Adviser Brent Scowcroft confirmed that the Gulf War allies were planning to establish a second no-fly zone in southern Iraq below the 32nd parallel to curb Saddam's ongoing military campaign against the Shiites. American, British, and French pilots would enforce a ban on Iraqi flights in the area, but there was not to be any prohibition, like the one in effect in northern Iraq, against all Iraqi military activity. This evidently would leave Saddam free to continue his military campaign against the Shiites with ground forces, although US officials hinted that they would turn up the pressure on Saddam in the southern no-fly zone if he did not ease up on the Shiites. "What we're trying to do," said Scowcroft, "is to protect minority groups…not to cause or encourage the split-up of Iraq."[14]

---

6   Ibid.

7   Bob Kerrey, "Finish the War: Liberate Iraq," *Wall Street Journal*, 12 September 2002, A14.

8   Caryle Murphy and Thomas W. Lippman, "'It's Important Work': US Still Committed to Protecting Kurds," *Washington Post*, 15 April 1994, A1.

9   John Lancaster, "Allies Declare 'No-Fly Zone' in Iraq," *Washington Post*, 27 August 1992, A1.

10   Ibid.

11   Ibid.

12   Newspaper Editorial, "Turn of the Screw in Iraq," *Washington Post*, 27 August 1992, A30.

13   No Author, "Saddam's Military Still Hamstrung by Beating It Suffered in Gulf War," *Christian Science Monitor*, 28 August 1992, No Page Number.

14   Gerald F. Seib, "Bush Set to Ban Iraqi Warplanes in Shiite Area – Order Could Go Out Today, Though Florida Visit Might Prompt a Delay," *Wall Street Journal*, 25 August 1992, A4.

Reaction from governments in the Middle East concerning the creation of the southern no-fly zone was far from enthusiastic. Scowcroft's assurances aside, several countries in the region were concerned that the plan would in fact cause the breakup of Iraq. Only Kuwait publicly endorsed the southern no-fly zone. Desert Storm allies Syria and Egypt were openly critical, while Bahrain and Saudi Arabia were silent but agreed to let US aircraft and ships use their facilities to enforce the new flight ban. Only British and French warplanes would join US planes in policing the southern zone.[15]

Dubbed *Operation Southern Watch*,[16] enforcement of the southern no-fly zone commenced on August 27, 1992, with allied pilots poised to turn back Iraqi civilian aircraft entering the zone and shoot down any Iraqi military jets or helicopters they encountered.[17] The potential for immediate conflict in the skies was quite real, as 20–30 flights by Iraqi planes and helicopters had been traversing the zone daily.[18] Although Saddam was continuing to use his force of 60,000 troops on the ground to persecute the Shiites, Bush administration officials remained publicly adamant that the zone was, as Marine Lieutenant General Martin Brandtner of the Pentagon Joint Staff put it, "a no-fly zone, not a security zone."[19] The president himself described the allied pilots' mission as one of "monitoring."[20] For its part, the Iraqi government vowed not to honor the new zone, which it considered "an aggressive act intended to partition Iraq along sectarian and ethnic lines."[21]

The realist motivation behind the southern no-fly zone became evident by the end of August 1992 when Bush administration sources started to describe the zone as the first step in a larger effort to put increasing pressure on Saddam's regime.[22] The new characterization of the policy in southern Iraq came in response to charges by members of Congress that the administration had no long-term Iraq policy and ought to be more assertive in building and arming an Iraqi expatriate government to someday replace Saddam.[23] National Security Adviser Scowcroft publicly acknowledged that the US and its allies might use military force in southern Iraq to

---

15   Caryle Murphy, "Iraq Threatens UN Expulsions Over Allied 'No-Fly Zone': Many Arabs Critical of Initiative," *Washington Post*, 26 August 1992, A7.

16   Caryle Murphy, "US Planes Begin Missions Over Iraq: Enforcement of 'No-Fly Zone' Starts Without Resistance," *Washington Post*, 28 August 1992, A1.

17   No Author, "World-Wide," *Wall Street Journal*, 27 August 1992, A30.

18   Gerald F. Seib, "Bush Set to Ban Iraqi Warplanes in Shiite Area – Order Could Go Out Today, Though Florida Visit Might Prompt a Delay," *Wall Street Journal*, 25 August 1992, A4.

19   John Lancaster, "Allies Declare 'No-Fly Zone' in Iraq," *Washington Post*, 27 August 1992, A1.

20   Ibid.

21   No Author, "Baghdad Vows to Resist Flight Ban 'in Due Time,'" *Washington Post*, 28 August 1992, A28.

22   John Lancaster, "US Moves to Toughen Iraq Stance: Flight Ban Called 1st Step in Campaign to Pressure Saddam," *Washington Post*, 29 August 1992, A1.

23   Ibid.

stop ground attacks against the Shiites.[24] "We're flying over there for a reason," said Scowcroft, "and that is to enforce compliance with Resolution 688."[25] Resolution 688, enacted soon after the Gulf War, had referred to Saddam's repression of his citizenry as "a threat to peace and security in the region."[26]

Saddam reiterated his view that the ratcheting up of the pressure on his southern flank was a US-orchestrated plot to "partition the region to seize control over its oil wealth."[27] Importantly, King Hassan II of Morocco voiced the similar and mounting reservations of several leaders in the Middle East who feared that greater Shiite autonomy in southern Iraq could split Iraq asunder and stoke aspirations of Shiite minorities in other countries in the region.[28] No shots had yet been exchanged between allied pilots and Iraqi forces in the southern no-fly zone, but America's increasingly muscular bid to contain Saddam was already proving divisive to the broad alliance of the Gulf War. That is where things stood as UN weapons inspectors, having just returned to Baghdad at the end of August 1992, continued their postwar mandate of rendering Iraq's military incapable of threatening its neighbors.[29]

The respite in the air over Iraq was not to last. On 11 September 1992, two US Air Force F-16 fighters intercepted an Iraqi F-1 Mirage fighter in the northern no-fly zone, the first incursion north of the 36th parallel since April of that year; moreover, a similar incident reported by a US pilot in the southern no-fly zone also was under investigation.[30] More Iraqi incursions occurred in late December 1992, as now lame-duck President Bush contemplated the transfer of power to his successor, Bill Clinton. A US F-16 shot down an Iraqi aircraft in the southern no-fly zone on 27 December,[31] and Iraqi warplanes darted into and retreated from the same zone over the next two days.[32] The systematic Iraqi violation of the no-fly zones presaged Saddam's disruption of UN food shipments to the Kurds in northern Iraq

---

24   No Author, "World-Wide," *Wall Street Journal*, 31 August 1992, A1.

25   Gerald F. Seib, "Scowcroft Warns Baghdad Not to Use Ground Forces Against Shiites in South," *Wall Street Journal*, 31 August 1992, A1.

26   Newspaper Editorial, "Review & Outlook," *Wall Street Journal*, 8 October 1992, A1.

27   Gerald F. Seib, "Scowcroft Warns Baghdad Not to Use Ground Forces Against Shiites in South," *Wall Street Journal*, 31 August 1992, A1.

28   William Drozdiak, "Moroccan Warns US About Iraq: King Hassan Cites Danger of Breakup From No-Fly Zone," *Washington Post*, 6 September 1992, A1.

29   Victoria Graham, "New UN A-Arms Team Arrives in Baghdad, Kuwaiti Policeman Killed in Border Clash," *Washington Post*, 1 September 1992, A13.

30   Barton Gellman, "US Intercepts Iraqi Jet in 'No-Fly Zone': F-16s Repel First Incursion Since April in Area Protecting Kurds," *Washington Post*, 11 September 1992, A26.

31   3Robert S. Greenberger, "US Jet Shoots Down Iraqi Plane After Violation of No-Fly Zone – UN Panel's Efforts to Set Air Accord for Bosnia Continue Amid Crisis," *Wall Street Journal*, 28 December 1992, A1.

32   John M. Goshko, "Iraqis Again Violate 'No-Fly' Zone Ban: Warplanes Retreat as US Fighters Move in to Intercept Them," *Washington Post*, 30 December 1992, A12.

during late December.[33] The aircraft carrier *Kitty Hawk* steamed into the Persian Gulf as the year ended,[34] and on 6 January 1993, the United States, Britain, France, and Russia presented Saddam's government with an ultimatum to remove newly deployed surface-to-air missiles from south of the 32nd parallel within 48 hours or face military action.[35]

Iraq's immediate response was to proclaim its right to position its surface-to-air missiles anywhere within its borders, although it did not refuse to comply with the allied edict.[36] As the deadline for Iraqi compliance passed on 8 January, it appeared that Iraq was moving its SA-2 and SA-3 missile batteries northward, and the allies took no military action.[37] Undeterred, Iraq next informed the UN that it would bar weapons inspectors from flying over or landing in Iraq, and the UN Security Council responded with a stern but nonbinding statement instructing Iraq to live up to its obligations under UN resolutions.[38] Capping off Baghdad's flurry of bad behavior, Iraqi military personnel crossed the border into Kuwait on January 10 and seized a cache of Silkworm missiles abandoned there after the Gulf War and watched over ever since by the UN[39]

Iraq had gone to the brink and stepped back, part of a pattern of behavior that US officials by now had labeled "cheat and retreat."[40] By provoking crises and portraying Iraq as the victim of unlawful behavior by President Bush and his allies, Saddam hoped to distract his subjects from domestic economic and social woes and focus their animus on the West.[41] The cycles also served to highlight to the world the allegedly sanction-induced suffering of Iraqis, to keep the Iraqi military busy with meeting immediate external challenges, and to breed in ordinary Iraqis a sense of gratitude to Saddam for repeatedly averting general war.[42] Saddam had become quite skilled at setting the agenda in his relations with the West, but the hammer was about to fall on his regime in a way that it had not during the nearly two years since the

---

33   No Author, "Iraq Steps Up Flight Violations: Saddam's Mischief Gains Attention, Slowly," *Christian Science Monitor*, 31 December 1992.

34   John M. Goshko, "Iraqis Again Violate 'No-Fly' Zone Ban: Warplanes Retreat as US Fighters Move in to Intercept Them," *Washington Post*, 30 December 1992, A12.

35   Ann Devroy and Julia Preston, "Iraq Given Ultimatum On Missiles: Allies Order Removal From 'No-Fly Zone' Within 48 Hours," *Washington Post*, 7 January 1993, A1.

36   No Author, "World-Wide," *Wall Street Journal*, 8 January 1993, A1.

37   Ann Devroy and Barton Gellman, "US, Allies Let Deadline Pass: Iraq Is Said to Move Missiles," *Washington Post*, 9 January 1993, A1.

38   Ibid.

39   William Drozdiak, "Iraqis Seize Arms Interned in Kuwait: US Protests Raid at UN Border Post," *Washington Post*, 11 January 2003, A1.

40   R. Jeffrey Smith, "'Cheat and Retreat' Is Familiar by Now," *Washington Post*, 9 January 1993, A1.

41   Ibid.

42   Nora Boustany, "Saddam's Calculated Jabs: Messages Seen Aimed at Iraqis and World," *Washington Post*, 12 January 1993, A1.

Gulf War. The last straw was evidence suggesting that the Iraqi military had begun to deploy surface-to-air missiles in the northern no-fly zone.[43]

On 13 January 1993, President Bush ordered US warplanes to bomb Iraqi air defense targets in the southern no-fly zone. Involving more than 100 aircraft, the joint operation was designed to remind Saddam that the international community was still capable of containing him.[44] Allied pilots targeted six locations housing four SA-3 mobile surface-to-air missile sites and four air defense command bunkers.[45] The president also accelerated the scheduled deployment of a battalion of 1,000 US soldiers to Kuwait to underscore his seriousness.[46] The air operation was a significant one, and it appeared to wring some concessions from the Iraqis, with Baghdad pledging to cease its forays into Kuwait and allow UN flights into Iraq.[47] Yet behind the scenes, the coalition that carried out the assault was showing signs of age. The Bush administration initially had envisioned the air campaign as a 2–3 day operation that would go after airfields, weapons plants, and various headquarters in Baghdad, yet there was not sufficient consensus among the allies to bring off such a plan.[48] China, a permanent member of the UN Security Council, by now considered the southern no-fly zone to be a Western creation lacking formal UN backing, and various developing nations were uneasy with the idea that the US and its allies could tell a country where to position military equipment on its own territory.[49]

On the whole, Saddam remained unchastened. Iraq refused to return the Silkworm missiles it had plundered from Kuwait, and despite disassembling three surface-to-air missile batteries that had survived the air attacks, the regime did not back down from its stance that it could position such missiles anywhere on its soil.[50] Nor did Iraq permanently renounce its claims to materiel at its former naval base at Umm Qasr, which soon was to become a part of Kuwait, and even the new openness to UN fights was to unfold on a "case-by-case" basis.[51] Finally, Iraq dragged its feet in relinquishing its police posts in territory to be ceded to Kuwait.[52] The UN Security

---

43   Newspaper Editorial, "Iraqi Brinksmanship," *Christian Science Monitor*, 13 January 1993.

44   Gerald F. Seib, "Desert Reprise: Allied Air Raid on Iraq May Subdue Baghdad, Helping Clinton Team," *Wall Street Journal*, 14 January 1993, A1.

45   Barton Gellman and Ann Devroy, "US Delivers Limited Air Strike on Iraq: Bush Sends Battalion to Kuwait; Baghdad Appears to Make Concessions," *Washington Post*, 14 January 1993, A1.

46   Ibid.

47   Ibid.

48   Ibid.

49   Gerald F. Seib, "Desert Reprise: Allied Air Raid on Iraq May Subdue Baghdad, Helping Clinton Team," *Wall Street Journal*, 14 January 1993, A1.

50   Barton Gellman and Julia Preston, "Targets in Iraq Missed, Building Hit, US Says," *Washington Post*, 15 January 1993, A1.

51   Ibid.

52   Ann Devroy and Julia Preston, "Allies, Iraq Again Near Brink Over UN Inspector Flights: Iraq Says It Can't Guarantee Safety of UN Flights," *Washington Post*, 16 January

Council was unsatisfied with Saddam's determination to impose new limits on its flights into Iraq,[53] and the Bush administration was equally nonplused with the dictator's new threats on January 16 to shoot down allied aircraft over both no-fly zones.[54] And so the president ordered another round of military strikes against Iraq.

On 17 January Iraqi air defense forces in the northern no-fly zone locked radars on or fired on American, British, and French jets on five occasions. US aircraft responded by downing one Iraqi MiG-23 and bombing an SA-6 surface-to-air missile site. The main action occurred outside the no-fly zones, eight miles southeast of Baghdad, where 40 US cruise missiles slammed into a $6 billon complex of more than 20 buildings suspected of housing elements of Iraq's nuclear program. Britain, France, and Turkey voiced support for this operation, but the White House found itself on the defensive about whether British Prime Minister John Major had been hesitant to commit to either this action or the earlier one on 13 January.[55]

The next day, eighteen US and British planes bombed Iraqi sites in the southern no-fly zone that had not been destroyed in the 13 January strike while French planes provided cover.[56] US jets also struck antiaircraft sites in the northern no-fly zone.[57] The attacks in the south, which were the first daylight bombing runs since the Gulf War, put Iraq's air defenses there out of commission.[58] The air raids of 14 January were the final military actions of the George H.W. Bush administration against Iraq. The US military remained poised to take defensive measures, if necessary, but as a senior Bush administration official put it, "Our watch is over."[59] The president spent much of his last full day in office working the phones, thanking allies for their support on Iraq, and leaving it to his successor to chart the future course of US policy toward Iraq.[60] In the last of his periodic reports on Iraq, required under the congressional authorization for the use of force for the Gulf War, Bush also thanked the US Congress for its support.[61] Bush also noted in this final report that

---

1993, A1.

53   Trevor Rowe and Barton Gellman, "UN Rejects Iraq's Flight Restrictions: Bush, Security Aides Hold Consultations as Likelihood of New Military Strike Grows," *Washington Post*, 17 January 1993, A1.

54   No Author, "Key Events in Iraq Confrontation," *Wall Street Journal*, 21 January 1993, A1.

55   Ann Devroy and Barton Gellman, "US Attacks Industrial Site Near Baghdad: MiG Downed as Gulf Allies Display Might," *Washington Post*, 18 January 1993, A1.

56   No Author, "Key Events in Iraq Confrontation," *Wall Street Journal*, 21 January 1993, A1.

57   Ibid.

58   Barton Gellman and Ann Devroy, "US, Allied Jets Batter Iraq's Air Defenses," *Washington Post*, 19 January 1993, A1.

59   Ibid.

60   Ibid.

61   No Author, "Bush's Last Message to Hill Is About Iraq," *Washington Post*, 21 January 1993, A18.

he endorsed "the efforts of the Iraqi Congress [an Iraqi exile group in Britain] to develop a broad-based alternative to the Saddam regime."[62]

Saddam spent the last day of Bush's presidency looking to the future, trying desperately to open a new chapter in Iraq's relationship with the US and its allies. Although reiterating its opposition to the no-fly zones, Baghdad declared a cease-fire on all western warplanes patrolling them, and dropped all conditions on UN flights into Iraq.[63] The Iraqi dictator hoped that these concessions would provide a breathing space for the President-Elect to ease the conflict, but Clinton showed little interest. In response to a question by CBS News, Clinton answered: "My view is that it is almost inconceivable that we can have good relations with Iraq with [Saddam] there because he has given no indication that he is capable of being a reliable member of the community of nations."[64] As Clinton took his oath of office, Saddam was as firmly ensconced in power in Baghdad as ever, and the Gulf War coalition was fraying. Reports trickled out of Russia, Turkey, and Egypt that those countries' governments were increasingly unhappy about the protracted military confrontation with Iraq.[65] In Europe and the Arab world, officials charged that Washington had no coherent long-term strategy to handle Iraq, and that the US increasingly was exceeding its claimed UN mandate.[66]

Clinton's First Term

Clinton's foreign policy team laid out three possible courses of action toward Iraq: the new president could tighten the military screws on Saddam and seek to drive him from power; he could seek to contain Iraq through diplomacy while patching up relations with US allies; or he could play realpolitik in the Gulf by reaching a triangular accommodation among the US, Iraq, and Iran.[67] Urging a more assertive policy toward Iraq, columnist Jim Hoagland offered prescient words as the Clinton administration got underway:

> Clinton's behavior is more likely to be affected by these late strikes [by George H.W. Bush] than is Saddam's. Politically it will now be difficult for the new American president

---

62   Ibid.

63   R. Jeffrey Smith and Julia Preston, "Baghdad Declares Goodwill Cease-Fire: Clinton Granted Time to Weigh Curbs," *Washington Post*, 20 January 1993, A1.

64   Ibid.

65   Caryle Murphy, "Attacks May Have Strengthened Saddam: Limited Campaign Leaves Iraqi With Image of a Leader Who Has Successfully Defied US," *Washington Post*, 20 January 1993, A24.

66   R. Jeffrey Smith and Julia Preston, "Baghdad Declares Goodwill Cease-Fire: Clinton Granted Time to Weigh Curbs," *Washington Post*, 20 January 1993 A1.

67   Stephen Rosenfeld, "The Legacy From Bush," *Washington Post*, 22 January 1993, A21.

to be any less assertive than Bush in defending the no-fly zones in southern and northern Iraq and the right of the UN inspectors to enter Iraq.[68]

Evaluation of various strategic approaches to Iraq immediately took a back seat to actual events within the country. Skirmishes in the southern no-fly zone on 21 January and in the northern no-fly zone on 22 January elicited bombing of Iraqi radar sites that had locked on to US planes, and on 23 January antiaircraft fire at three US planes in the southern no-fly zone prompted retaliatory bombing of the Iraqi position.[69] Such episodes then stopped, and Iraq announced on 1 February that it was shutting down its radar in both no-fly zones, ostensibly so that Saddam's cease-fire of January 19 could be preserved.[70] This ushered in a period of relative calm, with Saddam praising Clinton's "anti-war past" on 14 February and urging the President to seek a more peaceful accommodation with Iraq.[71]

In mid-March 2003, the Clinton administration concluded its review of policy toward Iraq. Saddam's charm offensive had not produced much movement on Washington's part. The president would maintain the pressure on Saddam, but avoid calling explicitly for Saddam's removal as President Bush had done. One official concluded that "we cannot say that we are anywhere near the point yet where a viable alternative to Saddam can be found." The policy line would still be a hard one, if less personal. To make the point, the administration released a Pentagon report that detailed Iraqi torture of Kuwaiti citizens during the Gulf War. Despite the respite of the past two months, US officials expected that Saddam would soon engineer new provocations if UN sanctions on Iraq were not eased.[72]

Noting Iraqi noncompliance with UN resolutions, the US in late March supported the extension of economic sanctions against Iraq for a minimum of 60 days.[73] True to expectations, by 9 April Iraqi antiaircraft guns were firing at US planes in the northern no-fly zone and the US was responding with cluster bombs.[74] In mid-April, US planes bombed an Iraqi antiaircraft site slightly south of the northern no-fly zone after being illuminated by radar while patrolling the zone.[75] In mid-May, US jets

---

68   Jim Hoagland, "Crank Up To Bury Saddam," *Washington Post*, 21 January 1993, A23.

69   Howard Kurtz, "Jets Targeted By Iraqi Fire, Official Says: Navy A-6 Intruder Responds With Bomb," *Washington Post*, 24 January 1993, A21.

70   Nora Boustany, "Iraq Said to Shut Down Radar to Prevent New Confrontations," *Washington Post*, 2 February 1993, A14.

71   Nora Boustany, "Saddam: Clinton's 'Anti-War Past' Is a Good Thing," *Washington Post*, 15 February 1993, A29.

72   John M. Goshko, "US Pressure on Iraq Due to Continue," *Washington Post*, 21 March 1993, A37.

73   John Lancaster and R. Jeffrey Smith, "US Jets Bomb Iraqis After Being Fired On: Planes Patrolling Northern 'No-Fly Zone' Attack Antiaircraft Guns Near Saddam Dam," *Washington Post*, 10 April 1993, A12.

74   Ibid.

75   Guy Gugliotta, "US Jets Attack Iraqi Radar Site: Facility Outside 'No-Fly Zone' Said to Have Taken Threatening Action," *Washington Post*, 19 April 1993, A19.

patrolling the southern no-fly zone were fired at from the ground on three occasions but did not shoot back.[76]

All of these incidents were relatively minor, for Saddam was focusing on consolidating his power inside Iraq, particularly in the Shiite south. There the dictator's regime had reconstructed its security apparatuses, was detaining and executing dissenting youths quite efficiently, and was using food rations to inculcate loyalty. Civil servants had been bought off with higher salaries, and tribal and clan leaders had been co-opted with praise and resources and enlisted in the fight against the Shiite resistance.[77]

Things were fairly quiet until 11 July, when UN weapons inspectors left Iraq for a while after being prevented from securing two missile test facilities.[78] Predictably, Saddam's discontent with limits on Iraq's sovereignty translated into incidents in the no-fly zones. On 29 July, US jets bombed Iraqi antiaircraft sites in the southern no-fly zone after being illuminated by radar.[79] US jets hit a similar site in the northern no-fly zone on 19 August after being fired upon from the ground.[80] Such incidents in Iraq's skies occurred intermittently throughout the rest of 1993.

A particularly troubling note punctuated the year's end when twice Iraqi forces fired upon a US-led ground patrol in northern Iraq.[81] None of the American, French, and Kurdish troops was injured, but the event marked the first time that Iraqi forces had fired on coalition ground troops since the end of the Gulf War.[82] Saddam, having achieved what the US dubbed "technical compliance" with UN resolutions on his weapons programs, was increasingly angry with American resistance to the resumption of Iraqi oil sales.[83] US Secretary of State Madeleine Albright enunciated the Clinton administration's position by setting forth further preconditions for supporting such oil sales: Iraqi recognition of Kuwait's independence and an end to repression of the Kurds in the north and Shiites in the south.[84] Perhaps surprisingly, the president did not order military retaliation for the gunfire episode in northern Iraq.

A tragic friendly-fire incident in the northern no-fly zone dominated the news from Iraq in mid-April 1994. Two US fighters mistook two US UH-60 Black Hawk helicopters for Russian-made Hind helicopters and shot them down, killing a total

---

76   No Author, "US Jets Fired Upon By Iraqis," *Washington Post*, 21 May 1993, A31.

77   Caryle Murphy, "Firm Hand of Saddam Has Cowed Iraq's Once-Rebellious Shiite South," *Washington Post*, 29 June 1993, A14.

78   Nora Boustany, "UN Team Rebuffed By Iraq: Missile Site Standoff Draws US Warning," *Washington Post*, 12 July 1993, A1.

79   No Author, "World-Wide," *Wall Street Journal*, 30 July 1993, A1.

80   No Author, "World-Wide," *Wall Street Journal*, 19 August 1993, A1.

81   Barton Gellman, "US-Led Patrol Is Fired On in North Iraq: No Casualties Reported in Security Zone 'Harassment' Incident," *Washington Post*, 23 December 1993, A15.

82   Ibid.

83   Ibid.

84   Ibid.

of 26 people.[85] The dead consisted of 15 Americans, 5 Kurds, 3 Turks, 2 British citizens, and 1 Frenchman who were part of the 1,700 personnel now serving with the Military Coordination Center near Zakhu as observers and liaisons engaged in the protection of the Kurds.[86] The incident was a reminder that, more than three years after the Gulf War, the US was still expending significant money—and blood—to contain Saddam.[87] Yet the Clinton administration was undeterred in pursuing its main objectives vis-à-vis Iraq: keeping the military and political pressure on Saddam while protecting the Kurds to prevent them from once again fleeing in huge numbers into neighboring countries.[88] With roughly 100,000 reasonably well-equipped Iraqi troops positioned along a 180-mile segment of the northern no-fly zone's southern border, only a few allied ground observers and the constant vigilance of allied pilots stood between Saddam and his re-conquest of Kurdistan.[89]

The costs of the no-fly zones and America's unfinished business with Saddam were growing, and so were fissures within the old Gulf War alliance. In late April 1994, Turkey announced that it would compensate Iraq with humanitarian aid in return for over 8 million barrels of oil that had been trapped in a shut-off Turkish pipeline since the fall of 1990 and which Turkey now wanted to refine. This was a technical violation of the sanctions against Iraq, but US officials did not consider it worth a major scrape with Ankara that might jeopardize basing rights for US, British, and French aircraft at Incirlik.[90]

By mid-October 1994, Saddam had repositioned some of his elite military units uncomfortably close to the border with Kuwait, prompting President Clinton to order a major buildup of US forces in Kuwait and pledge to send as many as 200,000 troops to the region if necessary.[91] France openly criticized the president's motives for the move, attributing it more to the political needs of vulnerable Democratic congressional candidates as midterm elections approached than to any objective Iraqi threat.[92] France contributed only a single navy frigate to the buildup in the Persian Gulf and vowed that its forces would only participate in military action sanctioned by the UN Security Council.[93] The crisis passed without any precipitant action by

---

85   Thomas E. Ricks, "US Fighters Accidentally Shoot Down Two American Helicopters Over Iraq," *Wall Street Journal*, 15 April 1994, A10.

86   John F. Harris and John Lancaster, "US Jets Over Iraq Mistakenly Down Two American Helicopters, Killing 26: Officials Set Investigation of Accident," *Washington Post*, 15 April 1994, A1.

87   Caryle Murphy and Thomas W. Lippman, "'It's Important Work': US Still Committed to Protecting Kurds," *Washington Post*, 15 April 1994, A1.

88   Ibid.

89   Ibid.

90   Caryle Murphy, "Turkish-Iraqi Oil Plan Raises Sanctions Issues," *Washington Post*, 29 April 1994, A46.

91   William Drozdiak, "France Implies Domestic Politics in US Sparked Response to Iraq," *Washington Post*, 13 October 1994, A29.

92   Ibid.

93   Ibid.

Saddam, but it illustrated that he still had the power to make US policymakers dance to his tune.

Throughout the spring of 1995, Washington and Baghdad remained locked in a test of wills, although events over the no-fly zones flared only occasionally. In the south, the Shiites were largely subjugated. In the north, where *Operation Provide Comfort* continued, the Kurds were preoccupied with political infighting. The US thus continued to contain Saddam, waiting for some change within Iraqi politics that would bring about his demise.

US-Iraq relations during the spring and summer of 1996 were dominated by Saddam's belligerence toward UN weapons inspectors. In March, Saddam refused to allow the inspectors access to several weapons program-related facilities including one government ministry and buildings of both the Republican Guard and Saddam's special presidential guard. A formal demand by the UN Security Council ultimately got the inspectors inside the facilities in question, but anything of interest once there was long gone. Weeks later, Deputy Prime Minister Tariq Aziz declared that no further inspections of government ministries and security facilities would be permitted.[94]

In March 1996, Jordan, which had broken with the US over the Gulf War, allowed US warplanes enforcing the northern no-fly zone to begin flying from its soil. Amman's policy change was a sure sign that the two countries were patching up their relationship, and it came at a time when the US was in need of airbases in addition to Incirlik to patrol northern Iraq.[95]

In mid-June 1996, Saddam denied UN weapons inspectors' access to all facilities in Iraq. UN disarmament chief Rolf Ekeus of Sweden went to Baghdad for meetings and discovered that Saddam's approach to this crisis was unique: Iraq was defying, without any nuance or qualification, Resolution 687, which required Iraq to end its weapons of mass destruction programs. The US and its Gulf War allies thus faced the choice of allowing Iraq to rearm or using massive force to make Baghdad comply with the resolution. Just when the allies were preparing to step over the brink, Saddam blinked once again, and the crisis eased.[96]

By early September 1996, Saddam's ground forces were the focus of international worry, making inroads once again into his traditional killing grounds in Kurdistan. In a macabre twist, one of two warring Kurdish factions had asked Iran for military aid, and the other faction had then asked Saddam to intervene on its side.[97] Into Saddam's lap had fallen something he could not have anticipated—an invitation by Iraqis to reestablish a military presence in the northern Iraq, beneath the no-fly zone—and he

---

94   Richard C. Hottelet, "Saddam: A Compulsive Gambler, and a Loser," *Christian Science Monitor*, 26 June 1996, 19.

95   No Author, "US Warplanes in Jordan," *Washington Post*, 13 April 1996, A26.

96   Richard C. Hottelet, "Saddam: A Compulsive Gambler, and a Loser," *Christian Science Monitor*, 26 June 1996, 19.

97   Gerald F. Seib, "Capital Journal: How to Turn Saddam's Gain Into New Pain," *Wall Street Journal*, 4 September 1996, A16.

complied.[98] Iraqi tanks, artillery, and 30,000–40,000 elite Republican Guard troops stormed into Kurdistan[99] en route to Irbil and other population centers.[100]

The UN responded by suspending a resolution it had passed earlier in the spring paving the way for Iraq to sell up to 700,000 barrels of oil each day to purchase food and medicine.[101] The resolution's suspension left Iraq's economy no way to break out of its isolation.[102] The response by the US, however, was both militarily fierce and strategically innovative. The US announced that effective at noon on 3 September it was expanding the southern no-fly zone northward by about 70 miles, from the 32nd to the 33rd parallel, to just south of Baghdad's suburbs.[103] The two no-fly zones would now cover 60 percent of Iraq.[104] In two successive unilateral military operations, the US on 2 September launched 27 cruise missiles from two Navy ships and two B-52 bombers at 14 air defense and command and control sites in the newly enlarged southern no-fly zone.[105] The next day, the US used a second volley of 17 cruise missiles from three surface ships and a submarine to mop up about half of these targets.[106] Taken together, the attacks were the largest use of force against Iraq since the Gulf War.[107]

By retaliating hundreds of miles away from the scene of Saddam's aggression, the Clinton administration had made a decision to fight on ground of its own choosing, protecting the Persian Gulf oil fields to the south of Iraq while wreaking heavy damage on Saddam's most valuable military assets.[108] Despite the president's insistence after the first strike that the campaign would "make Saddam pay a price" for his brutal drive into Kurdish population centers, the broader purpose was to damage what Clinton called the dictator's capacity to "threaten his neighbors and

---

98   Ibid.

99   Jonathan S. Landy, "Impact of Message Sent by Missile: Clinton May Gain Politically at Home, But Strike Sows Uncertainty in Mideast," *Christian Science Monitor*, 4 September 1996, 1.

100   Bradley Graham, "US Launches More Cruise Missiles Against Iraq; Air Defenses Near Baghdad Hit; 'No-Fly' Zone Extended in South," *Washington Post*, 4 September 1996, A1.

101   Ibid.

102   Ibid.

103   Ibid.

104   Dana Priest, "US Planes Intensify Iraq Strikes: Air Defense System is Primary Target," *Washington Post*, 2 March 1999, A1.

105   Bradley Graham, "US Launches More Cruise Missiles Against Iraq; Air Defenses Near Baghdad Hit; 'No-Fly' Zone Extended in South," *Washington Post*, 4 September 1996, A1.

106   Ibid.

107   Jonathan S. Landy, "Impact of Message Sent by Missile: Clinton May Gain Politically at Home, But Strike Sows Uncertainty in Mideast," *Christian Science Monitor*, 4 September 1996, 1.

108   Gerald F. Seib, "Capital Journal: How to Turn Saddam's Gain Into New Pain," *Wall Street Journal*, 4 September 1996, A16.

America's interests."[109] Rather than intervene on the ground in Kurdistan, and get tangled up between warring factions there, it was easier for the US to establish complete dominance of the skies in southern Iraq while offering increased protection to Kuwait and Saudi Arabia in the process.[110] The administration said nothing about the northern no-fly zone, which, of course, had originally been established to protect the Kurds.[111]

The US had been forced to go it alone militarily in the attacks of 2 and 3 September because not one ally was willing to offer assistance. Russia argued that the US should have given Saddam time to withdraw from Kurdistan before attacking, and France expressed "anxiety" over the unilateral US action.[112] Only Britain, Germany, Japan, and Canada voiced strong support for the raids.[113] Spain said it understood why the US had acted, but agreed with Russia that the timing was premature.[114] Asked on 4 September whether the Gulf War coalition was defunct, Clinton responded, "I don't think it's dead; I think quite the contrary," and indicated that Arab governments were more supportive behind the scenes than in their public comments.[115]

The attention of US policymakers in the coming days was on southern Iraq, not the north. Baghdad gave its pilots and air defense batteries a green light to go after allied planes policing the enlarged southern no-fly zone.[116] Skirmishes between Iraqi and allied planes took place over the southern no-fly zone on 4 September, and US planes continued to return fire against antiaircraft centers on the ground.[117]

Secretary of State Warren Christopher conceded that the US did not have any expectation Saddam would really withdraw from Kurdistan.[118] However, the US policy of seemingly trading protection of the Kurds in Iraq's north for complete

---

109   Bradley Graham, "US Launches More Cruise Missiles Against Iraq; Air Defenses Near Baghdad Hit; 'No-Fly' Zone Extended in South," *Washington Post*, 4 September 1996, A1.

110   Ibid.

111   Ibid.

112   Charles Trueheart, "Support for Strikes Falls Short of Gulf War Consensus; France, Russia Criticize US Action; Britain, Germany Call Move Justified," *Washington Post*, 4 September 1996, A19.

113   Jonathan S. Landy, "Impact of Message Sent by Missile: Clinton May Gain Politically at Home, But Strike Sows Uncertainty in Mideast," *Christian Science Monitor*, 4 September 1996, 1.

114   Charles Trueheart, "Support for Strikes Falls Short of Gulf War Consensus; France, Russia Criticize US Action; Britain, Germany Call Move Justified," *Washington Post*, 4 September 1996, A19.

115   John F. Harris and John Mintz, "US Airplanes Patrol Wider 'No-Fly' Zone," *Washington Post*, 5 September 1996, A1.

116   Bradley Graham, "US Launches More Cruise Missiles Against Iraq; Air Defenses Near Baghdad Hit; 'No-Fly' Zone Extended in South," *Washington Post*, 4 September 1996, A1.

117   John F. Harris and John Mintz, "US Warplanes Patrol Wider 'No-Fly' Zone," *Washington Post*, 5 September 1996, A1.

118   Ibid.

dominance in the south did not sit well with some analysts. Columnist Lally Weymouth observed that the Kurds were now vulnerable not just to Saddam's forces, but also to those of Turkey, which voiced an increasing interest in occupying parts of Kurdistan to prevent cross-border attacks by Kurdish guerrillas.[119] Indeed, Turkish planes would soon bomb guerrilla bases in northern Iraq while the US turned a blind eye.[120] Weymouth's judgment on the Clinton administration's handling of Iraq was clear and harsh:

> The United States needs to formulate a coherent policy to force Saddam from northern Iraq or to remove him from power. Air attacks should target Iraqi troops in the north or Baghdad itself. If the Iraqi dictator's actions spell the end of the protected northern zone, they constitute a tremendous setback for the United States. America's honor and prestige are at stake.[121]

Skirmishes over both no-fly zones were occurring with greater frequency and intensity by 11 September, prompting President Clinton to send additional F-117A jet fighters to Kuwait and move B-52 bombers closer to the theater in preparation for new and massive air strikes against Iraq.[122] The US military buildup continued for several days, but the president put plans for immediate operation on the back burner when Baghdad announced that it would no longer fire at planes policing the two no-fly zones.[123] Complicating matters was Kuwait's initial reluctance to accept a deployment of 5,000 US troops[124] to augment the 1,200 already there, a disagreement ultimately resolved by reducing the number to 3,500.[125]

The Clinton administration informed Iraq that it would not be sufficient simply not to target and fire at allied aircraft over the no-fly zones; in addition, certain antiaircraft equipment, including missiles, would have to be removed from the zones.[126] Calm prevailed for a time in the no-fly zones, but it was becoming clear by mid-October that Iraq had substantially rebuilt its air defense network in southern Iraq, including batteries of surface-to-air missiles, within two weeks of the strikes

---

119   Lally Weymouth, "Setback for the United States," *Washington Post*, 6 September 1996, A23.

120   William D. Hartung, "A Better Way in Iraq: The Code of Conduct Bill Could Help Elsewhere, Too," *Christian Science Monitor*, 9 September 1996, 19.

121   Lally Weymouth, "Setback for the United States," *Washington Post*, 6 September 1996, A23.

122   Bradley Graham, "US Readies for Airstrikes After Iraqi Attack on Jets," *Washington Post*, 12 September 1996, A1.

123   Carla Anne Robbins and Thomas E. Ricks, "US Builds Forces in Gulf, Puts Off Attack," *Wall Street Journal*, 16 September 1996, A3.

124   Ibid.

125   Dana Priest and John F. Harris, "US to Send More Troops to Kuwait: Additional Demands Are Issued to Saddam," *Washington Post*, 18 September 1996, A1.

126   Ibid.

of 2 and 3 September.[127] By early November 1996, as President Clinton was poised for reelection, Iraqi radars were once again illuminating US aircraft over the no-fly zones, and the pilots were responding with force.[128] Republicans in Congress, for their part, were complaining that the US had spent too much money on air strikes that had done only temporary damage.[129]

Clinton's Second Term

The year 1997 was one of occasional skirmishes over the Iraqi no-fly zones, but devoid of any major showdowns between Saddam and President Clinton. By early 1998, however, congressional Republicans and conservative think tanks intensified the pressure on Clinton to change the regime in Baghdad. Some proposals called for formally recognizing a provisional government, providing it with access to frozen Iraqi assets, and arming insurgents to capture oil fields in southern Iraq.[130] These proposals had an air of unreality about them, however, given that the divided and weak Iraqi opposition had not carried out any military operations against Saddam in almost three years.[131] Most Iraqi exiles had by now begun to assemble in London, under the banner of the Iraqi National Congress, headed by Ahmed Chalabi.[132]

By February 1998, the UN found itself locked in a new and protracted standoff with Saddam over access by weapons inspectors to his country's facilities. These repeated episodes illustrated the limits of aerial bombing to bring Saddam to heel. Despite maintaining no-fly zones over most of Iraq, and despite periodical punishment not only to Iraqi antiaircraft sites and even to the basic infrastructure of Saddam's regime, he still could precipitate crises whenever he wished.[133] Iraqi radar continued to lock onto allied jets patrolling the no-fly zones, prompting swift retaliation from the air,[134] but Iraq had not launched a surface-to-air missile against allied aircraft since late 1996.[135]

---

127   Dana Priest, "Iraq Rebuilt Missile System After US Attacks, Official Says," *Washington Post*, October 15, 1996, A12.

128   Robert Kilborn, Lance Carden, and Yvonne Zipp, "The News in Brief," *Christian Science Monitor*, 5 November 1996, 2.

129   Dana Priest, "Iraq Rebuilt Missile System After US Attacks, Official Says," *Washington Post*, 15 October 1996, A12.

130   Daniel Pearl, "West Tries to Energize Iraqi Opposition: Splintered Movement Shows Few Signs of Strength So Far," *Wall Street Journal*, 29 January 1998, 1.

131   Ibid.

132   Vernon Loeb, "Iraqi Opposition Waiting for a Role: Leaders Worry That Goal of Airstrikes is Not to Topple Saddam Hussein," *Washington Post*, 18 December 1998, A57.

133   Joseph C. Cyrulik, "So We Control the Air," *Washington Post*, 3 February 1998, A17.

134   Robert Kilborn, Lance Carden, and Caryn Coatney, "The News in Brief," *Christian Science Monitor*, 1 July 1998, 2.

135   Barton Gellman, "US Planes Hit Iraqi Site After Missile Attack: Jets Were Fired On in 'No-Fly' Zone," *Washington Post*, 29 December 1998, A1.

By early August of 1998, Saddam was again massing troops in northern Iraq near the cities of Irbil and Dihok, using his renewed military presence there to harass the Kurds and also to exert pressure on Kurdish leaders.[136] More than one commentator questioned the Clinton administration's continuing strategy of retaliating in the south and center of Iraq for Saddam's transgressions in the northern no-fly zone. Peter W. Galbraith urged the administration to "declare that any Iraqi military incursion into Kurdish-held territory will be met by sustained bombing for as long as the attack continues. Saddam should know that potential targets will include the forces moving north and military assets throughout the country."[137]

In mid-November 1998, Clinton planned and then called off an air campaign against Saddam's regime, but he simultaneously took a new step by calling for regime change in Baghdad. The president endorsed the just-enacted Iraqi Liberation Act, which sought to encourage Iraqi opposition factions in the north and south to coalesce into a coherent force capable of overthrowing Saddam. The Iraqi Liberation Act authorized $97 million in US military aid to the Iraqi opposition.[138]

Things finally came to a head militarily in mid-December 1998 when President Clinton ordered *Operation Desert Fox* against Saddam's regime. Over the course of 70 hours, US and British forces dropped over 600 bombs and launched more than 400 cruise missiles on targets in Iraq, with the operation concluding on 19 December.[139] Conjecture differed on whether Saddam's regime had been shaken by the assault, or strengthened by his ability to survive it.[140]

Iraq quickly vowed that UN weapons inspectors would not be allowed back in Iraq,[141] threatened the future of both UN relief efforts and the oil-for-food program,[142] and by 26 December was vowing to fire on allied warplanes in its no-fly zones "at will."[143] Saddam also was working harder than ever to wriggle out from under the UN sanctions regime, seeking to portray Iraq as a victim of US and British aggression and appealing to Arab countries to break the UN economic embargo.[144] The debate

---

136   Peter W. Galbraith, "A New Line in the Sand," *Washington Post*, 9 August 1998, C7.

137   Ibid.

138   Vernon Loeb, "Iraqi Opposition Waiting for a Role: Leaders Worry That Goal of Airstrikes Is Not to Topple Saddam Hussein," *Washington Post*, 18 December 1998, A57.

139   Thomas E. Ricks, "Persian Gulf, US Danger Zone: Military Has Been Committed to Hot Spot Despite Risk," *Washington Post*, 15 October 2000, A1.

140   Scott Peterson, "Iraq Sees Battles With US as a Help: It Plans to Fire on US War Jets in the No-Fly Zones in a Strategy Seen as Boosting Chances of an End to Sanctions," *Christian Science Monitor*, 28 December 1998, 1.

141   Ibid.

142   Barton Gellman, "US Planes Hit Iraqi Site After Missile Attack: Jets Were Fired On in 'No-Fly' Zone, *Washington Post*, 29 December 1998, A1.

143   Scott Peterson, "Iraq Sees Battles With US as a Help: It Plans to Fire on US War Jets in the No-Fly Zones in a Strategy Seen as Boosting Chances of an End to Sanctions," *Christian Science Monitor*, 28 December 1998, 1.

144   Ibid.

in the UN over the future of the sanctions regime predictably pitted the US and Britain against Russia, China, and France. Interestingly, Baghdad aimed most of its vitriol against the latter three nations, charging that they were not doing enough to champion its cause.[145] Iraq, in the words of one UN diplomat, had "embarked on a policy I might call total resistance."[146]

As 1998 drew to a close, the US and Iraq were locked in a "military and diplomatic cat-and-mouse game" that promised to stretch far into the future.[147] By early January 1999, Iraqi planes were routinely entering the no-fly zones to confront US and British jets.[148] The Clinton administration's interest in getting UN weapons inspectors back into Iraq was waning, in part because their absence from Iraq provided a helpful justification for keeping economic sanctions against Baghdad in place.[149] And the constant exchanges of fire in the no-fly zones provided an opportunity to materially damage Iraq's antiaircraft capabilities, choke off training and deployment opportunities for the Iraqi air force, and continuously gather intelligence on the Iraqi military.[150] The US and Britain had commenced a "low-level war of attrition" against Saddam designed to contain him while providing a growing opening to internal opposition to his regime.[151] In contrast with past military action, American and British bombing no longer sought to wring specific concessions from the Iraqi dictator.

As Iraq's intransigence intensified, and as Saddam's spokesmen openly challenged Kuwait's right to statehood, critics questioned whether the Clinton administration's approach to Iraq was anything more than a dead end. Of America's propensity to bomb targets in the no-fly zones and use its veto in the UN Security Council to keep in place economic sanctions against Baghdad (which France now proposed lifting) the *Washington Post* editorialized, "Both have about them the forlorn air of holding actions. Neither is likely to ensure Saddam Hussein's isolation, hasten his downfall or eradicate his weapons of mass destruction."[152]

---

145   Ibid.

146   Barton Gellman, "US Planes Hit Iraqi Site After Missile Attack: Jets Were Fired On in 'No-Fly' Zone, *Washington Post*, 29 December 1998, A1.

147   Robert S. Greenberger, "US Jets Clash With Iraq's Air Defense: Face-Offs Likely to Persist In the Coming Months, UN to Resume Debate," *Wall Street Journal*, 29 December 1998, 1.

148   Robert S. Greenberger and Thomas E. Ricks, "US Fighter Jets Fire at 8 Iraqi Planes: Dictator Urges Arab Revolt Against US," *Wall Street Journal*, 6 January 1999, 1.

149   Barton Gellman, "US Planes Hit Iraqi Site After Missile Attack: Jets Were Fired On in 'No-Fly' Zone," *Washington Post*, 29 December 1998, A1.

150   Robert S. Greenberger, "US, Iraq Again Trade Hostile Fire," *Wall Street Journal*, 31 December 1998, p. 1.

151   Jonathan S. Landy, "Saddam Maneuvers to Win Arab Sympathy: Behind Iraqi Leader's Skirmishes With US Is Attempt to Split West and Bolster His Standing," *Christian Science Monitor*, 4 January 1999, 2.

152   Newspaper Editorial, "Rewarding Saddam Hussein," *Washington Post*, 17 January 1999, B6.

By the end of January 1999, the US and British warplanes had bombed Iraqi targets more than 20 times since the end of *Operation Desert Fox*.[153] But despite the Clinton administration's new touting of "regime change" as a solution for Iraq, there was no sign that Iraqi opposition forces would ever be in a position to supplant the Iraqi leader.[154] Even the UN appeared to have given up on reestablishing weapons inspections in Iraq.[155] Perhaps most importantly, at the end of January President Clinton granted US pilots much greater latitude to attack Iraq's air defense system.[156]

Searching desperately to open a fissure in the US-led coalition against Iraq, Saddam sent his deputy prime minister, Tariq Aziz, to meet with Turkey's leadership in mid-February 1999. Baghdad's hope was that Ankara, which had been increasingly critical of US and British air strikes in the no-fly zones, would sever the use of Incirlik air base by allied pilots to patrol the northern no-fly zone.[157] Instead, and despite both intensifying military confrontations in the skies over Iraq and claims by Saddam that US and British bombing was killing Iraqi civilians, the Turks rebuffed Aziz, telling him Iraq must comply with the UN disarmament resolutions.[158]

On 1 March 1999, allied pilots finished two days of bombing in the no-fly zones that was the heaviest military action against Iraq since *Operation Desert Fox*. The US was slowly increasing both the kind of Iraq targets it was hitting and the number of bombs it dropped on them.[159] A total of more than 50 air strikes had now been carried out since *Operation Desert Fox*, and the latest bombing runs had even knocked an oil pipeline out of commission in northern Iraq.[160] Iraq's air defense network and military communications facilities were taking a beating. The Pentagon now estimated that 20 per cent of Iraq's surface-to-air missiles had been destroyed, while almost all of those remaining had been withdrawn into the center of the country.[161] The US was prosecuting with increased determination its low-level air war with Iraq and trying to attract little attention from the world community in the process.[162]

---

153   Carla Anne Robbins and Thomas E. Ricks, "US Effort to Curb Iraq Is Fraught With Risks," *Wall Street Journal*, 29 January 1999, A13.

154   Ibid.

155   Ibid.

156   Dana Priest, "US Planes Intensify Iraq Strikes: Air Defense System is Primary Target," *Washington Post*, 2 March 1999, A1.

157   Hugh Pope, "Iraq's Aziz Plans to Visit Turkey in Possible Bid to Blunt Airstrikes," *Wall Street Journal*, 11 February 1999, 1.

158   Howard Schneider, "Iraq Threatens Broader Attacks: Turkey Is Named a Missile Target For Assisting Allied Air Patrols," *Washington Post*, 16 February 1999, A11.

159   Thomas E. Ricks, "US Executes Airstrikes Against Iraq: Regional Politics Appear to Have Role," *Wall Street Journal*, 2 March 1999, 1.

160   Ibid.

161   Ibid.

162   Dana Priest, "US Planes Intensify Iraq Strikes: Air Defense System is Primary Target," *Washington Post*, 2 March 1999, A1.

Despite its aggressive military approach to Iraq, the Clinton administration fielded heavy criticism from conservatives who argued that it had not moved decisively enough to implement the Iraqi Liberation Act. In February 1999 the President had designated seven groups as candidates to receive arms and training, and he put in place an official to coordinate the effort. But, skeptical of the Iraqi opposition's capabilities, Clinton was slow to actually disburse any funds.[163]

In late June 1999, Clinton responded to requests from the Pentagon by granting US pilots in Iraq greater authority "to protect themselves and their missions."[164] By mid-August 1999, Iraq was routinely highlighting the toll taken on civilians by the less restricted bombing campaign by the US, claiming that 134 Iraqi civilians had been killed by 17 August.[165] Retribution for Iraqi radar illumination or targeting of a US aircraft, or a direct challenge by an Iraqi plane, now would often bring retaliatory bombing of Iraqi targets hours later in a separate sector of the no-fly zone in question.[166] By the end of August 1999, US and British aircraft had flown 10,000 combat and combat-support sorties over Iraq since *Operation Desert Fox* and had dropped over 1,000 bombs and missiles on more than 400 targets.[167]

On 31 October 1999,[168] Congress followed up on its initial spadework under the Iraqi Liberation Act by appropriating an additional $8 million to the Iraqi opposition.[169] The Band-Aid was but the latest confirmation that America's interest in helping the Iraqi opposition was too little, too late.[170] No amount of bombing in the no-fly zones could cover up the fact that President Clinton's pledge of December 1998 that his administration would "strengthen our engagement with the full range of Iraqi opposition forces" had come to naught.[171] Despite the presence of an Iraqi opposition headquarters in London, there existed beneath the no-fly zones no organized opposition with even a faint hope of endangering Saddam's regime.[172]

---

163   Jonathan S. Landy, "Who's Winning Quiet War in Iraq? Pentagon Steps Up Airstrikes Against Iraq In an Intensified Effort to Contain – and Possibly Remove – a Wily Saddam," *Christian Science Monitor*, 4 March 1999, 1.

164   Robert Suro, "US Air Raids on Iraq Become an Almost Daily Ritual: As Fighters Retaliate for Threats, Mission Faces Allies' Questions," *Washington Post*, 30 August 1999, A3.

165   No Author, "World In Brief," *Washington Post*, 18 August 1999, A16.

166   Robert Suro, "US Air Raids on Iraq Become an Almost Daily Ritual: As Fighters Retaliate for Threats, Mission Faces Allies' Questions," *Washington Post*, 30 August 1999, A3.

167   Ibid.

168   Bob Kerrey, "Finish the War: Liberate Iraq," *Wall Street Journal*, 12 September 2001, A14.

169   Daniel Byman, "All Talk, No Action May Be Best With Iraq," *Washington Post*, 2 January 2000, B4.

170   Ibid.

171   Ibid.

172   Ibid.

Saddam showed no new signs of flexibility with respect to arms inspections in 2000, saying in April of that year that a halt to US bombing in the no-fly zones and an end to aid to the Iraqi opposition were preconditions to the reintroduction of UN weapons inspectors. Neither France nor Russia was willing to lean on Baghdad to renew weapons inspections. As Sergei Lavrov, Russia's ambassador to the UN put it: "The Security Council never authorized creation of any no-fly zones ... and the Security Council never presented the task of undermining the regime in Baghdad."[173]

Indeed, Iraq increasingly was exploiting the bombing in the no-fly zones for sympathy on the world stage. By mid-June 2000, Iraq's air defense command claimed that US and British bombings during the 18 months since *Operation Desert Fox* had killed 300 Iraqis (including more than 200 civilians) and injured more than 800. In the more than nine years of the no-fly zones' existence, more than 280,000 sorties had been flown to enforce them, with no aircraft lost to Iraqi fire.[174]

By August 2000, as the 10th anniversary of UN-imposed economic sanctions against Iraq approached, certain segments of global public opinion had come to associate the enforcement of the no-fly zones with the sanctions as wreaking devastation on ordinary Iraqis rather than on Saddam's regime. Illustrative of this trend was a demonstration in front of the White House where protesters claimed that more than 1 million Iraqis had died due to malnutrition and a shortage of medical supplies over the past decade. Iraqi children, the protesters pointed out, were bearing the burden of Saddam's misbehavior.[175]

In September 2000, Saddam was still lashing out against the enforcement of the no-fly zones, taking advantage of a Labor Day pause in US enforcement of them to send one of his fighters into not only Iraqi but also Saudi Arabian air space. Coming in tandem with new claims by Saddam that Kuwait was tapping oil deposits that belonged to Iraq, it appeared that the Iraqi dictator was straining more erratically against the tethers of American and British containment. More worrisome was Iraq's alleged abuse of the UN oil-for-food program to import luxury items for Saddam's Baathists while selling food and medicine abroad rather than using them for the Iraqi people. And, with UN weapons inspectors now having been absent from Iraq for nearly two years, there was no way to tell how much rebuilding and concealment Saddam had been able to do with respect to his weapons of mass destruction programs.[176]

---

173   Colum Lynch, "US Strikes, Iraqi Arms Compliance Are Linked," *Washington Post*, 14 April 2000, A21.

174   Edward Cody, "Under Iraqi Skies, a Canvas of Death: Tour of Villages Reveals Human Cost of US-Led Sorties in 'No-Fly' Zones," *Washington Post*, 16 June 2000, A1.

175   David Montgomery, "Bread and Sympathy Offered for Iraq: 104 Protesters Arrested at White House Seeking End to Decade-Long Embargo," *Washington Post*, 8 August 2000, B3.

176   Newspaper Editorial, "Saddam's Winning Wars," *Washington Post*, 25 September 2000, A20.

It appeared in autumn 2000 that the international sanctions regime against Iraq was coming unstuck. Civilian flights from Russia, France, Jordan, and Yemen started to land at Baghdad's Saddam International Airport. Although neither France nor Russia was ready to resume trading with Iraq, and several countries would not grant permission for civilian planes to fly over their territory en route to Iraq, some Arab nations opened their borders to travel to and from Iraq while reopening embassies in Baghdad. One senior US official nonetheless claimed that it was "premature to conclude that the sanctions are crumbling." The question of whether Saddam was reconstituting his weapons of mass destruction remained unanswerable.[177]

By late October 2000, as President Clinton's two would-be successors awaited the imminent verdict of the American people at the polls, enforcement of the no-fly zones in Iraq was costing the US $1 billion per year.[178] As well, the US found itself increasingly alone on Iraq policy. The bombing campaign in the no-fly zones truly had become, for all intents and purposes, an American undertaking.[179] The Clinton administration, seeking to avoid a last major confrontation with Saddam, consented to the transit of the no-fly zones by Iraqi commercial flights, provided that Iraq provide 48 hours advance notice.[180] The US also went along with the UN's decision to allow Iraq's oil sales on the world market to be made in euros rather than dollars.[181]

The Clinton administration's policy of frequent military strikes in the no-fly zones had loosened the anti-Saddam coalition in the UN and given Iraq a new victim status in the eyes of some.[182] The question remained as to whether Vice-President Al Gore (with his ties to Clinton's Iraq policy) or Texas Governor George W. Bush (having surrounded himself with some of the same men who had advised his father to leave Saddam in power at the end of the Gulf War) would turn over a new leaf.[183] By Election Day, neither man had offered a compelling plan for reinvigorating US policy toward Iraq.[184]

---

177   Colum Lynch, "US Says Sanctions on Iraq Not Crumbling," *Washington Post*, 30 September 2000, A16.

178   Neil King, Jr., "New Iraq Policy: Yes, More Mr. Nice Guy," *Wall Street Journal*, 1 November 2000, A23.

179   Thomas E. Ricks, "Containing Iraq: A Forgotten War – As US Tactics Are Softened, Questions About Mission Arise," *Washington Post*, 24 October 2000, A1.

180   Neil King, Jr., "New Iraq Policy: Yes, More Mr. Nice Guy," *Wall Street Journal*, 1 November 2000, A23.

181   Ibid.

182   Ibid.

183   Newspaper Editorial, "Saddam's Winning Wars," *Washington Post*, 25 September 2000, A20.

184   Ibid.

George W. Bush's Administration

Of all the challenges facing President-Elect George W. Bush, none was more difficult than formulating policy toward Iraq. As Gerald F. Seib put it as the protracted post-Election Day drama of the 2000 presidential contest began to unfold, "America's most implacable foe is Iraq, and American policy toward Iraq is falling apart."[185] Despite growing disquiet amid Arab and European countries, Bush administration officials gave every signal that they intended to continue a tough policy toward Saddam.[186] US and British enforcement of the no-fly zones, and bombing missions there, continued to be the most visible sign of America's hard-edged approach to Iraq, with the numbers of sorties flown and dollars expended climbing steadily as 2001 got underway.[187] Iraq continued to draw international attention to the number of civilians killed by allied raids, with the US stating that allied pilots were quite cautious in their targeting but admitting that occasional errors occurred.[188]

Secretary of State Colin Powell was the leading voice of caution within the Bush administration where Iraq was concerned. With even the British tiring of the tedious business of enforcing the no-fly zones, and three of the five permanent members of the UNSC (France, Russia, and China) joining the rising chorus of Arab and African countries seeking to end economic sanctions against Baghdad, Powell believed a different tack was necessary. The Secretary of State favored building a new consensus in the UN around a system of more focused sanctions that would keep militarily useful items out of Saddam's hands while letting more consumer goods reach the Iraqi people. What went unsaid was Powell's apparent acceptance of the widely held view that UN weapons inspectors would not be getting back into Iraq.[189]

Hawkish Secretary of Defense Donald Rumsfeld was already deep into a comprehensive review of US policy toward Iraq when events in the no-fly zones provided his effort with greater impetus. By February 2001, Iraqi anti-aircraft units in both no-fly zones were behaving more aggressively than they had since the end of the Gulf War in 1991. Iraq's inventory of SA-6 missile batteries had suddenly jumped from just fewer than ten to approximately three-dozen, with the influx evidently coming from Serbia and Ukraine. Britain, concerned about mounting risks to its pilots over Iraq, was quietly pressing the Bush administration for a clearer strategy toward the ongoing military containment of Iraq.[190]

---

185   Gerald F. Seib, "A New President, and Four Choices He Can't Dodge," *Wall Street Journal*, 8 November 2000, A28.

186   Cameron W. Barr, "Blurry Edges of a Hard Line on Iraq: Convinced Iraq Is Rebuilding Military Programs, the US Is Enforcing No-Fly Zones – But With Disputed Accuracy," *Christian Science Monitor*, 25 January 2001, 1.

187   Ibid.

188   Ibid.

189   Jane Perlez, "The General Picks Up Where He Left Off," *New York Times*, 28 January 2001, 4.5.

190   Jim Hoagland, "A Risky No-Fly Zone Over Iraq," *Washington Post*, 11 February 2001, B7.

The new president's first major military action against Iraq was not long in coming. On 17 February 2001 24 US and British planes used long-range precision guided weapons to bomb five radar sites just south of Baghdad in the northern most part of the southern no-fly zone. US intelligence had discovered that Iraq was very close to connecting the nodes of its air defense system with subterranean fiber-optic cables, which explained the recent change in tactics. Bush called the bombing "routine," but diplomats the world around saw the action as a sure sign that his administration was preparing to embark on a collision course with Saddam.[191]

Bush administration officials soon let it be known that Chinese military and civilian workers had been helping Baghdad upgrade Iraq's air defenses by installing the fiber-optic cables in question. China's behavior was in direct violation of the UN sanctions regime still in place against Iraq, and it had enabled Baghdad to identify, target, and fire at allied planes with much greater accuracy. Baghdad's stepped-up activities in the no-fly zones, combined with China's role in them, were increasingly undermining Powell's efforts to steer the administration away from a war with Iraq, despite his recent statement that if Iraq obeyed UN sanctions, it could "become a progressive member of the world community."[192]

The Bush administration quickly called on Beijing to answer allegations that it had assisted in the modernization of Iraq's air-defense system by installing fiber-optic cables, but the Chinese government was mute.[193] The controversy had an air of newness about it, but the US had been working for years through the UN Sanctions Committee to prevent the sale of advanced telecommunications equipment to Baghdad by China, France, and Russia.[194] In fact, this was the third time that the US had raised the issue with China. The Clinton administration had privately dispatched a state department official to Beijing to approach China about the matter in early January 2001, and the new Bush administration had communicated its concern to the Chinese government a few weeks later.[195]

Opinion abroad, and particularly in the Middle East, took a decidedly negative turn in response to the latest bombings in the no-fly zones. Arab leaders and the Arab street questioned the claim by the US and Britain that the two nations were enforcing the no-fly zones (which were neither created nor endorsed by the UN) ostensibly to strengthen the UN, while the US nonetheless felt free to ignore actual UN resolutions concerning Israel's occupation of Arab territory.[196] Before the end of

---

191   Thomas E. Ricks, "American, British Jets Hit 5 Antiaircraft Sites in Iraq: Baghdad Area Bombed in Biggest Airstrike in 2 Years," *Washington Post*, 18 February 2001, A33.

192   Gregg Jaffe and Neil King, Jr., "US Says China Aided Iraq's Air Defense," *Wall Street Journal*, 20 February 2001, A4.

193   Neil King, Jr., and Greg Jaffe, "US Wants China to Answer Allegations it Helped Iraq Upgrade its Air Defense," *Wall Street Journal*, 21 February 2001, A10.

194   Ibid.

195   Steven Mufson and Thomas E. Ricks, "US to Protest China's Aid on Iraq's Anti-Aircraft System," *Washington Post*, 21 February 2001, A2.

196   Michael Theodoulou, "US Attack on Iraq Keeps Ricocheting: Arab Leaders Said the Bombing Last Friday Is Hardening Anti-US Sentiments in the Region," *Christian Science*

February 2001, Robert A. Pape, author of *Bombing to Win* and one of the foremost experts on strategic bombing delivered a damning verdict on the status of US policy toward Iraq:

> America's policy to contain Iraq is unraveling. The package of coercive levers used in the 1990s, economic sanctions, weapons inspections and the no-fly zones, is coming unglued. Indeed, this containment policy has not succeeded in its goals of ridding Iraq of weapons of mass destruction or ousting Saddam Hussein. The policy only antagonizes our coalition allies, and it should be abandoned.[197]

Pape endorsed focusing America's Iraq policy on reassuring allies to maintain a diplomatic coalition that would at least ensure the long-term presence of US military forces in the Middle East. Then, at least, the US would be in a position to deter Saddam from attacking his neighbors—and to confront him if deterrence were to fail.[198]

Periodic air strikes by the US and Britain continued into the spring of 2001,[199] but the rationale provided by the Bush administration was increasingly under fire. In June, as the UNSC unanimously nominated Secretary General Kofi Annan to serve a second five-year term, the Ghanaian diplomat spoke out against American and British bombings in the no-fly zones. Annan said that the Washington and London could not claim to be acting under the legal authority of the UN[200] In late July, an Iraqi missile nearly hit a high-altitude U-2 spy plane in the southern no-fly zone,[201] prompting Bush administration officials to let out word in early August that they were preparing to choose a more assertive policy toward Iraq.[202]

It was at this point that President Bush, chairing a formal meeting of the National Security Council, embraced the first phase of a larger plan designed to culminate in regime change in Baghdad, with more aggressive enforcement of the no-fly zones as the starting point.[203] Evidence of the toughening US policy was not long in coming, with US and British jets attacking three Iraqi air defense sites on 10 August

---

Monitor, 21 February 2001, 1.

197   Robert A. Pape, "Our Iraq Policy Is Not Working," *New York Times*, 24 February 2001, A13.

198   Ibid.

199   No Author, "World Briefing Middle East: Antiaircraft Positions Bombed," *New York Times*, 24 May 2001, A8.

200   Colum Lynch, "UN Security Council Unanimously Backs Annan: General Assembly Is Expected to Give Ghanaian a Second Term as Secretary General," *Washington Post*, 28 June 2001, A21.

201   No Author, "Iraqi Missile Nearly Hits Spy Plane," *Washington Post*, 26 July 2001, A4.

202   Alan Sipress, "Presidential Pressure Point: Arab-Israeli Conflict Could Undercut Policy on Mideast, Iraq," *Washington Post*, 6 August 2001, A1.

203   Jim Hoagland, "Nothing Comes From Nothing in the Middle East," *Washington Post*, 9 August 2001, A19.

2001.[204] With Secretary of State Powell's bid to establish a renewed UN sanctions regime now foundering, neoconservatives in the Bush administration, led by Deputy Defense Secretary Paul Wolfowitz, were hard at work on achieving their long-held goal of getting rid of Saddam Hussein.[205]

The dangers of the new, more confrontational approach were soon evident in both the no-fly zones and in the UN. Before the end of August 2001 the US lost a Predator spy drone over the southern no-fly zone, the first loss of a Western aircraft since the terrible friendly-fire incident that had destroyed two US helicopters in the northern no-fly zone in 1994.[206] (Defense Department officials would later confirm that a second Predator had been lost to Iraqi antiaircraft fire in the late summer of 2001.)[207] As summer turned to autumn, and the world reacted to the tragedy of 11 September 2001, President Bush was discovering that if he wished to set the stage for a military showdown with Saddam, he would have his work cut out for him to gather support from wary countries in the UN By late November 2001, as US and British jets bombed targets in the southern no-fly zone, the President was arguing that Saddam must allow UN weapons inspectors back into Iraq, a strong indication that he intended to link a military campaign against Iraq to the broader war on terror.[208]

In his State of the Union address in January 2002, President Bush labeled Iran, Iraq, and North Korea as an "axis of evil," and discussion among military analysts turned to when and how, not whether, the US would go to war against Iraq.[209] At roughly the same time as his State of the Union address, Bush signed a secret order instructing the CIA to commence a broad secret program to overthrow Saddam Hussein.[210] Yet during the spring of 2002, things were quieter in the no-fly zones than they had been during much of 2001. Iraqi maneuvering of surface-to-air missiles in both no-fly zones in April 2002 prompted US and British air attacks, but the bombings in the south were the first since January, and the bombings in the north were the first since February.[211] By mid-summer of 2002, however, a re-intensified allied air campaign

---

204   Thomas E. Ricks, "US, British Jets Attack Three Iraqi Air Defense Sites," *Washington Post*, 11 August 2001, A18.

205   Jane Perlez, "3 Iraqi Sites Bombed," *New York Times*, 12 August 2001, 4.2.

206   Greg Jaffe, "Spy Plane's Disappearance Over Iraq Highlights US Dilemma on No-Fly Zones," *Wall Street Journal*, 28 August 2001, A16.

207   Karen DeYoung and Thomas E. Ricks, "Iraqis Down Reconnaissance Drone: US Calls Incident Part of Baghdad's 'Campaign of Military Aggression,'" *Washington Post*, 24 December 2002, A11.

208   Robert S. Greenberger and Alix M. Freedman, "Campaign Against Terrorism: For Bush, Pushing Iraq on Inspections Will Require Courting Support at UN," *Wall Street Journal*, 28 November 2001, A4.

209   Walter Pincus and Karen DeYoung, "Anti-Iraq Rhetoric Outpaces Reality: Military Not Primed for New War Soon," *Washington Post*, 24 February 2002, A1.

210   Bob Woodward, "President Broadens Anti-Hussein Order: CIA Gets More Tools to Oust Iraqi Leader," *Washington Post*, 16 June 2002, A1.

211   James Dao, "US Says Iraq Moved Missiles to No-Fly Zone," *New York Times*, 23 April 2002, A13.

focusing on the southern no-fly zone was underway, with bombings becoming quite regular during the month of July.[212]

In fact, the new air offensive in the no-fly zones was the de facto opening of the war to depose Saddam. The regular bombings, especially in southern Iraq, gave the Pentagon plenty of intelligence as well as an opportunity to take apart Iraqi air defenses. Allied pilots were sharpening their skills for all-out war, keeping close tabs on Saddam's military assets, and clearing a swath of southern Iraq of the tanks and armored personnel carriers that the Iraqi army would need to resist an American and British ground invasion from Kuwait. To be sure, Iraqi military forces in the southern no-fly zone were learning something about allied military capabilities and how to evade them, but the neutralization of Iraqi air defenses there more than compensated for this negative side effect.[213]

If any doubts still existed that the US was on the road to war with Iraq, Vice President Dick Cheney erased them with a speech to a Veterans of Foreign Wars audience in Nashville on 26 August 2002. Cheney stated that Saddam's possession of weapons of mass destruction was a fact, as was the Iraqi dictator's plotting to use them against the US and its allies.[214] The Vice President also said that weapons inspectors, if they could be readmitted to Iraq, would never be able to locate Saddam's hidden arsenal.[215] Cheney's speech prompted conservative publisher William Kristol to call for a congressional authorization for the use of force against Iraq: "The debate in the administration," concluded Kristol, "is over."[216] As if to confirm Kristol's verdict, a few days later, in an interview with the *BBC*, National Security Adviser Condoleezza Rice also made a pitch for a unilateral attack on Iraq.[217]

In September 2002, incidents between Iraqi forces and allied aircraft in the no-fly zones were becoming still more frequent, and allied retaliatory bombings increasingly were utilizing precision-guided weapons.[218] Pentagon officials denied stepping up the number of patrols and attacks in the no-fly zones but conceded that US pilots had targeted Iraqi air defenses 34 times in 2002,[219] thus surpassing the

---

212   No Author, "US Planes Strike Radar Unit in Iraq," *Washington Post*, 16 July 2002, A14; No Author, "World in Brief," *Washington Post*, 24 July 2002, A14.

213   Vernon Loeb, "'No-Fly' Patrols Praised: US Says Effort Pressures Iraq, Yields Intelligence," *Washington Post*, 26 July 2002, A23.

214   Dana Milbank, "Cheney Says Iraqi Strike Is Justified: Hussein Poses Threat, He Declares," *Washington Post*, 27 August 2002, A1.

215   Ibid.

216   Ibid.

217   William Raspberry, "Bush's Reverse Psychology," *Washington Post*, 3 September 2002, A17.

218   No Author, "Allied Aircraft Hit Air Defenses In Southern Iraq," *Washington Post*, 26 September 2002, A28.

219   Rajiv Chandrasekaran, "Baghdad Is Planning for Urban Warfare: Strategy Opposite of Gulf War Approach," *Washington Post*, 27 September 2002, A1.

total number of air strikes for each of the preceding two years,[220] with nine strikes occurring in September 2002 alone.[221] One raid utilized 100 allied planes was designed to signal Baghdad that the US and Britain could expand the scope of the air campaign with ease at any time.[222] The sudden increase in allied bombing was no accident, as Defense Secretary Rumsfeld had just given allied pilots the green light to target a broad spectrum of Iraqi air defense targets of high value, rather than just retaliating narrowly in response to specific provocations.[223]

Some members of Saddam Hussein's regime now had little doubt of what ultimately was in store for Iraq. One Iraqi official said of the allies' creeping air offensive: "Their first step is destroying all our installations in the north and south through the excuse of protecting their so-called no-fly zone."[224] Speculation swirled in the West that Iraq's response to the allies' clear air supremacy, if war came, might be to mass its forces in population centers and attempt to lure the allies into urban warfare.[225] (Thankfully, such urban warfare scenarios never really materialized.)

On 31 September 2002 Defense Secretary Rumsfeld made an argument about the no-fly zones that no US government official ever had: US and British planes were in fact performing "aerial inspections" under UNS.C. Resolution 687 (passed in 1991), which required Iraq to admit UN weapons inspectors to oversee and certify the country's disarmament. Until this point, the US had always claimed that UN Security Council Resolution 688 (also passed in 1991), which sought to protect Iraqi citizens from attacks by the Iraqi military, justified enforcement of the no-fly zones. Kenneth M. Pollack, director of research at the Brookings Institution's Saban Center for Middle East Policy, noted, "This is the first time the US government has ever tied [the no-fly zones] to enforcement of the inspection provisions of 687."[226]

By early October 2002, US planes over the southern no-fly zone had initiated an intensifying program of psychological pressure on the Iraqi military there in

---

220   No Author, "US Asserts Role for Planes Over Iraq: 'Aerial' Surveillance for Weapons is Valid, Rumsfeld Says," *Washington Post*, 1 October 2002, A13.

221   Rajiv Chandrasekaran, "Baghdad Is Planning for Urban Warfare: Strategy Opposite of Gulf War Approach," *Washington Post*, 27 September 2002, A1.

222   Scott Peterson, "US Sliding Into War With Iraq? Airstrikes in the No-Fly Zones – and Iraqi Counterattacks – Are Intensifying," *Christian Science Monitor*, 8 October 2002, 1.

223   Karen DeYoung and Thomas E. Ricks, "Iraqis Down Reconnaissance Drone: US Calls Incident Part of Baghdad's 'Campaign of Military Aggression,'" *Washington Post*, December 24, 2002, A11; Vernon Loeb, "Airstrikes in Southern Iraq 'No-Fly' Zone Mount: Attacks' Growing Precision and Scope May Aid Invasion," *Washington Post*, 15 January 2003, A1.

224   Rajiv Chandrasekaran, "Baghdad Is Planning for Urban Warfare: Strategy Opposite of Gulf War Approach," *Washington Post*, 27 September 2002, A1.

225   Ibid.

226   No Author, "US Asserts Inspection Role for Planes Over Iraq: 'Aerial' Surveillance for Weapons Is Valid, Rumsfeld Says," *Washington Post*, 1 October 2002, A13.

response to the more frequent antiaircraft fire.[227] Allied planes dropped leaflets that sought to dissuade Iraqi soldiers from tracking or firing on them, warning of quick and deadly retribution, while planting the seed of the notion that surrender might be the best course in the event of a US-led invasion.[228] By November, leaflets were being dropped on southern Iraq instructing Iraqi soldiers not to repair installations bombed by allied jets and stating that the US and British enforcement of the no-fly zones was intended to protect the Iraqi people.[229]

The air war in the no-fly zones was the opening salvo of *Operation Iraqi Freedom*, which was still months away. In addition to targeting missile launchers, allied pilots were hitting the command centers and communications networks that were the lynchpins of the Iraqi air defense system.[230] One lesson that many military strategists had drawn from the effectiveness of earlier military campaigns in Kosovo and Afghanistan was that it was best to liquidate the enemy's air defenses before undertaking a full-out air offensive—a tenet now being put into practice once again in Iraq.[231] The US also was also using aerial missions in the no-fly zones to identify likely hiding spots for Scud missile launchers, in hopes of disabling the missiles just before hostilities formally commenced, thus averting attacks on Israel and other countries proximate to Iraq.[232]

On 8 November 2002, after much diplomatic wrangling, the UN Security Council unanimously passed a resolution calling for Iraq to readmit weapons inspectors and disarm.[233] The resolution had the effect of putting confrontations in the no-fly zones front and center on the world political stage as Iraqi antiaircraft batteries began firing at allied aircraft with new intensity. Some elements of the Bush administration flirted with the idea of claiming that Iraqi provocations in the no-fly zones were serious enough violations of the new Security Council resolution to require consideration at the UN of general military action against Iraq.[234] Civilian leaders at the Pentagon took a hard line on the matter, but the military brass and the State Department did not consider anything taking place in the no-fly zones to be an adequate justification for

---

227   No Author, "Leaflets Warn Iraq Not to Target Allied Jets," *Washington Post*, 4 October 2002, A22.

228   Ibid.

229   No Author, "Leaflets, Bombs Dropped on Iraq: US Warns Against Rebuilding Site; Civilians Reported Killed," *Washington Post*, 29 November 2002, A16.

230   Scott Peterson, "US Sliding Into War With Iraq? Airstrikes in the No-Fly Zones – and Iraqi Counterattacks – Are Intensifying," *Christian Science Monitor*, 8 October 2002, 1.

231   Ibid.

232   Greg Jaffe, "Iraq's Scuds Still Keep Pentagon Guessing: High-Tech Gear May Foil Mobile Missiles' Use, But Nightmare Scenarios Haunt Officials," *Wall Street Journal*, 15 October 2002, A4.

233   Hugh Pope and Christopher Cooper, "Opinions Split on Iraq's No-Fly Zones," *Wall Street Journal*, 20 November 2002, A18.

234   Ibid.

war.[235] The international community, and the Secretary General of the UN, simply did not believe that the dust-ups in the no-fly zones constituted a "material breach" of the UN resolution in question.[236]

In early December 2002, as US troop strength in the Persian Gulf approached 60,000 and the sinews of war flowed into the region, events in the no-fly zones continued to escalate and the likelihood of war continued unabated.[237] Shortly before Christmas, an Iraqi plane managed to shoot down an Air Force Predator drone over southern Iraq, the first successful Iraqi air-to-air attack of any kind since the Persian Gulf War.[238] Air defense communication and command and control facilities in southern Iraq remained the central, but hardly the only, targets for allied pilots both before and after Christmas.[239] Perhaps most crucially, the US was now using Iraqi fire against allied jets in the northern no-fly zone as justification for retaliatory strikes in the southern no-fly zone to take apart the Iraqi air defense system in the area.[240]

In February 2003, Turkey, which had long placed restrictions on the types of targets allied aircraft could hit in the northern no-fly zone, gave allied pilots greater latitude.[241] Ankara had by now accepted war as inevitable, and it wanted to make sure that Baghdad did not fire Scuds and other surface-to-surface missiles its way when the shooting started.[242] When war came, though, Ankara not only refused to let US forces to use Turkish soil as a staging ground to invade Iraq but also denied allied requests to fly combat missions from Incirlik as part of Operation Iraqi Freedom.[243]

By mid-March 2003, approximately 170,000 American and British forces were massed in Kuwait and ready to launch an offensive. In the days before President Bush delivered his 48-hour ultimatum to Saddam Hussein on 17 March 2003, allied warplanes repeatedly hit mobile radar targets in western Iraq and communications facilities near Basra.[244] And slightly before the deadline for war arrived on 19 March,

---

235   Ibid.

236   No Author, "Leaflets, Bombs Dropped on Iraq: US Warns Against Rebuilding Site; Civilians Reported Killed," *Washington Post*, 29 November 2002, A16.

237   Linda Feldmann, "US Jockeys to Keep Trigger for War at Hand: Administration Steps up Pressure on Iraq as the UN's December 8 Deadline Nears," *Christian Science Monitor*, 4 December 2002, 1.

238   Karen DeYoung and Thomas E. Ricks, "Iraqis Down Reconnaissance Drone: US Calls Incident Part of Baghdad's 'Campaign of Military Aggression,'" *Washington Post*, 24 December 2002, A11.

239   No Author, "Allied Planes Attack Site in Iraq's 'No-Fly' Zone," *Washington Post*, 27 December 2002, A12.

240   Vernon Loeb, "Airstrikes in Southern Iraq 'No-Fly' Zone Mount: Attacks' Growing Precision and Scope May Aid Invasion," *Washington Post*, 15 January 2003, A1.

241   Robert Burns, "Franks Won't Guarantee Human Shields' Safety," *Washington Post*, 27 February 2003, A20.

242   Ibid.

243   Greg Jaffe, "In Massive Shift, US Is Planning to Cut Size of Military in Germany," *Wall Street Journal*, June 10, 2003, A1.

244   Greg Jaffe and Neil King, Jr., "Endgame: Ceasing Diplomacy, US Nears War; Bush Declares Deadline for Hussein Exit as UN Pulls Personnel; Military Gears Up for Attack,"

the US and British planes even pounded Iraqi field artillery in southern Iraq—something that had not occurred since the Gulf War.[245] Finally, allied jets scattered more than 1.98 million propaganda leaflets over 29 locations in southeastern Iraq, bringing the total number of leaflets dropped in 2003 to 17 million.[246] Twenty-two days after *Operation Iraqi Freedom* commenced, Baghdad fell to allied forces.[247] The war, writ large, had unfolded quickly once it finally commenced, but it had incubated in miniature for more than a decade in the no-fly zones of Iraq.

Conclusion

As allied ground forces in Iraq were making the transition from war fighting to occupation and reconstruction, the Bush administration announced in late April 2003 that the US military would cease operations in Saudi Arabia before the year's end. Between August 1992 and *Operation Iraqi Freedom*, allied warplanes had flown from Prince Sultan Air Base in Saudi Arabia to patrol the southern no-fly zone, with the US Air Force alone flying 286,000 such sorties.[248] At the peak of *Operation Iraqi Freedom*, 200 US aircraft were based at Prince Sultan, but in a matter of months there would be none, for there was no longer a southern no-fly zone to patrol.[249] Similarly, the US Combined Air Operations Center in Saudi Arabia was scheduled for transfer to nearby Qatar.[250] All of the 4,000 to 5,000 US military personnel would be leaving Saudi Arabia.[251]

Because there was no longer a no-fly zone over northern Iraq, either, a similar drawdown of the US military presence in Turkey was also underway during April 2003. US warplanes left Incirlik for the US[252] No more than 500 of the 3,000 US Air Force personnel previously based at Incirlik to enforce the northern no-fly zone

---

Wall Street Journal, March 18, 2003, A1.

245   Helene Cooper, Yaroslav Trofimov, Hugh Pope, and David S. Cloud, "US Launches War on Iraq With Limited Attack: President Predicts a 'Broad and Concerted Campaign'; In Opening Salvo, US Hits 'Targets of Opportunity'; Early Attempt on Leaders of Nation Follows a Day of Massive Mobilization; Instructions for Surrender," *Wall Street Journal*, 20 March 2003, A1.

246   Ibid.

247   Merrill A. McPeak, "Leave the Flying to Us," *Washington Post*, 5 June 2003, A33.

248   Vernon Loeb, "US Military Will Leave Saudi Arabia This Year," *Washington Post*, 30 April 2003, A1.

249   Ibid.

250   Ibid.

251   Greg Jaffe, "In Massive Shift, US Is Planning to Cut Size of Military in Germany," *Wall Street Journal*, 10 June 2003, A1.

252   Seth Stern, "New Map for US Outposts: Pentagon Announces Pullout From Saudi Bases and Plots Other Long-Term Shifts," *Christian Science Monitor*, 1 May 2003, 2.

ultimately would remain, with the exact figure subject to the status of Turkish-American relations and military cooperation.[253]

In the summer of 2003, Lieutenant General Michael Moseley, who oversaw air operations in Iraq before and during *Operation Iraqi Freedom*, confirmed what had become conventional wisdom among military analysts and astute observers of US policy toward Iraq: the US had indeed stepped up surveillance over southern Iraq in autumn 2001 and commenced by summer 2002 a bombing campaign explicitly designed to prepare the way for war with Iraq. General Tommy R. Franks, the top US commander in the Middle East, had given Moseley permission in November 2001 to map Iraq's air defense network with an eye toward hitting a broader array of targets in southern Iraq by the following summer. Moseley concluded that this campaign had sufficiently degraded Iraqi air defenses so that no "preliminary air effort" was necessary when it came time to launch *Operation Iraqi Freedom*.[254]

So ends the storied role of the Iraqi no-fly zones in US foreign policy. Created to protect Iraq's ethnic minorities and contain Saddam Hussein, they soon became the primary Western lever to punish him for his transgressions, and finally, to commence a war with the explicit purpose of unseating him. The no-fly zones were expensive in dollars and the demands they placed on the US military over more than a decade following the end of the Cold War, but their greatest cost was as a symbol of perceived US hostility towards and designs on a country in the heart of the Islamic world. No longer can bin Laden or anyone else cite as a grievance the presence of US forces on Saudi soil, in proximity to the holy sites of Mecca and Medina, to enforce a no-fly zone over Iraq. Of course, the US-led occupation of Iraq ensures that people everywhere looking for new grievances against the US will need to overturn few stones to find them.

---

253   Greg Jaffe, "In Massive Shift, US Is Planning to Cut Size of Military in Germany," *Wall Street Journal*, 10 June 2003, A1.

254   Bradley Graham, "US Moved Early for Air Supremacy: Airstrikes on Iraqi Defenses Began Long Before Invasion, General Says," *Washington Post*, 20 July 2003, A26.

Chapter 10

Iraq and the Evolution of American Strategy

Steven Metz[1]
Army War College

Introduction

The conflict with Iraq has been one of the longest in American history, beginning in 1991 with no end in sight. It emerged from an the unfortunate interplay of several trends and conditions: the end of the Cold War, the repression and aggression of Saddam Hussein, the increasing importance of petroleum from Southwest Asia to much of the world, and, more recently, the explosion of Islamic radicalism. Together, these have propelled Iraq to the forefront of US national security strategy.

America's conflict with Iraq occurred at a seminal time in the evolution of US national security and military strategy as Washington scrambled to adjust to and manage the post-Cold War world. It has thus been a laboratory and a locomotive for broad strategic changes and a laboratory for strategic assumptions, new military technologies and operational innovations. With each phase of the conflict with Iraq, the US military and Department of Defense derived "lessons" which shaped the trajectory of military change. The content of these lessons provided the foundation and fuel for broader change in grand strategy.[2]

In the post-Cold War world, the United States developed a military strategy designed to promote stability in vital regions of the world. It was to capitalize on qualitative advantages on the part of the American military—both technological and human—to prevent or thwart aggression and attain a significant, preferably decisive victory, within a short period of time and with the minimum blood cost. Iraq under Saddam Hussein provided the perfect opponent for such a strategy. He

---

1   The opinions in this chapter are solely those of the author and do not reflect official positions of the US Department of Defense of the US Army War College.

2   "Grand strategy" is the synchronization of all elements of power—military, political, economic, psychological, and moral—in pursuit of objectives. "National security strategy" is a subset of this, and "military strategy" is a subset of national security strategy which defines when, why, and how armed force will be used, and the size and composition of the armed forces. Congress requires the President to publish an unclassified National Security Strategy on an annual basis, and the Chairman of the Joint Chiefs of Staff periodically publishes an unclassified national military strategy. There is no formal statement of American grand strategy.

was clearly aggressive, thus helping solidify support for the use of force by the US public and America's allies. In addition, Hussein relied on Soviet equipment and operational methods which the American military thoroughly understood. He was unambiguously evil yet predicable and familiar. In many ways, Saddam Hussein was the ideal enemy for the United States.

Unfortunately, Hussein's removal did not end America's involvement in Iraq but shifted it away from the unambiguous and the familiar. Suddenly, the United States was not facing a "perfect" enemy. From 1991 to 2003, the Iraq conflict validated America's assumptions about the nature of the global security environment and the appropriate strategy for it. Iraq since 2003 has confounded these assumptions and served as a catalyst for a deep re-evaluation of American strategy. Its results, whatever they are, will be far reaching. Iraq has thus shaped American strategy not only in the "post Cold War" period, but also is doing so in the era of terrorism.

The First War With Hussein

The collapse of the Soviet Union during the administration of George H.W. Bush undercut the foundation of American national security and military strategy. Everything the United States had prepared for was gone. This forced deep debate, revision and introspection. In the broadest sense, the United States sought answers to four vital strategic questions: First, what is the appropriate American role in the world? Second, why and when should American military power be used? Third, how should American military power be used? And fourth, what is the appropriate size and configuration of the US military?

The Bush administration (and most of Congress and the American public) believed that even in the absence of the Soviet Union, the United States should remain actively engaged in the world, engineering or preserving stability. The President talked of a "new world order" with the United States as the only superpower, but one committed to democracy, human rights and open economies. The goal was, according to Bush, world "where diverse nations are drawn together in common cause to achieve the universal aspirations of mankind—peace and security, freedom, and the rule of law."[3] Freed from the Cold War stalemate, the President and his advisers thought, the United Nations could finally play the role it was designed for, particularly in regions and conflicts outside the direct interest of the United States. However, the administration did not intend to rely solely on international cooperation. As indicated in an early draft of the 1992 Defense Planning Guidance, it was also concerned with safeguarding US national interests and preventing the emergence of rivals (whether a revived Russia, China, or even a coalition of former allies), and was willing to undertake unilateral action in pursuit of these goals if necessary.[4]

---

3   President George H.W. Bush, State of the Union Address Before a Joint Session of Congress, 29 January 1991.

4   Barton Gelman, "Pentagon War Scenario Spotlights Russia," *Washington Post*, 20 February 1992; and Patrick E. Tyler, US Strategy Plan Calls for Insuring No Rivals Develop,"

Within this construct, the primary purpose of American military power was to deter or defeat aggression by regional dictators—what would later become known as "rogue" states—and, to a lesser extent, to support multinational and United Nations efforts to resolve local conflicts. In other words, America would retain the world's preeminent military but would be so responsible in its use that potential competitors would see no purpose in challenging the United States.

How to use force was a sticky issue for the Bush administration. While the military had undergone an extensive enlargement and rejuvenation of morale during the Reagan administration and fielded a number of important new weapons systems such as the B-1, F-16 and F-15 aircraft, the Navy's Ticonderoga class cruisers, and the Army's M1 Abrams tank, M2 Bradley fighting vehicle, Multiple Launch Rocket System (MLRS), Patriot Air Defense System, and AH-64 Apache attack helicopter, unease with the use of military power lingered from Vietnam among both the Congress and the American public. Thinking in the Bush administration largely held to what was widely known as the "Weinberger principles." In a November 1984 speech at the National Press Club, Reagan's Secretary of Defense Caspar Weinberger contended that any use of military power must pass six "tests": the vital national interests of the United States or its allies must be at stake; the United States must be committed to winning; there should be clearly defined political and military objectives; the relationship between the objectives and the forces committed must be continually reassessed and adjusted if necessary; there must be a reasonable assurance of support from the Congress and the American public; and commitment of US forces to combat must be a last resort. The most powerful advocate for this type of approach within the Bush administration was General Colin Powell, Chairman of the Joint Chiefs of Staff, who had been Weinberger's military assistant in 1984.

The size and configuration of the American military remained an issue of debate throughout the G.H.W. Bush administration. The military rejuvenation of the 1980s had come not only through increased defense budgets, new weapons systems and new operational concepts," but also through a renewed emphasis on conventional state-on-state warfighting.[5] Within the military the idea had arisen that while involvement in what had become known as "low intensity conflict"—counterinsurgency, peacekeeping, counterterrorism, and support to insurgency—was necessary, it could be corrosive to the military and to military's relationship with the American people. The military would undertake low-intensity conflict when ordered to, but greatly preferred to prepare for and focus on the less politically complex

---

New York Times, 8 March 1992. After this draft was leaked and published by the *New York Times* and *Washington Post*, the Department of Defense re-wrote it with greater stress on cooperation with allies and less on sustaining American dominance. See Barton Gelman, "Pentagon Abandons Goal of Thwarting Allies," *Washington Post*, 24 May 1992.

5   One of the most important of the new operational concepts was AirLand Battle— the Army and Air Force's shared central concept for conventional warfighting operations. This was codified in the Army's Field Manual 100-5, Operations, 1982. See John J. Romjue, From Active Defense to AirLand Battle: The Development of Army Doctrine 1973–1982 (Fort Monroe, VA: Historical Office, US Army Training and Doctrine Command, 1984).

and ambiguous conventional, large-scale combat. Phrased differently, the military, particularly the Army, Air Force, and Navy, developed a "conventional mindset." This had multiple effects which were only beginning to emerge in the early 1990s, including a personnel system where a concentration on conventional warfighting was the surest path to senior rank, massive investment in advanced technology designed to defeat an opposing state military, and the first emergence of the idea that airpower had superseded landpower as the most decisive component of armed conflict. These issues would be played out throughout America's long conflict with Iraq. But in a very real sense President Ronald Reagan had set the stage for the first war of Iraq by leading a renewal of the American sense of purpose and confidence in the use of its military. All that was missing was a chance to demonstrate what the United States and its armed forces could do in pursuit of the new world order.

Since the late 1970s, the United States viewed Iran as the major threat to stability in the volatile and important Gulf region. Continuing the "Nixon doctrine" of relying on proxies to preserve regional balances, the United States developed a security relationship with Saddam Hussein's Iraq to counterbalance Teheran. It was less than an embrace—no American leader had illusions about Hussein's repression and aggression. But in a region overflowing with problems, Hussein was seen as the lesser evil. The Bush administration assumed that war weariness, diplomacy, and the need for reconstruction assistance would restrain Iraq.[6]

By 1990, however, American defense officials were concerned with threatening and aggressive noises coming from Baghdad. Iraq's long war with Iran in the 1980s had bled its economy and led to a bloated military that further inhibited what had previously been a robust rate of development. As Michael Gordon and Bernard Trainor phrase it:

> Iraq's deteriorating economy created an incentive for it to keep its military strong. Unemployment was high, and Iraq's economy could not easily accommodate the strains of large-scale military demobilization, which also threatened social unrest. As the economic vise tightened, Iraq began to view its military might not as an impediment to the rebuilding of the country, but as a way to compel its neighbors to contribute to Iraq's reconstruction and economic development or to grab their wealth if they resisted.[7]

As Hussein became increasingly bellicose, the US Central Command (CENTCOM)— the military headquarters responsible for southwest Asia—began contingency planning to defend US allies and interests on the Arabian Peninsula (which is normal activity for regional combatant commands during times of tension or crisis).[8] On 2 August 1990, Iraqi forces invaded Kuwait. They quickly routed the small, unprepared Kuwaiti military and occupied the country. Hussein declared part of Kuwait to be part of Basra province, the rest Iraq's 19th province; he also threatened

---

6   Michael R. Gordon and Bernard E. Trainor, *The Generals' War: The Inside Story of the Conflict in the Gulf* (Boston: Little, Brown, 1995), 9–11.

7   Ibid., 9.

8   Ibid., 29.

missile attacks against Israel and Saudi Arabia if challenged.[9] Since he was known to have an extensive array of Soviet bloc missiles and, during his war with Iran in the 1980s, had armed them with chemical warheads, this was taken very seriously. The United States and Kuwait immediately asked the United Nations Security Council to intervene. SC (Security Council) Resolution 660 condemned the invasion and demanded withdrawal; four days later SC Resolution 661 established economic sanctions on Iraq. Hussein, though, reiterated his longstanding position that Kuwait was historically part of Iraq and gave no sign of submission to the United Nations.

For the Bush administration, two things were at stake, one tangible, one symbolic. Some administration Bush officials, concerned by an ominous CIA analysis which concluded that Hussein's forces could be in Riyadh in three days, felt that the invasion of Kuwait would be followed by armed intervention into Saudi Arabia.[10] Control of even the northern oil fields of Saudi Arabia would give Hussein a stranglehold over the world's petroleum supply. According to the US Department of Defense's official history of the Gulf War, such an invasion was "deemed possible both by the United States and Saudi Arabia."[11] At the same time, Hussein's blatant aggression was a blow to President Bush's vision of a new world order, particularly the idea that the forcible seizure of territory was unacceptable in the modern era.

Senior administration officials were initially torn on the appropriate response.[12] General Powell urged caution, favoring a robust defense of Saudi Arabia.[13] The American people, he believed, might not support military action to restore the Kuwait royal family. "We can't make a case for losing lives for Kuwait," Powell argued, "but Saudi Arabia is different."[14] Quickly, though, President Bush, swayed by arguments such as those of British Prime Minister Margaret Thatcher who compared the invasion to Nazi aggression in both strategic and ethical terms and by the immense strategic importance of Saudi Arabia, decided that, his words, the invasion "will not stand." By clearly implying that the objective was not simply the defense of Saudi Arabia but also the liberation of Kuwait, this ended debate within the administration concerning the ultimate goals. The question was how to use the American military to assure it.

Reversing cross-border aggression is a very difficult task but had been a longstanding planning scenario for the US military. For decades it had planned to rapidly mobilize and deploy forces to Europe which would, in conjunction with NATO allies and US units already there, counter a Warsaw Pact invasion of West

---

9   Thomas A. Keaney and Eliot A. Cohen, *Revolution in Warfare: Air Power in the Persian Gulf* (Annapolis, MD: Naval Institute Press, 1995), originally published as the *Gulf War Air Power Summary Report*, 4.

10   Bob Woodward, *The Commanders* (New York: Touchstone, 1991), 237.

11   US Department of Defense, *Conduct of the Persian Gulf War*, Final Report to Congress, April 1992, 31. (Henceforth *Conduct of the Persian Gulf War*).

12   See Woodward, *The Commanders*, 203–46.

13   James Mann, *Rise of the Vulcans: The History of Bush's War Cabinet* (New York: Penguin, 2004), 184; Woodward, *The Commanders*, 229.

14   Quoted in Gordon and Trainor, *The Generals' War*, 33.

Germany. Annual "Reforger" (return of forces to Germany) exercises tested the plans. Much of the military's doctrine was designed for this sort of task. While Southwest Asia had not been the focus of as many exercises and as much planning as Europe, CENTCOM had developed plans for defending America's friends in the Gulf ever since it was created in 1983. One of these (Operations Plan 90-1002) served as the basis for the response to Iraq's invasion of Kuwait.[15]

The initial task was preventing Iraq from seizing Saudi oil fields. Five days after the invasion of Kuwait, the first US forces—F-15C fighter aircraft, RC-135 reconnaissance planes, and E-3 Airborne Warning and Control System aircraft—arrived as part of *Operation Desert Shield*. Naval forces (including carrier battle groups) and rapidly deployable land units such as parts of the Army's 82d Airborne Division soon followed. For a number of weeks, though, there was a "window of vulnerability": even though American and other forces were pouring into Saudi Arabia, they would have been hard pressed by the three armored and two mechanized divisions Iraq had in Kuwait if Hussein continued to press southward.[16] As Bob Woodward noted, in the first three or four weeks, American forces were "naked and excruciatingly vulnerable."[17] By October, though, units such as the 24th Infantry Division (Mechanized), 3d Armored Cavalry Regiment, and 1st Cavalry Division had arrived. In conjunction with American airpower, these forces could have repulsed an invasion of Saudi Arabia.

The failure of Iraq to enter Saudi Arabia in August and September suggests that this was never Hussein's intention.[18] Most likely, he concluded that he would face tolerable pressure by taking Kuwait which was, in Bob Woodward's words, "small, unpopular, and an afterthought in the region" but had to know that Saudi Arabia was a different matter.[19] In a broad sense, his strategy was similar to that of the Japanese in World War II: seize territory quickly then make recapture so costly that the United States would negotiate a settlement. Like all militaries, the Iraqi army planned to "fight the last war." As Gordon and Trainor note, "Iraqi commanders intended to fight the same type of war they waged against Iran, a grinding battle of attrition with high casualties on both sides that would nullify the American hopes to win a quick victory with high-technology weapons."[20] Both the Japanese and Hussein underestimated American will, but at least Hussein did not, like the Japanese, over-extend while flush with initial victories.

With diplomatic efforts to reverse the invasion making little progress, President Bush announced in November 1990 that he intended to send enough military force to the Gulf to undertake offensive operations.[21] By January, the coalition had nearly

15   Woodward, *The Commanders*, 220.
16   *Conduct of the Persian Gulf War*, 37.
17   Woodward, *The Commanders*, 278.
18   Keaney and Cohen, *Revolution in Warfare*, 4.
19   Woodward, *The Commanders*, 262.
20   Gordon and Trainor, *The Generals' War*, 163.
21   *Conduct of the Persian Gulf War*, 65.

1800 combat aircraft from twelve countries, a huge naval forces (mostly but not exclusively American), and 540,000 troops from thirty-one countries.[22] The US Defense Intelligence Agency estimated that Iraq had about 540,000 troops in Kuwait and southern Iraq, with 4200 tanks and 3100 artillery pieces.[23] And the political stage was set: in January, Secretary of State James Baker warned Iraqi Foreign Minister Tariq Aziz that Baghdad's only options were unconditional withdrawal from Kuwait or armed conflict.[24] On 12 January 1991 Congress authorized President Bush to use force to liberate Kuwait.[25]

Military planning had been underway since the summer of 1990. CENTCOM, under the command of General Norman Schwarzkopf, developed the war plan with regular briefings to and guidance from General Powell, Secretary of Defense Dick Cheney, and President Bush as well as constant coordination with coalition political and military leaders. The warfighting plan consisted of four phases: a strategic air campaign to disrupt Baghdad's command and control of deployed forces; air strikes to suppress Iraqi air defenses, preparation of the battlefield through air strikes and other long range fires (directly at fielded forces, including units in Kuwait and elite Republican Guard divisions in southern Iraq), and ground operations to expel the Iraqi forces from Kuwait.[26]

When all diplomatic efforts failed, the air campaign began on January 16 with strikes on Iraqi air defense networks by Army attack helicopters and on command targets in Baghdad by F-117A Nighthawk stealth fighter-bombers.[27] Within days a wide range of US Air Force, Navy and Marine, and coalition fixed wing aircraft as well as Army attack helicopters destroyed the Iraqi air defense system and began systematically crushing command and control networks, other targets important to the Hussein regime, and Iraqi forces in the field. This massive air armada included not only fighter-bombers, but also strategic bombers such as the B-52 and B-1 originally designed for nuclear attacks against the Soviet Union.

Despite stunning successes by coalition flyers, the hopes of airpower advocates that this alone would defeat Iraq proved unfounded. There were several reasons for this. Hussein's decision to fire Scud ballistic missiles at Israel raised fears that the Israeli government would strike back, thus endangering the cohesion of the coalition whose Arab partners did not want to be consider allies of Jerusalem. As Secretary of

---

22   Keaney and Cohen, *Revolution in Warfare*, 6–7.

23   While these numbers were used by American planners, post-war analysis suggested they were inflated with perhaps 336,000 Iraqis in theater. (Keaney and Cohen, *Revolution in Warfare*, 7–9).

24   Gordon and Trainor, *The General's War*, 196–8.

25   House Joint Resolution 77 (H. J. Res. 77) and Senate Joint Resolution 2 (S. J. Res. 2), 12 January 1991

26   Major General Robert H. Scales, Jr., *Certain Victory: The US Army in the Gulf War* (Washington: Brassey's, 1997), pp. 103–155; and *Conduct of the Persian Gulf War*, 65–77.

27   The F-117A flew approximately 1,300 sorties and scored direct hits on 1,600 high-value targets in Iraq. It was the only US or coalition aircraft to strike targets in downtown Baghdad.

Defense Cheney said in a meeting, "The number one priority is to keep Israel out of the war."[28] This caused many aircraft to be shifted from strategic targets to searching for Scud launchers in Iraq's western desert. Second, the massively complex process of developing the daily air tasking order (ATO) meant that targets were often not hit until days after they were identified, allowing the Iraqis to move them. And, most of all, the Hussein regime simply proved too determined and resilient to collapse under even massive air attack.

By February, coalition ground forces were prepared to attack. The XVIII Airborne Corps, VII Corps (including the U.K 1st Armored Division), and French 6th Light Armored Division were on the western flank of the theater. Joint Forces Command-North in the center included the 3rd Egyptian Mechanized Division, the 4th Egyptian Armored Division, the 9th Syrian Division, the Egyptian Ranger Regiment, the Syrian Special Forces Regiment, the 20th Mechanized Brigade, Royal Saudi Land Forces (RSLF), the Kuwaiti Ash-Shahid and Al-Tahrir Brigades, and the 4th Armored Brigade (RSLF). The First Marine Expeditionary Force (I-MEF) on the coalition's right included the 1st and 2d Marine divisions and the "Tiger Brigade" of the US Army's 2d Armored Division. The right flank was anchored by the Joint Forces Command-East with units from Saudi Arabia, the United Arab Emirates, Oman, Bahrain, and Kuwait.

Ground operations began on 24 February 1991. The Iraqi army remained in defensive positions, attempting to replicate the success they had in Hussein's war with Iraq when Teheran's poorly trained forces were lured into "kill boxes." But the American-led coalition was not the Iranian military. Faced with immense and coordinated speed and firepower, some Iraq units, eroded by the air campaign and long deployment, crumbled quickly; others fought, some tenaciously. When possible, coalition land forces bypassed and cut them off. Any which moved or could be found were destroyed by airpower. After only 100 hours of combat, coalition forces on the left flank struck deep and nearly encircled the Iraq forces. Iraqi defenses in Kuwait City collapsed and began a precipitous withdrawal. Many were destroyed by coalition air forces during the retreat. US Marines, with Arab coalition forces, liberated Kuwait City by 27 February. That day, President Bush announced a cease fire.

The rapid and crushing defeat of the large, battle-tested Iraqi military demonstrated that the renaissance of the American military begun in the 1970s had borne fruit. The all-volunteer military performed superbly with a high degree of cohesion and professionalism, and the ability to master advanced technology.[29] The investment in recruiting, educating, and developing high quality troops, in new weapons systems and improved command and control, and development of new doctrine generated one of the most stunning victories in the history of American landpower.[30] American

---

28   Quoted in Gordon and Trainor, *The Generals' War*, 234.

29   Gordon and Trainor, *The Generals' War*, 470–71.

30   Scales, *Certain Victory*, 5–36, 361–82; Gregory Fontenot, E.J. Degen, and David Tohn, *On Point: The US Army in Operation Iraqi Freedom* (Fort Leavenworth, KS: Combat

airpower dominated the battlefield. Air platforms and systems developed in the 1970s and 1980s worked nearly flawlessly. While only a small proportion of the munitions dropped were precision guided, those used were impressive. According to Lt. Col. Edward Mann of the US Air Force:

> ... dramatic video images made clear that it no longer took hundreds of bombers dropping thousands of bombs or even tens of bombers dropping scores of bombs to destroy a single target. Now one aircraft, often delivering only one weapon, could destroy one target (or at least one "aiming point"). Bombing has become so precise that weapon systems can routinely identify not just the building or the room, but the corner of the room that will bring everything down--even the vent shaft that will put the bomb inside the shelter.[31]

Other lessons from America's first war with Iraq, however, were not so rosy. On the purely military level, cooperation between air and ground forces was as effective as it ever had been in history, but clearly needed more effort to attain its full potential.[32] For all of the tremendous improvements in airpower, it could not attain strategic success on its own. As Gordon and Trainor note:

> In the final analysis, the air war had confirmed the Air Force's growing ability to destroy targets deep in the enemy heartland and on the battlefields. By late February, however, airpower's success in crippling Iraq had not led to a political success comparable to it military success. Airpower had yet to do what ground power had habitually done—change the political equation as a function of that power.[33]

While airpower advocates contended that the shortage of precision guided munitions and inadequate methods for battle damage assessment kept airpower from attaining strategic success, most military and strategic analysts felt that *Desert Storm* re-demonstrated the lessons of World War II and Vietnam: airpower could be vitally important, perhaps even militarily decisive, but could not bring ultimate victory by itself.

In the broadest level, the first war with Iraq showed that even America's great military prowess did not guarantee strategic success (defined as attainment of a war's political objectives). It later became widely accepted that President Bush's decision to stop the offensive was, in Jeffrey Record's words, based on "an erroneous picture of the battlefield."[34] In particular, the President thought the Republican Guard divisions, which were central to Hussein's power, were more damaged than they actually were. This mistake became clear soon after the cease fire. From the beginning, Saddam

---

Studies Institute, 2004), 4–26.

31   Edward Mann, "One Target, One Bomb: Is the Principle of Mass Dead?" *Airpower Journal*, 7, 1, Spring 1993, 17, 39.

32   Gordon and Trainor, *The Generals' War*, pp. 471–3; Williamson Murray and Robert H. Scales Jr., *The Iraq War* (Cambridge, MA: Belknap, 2003), 11.

33   Gordon and Trainor, *The Generals' War*, 331.

34   Jeffrey Record, *Dark Victory: America's Second War Against Iraq* (Annapolis, MD: Naval Institute Press, 2004), 4.

Hussein refused to comply with the terms of the cease-fire—something that would continue for the remainder of his time in power.[35] It was, according to retired Army Colonel Douglas Macgregor, *Desert Storm* was "an unfinished war or, more precisely, a strategic defeat for American arms."[36] Similarly, one of the first major books to appear after the war labeled it "triumph without victory."[37]

There are political explanations for the willingness to accept partial victory. After the trauma of Vietnam, the United States had taken steps to make the use of force palatable to the public making it more precise and rapid, and focusing on engagement with the armed forces of evil enemy states as far as possible from civilians. The American public, it was thought, has little tolerance for protracted, morally ambiguous conflicts involving extensive suffering by non-combatants. The conundrum was that this approach to war increased the chances of public support but simultaneously limited the ability to attain the ultimate strategic objectives. The "Powell doctrine" which had emerged from the Weinberger principles for the use of force and codified this approach to warfighting, had severe limitations.[38] In fact, Saddam Hussein quickly recognized this, assessed it as a major weakness of the United States, and used it as a shield in his struggle with Washington. Still, the image of *Desert Storm* held by the American public was not one of strategic failure, but of the overwhelming battlefield victory. This created an expectation that whenever the US military was used, the results would be quick and at a low blood cost to the United States. Ironically, this meant that despite all of the improvements made in the US military in the years before the war with Iraq, there were limited conditions under which it could be used.[39]

Conflict Without War

Two broad issues dominated the strategic agenda during the Clinton administration: the appropriate size of the US military and its involvement in peacekeeping. While the conflicts in Somalia and the Balkans drove the latter, Iraq continued to shape thinking about the size of the military. Entering office, President Clinton and his top advisers believed that the US military was too large, contained the wrong capabilities, and was too expensive.[40] The United States, they felt, could remain a

---

35   Thomas Donnelly, *Operation Iraqi Freedom: A Strategic Assessment* (Washington, DC: American Enterprise Institute, 2004), xii–xiv.

36   Douglas Macgregor, "America's Unfinished War—And the Effort to Redeem It," *Chicago Tribune*, 13 March 2005.

37   *Triumph Without Victory: The Unreported History of the Persian Gulf War* (New York: Times Books, 1992).

38   Gordon and Trainor, *The Generals' War*, 488–9.

39   Grant T. Hammond, "Myths of the Gulf War: Some 'Lessons' Not to Learn," *Airpower Journal*, 12, 3, Fall 1998, 11.

40   See John T. Correll, "The Base Force Meets Option C," *Air Force Magazine*, Vol. 74, No. 6, June 1992; and Les Aspin, "National Security in the 1990s: Defining a New Basis

global power with substantially lower levels of defense by working with partners, allies and the United Nations.[41] The framework was a strategy of "engagement and enlargement." The stress on "engagement" was intended to both reassure friends and enemies that the United States would remain active, and to counter sentiment for withdrawal among the American people. "American leadership in the world," the Clinton strategy held, "has never been more important."[42] "Enlargement"—a concept advocated most persistently by National Security Advisor Anthony Lake— committed the United States to expanding the community of market democracies in order to augment American security and prosperity.

To reflect President Clinton's wider national security strategy, Secretary of Defense Les Aspin instigated what became known as the "Bottom Up Review" (BUR) immediately upon assuming leadership of the Pentagon. Like the Bush strategy that preceded it, the BUR stressed the complexity and unpredictability of the new security environment. It committed the US military to two sorts of activities: prevention and partnership. Prevention was the use of the military and other elements of the Department of Defense to attempt to forestall armed conflict by promoting democracy, economic growth, economic reform, human dignity, and the peaceful resolution of disputes. Partnership linked the US military to those of other countries, particularly ones undergoing the transition to democracy. The BUR, however, did not abandon the stress on major regional war against opponents like Iraq. Even the number of such wars used for planning and force development remained the same. The BUR stated:

> It is prudent for the United States to maintain military power to be able to win two major regional conflicts that occur nearly simultaneously. With this capability, we will be confident, and our allies as well as potential enemies will know, that a single regional conflict will not leave our interest and allies in other regions at risk.[43]

The BUR considered Iraq and North Korea the most likely aggressors which might cause a "major regional conflict" (MRC).[44] Such aggression would take the form of an armor-heavy, combined arms offensive against the outnumbered forces of a neighboring state friendly to the United States with only limited US military forces in the region before hostilities and Washington acting as leader of a coalition. The

for US Military Forces," briefing to the Atlantic Council of the United States, Washington, DC: House Armed Services Committee, 6 January 1992.

41   Daniel Goure and Jeffrey M. Ranney, *Averting the Defense Train Wreck in the New Millennium* (Washington, DC: Center for Strategic and International Studies, 1999), 23.

42   *A National Security Strategy of Engagement and Enlargement* (Washington, DC: The White House, July 1994), 1.

43   Secretary of Defense Les Aspin, *Report on the Bottom-Up Review* (Washington, DC: Department of Defense, 2003), Section II, "A Defense Strategy for the New Era."

44   John F. Troxell, *Force Planning in an Era of Uncertainty: Two MRCs as a Force Sizing Framework* (Carlisle Barracks, PA: US Army War College Strategic Studies Institute, 1997), 11–12.

American response would involve four phases: (1) halt the invasion; (2) build up US combat power in the theater while reducing the enemy's; (3) decisively defeat the enemy; and (4) provide for post-war stability. To counter an MRC, the US military would need a force package composed of 4–5 Army divisions, 4–5 Marine Expeditionary Brigades, 10 Air Force fighter wings, 100 Air Force heavy bombers, 4–5 Navy aircraft carrier battlegroups, and various special operations forces. In other words, *Desert Storm* served as the planning template for major wars. Major wars, in turn, formed the centerpiece of US military strategy. The logic behind this was that such conflicts would be the most dangerous kind that the US military would face, and if the US military prepared for them, it would by default be prepared to handle other kinds.

While Clinton's grand strategy linked the military to American national interests, initially it was vague on the priority assigned to various interests. In the 1995 edition of the National Security Strategy, President Clinton distinguished *vital* interests (those for which the United States would be willing to use force unilaterally), *important* interests (those for which the United States would use force in conjunction with partners); and *humanitarian* interests (those for which the large scale use of force was not appropriate).[45] In 1996, Secretary of Defense William Perry began to describe US military strategy as one of "prevent, deter, defeat." While this language certainly did not reflect any radical transition in strategic thinking, it did have serious implications. As Perry phrased it, the Clinton strategy placed "renewed" emphasis on prevention by using the US military in ways that might limit the chances of future conflict.[46] Preventive defense was to include four "core activities": (1) working with the successor states to the Soviet Union to reduce the nuclear threat; (2) limiting proliferation of weapons of mass destruction; (3) encouraging newly independent and newly democratic states to restructure their defenses; and (4) establishing cooperative military-to-military ties with states which were not traditional American allies or coalition partners. Preventive defense represented the beginning of what would become known as "shaping" activities for the armed forces.

While Clinton's grand strategy matured, the US military worked to develop concepts of future warfare and a framework for the force it required. *Desert Storm* was always a backdrop, serving as a model for future wars. One of the most important steps in this process was the publication of *Joint Vision 2010* by General John Shalikashvili, Chairman of the Joints Chiefs of Staff. JV 2010—to use the document's popular name—was to serve as "the conceptual template for how America's Armed Forces will channel the vitality and innovation of our people and leverage technological opportunities to achieve new levels of effectiveness in joint warfighting."[47] The

---

45   *A National Security Strategy of Engagement and Enlargement* (Washington, DC: The White House, February 1995), 12.

46   Secretary of Defense William J. Perry, *Annual Report to the President and the Congress* (Washington, DC: Department of Defense, March 1996), viii.

47   *Joint Vision 2010* (Washington, DC: The Joint Staff), n.d., 1. JV 2010 was published in 1995 but, for reasons known only to General Shalikashvili and the Joint Staff, does not

focus was purely operational: JV 2010 did not analyze the changing political, social, economic, and normative framework of armed conflict at the end of the 20th century. There were, however, some important implied beliefs about the use of military force, specifically the challenges to its political usability and legitimacy that resulted from the information revolution and global interconnectedness.[48] According to JV 2010, the solutions to these challenges were greater speed and precision. A US military able to defeat any opponent quickly with minimum collateral damage and American casualties would be politically usable. To operate on a lethal battlefield where precision weapons, weapons of mass destruction, and various types of missiles were common, the US military would need increased stealth, mobility, dispersion, and higher operational tempo. Four key technologies—low observable/masking technologies, "smarter" weapons, long-range precision capabilities, and information technology—were central. "Superior technology," the Joint Staff contended, "has been a cornerstone of US *NMS* [National Military Strategy] since the dawn of the Cold War and will remain so through the year 2010."[49]

The central concept of JV 2010 was "full spectrum dominance"—superiority over any opponent in any type of military operation. While stressing that this was only possible by retaining the high quality levels of people, leadership, and training, the focus of JV 2010 was using information superiority to gain full spectrum dominance via four operational concepts:

> *Dominant maneuver*: the multidimensional application of information, engagement, and mobility to position and employ widely dispersed joint air, land, sea, and space forces.
> *Precision engagement*: a system of systems that enables US forces to locate objectives or targets, generate the desired effect, assess the level of success, and reengage.
> *Full-dimensional protection*: control of the battlespace to maintain freedom of action during deployment, maneuver and engagement, while providing multi-layered defenses.
> *Focused logistics*: the fusion of information, logistics, and transportation technologies to provide rapid crisis response, track and shift assets even while enroute, and directly deliver tailored logistics packages and sustainment.

In the broadest sense, though, JV 2010 represented the codification of the idea that a revolution in military affairs (RMA) was underway, and that its essence was information technology.[50]

---

indicate a publication date anywhere in the printed version. The concepts in JV 2010 were elaborated in *Concept for Future Joint Operations: Expanding Joint Vision 2010* (Washington, DC: Joint Chiefs of Staff, May 1997).

48   This is explored in detail in Steven Metz, *Armed Conflict in the 21st Century: The Information Revolution and Post-Modern Warfare* (Carlisle Barracks, PA: Strategic Studies Institute, 2000), 5–25.

49   *Concept for Future Joint Operations: Expanding Joint Vision 2010* (Washington, DC: Joint Chiefs of Staff, May 1997), 24.

50   For assessments and explanations of the official DOD view of the RMA, see Metz, *Armed Conflict in the 21st Century*, pp. 27–40; Colin Gray, *The American Revolution in Military Affairs: An Interim Assessment* (Camberley, UK: Strategic and Combat Studies

In the FY 1994 Defense Authorization Bill, Congress directed the Secretary of Defense to conduct a "fundamental and comprehensive examination of America's defense needs" every 4 years, with the first due in 1997. The Quadrennial Defense Review (QDR) report was released in May of that year and offered insights into the logic and key concepts of the Clinton Strategy. The 1997 QDR retained the "two MRC" force shaping yardstick.[51] "If the United States were to forego its ability to defeat aggression in more than one theater at a time," the QDR report stated, "our standing as a global power, as the security partner of choice, and as the leader of the international community would be called into question ... A one-theater war capacity would risk undermining both deterrence and the credibility of US security commitments in key regions of the world."[52] After sometimes-intense debate over the sequencing of the two MRCs, the QDR settled on the phrase "nearly simultaneous." It also introduced another crucial idea: "preparing now for an uncertain future." By 1997 most of the American defense community agreed that an historic revolution in military affairs was underway.[53] Led by people like Andrew Marshall, (director of the Pentagon's Office of Net Assessment), Andrew Krepinevich (Center for Strategic and Budgetary Analysis), and Admiral William Owens (former Vice Chairman of the Joint Chiefs of Staff), the concept of military revolutions has gone from the fringe to the foundation of US military thinking. This made perfect sense since the type of military revolution that the Pentagon had begun to pursue meshed with so many elements of the American strategic culture including a never-ending quest for technological solutions to problems, the desire for continuous improvement, the tendency to use qualitative superiority to keep human costs low and thus retain political support for engagement, and the perceived need for US military preponderance. The QDR, along with JV 2010, codified this version of the RMA in American military strategy. It described three "alternative paths" to the future. One was to focus on the near-term, minimizing the money and effort devoted to preparing for the long-term. The second path was to accept greater near-term risk by further reducing the size of the military, thus freeing money for exploiting the RMA. The third was to balance current demands and an uncertain future, combining modest

---

Institute, 1997); and Bill Owens, *Lifting the Fog of War* (New York: Farrar, Straus, Giroux, 2000).

51   The ability to fight two major regional wars remained part of American military strategy until the George W. Bush administration. For a full assessment see Steven Metz, ed., *Revising the Two MTW Force Shaping Paradigm* (Carlisle Barracks, PA: US Army War College Strategic Studies Institute, 2001).

52   Secretary of Defense William S. Cohen, *Report of the Quadrennial Defense Review* (Washington, DC: Department of Defense, May 1997), Section III.

53   Some analysts argue that the real revolution took place in the 1980s and thus the Clinton era simply represented a time of consolidation and exploitation. See, for instance, Ralph Peters, "After the Revolution," *Parameters*, Vol. 25, No. 2, Summer 1995, 7–14; and David Jablonsky, *The Owl of Minerva Flies at Twilight: Doctrinal Change and Continuity and the Revolution in Military Affairs* (Carlisle Barracks, PA: US Army War College Strategic Studies Institute, 1994).

force reductions with steady technological progress. Of course, this sort of analysis was "cooked." The technique of devising three options, one calling for doing less of what is already being done, one calling for doing more, and one calling for a continuation of existing actions is common among bureaucracies not committed to substantial change. Clearly no rational decisionmaker would choose anything other than the "balanced" approach which was defined as what the Department of Defense was already doing.

The Clinton administration thus considered Hussein enough of a threat to use renewed war with Iraq as a force sizing yardstick and a scenario for military wargames, but not enough to justify outright intervention. As General (ret) Wesley Clark notes,

> ... the threat from Iraq came to assume a major role in US defense planning. A refight of Desert Storm was one of only two scenarios that could be publicly cited to justify large military forces ... By the late 1990s the Persian Gulf had been designated for planning purposes as one of two Major Theaters of War, and systematic investments were undertaken to strengthen logistics, communications, and intelligence in preparation for possible conflict there. In addition, scenarios from hypothetical war in Iraq were used in requirements studies, weapons procurement, force designs, and training.[54]

Clinton's strategy toward Iraq was based on containment and deterrence, and on preserving the *Desert Storm* coalition. As part of this, the administration expanded security ties to the Gulf States, providing trainers, selling equipment, augmenting military-to-military cooperation through things like staff talks, combined exercises, and expanded slots for Gulf militaries at American military schools, and increasing its military presence in Kuwait. The United States continued to support the slate of sanctions imposed on Iraq after the 1991 war.[55] When necessary, the Clinton administration used military power, particularly airpower. When Hussein supported a 1993 attempt to kill former President George H.W. Bush during a trip to Kuwait, Clinton struck Iraqi intelligence headquarters with Tomahawk cruise missiles. In 1994, worsening economic and security conditions inside Iraq led Hussein to deploy troops to the border with Kuwait, apparently hoping to erode the Gulf States' backing for the sanctions. Clinton then ordered Operation *Vigilant Warrior* which significantly increased the American military presence in the region.[56] American and British warplanes patrolled the "no fly" zones in the north and south of Iraq (the former—*Operation Northern Watch*—to prevent from Hussein from using his air force against the Kurds, the latter—*Operation Southern Watch*—to do the same for Iraqi Shiites).

---

54   Wesley K. Clark, *Winning Modern Wars: Iraq, Terrorism, and the American Empire* (New York: Public Affairs, 2003), 6.

55   For a comprehensive treatment, see Sarah Grahm-Brown, *Sanctioning Saddam: The Politics of Intervention in Iraq* (London: I.B. Tauris, 1999).

56   Donnelly, *Operation Iraqi Freedom*, 11.

By the second Clinton term, the United Nations Security Council, worried about the human costs of sanctions which Hussein was amplifying and manipulating as a political tool, established the oil for food program to provide Iraq a source of foreign currency to be used for humanitarian purposes. In reality, much of this was siphoned off and used for the Iraqi military, rewards to the regime's cronies, and luxury purchases by Hussein and his immediate family. Hussein continued to deceive and limit UN weapons inspectors and chip away at the sanctions. In 1998 the Clinton administration launched *Operation Desert Fox* in which US aircraft attacked various Iraqi facilities, including suspected sites for the production and storage of weapons of mass destruction. When Iraq challenged the attacks, the United States and United Kingdom changed their rules of engagement and began attacking Iraqi anti-air radars which illuminated coalition planes and other air defense targets.[57] The result was an almost continuous bombing campaign. This approach did help deter Hussein from cross-border invasions, but did not attain America's wider strategic objectives including the destruction of weapons of mass destruction and a diminution of internal repression. When Congress passed the Iraq Liberation Act of 1998, removal of the Hussein regime became official US policy, but the Clinton administration continued to seek this through containment, sanctions, and pressure rather than the direct application of military force.

Despite the presence on the Republican ticket of Dick Cheney, one of the architects of the 1991 war against Hussein, Iraq did not play a leading role in George W. Bush's 2000 campaign. His major defense proposals were ending or limiting American involvement in protracted peacekeeping operations like the Balkans, containing China, building a national missile defense system, and speeding the transformation of the American military to capitalize on the revolution in military affairs.[58] Like many conservatives, Bush was concerned that the defense cuts of the 1990s had gone too far, allowing American power to atrophy. As one major report expressed it,

> At present the United States faces no global rival. America's grand strategy should aim to preserve and extend this advantageous position as far into the future as possible … But years of cuts in defense spending have eroded the American military's combat readiness, and put in jeopardy the Pentagon's plans for maintaining military superiority in the years ahead. Increasingly, the US military has found itself undermanned, inadequately equipped and trained, straining to handle contingency operations, and ill-prepared to adapt itself to the revolution in military affairs.[59]

During the first months of the new administration, Secretary of Defense Rumsfeld, who was convinced the military was "hidebound and outdated, still equipped, trained

---

57   Clark, *Winning Modern Wars*, 5–8.

58   James Kitfield, *War and Destiny: How the Bush Revolution in Foreign and Military Affairs Redefined American Power* (Washington, DC: Potomac Books, 2005), 5–6.

59   *Rebuilding America's Defenses: Strategy, Forces and Resources For a New Century*, a report of the Project for the New American Century, September 2000, i.

and organized to fight old enemies," poured his immense energy into accelerating the pace of military transformation.[60]

As the Bush administration took shape, though, there were signs that patience with Hussein's deception, disregard for UN resolutions, and repression would be limited. Donald Rumsfeld, Deputy Secretary of Defense Paul Wolfowitz, Deputy Secretary of State Richard Armitage, and Richard Perle, chairman of the Pentagon's Defense Policy Board had been among those lobbying the Clinton administration for firmer action against Hussein.

President Bush's world view and grand strategy were, of course, irrevocably altered by the terrorist attacks of 11 September 2001. Most important, he considered the United States to be at war and thus in need of bold, dramatic strategic actions. According to Bush, the gravest danger faced by the United States "lies at the perilous crossroads of radicalism and technology." "For much of the last century," he continued, "America's defense relied on the Cold War doctrines of deterrence and containment. Deterrence—the promise of massive retaliation against nations— means nothing against shadowy terrorist networks with no nation or citizens to defend. Containment is not possible when unbalanced dictators with weapons of mass destruction can deliver those weapons on missiles or secretly provide them to terrorist allies."[61] Of course, deterrence and containment per se are not Cold War doctrines, and there is no example of an "unbalanced dictator" launching a strike with weapons of mass destruction outside conventional war or providing them to terrorists. One of the key components of strategy is always deciding how much risk is acceptable by balancing it against anticipated benefits. During the Cold War, for instance, the United States was willing to risk a nuclear exchange with the Soviet Union and, later, China because the chances of this happening were remote and the costs of eradicating the threat large. President Bush shifted this risk equation by contending that the fact that dictators *could* provide weapons of mass destruction was unacceptable. Potential rather than motive or demonstrated intent was enough to inspire action. For the first time, American policymakers assumed the nation's enemies were irrational and thus not bound by the traditional logic of strategy which held that courses of action should be assessed by measuring expected gains against expected risks and costs.

In September 2002 the Bush administration issued a formal national security strategy which expanded its thinking. The United States, it stated, was "fighting a war against terrorists of global reach. The enemy is not a single political regime or person or religion or ideology. The enemy is terrorism— premeditated, politically motivated violence perpetrated against innocents."[62] This "deadly new challenge" emerged "from rogue states and terrorists"—in other words, the danger was the

---

60   Bob Woodward, *Bush At War* (New York: Simon and Schuster, 2002), 22.

61   President George W. Bush, Remarks at the 2002 Graduation Exercise of the United States Military Academy, West Point, NY, 1 June 2002.

62   *National Security Strategy of the United States* (Washington, DC: The White House, September 2002), 5.

nexus of a new threat—increasingly dangerous global terrorist networks—and old ones—rogue states. The United States must thus "be prepared to stop rogue states and their terrorist clients before they are able to threaten or use weapons of mass destruction against the United States and our allies and friends ... We cannot let our enemies strike first"[63] The war on terrorism, which President Bush labeled "an inescapable calling of our generation," sought to strike directly at terrorist networks in order to disrupt and destroy them, protect the American homeland, and create a global anti-terrorist environment.[64] This last element brought Iraq to fore of the administration's thinking.

Iraq fueled one other important trend in American strategy: a shift in thinking about war objectives. During the Cold War, the notion of "limited war" dominated American thinking. The idea was that in a nuclear world, decisiveness in the sense of utterly defeating an opponent's armed forces, occupying its territory, and changing its political structure was infeasible and unacceptably dangerous. For decades, the implied or stated military objectives in American strategy concerned the restoration of the *status quo ante bellum*. Had a war between the Warsaw Pact and NATO ever occurred, for instance, it probably would have ended with a restoration of the inter-German border, not with a NATO march on Moscow and an occupation of the Soviet Union. This idea of limited military objectives continued in the post-Cold War (i.e. pre-11 September) era. The 1997 National Military Strategy of the United States, for instance, stated:

> In the event of armed conflict, US Armed Forces will render an adversary incapable of armed resistance through destruction of his capacity to threaten our interests or by breaking his will to do so. This sets the military conditions for winning the peace. In conducting combat operations, the United States will use all means available, commensurate with the national interest at stake, the risks involved, and international law. We will endeavor to commit decisive force to ensure that we achieve the objectives established by the NCA [National Command Authorities—the President and Secretary of Defense] and conclude hostilities in the shortest time possible and on terms favorable to the United States.[65]

The post-11 September National Military Strategy, by contrast, said,

> Where necessary, commanders' plans will include options to rapidly transition to a campaign to win decisively and achieve enduring results. The capabilities required for major combat operations must be applicable to the full spectrum of threats ranging from state to non-state adversaries employing traditional and/or asymmetric capabilities. A campaign to win decisively will include actions to: destroy an adversary's military capabilities through the integrated application of air, ground, maritime, space and information capabilities; and

---

63   Ibid., 14, 15.

64   President George W. Bush, remarks from the White House on Operation Iraqi Freedom and Operation Enduring Freedom, Washington, DC, March 19, 2004. For details on the counterterrorism strategy, see *National Strategy For Combating Terrorism* (Washington, DC: The White House, February 2003).

65   *National Military Strategy* (Washington, DC: The Joint Staff, 1997).

potentially remove adversary regimes when directed. Such campaigns require capabilities for conventional warfighting, unconventional warfare, homeland security, stability and post-conflict operations, countering terrorism and security cooperation activities.[66]

Similarly, the 2001 Quadrennial Defense Review Report—released a few weeks after the terrorist attacks on New York and the Pentagon—formally shifted the force planning standard from fighting two simultaneous regional wars to the defeating aggression in "overlapping major conflicts" with the ability to undertake decisive victory, to possibly including regime change and occupation, in one of them.[67]

Clearly the fact that the 1991 war with Iraq had brought military triumph but, by leaving Hussein in power, not strategic success haunted American leaders and drove this evolution in strategy. President Bush and his advisors had concluded that in the post-11 September world, instability and the root causes of indirect aggression (which often took the form of terrorism) must be ameliorated, not simply contained. If the root causes are not addressed, the problem will eventually re-emerge. In discussing the Middle East, for instance, President Bush stated

> As long as that region is a place of tyranny and despair and anger, it will produce men and movements that threaten the safety of Americans and our friends. We seek the advance of democracy for the most practical of reasons: because democracies do not support terrorists or threaten the world with weapons of mass murder.[68]

Aggression flowing from internal instability thus demands the actual *transformation* of an unstable or aggressive state into one which is both stable and willing to adhere to the norms of the international community. The challenge, then, was to develop the means and concepts to implement this idea.

The Second War With Hussein

No one other than those very close to President Bush and privy to private discussion fully understands why he chose to make America's conflict with Iraq a central part of the war on terrorism. Hussein certainly supported some terrorist movements and may have had some ties to al Qaeda, but he was not a central cog in global terrorism.[69] His

---

66   *National Military Strategy of the United States* (Washington, DC: The Joint Staff, 2004), 14.

67   *Quadrennial Defense Review Report* (Washington, DC: Department of Defense, 30 September 2001), 17.

68   President George W. Bush, remarks on Winston Churchill and the War on Terror, Library of Congress, Washington, D.C., 4 February 2004.

69   Some analysts argue that the relationship between Hussein and al Qaeda was more extensive than is generally thought. See, for instance, Stephen F. Hayes, *The Connection: How al Qaeda's Collaboration With Saddam Hussein Has Endangered America* (New York: Harper Collins, 2004). Others such as Richard Clarke, the counter-terrorism director on the National Security Council at the time of the 11 September attacks, do not consider this

demise in itself did not decisively damage to al Qaeda, America's primary enemy. The assertion that Hussein *could* provide weapons of mass destruction is technically true, but there is no evidence that he intended to do so. Plus, this argument is made even more implausible by the fact that the use of weapons of mass destruction provided to terrorists by Hussein could probably be traced back to Baghdad, thus leading to the certain demise of the regime. In all of his evil behavior, Hussein had never shown himself to be suicidal.

Rather than being built on clear, linear logic or a "smoking gun," the administration's case for war against Iraq was like a courtroom argument where a number of facts, none of which were convincing in isolation, were, when combined, held to constitute a valid rationale. The central components of the President's argument included:

> Hussein's regime was an "aggressive threat" which accepted no "law of morality" and was unlimited in its ambitions; Hussein had not proven that he complied with the commitments made after the 1991 war to disarm, end the production of biological and chemical weapons and pursuit of nuclear weapons; stop support to terrorism, and stop repression of his own people.

While the existing threat to regional stability and other US interests posed by Iraq was tolerable, the assumption was that it was on the rise. Better to resolve the issue now, the administration though. As President Bush explained:

> If we fail to act in the face of danger, the people of Iraq will continue to live in brutal submission. The regime will have new power to bully and dominate and conquer its neighbors, condemning the Middle East to more years of bloodshed and fear. The regime will remain unstable—the region will remain unstable, with little hope of freedom, and isolated from the progress of our times. With every step the Iraqi regime takes toward gaining and deploying the most terrible weapons, our own options to confront that regime will narrow. And if an emboldened regime were to supply these weapons to terrorist allies, then the attacks of September the 11th would be a prelude to far greater horrors.[70]

Given that upholding the authority of the United Nations or ending the suffering of people in far away countries had not been at the center of the Bush strategy to that point, part of this rationale rings hollow. The most plausible explanation for President Bush's decision to remove the Hussein regime has two parts. First, the Administration may have concluded that Southwest Asia was vital not only to the United States, but also to the world, and that the region would never be stable so long as Hussein was in power. The existing sanctions and containment regime was

---

relationship important. (See Richard A. Clarke, *Against All Enemies: Inside America's War on Terror* (New York: Free Press, 2004).

70   President George H. Bush, remarks at the United Nations General Assembly, 12 September 2002.

crumbling and showed little promise of removing him.[71] And—importantly—the post 11 September political climate in the United States and around the world provided a window of opportunity where Hussein's removal would garner public support. Even if the threat from Hussein was not increasing, the chance of being able to remove him was diminishing.

Second, the President did view global terrorism systemically. He understood that simply to destroy existing terrorists without changing the underlying conditions which led them to violence would be ineffective. Despite what terrorist leaders like Osama bin Laden said, President Bush did not believe that it was American policies in the Islamic world which generated terrorism, but instead the frustration and anger arising from the lack of political openness there.[72] This argument, made most ardently by former Deputy Secretary of Defense Paul Wolfowitz and others grouped under the label "neoconservatives," held that the ultimate solution to the challenge of terrorism was democracy in the Islamic world.[73] "Iraq," said Dr. Wolfowitz, "is part of the global war on terrorism because Iraq represents one of the first and best opportunities to begin building what President Bush has referred to as a better world beyond the war on terrorism. If Saddam Hussein is a danger and a support to terrorists and an encouragement to terrorist regimes, conversely his demise will open opportunities for governments and institutions to emerge in the Muslim world that are respectful of fundamental human dignity and freedom and that abhor the killing of innocents as an instrument of national policy."[74] According to President Bush, "A democratic revolution that has reached across the globe will finally take root in the Middle East. The stagnation and isolation and anger of that region will give way to progress and opportunity. America and the world will be safer from catastrophic violence because terror is not the tool of the free."[75] In other words, Iraq was to be

---

71   This is covered in detail in Kenneth M. Pollack, *The Threatening Storm: The Case for Invading Iraq* (New York: Random House, 2002), 211–42. Pollack's book was influential during the debate over the appropriate action against Iraq. He later admitted that some of the information on which he built his analysis was flawed. See Kenneth M. Pollack, "Spies, Lies, and Weapons: What Went Wrong," *Atlantic Monthly*, January/February 2004.

72   The most detailed case for taking bin Laden at his word when he says that it is Western policies rather than the Western political system which inspires anger in the Islamic world is made by Michael Scheuer (writing under the pseudonym "Anonymous") in *Through Our Enemies' Eyes: Osama bin Laden, Radical Islam, and the Future of America* (Washington, DC: Brassey's, 2001) and *Imperial Hubris: Why the West Is Losing the War on Terror* (Washington, DC: Brassey's, 2004).

73   Todd S. Purdum, *A Time of Our Choosing: America's War in Iraq* (New York: Times Books, 2003), pp. 12–16; and, Kitfield, *War and Destiny*, 66–79.

74   Deputy Secretary of Defense Paul Wolfowitz, remarks at the Fletcher Conference, Ronald Reagan Building and International Trade Center, Washington, DC, Wednesday, 16 October 2002.

75   President George W. Bush, "Turning Back the Terrorist Threat: America's Unbreakable Commitment," address at the Heritage Foundation, Washington, DC, 19 November 2003.

a laboratory for open government in the Arab world, and a catalyst for what the Administration hoped would be broader and deeper changes eventually shattering the system that generated terrorists. As Thomas Donnelly notes,

> ... the Bush administration's determination to remove Saddam Hussein had less to do with his regime's armaments than its character. It was, in the president's reckoning, the despotic nature of the Iraqi regime that was the source of danger. More than any other country in the region, Saddam Hussein's terror state epitomized the broader political dysfunction responsible for the phenomenon of Islamic terrorism ... Iraq, in short, was always about more than weapons. It was about Saddam Hussein and the failure of the United States—for the past sixty years—to confront the political sinkhole created by the tyrants of the Middle East.[76]

The administration never fully explained why it believed that the absence of democracy motivated al Qaeda rather than the reasons given by bin Laden and his associates.[77] It did not explain why new, fragile democracies created in the Middle East would constrain the anti-Americanism that was rampant among the people of that region. Nor did it account for terrorism arising from open societies such as Europe.

Still, by late 2002 President Bush had built enough political support to undertake military action against Iraq, at least within the United States (international support did not come close to matching the near-unanimity for action against Iraq's invasion of Kuwait in 1990). On October 2 of that year a Joint Resolution of Congress stated "Iraq both poses a continuing threat to the national security of the United States and international peace and security in the Persian Gulf region and remains in material and unacceptable breach of its international obligations by, among other things, continuing to possess and develop a significant chemical and biological weapons capability, actively seeking a nuclear weapons capability, and supporting and harboring terrorist organizations ..."[78]

Organizationally, little had changed in the US military since the 1991 war.[79] The US Central Command, now under the command of General Tommy Franks—a popular, professional officer—had responsibility. But while Normal Schwarzkopf was able to exercise direct personal command of the planning and warfighting in 1990–91, Franks was also responsible for the ongoing war in Afghanistan. He therefore designated Army Lieutenant General David McKiernan Combined Forces

---

76   Donnelly, *Operation Iraqi Freedom*, 26.
77   Michael Scheuer, one of the more astute observers of al Qaeda first as a CIA analyst and later as an author, contends that bin Laden is drive by six US policies he sees as anti-Muslim: 1) support for Israel; 2) the presence of American troops on the Arabian peninsula; 3) occupation of Iraq and Afghanistan; 4) support for Russia, China, and India in their conflicts with Muslim minorities; 5) pressure on Arab oil producers to keep petroleum prices low; and 6) support for apostate, corrupt, and repressive Muslim governments. (Anonymous, *Imperial Hubris: Why the West Is Losing the War on Terror* [Washington, DC: Brassey's, 2004], 241.)
78   2 October 2002.
79   Murray and Scales, *The Iraq War*, 63.

Land Component Commander (CFLCC)—a choice which Murray and Scales called "inspired"—and delegated control of the land war to him.[80] In many ways, the planning for *Operation Iraqi Freedom* was unusual since the conflict was a reprise. As retired General Wesley Clark notes, "Usually, militaries fight wars they haven't prepared for. This one would be different. General plans had been in place for a decade, backed up by substantial preparations."[81] In fact, a 1996 plan which was basically a replay of *Desert Storm* was used to provide the initial baseline.[82] What had changed—and what eventually allowed a campaign very different than *Desert Storm*—was the effectiveness of the US military after a decade of reform and transformation.

Detailed planning began in January 2002 with a series of meetings between General Franks and Secretary of Defense Donald Rumsfeld.[83] They agreed that Baghdad was Hussein's "center of gravity" but the US military must destroy Iraq's ground forces and various targets which allowed the regime to function before seizing the capital. Initially the major points of dissension were the size of the force package and the speed of the operation. Rumsfeld pushed Franks for the smallest possible force package and fastest possible operational pace while the CENTCOM commander favored a larger force and slower advance in order to minimize risk.[84] Since assuming leadership of the Department of Defense, Rumsfeld had been convinced that the uniformed military was too risk averse. The Secretary was willing to accept greater operational risk in exchange for efficiency and, he believed, for other strategic benefits that accrued from using the smallest possible military force in the quickest way possible.[85] During the development of the plan for intervention in Iraq, Rumsfeld pushed CENTCOM on this point.

According to Franks, he conceptualized the campaign in two dimensions. One consisted of "lines of operations"—operational fires, Special Forces operations, operational maneuver, information operations, support to Iraqi opposition groups, political-military operations, and civil-military operations to restore governance and services. The second dimension was the "slices" which must be controlled or eliminated to remove the Hussein regime: the leadership itself, internal security and intelligence services, the Republican Guard and Special Republican Guard divisions, selected regular army forces, key territory, infrastructure, civilian population, and the regime's commercial and diplomatic leverage. Using a matrix based on these two dimensions, Franks developed a campaign with five fronts: information operations, Special Operations Forces activities in the western part of Iraq to prevent Scud

---

80   *Ibid.*, 60.

81   Clark, *Winning Modern Wars*, 9.

82   Donnelly, *Operation Iraqi Freedom*, 31.

83   The most detailed narrative of the planning process is in Bob Woodward, *Plan of Attack* (New York: Simon and Schuster, 2004).

84   Clark, *Winning Modern Wars*, 10.

85   Kitfield, *War and Destiny*, 143–7.

launches, Special Forces operations in the north to fix the Iraqi forces there, and—the key—a two pronged assault from Kuwait to Baghdad.[86]

Planning continued for more than a year. The primary work was done by CENTCOM planners with close coordination with other elements of the military such as the Joint Staff and the Services. Rumsfeld and his senior lieutenants provided frequent guidance, and President Bush was briefed on a regular basis. While this was, according to retired General Clark, one of the "most detailed and meticulous" military planning processes ever conducted, it was also characterized by the abandonment of normal procedures for force phasing—deciding which forces would arrive when—and the extensive use of individual Deployment Orders. Again, Rumsfeld felt that the military's methods of force deployment were too cumbersome for the type of fluid, fast-changing warfare he intended to use.[87] But the result, according to General Clark, was "patchwork process that interspersed early-deploying units with those needed later, delayed mobilization, hampered training, and slowed the overall deployments considerably."[88] It was not clear, in other words, that the advantages of deviating from normal planning methods outweighed the disadvantages.

The military which was to implement this plan was smaller but better than the one which had gone to war in 1991. A number of new technologies were in widespread use such as unmanned aerial vehicles for surveillance and target acquisition; nearly all of the munitions delivered by aircraft were precision guided; and the Blue Force Tracker system gave American commanders a much clearer picture of the disposition of both friendly and enemy forces. In addition, jointness—the working together of the services—and all forms of communication were vastly improved. The coalition to remove Hussein in 2003 was significantly smaller than the one to eject him from Kuwait in 1991 but, American policymakers felt, adequate for the task. The inability to use Saudi facilities and to enter Iraq from Turkey did create challenges. Even though Kuwait virtually turned over its port and airport facilities to the Coalition, these were barely adequate for the flow of forces and supplies.[89]

On 14 March 2003 final diplomatic efforts collapsed and President Bush gave Saddam Hussein 48 hours to leave Iraq. While the politics of the conflict had reached the boiling point, all American ground forces were not yet prepared for combat operations. The 101st Air Assault Division was only partially deployed; all of the equipment of the 4th Infantry Division—the Army's most advanced—had not arrived in Kuwait (since the 4th was initially planned to enter Iraq through Turkey); the 1st Armored and 1st Cavalry divisions had not begun deployment. But rather than wait for them and give Hussein more time to prepare, the President and Secretary of Defense opted for a "rolling start" using the forces on hand: Air Force and Navy air

---

86   Tommy Franks with Malcolm McConnell, *American Soldier* (New York: Regan, 2004), 339–96.

87   Kitfield, *War and Destiny*, 143.

88   Clark, *Winning Modern Wars*, 13–17. Interviews conducted by the author with CFLCC planners at Camp Doha, Kuwait, in April and May 2003 confirmed this assessment.

89   Clark, *Winning Modern Wars*, 22–3.

assets, multinational special forces, and a land component composed of the Army's 3d Infantry Division and a brigade of the 82d Airborne Division, the First Marine Expeditionary Force, the Marine Task Force Tarawa, and the British 1st Armored Division. The assault began on March 20th.

Iraq expected a lengthy air campaign before a ground invasion as in the 1991 war.[90] In reality, the two began almost simultaneously, prompted by concerns that Iraq would destroy its oil fields and river bridges to hinder the advance, and would strike at Coalition staging areas in Kuwait with missiles. While airpower struck targets across Iraq, Coalition special forces and Central Intelligence Agency were to seize high value targets, and the main ground attack was to come from the south with the British controlling the area around Basra, the Marines advancing on the Coalition's right (eastern) flank and Army units on the left. The two prongs then were to converge south and west of Baghdad to prepare for an assault on the capital.

Initially the ground units advanced rapidly with limited resistance and bypassed the major population centers. The Iraq army units deployed in the south were poorly equipped, supplied, trained, and led.[91] Their morale was very low and most surrendered or ran away at first contact with Coalition forces. At the same time, Coalition aircraft and missiles hammered Iraqi command and control and any military forces which moved or deployed in the open. Despite pre-conflict concerns, the Iraqis had not undertaken extensive efforts to sabotage petroleum facilities or infrastructure.[92]

The American forces encountered their first organized resistance near Najaf on 23 March. The regular Iraqi army division there fought harder than expected. But when attacked with precision, standoff fires (airpower as well as rocket and tube artillery) then with direct assaults with tanks and fighting vehicles, this Iraqi unit was soon demolished. Despite a sandstorm which slowed the advance, both Army and Marine units quickly approached Baghdad and began to encounter Republican Guard units. Before the war, Coalition planners expected little opposition from Iraq's regular army units. In fact, these were expected to surrender en masse. But, the Republican Guards and Special Republican Guards were expected to fight fiercely, to include urban combat in Baghdad. In reality, most of the elite units collapsed under pressure as quickly as regular ones. At the same time the 173d Airborne Brigade seized the important oil fields near Kirkuk, in Iraq's north. And, the chemical attacks which CFLCC expected as American forces approached Baghdad never occurred.[93]

---

90   Interviews by the author with Iraqi military prisoners ranging from sergeant to major general, Camp Buccanear Umm Qasr, April 2003.

91   Interviews by the author with Iraqi military prisoners, Camp Bucca near Umm Qasr, April 2003.

92   Interviews by the author with CLFCC planners, V Corps staff, and 3d Infantry Division commanders, Camp Doha, Kuwait and Baghdad, April–May 2003.

93   Interview by the author with Major General James D. Thurman, Director of Operations (C3) and Assistant Chief of Staff for the Combined Forces Land Component Command, Camp Doha, Kuwait, May 2003.

As US forces advanced, though, they did encounter an unexpected problem: fanatic paramilitary bands known as Saddam Fedayeen and Special Republican Guard units fighting as irregulars launched attacks against the very long and thinly guarded supply routes leading back to Kuwait and in cities with limited Coalition presence such as Nairiyah, Najaf, Samawah, Basra, and Umm Qasr. These units were no match for American combat formations. One soldier said that annihilating wave after wave Saddam Fedayeen in open pickup trucks from his Bradley Fighting Vehicle was so surreal that it reminded him of a video game.[94] But a few highly publicized attacks on poorly defended American supply convoys by the Iraqi irregulars did force CFLCC to shift some units earmarked for the assault on Baghdad to rear area security duties. This left only the 3d Infantry Division and the Marine Expeditionary Unit available for the final attack on the capital.[95]

The initial plan was for the Army heavy forces to seal off Baghdad and light forces from the 82d Airborne Division and 101st Air Assault Division to clear the city. But to capitalize on the momentum developed by American forces during the fierce battles outside Baghdad, the commander of the 3d Infantry Division approved a probing movement into the city by the division's 2nd Brigade Combat Team (Spartan Brigade) under the command of Colonel David Perkins.[96] In part this was inspired by a similar armored raid a few weeks earlier into the southern city of Najaf which led to the collapse of resistance there.[97] Perkins' raid met intense but ineffective Iraqi fire. This led the American commanders to conclude that the defense of Baghdad was much less organized and formidable than expected. Two days later, Colonel Perkins led a second "thunder run" and this time was given permission to stay in the center of Baghdad. This was the final psychological blow. Army and Marine units quickly occupied the city as Hussein's regime collapsed—thirteen years after his conflict with America began.

Military strategists began culling lessons from *Operation Iraq Freedom* literally before it was over. Most agreed that the operation once again demonstrated that airpower alone cannot crush a determined opponent. It was, beyond a doubt, absolutely vital to the battlefield success of the coalition. As Wesley Clark puts it, airpower "enabled the relatively small and compact US ground forces in Iraq to achieve extraordinary gains in ground combat."[98] But there is no evidence that even the massive and well-coordinated air attacks based on the concept of "shock and awe" could have shaken Hussein's hold on power without the land invasion. *Operation Iraqi Freedom* also suggested that the qualitative gap on the battlefield between the US military and other state militaries which fight conventionally had

---

94   Interview by the author with US soldiers from the 3d Infantry Division, Baghdad, May 2003.

95   Clark, *Winning Modern Wars*, p. 56; Murray and Scales, *The Iraq War*, 95.

96   Briefing from Colonel David Perkins to a research team which included the author at his headquarters, Baghdad, May 2003. See also David Zucchino, *Thunder Run: The Armored Strike to Capture Baghdad* (New York: Atlantic Monthly Press, 2004).

97   Kitfield, *War and Destiny*, 197–8.

98   Clark, *Winning Modern Wars*, 63.

increased during a decade of transformation and reform. However, two points are important. The Iraq military was inept, poorly led, poorly equipped, and demoralized. All indications are that until the very end of the regime, Hussein feared his own military more than he feared external actors and thus kept it weak. *Operation Iraqi Freedom* did not demonstrate that transformation lad led to a US military which could quickly dominate a proficient opponent. Second, *Operation Iraqi Freedom* did not show that America's tremendous battlefield advantage over conventional state militaries automatically leads to strategic success. In fact, the "war after the war" in Iraq has caused a serious reconsideration of the trajectory of American military transformation.

The War After the War

The United States did not anticipate major security problems in Iraq after the removal of Hussein. The expectations were that the regime was so deeply hated that, as Vice President Cheney put it, the Coalition would be welcomed as liberators by most Iraqis.[99] The American plan assumed that a significant proportion of the Iraqi security forces, both military and police, would remain intact and surrender to the Coalition.[100] After removing individuals with close ties to the Hussein regime, these organizations were to form the bedrock of the new Iraqi security forces. And the Bush administration believed that once Hussein was removed, the United Nations and other states would assume a major role in helping stabilize, reconstruct, and transform Iraq. John Lewis Gaddis wrote:

> The Bush administration believed that it could invade Iraq without widespread consent because it expected a replay of the Afghanistan experience: military resistance would quickly evaporate, Iraqis would welcome the Americans and their allies, and the victorious coalition would quickly install an Iraqi regime capable of controlling and rebuilding the country. Success on the ground, together with confirmation that Saddam Hussein did indeed have WMD, would yield the consensus that diplomacy had failed to produce. The occupation of Iraq would become a broadly supported international effort, even if the invasion had not been.[101]

Or, as Bob Woodward put, CENTCOM and the Administration believed "the more the US became involved, the less the people of Iraq would support the regime. This important argument was based less on solid intelligence from inside Iraq than the assumption about how people *should* feel toward a ruthless dictator."[102]

CENTCOM and the Department of Defense thus concluded that their mission was nearly over after the fall of Baghdad. In mid April, General Franks flew to

---

99   Interviewed by Tim Russert on "Meet the Press," 27 March 2003

100   Thurman interview.

101   John Lewis Gaddis, "Grand Strategy in the Second Term," *Foreign Affairs*, 84, 1, January/February 2005,

102   Woodward, *Plan of Attack*, 81.

the capital, told his subordinate commanders that he expected a functioning Iraqi government to be in place in 30 to 60 days, and instructed them to develop troop withdrawal plans.[103] Secretary of Defense Rumsfeld cancelled the deployment of some units still in the pipeline such as the 1st Cavalry Division.

The first indicator that events might not unfold this way came when Iraqi military and police units faded away rather than surrendering intact. According to Major General Buford Blount, commander of the 3d Infantry Division at the time, "the expectation was that a lot of the infrastructure there would be functioning, that 50 percent of the policemen would be present, and the government would still be there. There was not a police force. Everybody left."[104] Nor did the Iraqi army remain intact. In late April 2003, the Americans held only a few thousand former members of the Iraqi military at Camp Bucca out of the hundreds of thousands who had been in uniform as few weeks earlier.[105] A second ominous sign was massive looting, particularly in Baghdad, which followed the collapse of the regime. In part this was a venting of years of frustration but there were clear indications that some of the looting was organized. US military officials, for instance, concluded that Iranian gangs commissioned some of the criminals Hussein had released from prison earlier in the year to seize desired goods.[106] Adding to the problem, basic services were not restored for an extended period of time with persistent shortages of fuel and electricity.

Iraqis quickly began to lose patience with what they saw as the heavy handed and culturally insensitive nature of the American occupation. Beginning in June, there were sporadic attacks on Coalition forces. In July, General John Abizaid who replaced General Franks as CENTCOM commander, admitted "… we're fighting Baathist remnants throughout the country. I believe there's mid- level Ba'athist, Iraqi intelligence service people, Special Security Organization people, Special Republican Guard people that have organized at the regional level in cellular structure and are conducting what I would describe as a classical guerrilla-type campaign against us. It's low-intensity conflict, in our doctrinal terms, but it's war, however you describe it."[107]

Given the pathological nature of the Hussein regime, it was inevitable that the transition away from it was difficult, even violent. Coming out of decades of repression, government parasitism, and domination by a sectarian minority—the Sunnis—Iraqis were not prepared to operate a stable, open political system without

---

103   Michael R. Gordon, "The Strategy to Secure Iraq Did Not Foresee a Second War," *New York Times*, 19 October 2004, 1.

104   Quoted in Stephen J. Hedges, "Military Learns Tough Lessons," *Chicago Tribune*, 22 March 2004.

105   Briefings received and observation by the author during a visit to Camp Bucca, April 2003.

106   Interviews by the author with US Army Civil Affairs officers, Baghdad, May 2003.

107   General John Abizaid, statement at US Department of Defense news briefing, 16 July 2003.

tutelage. On the other hand, with nationalism amplified by the religious difference between the majority of Iraqis and most of the Coalition forces, a significant number of the Iraq people were unwilling to accept this. This was particularly true of Iraq's Sunnis who expected their privileged position to fade in a democratic Iraq which would be dominated by the Shiite majority. These dynamics, in combination, made armed conflict inevitable.

Still, several factors probably sped the spread of the insurgency, added fuel to it, or hindered the American response. One was reliance on flawed assumptions about what would happen after the fall of Baghdad. Even US commanders and policymakers admitted that many of these did not hold.[108] For instance, American planners appear to have underestimated the degree of instability that emerged when the old system collapsed.[109] The Iraqi military and police units did not remain intact and switch loyalties.[110] As a result, the United States did not have adequate forces on hand to deal with the massive looting and instability. The American military units present were exhausted after weeks of sustained combat. They were short of military police, intelligence units, engineers, civil affairs, light infantry, and other badly needed assets.[111] Coordination with other US government agencies also left much to be desired. The Department of Defense created the Organization for Reconstruction and Humanitarian Affairs (ORHA), which later became the Coalition Provisional Authority (CPA) to synchronize and coordinate the various components of stabilization and reconstruction. But this organization was understaffed, inadequately prepared, late to organize, and slow to deploy. Interface between the US military and

---

108   For instance, Lieutenant General William S. Wallace, former V Corps commander, quoted in Charlie Coon, "General: U.S Didn't Note Post-Invasion Iraq Power Shift Quickly Enough," *European Stars and Stripes*, 30 September 2004; Ann Scott Tyson, "Pentagon Official Admits Iraq Errors," *Washington Post*, 13 July 2005, 12.

109   Richard Wolffe and T. Trent Gegax, "The Best-Laid Plans," *Newsweek*, 21 July 2003, 32; Jonathan S. Landay and Warren P. Strobel, "US Lacked Plan B In Iraq," *Philadelphia Inquirer*, 13 July 2003; Mark Fineman, Robin Wright, and Doyle McManus, "Preparing For War, Stumbling to Peace," *Los Angeles Times*, 18 July 2003; Rowan Scarborough, "US Miscalculated Security For Iraq," *Washington Times*, 28 August 2003; Rowan Scarborough, "Defense Team Hit For Iraq Failures," *Washington Times*, 16 September 2003; Richard Lloyd Parry, "US Forces Chief Admits Mistakes in Iraq," *London Times*, 17 September 2003; Warren Vieth and Esther Schrader, "Iraq Estimates Were Too Low, US Admits," *Los Angeles Times*, 9 September 2003; Eric Schmitt and Joell Brinkley, "State Department Study Foresaw Trouble Now Plaguing Iraq," *New York Times*, 19 October 2003; Michael Elliott, "So, What Went Wrong?" *Time*, 6 October 2003, p. 30; John Barry and Evan Thomas, "The Unbuilding of Iraq," *Newsweek*, 6 October 2003; and, Gerard Baker and Stephen Fidler, "The Best Laid Plans?" *London Financial Times*, 4 August 2003.

110   Anthony H. Cordesman, *Iraq and Conflict Termination: The Road to Guerrilla War?* (Washington, DC: Center for Strategic and International Studies, 28 July 2003), 15.

111   Anthony H. Cordesman, *The Current Military Situation in Iraq* (Washington, DC: Center for Strategic and International Studies, 14 November 2003), pp. 26–8; and Larry Diamond, "What Went Wrong in Iraq," *Foreign Affairs*, 83, 5, September/October 2004.

CPA remained a persistent problem, with each grumbling that the other should be doing significantly more toward stabilization.[112]

In the broad sense, planning for the period after the collapse of the regime—"Phase IV" in military parlance—by both the military and CPA/ORHA was inadequate. The most detailed report of the post-regime planning has found:

> Post conflict stabilization and reconstruction were addressed only very generally, largely because of the prevailing view that the task would not be difficult. What emerged was a general set of tasks that were not prioritized or resourced ... No planning was undertaken to provide for the security of the Iraqi people in the post conflict environment, given the expectations that the Iraqi government would remain largely intact; the Iraqi people would welcome the American presence; and local militia, police, and the regular army would be capable of providing law and order ... Iraq demonstrates that the military mission of providing security in the post conflict environment is just as important to achieving a strategic victory, if not more important, than the military mission of winning decisive combat operations.[113]

This held at every level of the military. For instance, the official after action report of the 3rd Infantry Division stated "3ID (M) did not have a fully developed plan for the transition to SASO [security and stabilization operations] and civil military operations in Baghdad priority to entering the city.[114] Michael O'Hanlon of the Brookings Institution contends that Phase IV of *Operation Iraqi Freedom* was "the least well-planned American military mission since Somalia in 1993, if not Lebanon in 1983."[115] If anything, things were worse in CPA/ORHA and other agencies of the American government. As one State Department official put it, "We didn't go in with a plan. We went in with a theory."[116]

With hindsight, it is clear that the irregular conflict in Iraq actually began with the March and April battles against the Saddam Fedayeen. But by the beginning of the summer of 2003 it had mutated into an insurgency initially led by Former Regime Loyalists hiring out of work and angry ex-soldiers and security forces to undertake attacks, and quickly spreading among the Sunni Arab segment of the population.

---

112   Interviews by the author with CFLCC C9 and ORHA/CPA personnel, Baghdad, May 2003; and Lieutenant General David McKiernen, quoted in Ron Martz, "Power Vacuum Hurt in Iraq, General Says," *Atlanta Journal-Constitution*, 14 October 2004, 3B.

113   James Thompson, President and CEO of the RAND Corporation, "Iraq: Translating Lessons Into Future DoD Policies," memorandum to Secretary of Defense Donald Rumsfeld, 7 February 2005.

114   Third Infantry Division (Mechanized) After Action Report: Operation Iraqi Freedom, July 2003, 18.

115   Michael E. O'Hanlon, "Iraq Without a Plan," *Policy Review*, December 2004/ January 2005, 128,

116   Quoted in Joseph Galloway, et. al., "Errors Mar Military Win In Iraq," *Philadelphia Inquirer*, 17 October 2004, p. 1. During an interview with an official at CPA headquarters in Baghdad in May 2003, the author was told that the CPA strategic plan consisted of a few bullets on PowerPoint briefing charts.

Eventually it became clear that the insurgency was composed of four components, to some degree interlinked, to some degree competing: the tribal based nationalist insurgency in the Sunni dominated region north and northwest of Baghdad, with its vortex in Fallujah; the Sunni insurgent groups controlled by former military and security officials of the Hussein regime; foreign jihadists, most importantly the al Qaeda-associated group led by Abu Musab al-Zarqawi; and Shi'ite militia led by he radical Shi'ite cleric Moktada al-Sadr. These groups had diverse motives and objectives. The jihadists appear to want a Taliban-like Iraq to serve as a bastion for the wider global Islamist insurgency. The former Ba'athist officials seek a return to personal power. The "Sunni nationalists" are concerned restoring the domination of their confessional group over Iraq, particularly over the Shiite majority.

Throughout the summer and into the autumn of 2003, the insurgents in the Sunni Triangle developed increasingly sophisticated methods for attacking US forces using improvised explosive devices (IEDs), rocket propelled grenades, rockets, small arms, and mortars. Foreign jihadists began converging on Iraq and undertook a parallel campaign of suicide bombings aimed at both Iraqis and outsiders, including the headquarters of the United Nations in Baghdad.[117] In November 2003 the insurgents launched the first of what would be a series of offensives. It was crushed, but the skill and coordination of the movement was clearly growing.

Even though the US shifted its focus from directly crushing the insurgency to preparing the security forces of the new Iraqi government to do so in late 2003, it continued to become more deadly and effective. In April 2004 the fighting reached a new peak as US forces entered the city of Fallujah which was under the control of the insurgents. At nearly the same time, Sadr launched an insurrection across southern Iraq. Fallujah was a turning point in the insurgency as the guerrillas at least temporarily shifted from "shoot and scoot" attacks using rocket propelled grenades, mortars, small arms, and IEDs to set-piece small unit actions—what one military officer called "a stand-up fight between two military forces."[118] For the first time, the insurgents attempted to create and hold "liberated areas."[119] The spring battles also showed that the new Iraqi security forces, which were a cornerstone of US

---

117   Audrey Hudson, "Foreign Militants Converging, Making Iraq Terror Battlefield," *Washington Times*, 25 August 2003, p. 1; Michael Dobbs, "Foreign Islamic Militants Add To Coalition Worries in Iraq," *Washington Post*, 24 August 2003, A18; Neil MacFarquhar, "Rising Tide of Islamic Militants See Iraq as Ultimate Battlefield," *New York Times*, 13 August 2003, 1; Nicholas Blanford and Dan Murphy, "For Al Qaeda, Iraq My Be the Next Battlefield," *Christian Science Monitor*, 25 August 2003, 1; and Amy Goldstein, "Bush Cites 'Foreign Element' In Iraq," *Washington Post*, 23 August 2003, 16.

118   Quoted in Thom Shanker, "US Prepares a Prolonged Drive to Suppress the Uprisings in Iraq," *New York Times*, 11 April 2004. Also, Ann Scott Tyson, "Insurgents In Iraq Show Signs of Acting As a Network," *Christian Science Monitor*, 28 April 2004.

119   "The Iraq War's New Phase," Stratfor.com, 11 April 2004.

efforts to transform the nation, were far from ready to defend their nation against the insurgents. About half of the Iraqi forces fought.[120]

In June 2004 the handover of political authority from the Coalition Provisional Authority to a provisional Iraqi government was a psychological blow to the insurgents, but the violence continued. In November 2004, a second, better organized assault, led by US Marines, cleared the insurgent stronghold in Fallujah, but fighting spread to other cities, particularly Mosul.[121] While this ended any hope the insurgents may have had of creating "liberated areas," they were able to keep at least parts of Iraq in constant upheaval. In particular, increasingly sophisticated IEDs—with new designs continually appearing soon after coalition forces fielded effective countermeasures—and vehicle bombs (VBIEDs), either with suicide drivers or remote detonation means, caused casualties among both American forces and Iraqis supporting the new government.

The pattern of lull and escalation was repeated when national elections were held in January 2005. During the escalation, the insurgents continued to concentrate on "soft" targets, especially Iraqis who supported the Americans or were part of the new security forces, and on infrastructure attacks designed to prevent the stabilization of the new government.[122] In addition, there were signs that insurgent attacks on civilians, which normally targeted Shiites, were fueling sectarian tensions. In the spring of 2005 the US developed a new plan designed to shift responsibility for the counterinsurgency effort to Iraqi security forces within a year and begin a drawdown of the US military presence.[123] According to President Bush, "As Iraqis stand up, Americans and coalition forces will stand down ... the timetable depends on our ability to train the Iraqis, to get the Iraqis ready to fight."[124] Despite some indications that there were rifts, even armed clashes between components of the insurgency and optimistic statements from American officials just as General Richard Meyers

---

120   Deputy Secretary of Defense Paul Wolfowitz, Prepared Statement for the House Appropriations Committee, Foreign Operations Subcommittee, Washington, D.C., Thursday, 29 April 2004.

121   After two major battles, Fallujah had taken on "iconic" status among the insurgents. By the summer of 2005, there were signs that they would attempt to re-enter the city (John Hendren, "Falluja May Be in Rebel Sights," *Los Angeles Times*, 8 August 2005, 1).

122   "Iraq: Softer Targets and Countermeasures," Stratfor.com (Strategic Forecasting), 25 April 2005.

123   Greg M. Grant, "New Strategy Details Security Handover In Iraq," *Jane's Defence Weekly*, 27 April 2005, 5.

124   "President Bush Discusses Second Term Accomplishments and Priorities" Gaylord Texan Resort and Convention Center, Grapevine, TX, 3 August 2005. For assessments see Rowan Scarborough, "Task Force To Set Pace of Pullout," *Washington Times*, 30 July 2005, 1; Greg Jaffe, "Drawdown Talk May Spur Iraq Rebels," *Wall Street Journal*, 4 August 2005, 11; Philip Dine, "Talk of Troop Reduction in Iraq Cheers, Troubles Experts," *St. Louis Post-Dispatch*, 31 July 2005; Eric Schmitt, "Military Plans Gradual Cuts In Iraq Forces," *New York Times*, 7 August 2005, 1; and Robert Burns, "US Laying Groundwork For Iraq Pullout," *Washington Post*, 3 August 2005.

and Vice President Cheney, public and congressional support for the American involvement in the counterinsurgency was at a low by the summer of 2005.[125]

The strategy and operational lessons of the "war after the war"—a phrase popularized by Anthony Cordesman of the Center for Strategic and International Studies—were profound for the American military.[126] The 1991 and 2003 wars against Hussein's army showed that the reforms undertaken by the US armed services were on track. They validated the trajectory of defense transformation. The difficulty of stabilizing Iraq after the removal of the Hussein regime and of defeating the insurgency suggested that this trajectory needed adjustment. The 1991 and 2003 wars had shown potential adversaries that it was a very bad idea to fight the United States conventionally. Only "asymmetric" techniques stood a chance of success.[127]

In broad terms, the insurgency called into question the American "way of war" which had developed after Vietnam. In Ian Roxborough's words,

> The American way of war is characterized by an obsession with speed, firepower and decision. It is designed to overwhelm. Speed plus devastating firepower is intended to shock and crush an opponent, rather than simply grind him down or outmaneuver him. By operating at a faster tempo than the adversary, American military forces operation within the decision-cycle of their opponent, constantly throwing the adversary off balance. War is won with a decisive victory rather than as the result of a negotiated settlement. There is to be a clean end to the fighting and a clear division between war and peace.[128]

The "war after the war" in Iraq was, by contrast, characterized by ethical, legal and strategic ambiguity, asymmetric methods, fuzzy outcomes, and protracted struggle. Military action was inextricably intertwined with political, cultural, legal, informational, economic, and diplomatic efforts.

Debate within the US government, military, and strategic community has focused on three key questions: first, what is the appropriate American grand and military strategy for a strategic environment dominated by asymmetric, irregular conflict? Second, how should the US military be organized, trained, and educated for this new strategic environment? And third, how large should the US military be?

---

125   In April, General Meyers said, "I think we're definitely winning. I think we've been winning for some time." (Quoted in Bradley Graham, "Pentagon Plays Down New Rise In Iraq Violence," *Washington Post*, 27 April 2005, 16). In May, Vice President Cheney said, "I think they're in the last throes, if you will, of the insurgency." (CNN Larry King Live, interview with Vice President Dick Cheney, aired 30 May 2005.)

126   Anthony H. Cordesman, *The War After the War: Strategic Lessons of Iraq and Afghanistan* (Washington: Center for Strategic and International Studies, 2004).

127   For an assessment of US military thinking on asymmetry and asymmetric threats, see Steven Metz and Douglas V. Johnson II, *Asymmetry and US Military Strategy: Definition, Background, and Strategic Concepts* (US Army War College Strategic Studies Institute, 2001).

128   Ian Roxborough, "Iraq, Afghanistan, the Global War on Terrorism, and the Owl of Minerva," *Political Power and Social Theory*, Vol 16, 2003, 204–205.

The Bush administration has viewed the "war after the war" in Iraq as validation of its grand strategy. The President and his top advisers have held to the position that Iraq is the central theater in the global war on terrorism, that democracy is taking root there, and this will serve as a catalyst for wider change in the region, and democratic reform will undercut terrorism. The President said:

> Iraq is the latest battlefield in the war on terror. Foreign fighters are going into Iraq to fight coalition troops for a reason. They understand the stakes. A free Iraq in the heart of the Middle East will deal a serious slow to their hateful ideology. A democracy in the heart of the Middle East will be a major blow to their desire to spread an ideology that's hateful and dark and negative ... We have a strategy for success in Iraq.[129]

The idea that it is "better to fight them there than here" remains popular among Americans despite the fact that the vast majority of Iraqi insurgents, including the foreign jihadists, were not actively attacking the US before the intervention, thus supporting the argument that it increased terrorism rather than decreased. But while frustration has grown within the American public and Congress on the cost of the counterinsurgency in Iraq, debate over the logic of this grand strategy has been muted, particularly the idea that the absence of open government in the Islamic world is the cause of terrorism and the spread of democracy will cure terrorism.[130]

American military strategy has undergone more flux, but not a complete shift. Secretary of Defense Rumsfeld entered office convinced that the military, because of its inherent conservatism, had not fully capitalized on the revolution in military affairs. The military still preferred an approach that was too conservative and slow, and unnecessarily risk averse. The conservative "Powell Doctrine" which held that the US military should only be used when overwhelming force could be brought to bear stood in contrast to the "Rumsfeld Doctrine" which stressed the use of smaller numbers of ground forces operating at a very high operational tempo in intricate conjunction with airpower and special operations.[131] Secretary Rumsfeld was, as Greg Jaffe phrases it, "firm believer in the power of speed almost from the moment he took office."[132] He has asserted that the pace of the American advance into Iraq in 2003 prevented the destruction of the oil fields and other infrastructure, and stopped

---

129   "President Bush Discusses Second Term Accomplishments and Priorities."

130   There has been an increasing debate over what is seen as a mismatch between the stated objectives of the Bush grand strategy and the resources devoted to it. See, for instance, Stephen D. Biddle, *American Grand Strategy After 9/11: A Strategic Assessment* (Carlisle Barracks, PA: US Army War College Strategic Studies Institute, 2005).

131   For instance, Brad Knickerbocker, "How Iraq Will Change US Military Doctrine," *Christian Science Monitor*, 2 July 2004.

132   Greg Jaffe, "Rumsfeld's Push For Speed Fuels Pentagon Dissent," *Wall Street Journal*, 16 May 2005, 1.

the Iraqis from using chemical weapons.[133] Rumsfeld has even concluded that a faster advance into Iraq might have prevented or limited the insurgency.[134]

Critics, some within the military and others in the defense analytical community, have countered that a military strategy built on a minimum presence, maximum speed, and heavy reliance on technology can bring battlefield victory against a conventional opponents, but not ultimate strategic success, particularly against an enemy using asymmetric methods such as insurgency. Anthony Cordesman, for instance, writes,

> Military intervention cannot be the dominant means of exercising US military power; better ways must be found to use the threat of US military power to deter and contain asymmetric conflicts and new political and economic threats ... Military victory in asymmetric warfare can be virtually meaningless without successful nation building at the political, economic, and security levels. Stabilization operations—Phase IV operations— are far more challenging than fighting conventional military forces.[135]

As Antulio Echevarria explains, US military strategy has developed an effective "way of battle" but not a concomitant "way of war" which leads to the attainment of political objectives.[136] And, in Ian Roxborough's words

> the American military has come to adopt a Jominian, engineering approach to military operations. By this I mean that, instead of thinking of war as a clash of wills between two adversaries seeking to thwart each other, the American military tends to see war as the technical application of force to achieve a desired result. They are technocrats of violence. In this image, the adversary is an inert or resistant medium to be hammered into shape by American military power.[137]

While not jettisoning the emphasis on operational and strategic speed, Secretary Rumsfeld has begun redirecting the trajectory of American military transformation, shifting away from the focus on large-scale, conventional war toward more agile, specialized forces able to deal with irregular enemies like insurgents as well as catastrophic terrorist attacks using chemical, biological, or nuclear weapons.[138] The

---

133   For instance, Secretary of Defense Donald H. Rumsfeld, remarks at the Council on Foreign Relations, New York, NY, 27 May 2003.

134   Jaffe, "Rumsfeld's Push For Speed Fuels Pentagon Dissent."

135   Cordesman, *The War After the War*, 41.

136   Antulio J. Echevarria II, *Toward An American Way of War* (Carlisle Barracks, PA: US Army War College Strategic Studies Institute, 2004).

137   Roxborough, "Iraq, Afghanistan, the Global War on Terrorism, and the Owl of Minerva," 188–9.

138   See Greg Jaffe and David S. Cloud, "Pentagon's New War Planning To Stress Postconflict Stability," *Wall Street Journal*, 25 October 2004, 2; Jason Sherman, "US Seeks To Add Flex To Force," *Defense News*, 6 September 2004; Thomas E. Ricks, "Shift From Traditional War Seen At Pentagon," *Washington Post*, 3 September 2004, 1; Bradley Graham, "Pentagon Prepares To Rethink Focus on Conventional War," *Washington Post*, 26 January 2005, 2; Greg Jaffe, "Rumsfeld's Gaze Is Trained Beyond Iraq," *Wall Street Journal*, 9

assumption was that, for the time being, the United States faces almost no serious conventional threats from a state military. There are also signs that potential state enemies had concluded that confronting the United States with conventional military power was suicidal and thus had began preparing for irregular operations to deter American intervention and possibly defeat it if it occurred.[139]

The major thrust of this shift has been to more tightly link warfighting and postwar activities, and to alter or expand the skill set within the US military. For decades, focusing on conventional warfighting was the surest path to promotion within the US military, and thus this activity drew most of the energetic and talented officers. Rumsfeld and the leaders of the military services are now engineering a shift in which functions lead to strategic success such as counterinsurgency, counterterrorism, peace enforcement, and nation building is considered as prestigious and advantageous as conventional warfighting.

This has had the greatest impact on the Army since it is the service with the most direct responsibility for stabilization and the consolidation of strategic success after an armed conflict.[140] Under General Peter Schoomaker—an officer who spent most of his career in Special Forces and was brought back from retirement by Rumsfeld—the Army has embraced "modularity" which will give it a more flexible organizational method and allow it to tailor for irregular challenges by, for instance, adding more military police and civil affairs specialists, to a unit involved in stabilization or counterinsurgency.[141] The driving idea is that

> the combination of traditional and irregular threats will present the most demanding challenges to military effectiveness. However, because the nation cannot afford two separate armies, the Army must meet this requirement largely by increasing the versatility and agility of the same forces that conduct conventional operations.[142]

It remains to be seen, though, whether making Army units equally adept at conventional warfighting and irregular operations through changes in organization, training, and leader develop will work. Some analysts contend that a "jack of all trades is the master of none," and thus argue that the US military needs forces

---

December 2004, 4; and Mark Mazzetti, "Iraq War Compels Pentagon To Rethink Big-Picture Strategy," *Los Angeles Times*, 11 March 2005, 1.

139   "The Iraq Insurgency and the Lessons of War," Stratfor.com, 28 January 2005.

140   Knickerbocker, "How Iraq Will Change US Military Doctrine."

141   See Thom Shanker, "Army Is Designing Ways to Reorganize Its Forces," *New York Times*, 6 August 2003; Kim Burger, "New Directions For US Army," *Jane's Defence Weekly*, 27 August 2003; Greg Jaffe, "A Maverick's Plan To Revamp Army Is Taking Shape," *Wall Street Journal*, 12 December 2003, 1; and, Greg Jaffe, "As Chaos Mounts in Iraq, US Army Rethinks Its Future," *Wall Street Journal*, 8 December 2004, 1.

142   TRADOC (U.S Army Training and Doctrine Command) Pamphlet 525-3-0, *The Army In Joint Operations*, Version 2 (Fort Monroe, VA: Training and Doctrine Command, April, 2005), Chapter 2.

dedicated to stabilization operations and confronting other irregular challenges.[143] This debate may stretch on for years.

To master this new mode of war, the Army and Marine Corps are augmenting their ability to function in other cultures stressing language and cultural understanding.[144] Cultural anthropologists are in demand as consultants and advisers to the Department of Defense—something that hasn't happened since Vietnam. The driving idea is that stabilization operations and irregular conflict require close interaction between the military and the local population. The "war after the war" in Iraq has shown the problems that arise from a shortage of language capability and cross-cultural acumen.[145] And the problems from a shortage of cultural understanding do not only occur at the tactical level, but also shape strategic planning. The tendency of American strategists and policymakers is to "mirror image" and assume that other cultures have basically the same set of values, priorities, and perceptions as Americans. This certainly caused the adoption of what proved to be flawed assumptions about the way the Iraqi people would react to the American presence. As Ian Roxborough puts it,

> Many of the miscalculations made by American war planner derived from overly optimistic assumptions about Iraqi behavior. The implicit cognitive models used by war planners seem to have been based on questionable social science theories about Iraqi responses to the American-led attack. Underlying most of the American planning failures was a systematic failure of sociological analysis of the Iraqi regime of the social preconditions for the establishment of democracy in Iraq.[146]

Another dimension of this broad debate over American strategy concerns the role of special operations forces. As James Thompson of the RAND Corporation wrote, "US special operations forces need to be at the core of any successful counterterrorist and/or counterinsurgency strategy."[147] The Bush administration decided to increase the US Special Operations Command by 23,000 over a four year period, with additions in Army Special Forces, Civil Affairs, Psychological Operations troops, Special Forces aviation, and Navy Special Forces (SEALs).[148] Questions remain, though, as to how quickly the number of Special Forces can be expanded and how large this component of the military can become without an erosion of quality (since

---

143   See, for instance, Hans Binnendijk and Stuart Johnson, eds., *Transforming for Stabilization and Reconstruction Operations* (Washington, DC: National Defense University Center for Technology and National Security Policy, 2004).

144   Jaffe, "Rumsfeld's Push For Speed Fuels Pentagon Dissent."

145   Former Secretary of Defense Paul Wolfowitz began exploring the idea that all military officers should have language training (Jason Sherman, "Wolfowitz Approves Plan To Improve DOD's Foreign Language Skills," *Inside the Pentagon*, 10 March 2005, p. 1.)

146   Roxborough, "Iraq, Afghanistan, the Global War on Terrorism, and the Owl of Minerva," 194.

147   Thompson, "Iraq."

148   Donna Miles, "Special Ops to Increase Force Strength to Meet Terror War Demands," American Forces Information Service News Article, 25 April 2005.

only a few service members qualify for special operations forces and it takes a very long time to train them). In the short term, Thomas O'Connell, the top administration official overseeing the military's special operations forces, has expressed concern about the US Special Operations Command's ability to meet the requirements of the regional combatant commanders.[149]

This final issue is playing out on an even broader scale. Many critics in Congress and the strategic community have argued that the US military is simply too small to undertake protracted, manpower intensive operations such as Iraq on a global scale. This idea has come from across the political spectrum as well as from non-partisan sources. The Defense Science Board, for instance, warned in 2004 that the US military was too small to meet the nation's commitments.[150] Lieutenant General (now retired) John Riggs, head of the Army's futures program, stated in January 2004 that the Army was too small to do the jobs assigned it.[151] Senators Jack Reed (D-RI), Chuck Hagel (R-NE), Hillary Clinton (D-NY), John McCain (R-AZ), John Kerry (D-MA) and some other members of Congress have pushed for an increase in the size of the Army and Marine Corps.[152] And this idea has gained bipartisan support among major defense intellectuals such as Thomas Donnelly and Frederick Kagan of the American Enterprise Institute, Lawrence Korb of the Center for American Progress, and Michael O'Hanlon of the Brookings Institute.[153] As another sign of the strain on the US military, in the spring of 2005 General Richard Myers, Chairmen

---

149   Ann Scott Tyson, "Crunch Time For Special Ops Forces," *Christian Science Monitor*, 6 April 2004.

150   Mark Mazzetti, "US Military Is Stretched Too Thin, Defense Board Warns." *Los Angeles Times*, 30 September 2004. This was explained in *Transition To and From Hostilities*, Report of the Defense Board 2004 Summer Study (Washington, DC: Office of the Undersecretary of Defense for Acquisition, Technology, and Logistics, December 2004).

151   Tom Bowman, "3-Star General Says Army Is Too Small To Do Its Job," *Baltimore Sun*, 21 January 2004.

152   Reed introduced S. 530, 109th Congress, 1st session, 4 March 2005 which would increase the end strength of the Army and Marine Corps after fiscal year 2005. For analysis, see Mark Sappenfield, "Dueling Views on Army Size: Congress vs. Rumsfeld," *Christian Science Monitor*, 17 May 2005; and Peter Brownfield, "Debate Over Size, Shape of the Army," Foxnews.com, 20 August 2004.

153   Michael E. O'Hanlon, *Defense Strategy For the Post-Saddam Era* (Washington, DC: Brookings Institution Press, 2005); Lawrence J. Korb, "All Volunteer Army Shows Signs of Wear," *Atlanta Journal-Constitution*, 27 February 2005; Frederick W. Kagan, "The Army We Have," *The Weekly Standard*, 27 December 2004; and Thomas Donnelly, *The Military We Need: The Defense Requirements of the Bush Doctrine* (Washington, DC: American Enterprise Institute Press, 2005). On 28 January 2005 the Project for the New American Century—a conservative think tank which a number of senior officials in the Bush administration were affiliated with before assuming office—sent a letter to Congress signed by thirty six prominent defense experts including former senior policymakers and military flag officers advocating an increase in US ground forces. Other defense analysts support Secretary Rumsfeld's position that the United States does not need a larger military. See, for instance, Daniel Goure, "No To a Larger Army," Lexington Institute Issue Brief, 27 January 2005.

of the Joint Chiefs of Staff, announced that operations in Afghanistan and Iraq had strained the military to accept greater risk elsewhere in the world.[154] But, Secretary Rumsfeld insisted that the problem was not in the aggregate size of the military, but in inefficiencies within it—"how forces have been managed and the mix of capabilities at our disposal."[155] These, the Secretary stated, are being addressed.

Conclusion

During America's wars with Iraq in 1991 and 2003, Hussein acted as American policymakers and military strategists expected. The only major exception was his failure to use chemical or biological weapons in the 2003 war. From the Department of Defense's perspective, Hussein validated improvements in the military forces and refinements American strategy. He was thus the "perfect" enemy, unambiguously evil yet stupid enough to fight the way that the American military preferred. The "war after the war," however, was undertaken by an enemy the United States had difficulty understanding and was less prepared for. The Department of Defense had explored the defeat of Hussein's army through countless wargames and planning exercises but much less intellectual effort was expended exploring the difficulties of a major counterinsurgency in Iraq or a similar country. While the US military had developed impressive skills for multinational peacekeeping during the 1990s, particularly in operations in the Balkans and was able to adapt some of these to stabilization and counterinsurgency in Iraq, it was not fully prepared for a large-scale, protracted counterinsurgency campaign undertake with limited international support.

The Department of Defense and other government agencies have learned from the "war after the war" in Iraq. Many programs are underway to improve America's ability to undertake stabilization and counterinsurgency operations. But two huge questions remain. First, is reform—adjusting the trajectory of defense transformation enough or does the United States need a radical shift in the way it thinks about national security and military strategy? Ian Roxborough is right when he critiques the US military for an "engineering approach" to the use of force and when he notes that this is seldom effective in irregular conflicts like the "war after the war" in Iraq. But is this approach ingrained, even cultural? If so, it may beyond the ability of even the most energetic and brilliant leaders to change. Perhaps the only solution is to eschew involvement in protracted stabilization operations and irregular conflict. If so, this will require abandoning President Bush's grand strategy.

Second, even if the US military is able to reform itself into a force optimized for "Iraq style" conflicts, will this be what America needs in the future? There is an old saying that militaries—at least successful ones—tend to prepare to fight the last war rather than future ones. The United States spent much of the 1990s preparing to

---

154   Josh White and Ann Scott Tyson, "Wars Strain US Military Capability, Pentagon Reports," *Washington Post*, 3 May 2005, 6.

155   Donald H. Rumsfeld, "New Model Army," *Wall Street Journal*, 3 February 2004.

fight *Desert Storm* over but that led to precisely the type of force needed to, in effect, complete *Desert Storm* in the spring of 2003. When American leaders saw that the military was not optimized for actions such as the "war after the war" in Iraq, they engineered changes in that direction. The question is whether future armed conflict will, in fact, be similar to the "war after the war" in Iraq. Will the United States undertake large-scale, protracted stabilization and counterinsurgency operations with limited international support? If not, the lessons of the "war after the war" could be mislearned and the United States might find itself inadequately prepared for future wars, whatever shape they take. By the summer of 2005, this debate was already blossoming, particularly within the US Army with some strategic thinkers seeing Iraq as a model for the future, others convinced that large-scale, conventional war remained the Army's central concern.[156]

As it has since 1991, Iraq will continue to shape US national security and military strategy. If the "war after the war" has a positive outcome—successful stabilization under a progressive and open government—US policymakers and military leaders are likely to conclude that President Bush's grand strategy is validated and thus the only changes needed are reforms within the military and other components of the government to be more effective and efficient at stabilization and counterinsurgency operations. If the 'war after the war" in Iraq is not successful, it may unleash deep debate about existing grand strategy and ultimately lead to a very different national security and military strategy.

---

156   Greg Grant, "Iraq Reshapes US Army Thinking," *Defense News*, 29 August 2005, 1.

Conclusion

Getting There:
The Road to and the Aftermath of
the Second War in Iraq

John Davis
Howard University

Introduction

Irrespective of the contention that the 43rd President of United States had from the inception of his tenure in office a policy in place that called for the removal of Saddam Hussein, this study has endeavored to demonstrate that the process of renewed US-Iraqi hostilities were well underway long before "W" assumed the office of the president. Indeed, as presented in this study, evidence abounds that since the conclusion of *Operation Desert Storm*, forces indifferent to the polices of the 41st President George H.W. Bush, whether within the White House, the Office of Vice President, within the State Department, the CIA, and especially throughout the Pentagon, and even within the halls of the US Congress, these forces were opposed to the withdrawal of US forces in Iraq and more significantly were indifferent to leaving the regime in Iraq in place. Beginning with the presidency of Bill Clinton these same forces lobbied the new administration to institute an assertive policy of "rollback" that would end the threat posed by Iraq once and for all. This group of advisors and elements scattered throughout the bureaucracy—this includes neoconservative and non-neoconservative elements—that were committed to stepping up their efforts to remove the Iraqi leader. Many within these groups, most certainly the neoconservative elements, were unafraid to confront the president directly. This strategy culminated in a meeting with President Clinton which permitted the dominant elements of this group (the neoconservatives) to make their case for regime change. The conclusion of this meeting ended with the forces for regime change proving unsuccessful in their efforts to pressure the administration into accepting their agenda. Ultimately this group turned to allies in Congress which eventually led to the passage of the Iraq Liberation Act, legislation that laid the foundation for the eventual removal of Saddam Hussein, and which made regime change the official policy of the United States. Thus long before George W. Bush entered office, forces loyal to the president's agenda were already in place and amenable to his approach to dealing with Saddam.

This concluding chapter opens with an examination of the forces within each of the aforementioned three administrations that set the stage for a second war in Iraq. In particular, the opening section examines the political calculations and strategic options that eventually forced three US presidents to confront the threat posed by Iraq. The second and third sections of this chapter explore "the failure to learn lessons." The first of these two sections examines the prewar invasion failures that range from the role of coalitions, misreading of the Arab street, the role of intelligence, and postwar planning. In the third section, this chapter examines the postwar lessons with particular emphasis on post-conflict activities deemed essential to defeating an insurgency. The three primary post-conflict activities discussed in this study fall into three categories: (1) providing a secure and stable environment, (2) the cooperation and assistance of government agencies and coalition participation in postwar planning, and (3) the role of nation building. The final section of this chapter examines how the current administrations inability to learn the aforementioned "critical lessons" permitted the insurgency in Iraq to flourish.

Getting There: Political Calculations and US Strategic Options

Iraq presented three US presidents with an assortment of challenges. In the case of Bush I, the president's initial objective involved expanding the legacy of Ronald Reagan. President Reagan viewed Iraq as buffer against the Khomeni-led Shia revolution that emanated from Iran. By contrast the senior Bush wanted to transform Iraq into a strategic partner; a relationship that ended after Saddam Hussein invaded Kuwait. Thereafter, Bush viewed Iraq as a threat to the New World Order, a clear recognition the nascent entente between the US and Iraq had run its course. Subsequently, the president assembled a vast coalition to remove Iraqi forces from Kuwait. Once the Gulf War concluded the president had a fundamental query to consider: What's next in US-Iraqi relations? Unable to satisfactorily resolve this issue, it was up to Bush's successor, Bill Clinton, to confront this challenge. During Clinton's first term, the president enlisted a policy of comprehensive containment to keep Iraq "off the radar screen" so that the president could pursue and implement his expansive economic agenda. In Clinton's second term the president had finally resolved to confront the Iraqi threat. The method of choice involved a covert policy aimed at unseating the Iraqi dictator. Like his predecessor Clinton left the "unfinished business" associated with the Iraq threat to the next president. Coming into office the Bush II administration wrestled with a two policy choices: containment-plus or regime change. After 11 September the administration opted for regime change, which called for the use of US ground troops to remove Saddam Hussein. The next section provides a brief illustration of the political calculations and strategic options that were available to each US president as they confronted the challenge posed by Iraq.

Bush I: Triumph Without Victory

Since Iraq's invasion of Kuwait in 1990 three US presidents have been forced to confront the regional threat posed by Saddam Hussein to his neighbors as well as the threat to US and allied oil interests. In the aftermath of *Operation Desert Storm* the senior Bush and his advisors argued that the situation in postwar Iraq—humiliation on the battlefield, the belief that Saddam's grip on society had dramatically decreased and the growth and maturation of anti-Saddam elements in the southern and northern parts of the country, and the weakening of the Republican Guard—signaled that the end of the regime is highly likely. Moreover, though the president and members of the administrations war council repeated the refrain that the objectives of the administration were tied to the UN mandate that called for Iraq to withdraw their forces from Kuwait. In spite of the stated war aim, internally the administration concluded that since Saddam Hussein is the leader of Iraqi armed forces, it was thus appropriate to target and kill the Iraqi dictator. Similarly, on the eve of the ground war, the US military unleashed a new weapon (bunker busters) to target and kill Saddam in one of his many underground command bunkers. Thus despite statements to the contrary it was clear that the administration considered and exercised a policy of regime change.

As the realization that Saddam would hold onto power took hold within the administration, there was a scramble to form a consensus on a new approach to dealing with the Iraqi leader. In the midst of the debate over "what to do with Saddam" the administration had just completed discourse on another issue: war termination. No matter what statement had been given by administration officials, the decision to end *Operation Desert Storm* was based more on regional and international calculations and less on US political-military options. Thus the perceived reality of the gruesome scenes on the "highway to death" became the central impetus for ending the war. Thus the administration was concerned about regional and international perceptions of a US war machine indiscriminately killing Iraqi troops. These considerations had additional manifestations: the administration was concerned that the scenes on the highway of death could be used as propaganda fodder for radicalizing the Arab street, and therefore utilized as latent support for the regime in Iraq. This reality impacted the decision calculus to the extent the administration was concerned that certain states within the coalition may even withdraw if domestic sentiments within their countries produced a backlash for their support of the US-led operations against Iraq. Second, the administration had hoped that the regime in Iraq would fall but there was significant concern among senior advisors to Bush, particularly Secretary of State James Baker and National Security Advisor Brent Scowcroft which argued that in the absence of the Iraqi leader the Lebanization of Iraq (that the country would divide along constituent parts) could soon follow. Thus in the midst of these fears the strategic option to employ containment as a strategy to prevent future Iraqi aggression seemed plausible at the time, but this ad hoc decision had consequences for subsequent administrations. This option provided credence to the perception that Iraq had now become the problem for the next president, Bill Clinton.

Clinton: From Containment to the Iraqi Liberation Act

With respect to political calculations within the Clinton administration, the overwhelming perception is that containment would suffice. By following the previous administrations approach, with a few minor adjustments (what emerged as comprehensive containment), the president was free to purse other political objectives, such as the modification of NATO's mission, national building in Somalia, and Haiti. Though these were not considered issues of consequence, the president and his more "dovish" advisors had selected what they believed were "safe issues," problems that would not interfere with the president's domestic agenda. Unfortunately for President Clinton Saddam had his agenda ran counter to that of the United States, forcing the administration to eventually readdress policy calculations.

A separate faction produced an altogether different set of political calculations that would, if accepted, affect the president's domestic agenda. This faction called for rollback. Many of the officials were mid-level bureaucrats that were holdovers from the previous administration and had one objective: completing what Bush started, the unseating of the regime in Iraq. Some of those officials within this wing of the administration were senior officials, such as Vice President Al Gore, UN Ambassador Madeline Albright, Martin Indyk, the special assistant to the president for the Near East and South Asia, along with Bruce Riedel (then director of Persian Gulf Affairs), and Mark Parris, the deputy assistant secretary of state for the Near East, to name a few that also wanted to confront the regime in Iraq.

This collective debate was summed up this way in the editor's chapter (Infighting in Iraq): despite the infighting administration policy ultimately involved two issues— how much priority and the amount of resources (including political, diplomatic, and military) that the administration should employ to confront Saddam.[1] From another perspective there were those that argued that administration policy was confusing and amounted to a "half a policy on Iraq."[2]

In the final year of the first term the president encountered a host of criticism from the left and the right both of which clamored that administration policy is ineffectual and that US credibility had declined considerably with administration Iraq policy a central reason for this observation. Moreover, many within the executive branch (Pentagon and CIA) questioned the validity of sending in carrier battle groups in the Persian Gulf as an instrument of coercive diplomacy and not using American power. The end result, the international community questioned administration resolve. During the second term it appeared the president had decided to finally confront Iraq. Though administration policy appeared to have changed, this too was questioned. That is the administration accepted congressional adoption of the Iraq Liberation Act of 1998, but this legislation was far closer to republican formulations

---

1   Kenneth Pollack, *The Threatening Storm-The United States and Iraq* (New York: Random House, 2002), 56.

2   As quoted in Robert S. Litwak, *Rogue States and US Foreign Policy: Containment After the Cold War* (Washington, DC: Woodrow Wilson Center Press, 2000), 127.

about Iraq than administration policy (in time it became official US policy to end the regime in Iraq).

The administration's strategic options were limited in scope. Though it acknowledged the importance of comprehensive containment, the administrations rhetoric at times was consistent with rollback. On both accounts it appeared that the administration had neither a short term goal regarding Iraq or a long term one; this is true regardless of whether administration policy was that of containment or regime change. On the former, the administration did not learn a fundamental lesson left by the previous administration: that planning, serious planning about how to confront Iraq involved a number of procedures. The first concerned a consistent plan buttressed by presidential support; second, relying on myths is problematic; third, reliable intelligence and strategic military preparation were vital to implementing any policy initiative, and fourth, whatever the policy executive cohesion and resolve are critical to secure strategic objectives.

Bush II: The Bush Doctrine and Iraq

From the beginning of Bush II until the tragic events of 11 September the administration operated with conflicting political calculations. The pragmatic realists led by Powell endeavored to continue containment but under the guise of smart sanctions. Another dominant group in the administration led by neoconservatives Rumsfeld and Wolfowitz, and with assistance from Cheney argued that regime change represented the only viable policy for the administration. As mentioned in chapter 4 the policy review process was dominated by these two disparate political calculations. The internal discourse resulted in a stalemate that produced a continuation of the policies of Clinton: covert operations to unseat the regime and no-fly zones that continued the pressure on the regime in Iraq.

This compromise policy remained in place until 11 September. Thereafter a new debate over the political calculations and Iraq ensued. The same combatants began a new round of bureaucratic infighting. After the neoconservatives attempted to make Iraq the first phase in the war on terror, the Powell faction erupted arguing that no evidence of an al Qaeda-Iraq conspiracy existed and that if the administration went after Iraq the coalition which had just been assembled to confront al Qaeda, would dissipate. The president accepted Powell's argument but the strategic options with respect to Iraq were confusing: the administration made Afghanistan the first stop in the war on terror but the president gave Rumsfeld and CENTCOM the task to initiate planning for an invasion of Iraq.

As the Afghan phase of the war on terror concluded in December of 2001, the internal debate over Iraq moved to another level. In the January 2002 State of Union Address the president announced the "axis of evil," with Iraq named as one of three rouge states whose alleged possession of WMD—and that there was a likelihood that they would transfer such weapons to al Qaeda—made Saddam a threat to international security. With Iraq now in play the Bush Doctrine according to neoconservatives would have its first test. To maximize the strategic options for the president, the neoconservatives noted that Iraq represented the beginning of the transformation of the Middle East and the export of democracy in the region.

For the neoconservatives *Operation Iraqi Freedom* and the unseating of the Baathist regime symbolized the success of the Bush Doctrine. The success of military operation illustrated the strategic options selected by the president had transformed US foreign policy in general and the administration was now in a position to transform the always unstable Middle East. This triumphalism however was short lived as the postwar verities assumed center stage. Thereafter, the strategic options were altered drastically. First, there were many scholars that assumed that Syria or Iran would be the next phase in the war on terror. Second, the growing insurgency and the absence of a viable government (recognized as legitimate in the eyes of the Iraqi people) in the wake of the invasion only increased the disorder in Iraq. Similarly, the mounting coalition casualties and the increasing death toll among Iraqi civilians has all but ended talk of the next phase in the war on terror, and ushered in a polarizing debate within the American polity about the need for a viable exist strategy. The very fact that this debate continues is an indication that the strategic options as put forth by the neoconservatives has not come to fruition and is out of step with Iraqi and regional realities.

The Failure of Lessons Learned

This study indicated that US presidential policies in Iraq unearthed a startling conclusion: US presidents failed to learn critical lessons from previous American involvement in Iraq. As such a number of critical mistakes were repeated in Iraq. These mistakes involve a number of categories and consist of the following areas: coalition diplomacy, the misreading of the Arab Street, the role of intelligence, and postwar planning.

Coalition Diplomacy

As Lansford points out in Chapter 5, coalition diplomacy, or the lack thereof, is a critical feature of each of the presidential policies discussed in this study. Lansford conclusively argues that successful policy initiatives, as exemplified in the initial conflict with Iraq, could not have been possible without 'the broad and inclusive nature of the alliance' that had been constructed by the Bush I administration.

The features of the coalition themselves were historic. First, the coalition against Iraq included the former Soviet Union. This marked the first time that the US and the Soviets participated in a coalition since World War II. Second, the coalition included a number of Arab states. Of those states, the involvement and participation of Syria required a host of qualifications on the part of US officials. First administration officials had to address the concerns of Israel which questioned the necessity of the inclusion of Syria, an arch enemy of the Jewish state, to play any role in the coalition. The position of the administration was rudimentary: Arab states were required to apply legitimacy to coalition efforts to remove Iraqi forces from Kuwait. A supplemental reason asserts that Syria's involvement (a state which utilized the Baathist ideology) in the coalition enabled US planners to isolate and later contain Saddam Hussein.

These points aside the coalition had other features that separated them from other coalitions. As indicated in the chapter 5, the core components of the anti-Saddam coalition required that the alliance survive beyond the original mandate, or until after Iraq's forces withdrew from Kuwait. Thus as Iraqi forces vacated from Kuwait, officially the mandate for the coalition (the military aspect of the coalition) should have concluded. However, Saddam's survival, the specter of WMD in Iraq, the need for an inspection regime, the plight of the Kurd's in the north and Shiites in the south, and the evolution of the no-fly zones, augmented a new mission for the coalition: the need to contain Iraq. Thus this mission continued the coalition, albeit in a diminished form (each aspect of the coalition required the use of different states to carry out disparate missions, i.e., the no-fly zones involvement the US, Britain, and France, or in the event that Iraq launched a new war against Saudi Arabia, subsequent US military strategy called for a far smaller coalition than the one employed in *Desert Storm*).

In the final analysis the lesson was clear: in order to keep Saddam in his box, it was essential to do so with broad support. An additional lesson, one that evolved as a by-product of the first, asserts that building a coalition is itself significant but maintaining a coalition and redefining it to preserve disparate presidential policies would be a challenge. Confronting these two lessons is essential if the policies of Clinton and Bush II toward Iraq were to be successful. Non-compliance to these tenets could be problematic, and in the case of Bush II, fatal.

The Clinton administration's policies with respect to the coalition were fundamental: preservation. Like the Bush administration before it, Clinton's policy toward Iraq called for sustaining containment. The administration recognized the obvious: preserving the coalition is an essential prerequisite to the maintenance of containment. Unfortunately, the administration did not succeed in preserving the coalition.

A host of variables indicated that preserving the coalition for the Clinton administration was fraught with frustration and peril. The problem for the administration is that many components of the coalition envisaged dissipation. A few examples are instructive. With respect to the no-fly zones, the French had grown weary of participation and concerned about the strain that countless patrols had on their pilots. In time France withdrew their participation in the no-fly zones. Another issue that caused great angst for the administration concerned the UNSC debates regarding the future of UN sanctions. In the wake of the Gulf War many coalition partners questioned the validity of sanctions. The discourse surrounding the sanctions regime further divided the UNSC. In reality the debate encompassed the permanent members. In short, the Russians, Chinese, and French which opposed the continuation of the regime; whereas the US and Britain not only wanted to continue the regime but labored to strengthen it. Ironically these same states would play a pivotal role over the use of force in Iraq under the second Bush administration. Returning to the Clinton administration, the inability to preserve coalition cohesion forced the president to lead several US-led missions to sustain not only the anti-coalition, but containment itself (*Operation Desert Fox* being the most vivid example).

For Bush II, like Clinton, preserving the coalition produced tumult in the form of polarizing debates within administration over Iraq policy. From the start of the Bush administration the utility of coalitions caused extensive debate among the president's foreign policy advisors. The diplomatic perspective, led by Powell, recognized that coalitions remained a vital instrument of US policy toward Iraq. Similarly, the secretary argued that coalitions were essential tools for the US-led war on terror, and should the administration invade Iraq, coalitions were equally significant to preserve US credibility, flexibility and legitimacy in the region and in the world at large. By contrast, civilians in the Pentagon, led by Rumsfeld and Wolfowitz, with additional support from Vice President Cheney, noted that while coalitions are important, they should not become a divisive element in deciding whether the US should or should not use force. Thus as the latter faction gained control of US Iraq policy a new language emerged: "the coalition of the willing" as a substitute for the traditional coalition that was utilized in the first gulf war. In short, the use of the anti-Saddam coalition that had been erected against Iraq during Bush I had all but ceased to exist under Bush II. And the debate among permanent members of the UNSC that polarized the Clinton administration's efforts to preserve the coalition had moved to a new level of intensity after the passage of UNSCR 1441. Thereafter coalition diplomacy dissipated setting the stage for a reduced "coalition of the willing" as the Bush administration opted for regime change in Iraq.

Ironically, in the aftermath of *Operation Iraqi Freedom* the administration, largely through the efforts of Powell, tried to revive the coalition for a new mission: postwar reconstruction in Iraq. While there was success in this regard (a host of UN Security Council Resolutions were passed) and the administration did succeed in getting states to add their troops to the US-led military coalition in Iraq, the administration had failed to learn the two critical lessons mentioned earlier, and when it did do so, in the post-Saddam period, US credibility had taken a major hit and worse the US military had become occupation forces instead of liberators.

Misreading the Arab Street

All three US presidents considered the Arab street a central pivot in their policies toward Iraq. In the administration of Bush I, the president recognized the importance of having Arab states as participants in the ever-expanding coalition of states arrayed against Saddam Hussein. For participants in the August 1990 war councils following Iraq's invasion of Kuwait, it had become obvious that Arab coalition partners were central to administration objectives, which advisors to the president considered essential if the president had any hopes of placating the Arab street. This policy manifested itself in several forms. With respect to coalition diplomacy the administration thought it important that Arab states in the region demonstrate their collective voices that Saddam's act of aggression would not be tolerated. Similarly, the presence of Gulf States were deemed mission critical when the administration included Arab states as alliance partners in *Desert Shield*. And as *Desert Storm* unfolded the administration understood that it was essential that Arab states, more importantly Kuwaiti forces, liberate Kuwait City.

Though the administration worked diligently to demonstrate that the US presence in the region was that of liberating power and not a conquering one, there were elements that worked to disprove the administration rhetoric. In the first example, not all entities in the region accepted the US-led mission in the region. Yaser Arafat and his Palestinian brethren, along with Jordan sided with Saddam Hussein throughout the war. Second, during the war itself coalition aircraft hit their assigned military targets but Saddam in one well publicized event placed women and children in a bunker and unfortunately for the US, all in the facility were killed by American bombs. Saddam's propaganda machine went into overdrive assuring that extreme elements within the region would react indifferent to the US presence in the area. Third, the impact of sanctions arrayed against Iraq—and the fact that close to a million Iraqi's were killed[3] as a result served the purpose of anti-American elements, some of which called for joining in a anti-American jihad to remove US forces from the region. This strategy is a growing problem and was viewed this way:

> Saddam's goal was to foil the inspectors by gaining relief from sanctions without giving up his remaining weapons. His strategy was to publicize the hardships of Iraqi civilians in order to gain sympathy among Arabs … and to an extent he succeeded. Anti-Americanism will always find a receptive audience in some circles.[4]

Fourth, as the war concluded some US troops remained in the region, most notably in Saudi Arabia. Osama Bin Laden, the leader of the al Qaeda transnational terror network, used the presence of US troops in the region as evidence of an infidel occupation force determined to conquer Islamic territory. Thus this propaganda (and the draconian sanctions against Iraq) resulted in an increase in anti-Americanism throughout the region. The postwar "blowback" that developed as a result of the policies of the senior Bush would therefore greatly hamper the policies of Clinton and Bush II.

In the case of Clinton the continuation of the policies of the Bush I administration and the strengthening of sanctions regime greatly impacted administration policy. That said the realization of the cost of the sanctions (that fact that so many Iraq's died as a result of them) invariably impacted pro-US states in the region. The pressure for these states came in two forms: domestic and regional. In both cases the pressure

---

3   For more on this point see Robert W. Tucker and David C. Hendrickson, *The Imperial Temptation: The New World Order and America's Purpose*, (New York: Council on Foreign Relations Press, 1992).

4   As quoted in Robert J. Pauly, Jr., *US Foreign Policy and the Persian Gulf: Safeguarding American Interests Through Selective Multilateralism* (London: Ashgate, 2005), 72.

increased dramatically on these states to end their support for US-led sanctions, owing to the fact that such states did not want to be seen in collusion with a UN policy that was killing Arabs. Second, sanctions fatigue in general had undercut Clinton's policies to strengthen sanctions and the UNSC that was responsible for enacting and preserving them. Similarly, sanctions (with assistance from Saddam's and al Qaeda's propaganda machines) had reawakened the Arab street that the US-led sanctions were causing untold suffering which in the final analysis increased the anti-American hatred in the region.

Though Saddam had been successful in awakening the Arabs in the region to the plight of the Iraqi people, bin Laden reaped the long term rewards. These rewards came in several forms: the burgeoning anti-Americanism that continued to grow as a result of the US presence in the region and the impact of US-led sanctions acted as a recruitment tool for al Qaeda. Second, the fact that pro-western regimes were seen as supportive of US policies and the fact that they were corrupt helped to advance recruitment inside those countries. Viewed collectively, US forces in Saudi Arabia came under attack which resulted in the targeting of American military personnel stationed within the Kingdom.

Before tackling the Bush II administration it is essential to note that long before the current occupant of the White House entered office, it was salient that enmity toward the United States from the Arab street had already reached a fever pitch. Additionally, other than the aforementioned the reader should note that Arabs in the region (moderates and extremists) had grown increasingly frustrated with the US role as chief mediator in the Israeli-Palestinian dispute. As Elkawas points out there was a sense that 41 & 42 were overtly pro-Israel in their orientation and that US presidents were no longer interested in being honest brokers. When the administration of 43 began the Arab street's frustration only increased as the president elected not to intervene ("W" made it clear that unless both parties to the dispute reached a ceasefire the president made it clear he was not willing to expend the political capital in the form and manner of his predecessor Bill Clinton) as confidence building measures between the Israelis and Palestinians were undermined.

In the post-9/11 environment the anti-Americanism continued to increase. Troubling for the administration is that many Arabs celebrated the destruction of the World Trade Center and the attack on the Pentagon. The attacks were perceived as rightful punishment for US support for Israel and the perception the administration was unwilling to apply pressure on the Jewish state. Following the administrations decision to list Iraq as a member of the "axis of evil," regional public opinion of the US remained indifferent to American objectives.

Thus when *Operation Iraqi Freedom* commenced opposition to US policy intensified. When *Al Arabia* and *Al Jazeera* displayed footage of dead Iraqi civilians such pictures were used as propaganda by these and other news outlets as evidence of "the cruelty of infidel occupiers." Even worse for the administration concerns the fact that the administrations war to liberate Iraq has instead resulted in extremist Sunni elements from the region and elsewhere mounting a *jihad* to remove US occupation forces. The administration's goal of democratizing the region suffered a serious blow as these forces worked to unseat the Shia-led governments in Iraq that threatened Sunni-led Iraq and preeminence in the region. Worst for the administration is that the likes of Abu Zarqawi, the leader of an al Qaeda affiliated insurgency in Iraq, is determined to foment a religious civil war in Iraq that would end the democratic experiment in Iraq and threaten other such experiments in Lebanon and elsewhere.

These issues raise another question: why did the administration fail to learn the critical lessons of the Bush I administration? The senior Bush understood that US involvement in removing Saddam Hussein from Kuwait could not take place without regional participation and support both in building the case for war in the UN and for the war itself. Bush II ignored the advice of Secretary Colin Powell and former senior advisors that served his father, such as Brent Scowcroft, both of which cautioned that UN approval and regional support were vital before the US-led operations commenced. Such advice was ignored and the administration now finds itself swimming upstream in search of Arab support that remains tepid at best (a recognition that Jordan has decided to assist in the training of Iraqi police recruits). Thus while there has been a noticeable democratic movement afoot in the region, one could only imagine the pace of that movement if *Operation Iraqi Freedom* had been launched with Arab cooperation (many countries did provide overflight rights but there was no Arab presence in the coalition to unseat Saddam) and UN legitimacy.

The Role of Intelligence

The issue of intelligence is a consistent variable that impacted presidential policies in Iraq. In the case of Bush I, intelligence officials warned of an impending Iraqi intervention in Kuwait. Within the senior levels of the administration the analysis on Iraqi troop movements went unheeded due in part because the intelligence did not mesh with administration policy which viewed Iraq as a critical partner for regional stability.

Intelligence again surfaced and was in a position to positively impact administration policy. Schwarzkopf, the chief military planner within CENTCOM, incessantly reminded the international press that "the gate is closed," a reference to the US Army's efforts to destroy Republican Guard units as they raced across the Kuwaiti border for their bases in Iraq. Intelligence photos, despite Schwarzkopf's statements, indicated the US military failed to meet a critical objective:

> According to the CIA analysis of the photos, at least 365 of the tanks that escaped were T-72s that belonged to Saddam Hussein's Republican Guard. By the CIA's count, the Republican Guard divisions had begun the war with 786 tanks. That meant half the Republican Guard Armor got away. Since the Tawakalna and Medina divisions sought to hold off the Americans, Pentagon intelligence analysts later concluded that the Hammurabi Division escaped largely intact. According to intelligence estimates by the Defense Intelligence Agency, 70 percent of its troops managed to make their way north of the marshes.[5]

---

5   Michael R. Gordon and General E. Trainor, *The Generals' War: The Inside Story of the Conflict in the Gulf* (New York: Little, Brown, and Company, 1995), 429.

The point here is that in the confusion surrounding administration efforts to end the war, President Bush had undercut the ability of military commanders in the field from utilizing available intelligence to locate and to direct fire on Iraq's fleeing armored forces. This failing symbolized a major flaw in administration strategy: a policy predicated on the myth that Saddam would not survive the war.

When it became clear that Saddam not only survived the war but that he would survive a US-led rebellion within Iraq as well, President Bush signed a presidential finding authorizing the CIA "to create the conditions for the removal of Saddam Hussein from power."[6] In a great irony, the president, at the close of the administration, had therefore instructed US intelligence services to do what Bush claimed throughout *Desert Shield* and *Desert Storm* was not administration policy: unseat Saddam, a policy later referred to by Clinton and Bush as regime change.

As the ad hoc policy process unfolded at the close of the administration, containment became the buzzword that characterized US policy. To make this policy work the administration counted on intelligence. Indeed, intelligence performed a critical role in the surveillance of Iraqi forces within the no-fly zones in the south and in the north. That said the role that defined the intelligence community concerned the area of monitoring Iraqi weapons of mass of destruction. US intelligence in November of 1990 concluded that Iraq's nuclear scientists would not be in a position to build a nuclear weapon until the end of the decade. This time US intelligence, which prior to this point had made accurate assessments about Iraqi preparations for intervention in Kuwait, about their analysis that Saddam's major armored forces would survive US air strikes and attacks by US Army forces during the ground war, and also predicted Saddam's survival after the war, had been surprised to learn that the prewar assessments of Iraq's nuclear program had been woefully inept. The following excerpt exemplifies the point:

> Following the Gulf War, based on a variety of sources of intelligence including reporting from defectors, the Intelligence Community learned that Iraq's nuclear weapons program went "far beyond what had been assessed by any intelligence organization in 1990–1991. ... Thus after the war the Intelligence Community was surprised to discover the breadth of Iraq's nuclear weapons program, including the wide range of technologies Iraq had been pursuing for uranium enrichment, which in turn indicated that Iraq "had been much closer to a weapon than virtually anyone expected." This humbling discovery that Iraq had successfully concealed a sophisticated nuclear program from the US Intelligence Community exercised a major influence on the Intelligence Community's assessments throughout the early 1990s and afterwards.[7]

This point is instructive because the intelligence assessments during the pre-*Desert Storm* period were grossly inaccurate under Bush I; interestingly the consequences

---

6   Pollack, *The Threatening Storm*, 59.

7   As quoted in *The Commission on the Intelligence Capabilities of the United States Regarding Weapons of Mass Destruction*. Report of the President of the United States. 31 March 2005, 53–4.

for the president were minimal due in part because the war had concluded and US troops were withdrawing. Ironically, Bush II failed to learn this vital lesson. In other words prewar (prior to *Operation Iraqi Freedom*) assessments made by the intelligence community indicated that Iraq was reconstituting their nuclear program. This assessment according to United Nations Monitoring, Verification and Inspection Commission (UNMOVIC), The Iraq Survey Group (ISG), and The Commission on the Intelligence Capabilities, proved wrong. Unlike Bush I, Bush II would pay a major price with respect to presidential credibility, but equally significant US moral authority with respect to the war on terror suffered a major hit and has yet to recover.

There is another lesson the Bush II administration failed to learn: the importance of accurate intelligence. As the Commission on Intelligence Capabilities noted, much of what the intelligence community collected "had grave defects that should have been clear to analysts and policymakers at the time."[8] This failure was magnified because analysts did not "apply sufficiently rigorous tests to the evidence it collected." Lastly, the intelligence errors that were committed with respect to Iraq's nuclear programs were mild compared to analysts' assessments concerning Iraq's biological weapons:

> Virtually all of the Intelligence Community's information on Iraq's alleged mobile biological weapons facilities was supplied by a source, code-named "Curveball," who was a fabricator. ... Curveball was not the only bad source the Intelligence Community used. Even more indefensibly, information from a source who was *already known* to be a fabricator found its way into finished prewar intelligence products, including the October 2002 NIE (National Intelligence Estimate). This intelligence was also allowed into Secretary of State Colin Powell's speech to the United Nations Security Council, despite the source having been officially discredited almost a year earlier. This communications breakdown could have been avoided if the Intelligence Community had a uniform requirement to reissue or recall reporting from a source whose information turns out to be fabricated, so that analysts do not continue to rely on an unreliable report.[9]

The Commission on Intelligence Capabilities and the ISG reports suggests intelligence collection within the CIA was problematic. Unfortunately, the mandate of the Commission on Intelligence and the ISG, even if the final reports themselves were damaging, were nonetheless limited. Thus, neither report probed executive accountability or the role of other intelligence agencies.

On the latter, the "other intelligence agencies" suggested herein is a reference to the Office of Special Plans (OSP), a similar version in the Office of the Vice President (Cheney himself was highly influential) and directed by Cheney's chief of staff, Scooter Libby, and a less conspicuous form within the State Department, that was direct by John Bolton. The efforts of Cheney would lay the foundations that

---

8   Ibid., 48–9.
9   Ibid.

would allow these creations to flourish. A quote by Seymour Hersh exemplifies the point:

> [Kenneth Pollack] . . . told me that what the Bush people did was "dismantle the existing filtering process that for fifty years had been preventing the policymakers from getting bad information. They created stovepipes to get the information they wanted directly to the top leadership."[10]

The process of undermining the CIA did not end there. According to Pollack, "they always had information to back up their public claims, but it was often very bad information. They were forcing the intelligence community to defend its good information"[11] Unfortunately the agency had little time to correct the disinformation.

The OSP is a Pentagon creation with the expressed purpose to circumvent the usual procedures (such as vetting) that were hallmarks of the CIA and other intelligence agencies. As the pressure from Cheney mounted, the agency had lost its ability or resolve to resist the efforts of the OVP. It is in this environment that William Luti, the director of the OSP, used to continue the unraveling of US intelligence. With the CIA human intelligence non-existent within Iraq, the OSP turned to Iraqi defectors, the bulk of which were connected to INC, for what was believed to be critical information. Much of this information was utilized by Pentagon civilians but in many cases this information was directed to the OVP and then presented to the president as intelligence "with little prior evaluation from intelligence officials."[12] Collectively all three non-traditional bureaucratic institutions worked to dismantle intelligence procedures that were invented to prohibit raw intelligence from making its way into the hands of zealous policy-makers.

Collectively, these efforts assisted in the politicalization of intelligence that led to the absence of WMDs, despite the claims to contrary by the administrations prewar assessments in Iraq. Thus the sad conclusion is that the administration took the country to war on the strength of deficient intelligence; at worst, and as one of the memos in connection with the Downing Street Reports concludes, intelligence was fixed to support administration policy. The Downing memos on US intelligence further eroded the credibility of US intelligence. For the administration, the British reports aside, some of the most damaging information came from within the executive branch (a presidential sponsored Commission on Intelligence Capabilities) and from the report of the Iraq Survey Group. In the end the failure to learn about the appropriate use of intelligence had impacted three administrations and their policies toward Iraq. The administration—Bush II—that could have profited the most from "lessons learned" instead politicized intelligence like no administration in post-World War II history. The results of the failed lessons will likely reverberate for years to come.

---

10   Seymour Hersh, "The Stovepipe," *The New Yorker*, 27 October 2003. www. newyorker.comprintables/fact/031027fa_fact. Retrieved on 27 September 2005.
11   Ibid.
12   Ibid.

Postwar Planning

The issue of unseating Saddam Hussein produced constant discourse among officials of the Bush I, Clinton and Bush II administrations, and it appears that neither president nor those officials within their respective administrations understood the consequences of regime change. In the case of the senior Bush he failed to understand a number of important lessons. In the aftermath of the Bush administration's invasion of Panama (*Operation Just Cause*), for example, the president had to confront the age old dilemma associated with conflict termination. To place this issue in its appropriate context let us consider two instructive caveats, one by noted military historian and strategist Carl von Clausewitz and the second by B.H. Liddell Hart. On the former, Clausewitz warns that "No one starts a war—or rather, no one in his senses ought to do so—without first being clear in his mind what he intends to achieve by that war and how he intends to conduct it." Hart asserts that "if you concentrate exclusively on victory, with no thought for the after effect, you may be too exhausted to profit by the peace, while it is almost certain that the peace will be a bad one, containing the germs of another war."[13]

In the case of Panama the administration won a decisive military victory but failed to plan for the stabilization phase or conflict termination. In the wake of the military victory US forces were still in combat mode and failed to secure the country. This failure resulted in a wave of looting and chaos which left over 10, 000 Panamanians homeless.[14] In the end the failure to pacify the country resulted in the administrations initial encounter with postwar planning. The aftermath of the situation within Iraq after *Operation Desert Storm* indicated that the administration had failed to learn from a valuable case study on the need for postwar planning.

In the case of Iraq the Bush administration had no plan for which to conduct postwar peace. Given that the war concluded with rapidity (a situation that was repeated under "W"), which CENTCOM officials claim left them with little time to prepare for armistice talks with Iraqi leaders. An organization recognized for their ability to plan for contingencies, the obvious query is this: should not a plan have been in place, one that could have been updated as the situation warranted? The realities within Iraq indicated that a successful coup against Saddam in the wake of the conclusion of the first gulf war was such that pro-US opposition forces never stood a chance of unseating the Iraqi leader without direct US military assistance. And when Saddam's forces mounted a devastating counterattack the Bush administration reacted as if they were paralyzed, and when the shock subsided thousands of Shiites had lost their lives. In the aftermath of the failed insurrection the administration back pedaled making pronouncements that it did not call upon the Iraqi people "to

---

13   As quoted in William Flavin, "Planning Conflict Termination and Post-Conflict Success," *Parameters*, Autumn 2003, 95.

14   Thomas Donnelly, "Extracts from Lessons Unlearned," *The National Interest*, Summer 2000. http: www. ciaonet.org/olj/ni/ni_00dot01.html. Retrieved on 19 September 2005.

take matters into their own hands." The evidence suggests otherwise. The resulting calamity and the failure to learn from the mistakes in Panama, and later compounded in Iraq is due in part to the fact that "most of the senior Bush administration team during *Desert Storm* was the same as during *Just Cause*."[15] For the administration the failure to deal with postwar planning left the administration vulnerable on a number of fronts. On the first, the president himself acknowledged *Desert Storm* did not produce a triumphant peace. Additionally, the administration had to live with a negative legacy: triumph on the battlefield but because the Iraqi leader remained in power the president and senior officials, have in the aftermath of the war, been forced to listen to criticism that Iraq represented "unfinished business." Finally, the administration's post-conflict rhetoric was consistent with regime change but history notes the president failed in this regard. As a reminder of this failure Tariq Aziz, at that time the foreign minister of Iraq, made the following statement to Secretary Baker, "We will be here long after you're gone."[16]

Similarly, Clinton called for a covert campaign to unseat the regime but in the event that the regime fell, no preparations were begun to plan for life without Saddam. This statement requires qualification. In January 1999 the Clinton administration created the "Coordinator for the Transition in Iraq" position within the State Department. The position was headed by career diplomat Frank Ricciardone. The diplomat's responsibility however had less to do with postwar planning than to serve as the administrations chief liaison with the opposition forces within and outside Iraq. Still, the Clinton administration had itself left a number of valuable lessons for his successor, George W. Bush. The Iraqi example aside, the Clinton administration failed to plan for postwar peace in Bosnia and Kosovo, in each case US-led coalition forces had to confront looting, arson and revenge killings.

Long before the Clinton administration concluded, the senior Bush, with assistance from his national security advisor, Brent Scowcroft, provided a number of additional warning signs, that if accepted, may have ended talk of regime change, or at the very least forced subsequent presidents to have conclusive and substantive postwar planning in place long before the commencement of military operations. On the problems associated with regime change, Bush and Scowcroft wrote the following in 1998:

> While we hoped that popular revolt or a coup would topple Saddam, neither the US nor the countries of the region wished to see the breakup of the Iraqi state. We were concerned about the long-term balance of power at the head of the Gulf. Trying to eliminate Saddam, extending the ground war into an occupation of Iraq, would have violated our guideline about not changing objectives in midstream, engaging in "mission creep," and would have incurred incalculable human and political costs. Apprehending him was probably impossible. We had been unable to find Noriega in Panama, which we knew intimately. We would have been forced to occupy Baghdad and, in effect, rule Iraq. The coalition

---

15   Ibid.

16   James Baker, *The Politics of Diplomacy* (New York: G.P. Putnam & Son's, 1995), 442.

would instantly have collapsed, the Arabs deserting it in anger and other allies pulling out as well. Under those circumstances, furthermore, we had been self-consciously trying to set a pattern for handling aggression in the post-cold war world. Going in and occupying Iraq, thus unilaterally exceeding the U.N.'s mandate, would have destroyed the precedent of international response to aggression we hoped to establish. Had we gone the invasion route, the U.S. could conceivably still be an occupying power in a bitterly hostile land. It would have been a dramatically different—and perhaps barren—outcome.[17]

In the case of 43, in hindsight, it appeared the administration had learned of the importance of postwar planning. As noted in chapter 4, the department of State commissioned in the spring of 2002 The Future of Iraq Project. This decision by the department developed in recognition that regime change emerged as a far gone conclusion. Powell placed Thomas Warrick, formerly the department's special adviser to the Office of Northern Gulf Affairs, in charge of the States postwar planning efforts. Work on postwar planning continued until late 2002 when the Pentagon, which had become concerned that Powell would dominate reconstruction in Iraq, moved to end States' control. Thereafter, Rumsfeld made a personal plea to the president that the Pentagon should control postwar planning. This bureaucratic move undercut Powell (actually it ended The Future of Iraq Project altogether). It was at this point that the administration secretly pressed into service the Office of Reconstruction and Humanitarian Assistance (ORHA) on 20 January 2003. There were a number of critical issues that impacted ORHA. First, bureaucratic maneuvering commenced by Rumsfeld's Office of Special Plans (OSP) assured that no senior officials that worked on The Future of Iraq Project could work on the Pentagon-led postwar plans. Second, as a by-product of this decision an obvious problem emerged that would later hamper administration planning: the lack of personnel with expertise on Iraq and the staff itself was too small to adequately deal with the attendant problems of governing a country the size of Iraq. Third, according to David Phillips, a member of State department team, rather than build on States' efforts, the civilians in the Pentagon "discarded all of the . . . Project's planning."[18] This decision indicated the depth of bureaucratic infighting over Iraq policy. As Judith Yaphe, a leading expert on Iraq stated: "The Pentagon didn't want to touch anything connected to the Department of State." Fourth, another factor impacting administration planning concerned the dilemma posed by time. This point is instructive given that war preparations were in the final phase, and postwar planning remained in a state of flux. Even worse, with the war tentatively scheduled for March the Pentagon-led effort left no time to conduct any serious planning. A RAND Corporation memorandum to Secretary Rumsfeld sheds light on the Pentagon's failure:

> Post-conflict stabilization and reconstruction were addressed only very generally, largely because of the prevailing view that the task would not be difficult. What emerged was a

---

17   George Bush and Brent Scowcroft, *A World Transformed* (New York: Alfred A. Knopf, 1998), 489.

18   See David Rieff, "Blueprint for a Mess," *The New York Times*, 2 November 2003.

general set of tasks that were not prioritized or resourced. No planning was undertaken to provide for the security of the Iraqi people in the post-conflict environment, given the expectations that the Iraqi government would remain largely intact; the Iraqi people would welcome the American presence; and local militia, police, and the regular army would be capable of providing law and order. … Iraq demonstrates that the military mission of providing security in the post-conflict environment is just as important to achieving a strategic victory, if not more important, than the military mission of winning decisive combat operations.[19]

Finally, as we know the failure to have "a real postwar plan" thereafter handcuffed administration strategy. In the absence of a larger force presence in Iraq, US-led coalition forces have been confronted with a burgeoning insurgency that continues to inflict casualties on US forces and untold Iraqi civilian casualties. The larger issue is this: the failure to secure Iraq in the wake of the collapse of the regime has stalled the war on terror and caused disunity among Atlantic coalition partners.

Ultimate Failure and Aftermath: The Struggle to Confront the Postwar Insurgency

This chapter has endeavored to illustrate that the road to the second Iraq war has as its most central cause the failure to learn vital lessons. The lessons themselves have come in multiple forms: dealing with coalition diplomacy, misreading the Arab Street, avoiding the pitfalls associated with bureaucratic infighting, inappropriate use of intelligence, and the need for extensive postwar planning. These lessons aside, there were others alluded to but not completely fleshed out and consist of the following: war termination cannot super cede the completion of political objectives. The problem of war termination beset Bush I during *Desert Storm*. As mentioned in chapter 4 political leaders must be prepared to make the requisite preparation of the domestic and international polities. Having done so as the senior Bush himself lamented "let the politicians get out of the way and let the military fight the war, and let them fight it to win."[20] Similarly, Clinton repeated the same mistake in *Operation Desert Fox*, a four day operation that failed to meet its objectives. Moreover, the limited air and cruise missile attack achieved limited objectives.[21] The result of the campaign left Saddam emboldened and the Iraqi leader continued to flout US/UN efforts to return inspectors to Iraq.

Perhaps more astounding regards administration policy in Iraq which has been and continues to be driven by ideological dislocation. Remarkably and perhaps purposefully the president and his senior advisors lost comprehension of the

---

19   James Thompson, President and CEO of the RAND Corporation, "Iraq: Translating Lessons Into Future DoD Policies," memorandum to Secretary of Defense Donald Rumsfeld, 7 February 2005.

20   Colonel Mark Garrard, USAF, "War Termination in the Persian Gulf: Problems and Prospects," 4.

21   Pauly, *US Foreign Policy and the Persian Gulf*, 73.

aforementioned mistakes, therefore Bush II and company would in the end repeat all of them. A few examples are instructive. Perhaps most salient concerned the fact that the administration did not adroitly utilize intelligence; rather it politicized intelligence to achieve regime change. Second, as a by product of the former, because of the ideological zeal that drove administration policy, Bush II failed to utilize the example that defined his father's policy toward Iraq: multilateralism or the use of coalition diplomacy. Third, in a major blunder, even after Clinton's mistakes in Bosnia and Kosovo, Bush, after deciding to launch *Operation Iraqi Freedom*, the president missed the most significant educational lesson: securing the country. This miss-education of the president would prove the most costly, politically, strategically, and with respect to the loss of US military personnel and Iraqi civilians: shameful and in the view of some criminal. It is this very failure that is the focus of this concluding portion of this chapter.

The administration missed a host of critical warning signs; many of the caveats came from within the administration itself. The caveats go hand in hand with what is referred to in Pentagon parlance as Phase IV or Stabilization. Troop levels should be twice that of the invasion force, the importance of a doctrine that is utilized by all troops to combat the insurgency; politically there needs to be legitimacy within the Iraqi government, the importance of national building, and the training of indigenous forces.

The Post-Conflict Activities

For Clausewitz the last procedure for the regional commander is not the cessation of hostilities but rather "the last step is the effective implementation of post-conflict activities."[22] The most essential post-conflict activities for this study include the following: (1) providing a secure and stable environment, (2) the cooperation and assistance of governmental agencies (the interagency process) and coalition participation to ensure effectiveness, and (3) and national building.[23]

The Significance of a Secure and Stable Environment

Providing a secure and stable environment in Iraq should have been the essential variable in US planning for *Operation Iraqi Freedom*. History illustrates that establishing a postwar security environment was not a central priority in administration postwar planning. After the cessation of military operations occurred it had become painfully clear that US military forces were unprepared for the aftermath. As result US military forces, most specifically the Third Infantry Division which watched as looting and arson occurred throughout Baghdad in their area of responsibility. One

---

22   Lt. Colonel Michael R. Rampy, USA, "The Endgame: Conflict Termination and Post-Conflict Activities," *Military Review* (October 1992), 54.

23   Another important post-conflict activity is peacekeeping or what the military calls stability operations.

would be tempted to blame the task force commander but that would let others up the chain of command to escape responsibility.

In fact two individuals deserve blame: Rumsfeld and CENTCOM Commander General Tommy Franks. Rumsfeld had become a champion of transformation of the military—doing more with less. This process is real and important. The problem is that one should question the validity and wisdom of the strategy during the war on terror. Specifically, when the administration selected regime change in Iraq, two issues should have been clear: the number of troops in the country are essential to return stability to the country, and second, the failure to complete the first task could lead to instability which could set the stage for an insurgency, that if successful, could delay the next phase of the war on terror.[24]

In the wake of the celebratory atmosphere among US commanders and politicians in Washington, as disorder unfolded on the ground in Iraq, and events were captured by the major American and international news outlets, senior officials, Rumsfeld chief among them, stated because of the speed of the operation the US had been caught of guard. This excuse is unfathomable given the experiences in Bosnia and Kosovo (more so in Bosnia) where speed contributed to the successful execution of both operations but violence and disorder were visible in both theatres. It is interesting that many back then utilized the excuse that because of the speed the US military had been unprepared for the aftermath. That excuse was unacceptable then and even more so now. The reasons for the postwar chaos in Iraq involve both transformation and planning. On the former, transformation, this process by its very nature precluded the consideration of large troop concentrations. Recalling the planning and vetting process between Rumsfeld and Franks keep in mind that the secretary of defense incessantly forced the general to come back with smaller force levels, arguing that speed, larger than usual introduction of Special Forces and combined air-ground operations were considered enough to defeat Iraqi forces. With respect to the latter, planning itself for Iraq after Saddam was an eleventh hour consideration and was based on faulty intelligence (that coming from Ahmed Chalabi and the Iraq National Congress) and myth's about the Iraqi population (that Iraq would greet US forces as liberators and not occupiers) and the reliance on Iraqi militias that would assist in the stabilization of the country. These assumptions all proved wrong.

With respect to Franks' CENTCOM, the failures of this institution were varied, strategic, and unforgivable. The central mistakes are captured by the following excerpt:

> The full chronology of what happened is still far from clear, and it's far easier to accuse given US leaders that it is to understand what really happened or assign responsibility with any credibility. It is clear, however, that many of the key decisions involved were made in ways that bypassed the interagency process within the US government, ignored the warnings of US area and intelligence experts, ignored prior military war and stability planning by the US Central Command (USCENTCOM or CENTCOM), and ignored

---

24   Greg Jaffe, "Rumsfeld's Gaze Is Trained Beyond Iraq," *Wall Street Journal*, 9 December 2004, 4.

the warnings of policy makers and experts in other key coalition states like the United Kingdom.[25]

Additional blame belongs to the ideologues (the neoconservatives) who were so wedded to their war ideology that commonsensical mistakes were made. Even worse this group of individuals exercised so much power that they were able to bypass other centers of power in the US government. There arrogance however produced a host of fatal mistakes in Iraq:

> It is also clear that far too much credence was given to ideologues and true believers in the ease with which such a war could be fought and in effective nation building. These included leading neoconservatives in the Office of the Secretary of Defense, the Office of the Vice President, and some officials in the National Security Council, as well as in several highly politicized "thinktanks." The same was true of various Iraqi exile groups that grossly exaggerated the level of Iraqi popular support for a "liberating" invasion and ease with which Saddam Hussein's regime could be replaced, and underestimated both the scale of Iraq's ethnic and sectarian divisions and economic problems.[26]

In the firestorm that erupted in the US Congress, Senators and members of the House of Representatives from both political parties grilled Pentagon civilians and military planners of the operation as to why securing the country was such a low priority. The aforementioned excuse was again repeated until a senior military officer stepped forward to acknowledge the truth. General Eric Shinseki, the Army Chief of Staff, in a statement that infuriated Pentagon civilians, expressed misgivings about the size of the force owing to historical precedents which attenuate that post-conflict environments require the invading army increase to twice its original size in preparation for securing the country. To undermine the credibility of Shinseki, Rumsfeld and Wolfowitz collectively discredited the general, eventually forcing him to retire.

Those actions aside the verities on the ground in Iraq indicate that the general was right. The looting, arson, revenge killing were rampant in postwar Iraq, and there were other troubling issues that arose because of the lack of troop presence, including insurgents pillaging of weapons storage facilities, the movement of indigenous insurgents throughout the country, the influx of foreign fighters via porous borders, the increasing cooperation between local insurgents and foreign fighters, and the presence of foreign intelligence elements (Iranian, Syrian, Saudi, and even Egyptian) that according to sources assisted the growth of the insurgency.[27] These forces and there activities were allowed to flourish because the US troop presence was too small.

---

25   Anthony H. Cordesman, "Iraq's Evolving Insurgency," Center for Strategic and International Studies, Working Draft: Updated as of 19 May 2005, 6.

26   Ibid.

27   See Yoseff Bodansky, *The Secret History of the Iraq War* (New York: Harper Collins, 2004).

Post-Conflict Interagency and Coalition Cooperation

Another essential post-conflict activity involves the cooperation between relevant agencies to assist in the management of security situation within Iraq could, if instituted quickly, have led to dramatically dissimilar results within the country. On both fronts the Bush administration failed to learn a critical lesson: that absent interagency cooperation in Iraq and coalition collaboration the security situation is likely to face unnecessary problems and stress, that over time could produce fissures of fragmentation within Iraqi society, thereby laying the evolution for civil war, or as will be discussed later, opportunities for the insurgency to exploit. Thus the absence of coalition cooperation invariably disrupts counterinsurgency. This point has been expressed another way:

> The United States and its close coalition partners must assure unity of effort across all of the governmental agencies involved. Counterinsurgency is not as exclusively or even predominantly a military function but demands the seamless integration of informational, political, social, cultural, law enforcement, economic, military, and intelligence activities.[28]

The postwar interagency process had been eviscerated long before the second Iraq war. As noted in Chapter 4 the bureaucratic infighting in the administration was so intense that it caused fragmentation within the policy process, so much so that when the post-conflict activities commenced the turf wars had precluded any real cooperation among the two principle departments deemed critical for successful postwar stability: State and Defense.

The relevant debate and absence of cooperation between State and Defense covered two critical areas: ORHA and whether the UN should be permitted a role in postwar Iraq. On the former, the ORHA is a brainchild of the Pentagon; a mechanism, much like the Office of Special Plans (which usurped many intelligence responsibilities from the CIA), was used to obstruct and eventually eclipse the State departments' traditional role in reconstruction. For Powell, Rumsfeld, Wolfowitz and Cheney, the debate was far more intense and the outcome of which significantly impacted post-conflict activities.

Much of this debate had its roots in the closing days of *Operation Desert Storm.* In the war council concerning discourse concerning when and where to conclude the ground war, Cheney and Wolfowitz in particular, remember the power and authority that accrued to Powell on this question, and now, with the assistance of Rumsfeld both were determined to prevent the secretary of state from assuming such power and prominence under Bush II. On the eve of the second war with Iraq, Rumsfeld, with assistance from Cheney, requested and received complete authorization and control over postwar reconstruction in Iraq. Thus the troika of Rumsfeld, Wolfowitz, and Cheney prevented Powell's Iraq experts from participating in ORHA. Even worse as

---

28   Steven Metz, "Insurgency and Counterinsurgency in Iraq," *The Washington Quarterly*, Winter 2003–2004, 33.

the war concluded, ORHA, which as late of April of 2003, began to operate in Iraq had at this time communicated directly with Rumsfeld and refused observations and input from Powell. The result of this bureaucratic tug of war prevented the inclusion of critical aspects of The Future of Iraq Project, especially the exclusion of many of Iraq's political *intelligentsia* participation in the Interim Iraq Government that left the civilians in the Pentagon free to exploit their relationship with Ahmed Chalabi.

The episode mirrored many other debates that precluded interagency cooperation in other areas that include some of Iraq's most vital problems: what elements of Iraq's bureaucracy should be slated for de-Baathification, the same is true for the ranks within the Iraqi armed forces and intelligence, to work to repair Iraq's electrical power grids as well as the need for upgrades on power stations, all as we will see, impacted post-conflicted activities that retarded efforts to eliminate a nascent insurgency.

The second element in the interagency bureaucratic debate over Iraq's future concerned the role and participation of the UN and coalition partners. Powell and his deputy Richard Armitage argued from the end of major combat operations that UN participation was required for the passage of UNSC resolutions to legitimize the US efforts in Iraq as well as to provide a cover for coalition troops and those Powell thought essential during the stabilization phase. By contrast Pentagon civilians and Cheney argued that over time it may be possible to include the UN and other coalition partners, but since many states (the French and Germany in particular) chose to obstruct US-led efforts it made little sense from their perspective to enlist UN and allied participation in Iraq.

In time the troika recanted allowing participation from the UN. Ironically, after the insurgency gathered strength and began to inflict heavy casualties on US-led coalition forces in Iraq, and following a truck bombing of UN headquarters, Rumsfeld, Wolfowitz, and Cheney recognized in August of 2003 the need for legitimacy would be beneficial to administration efforts to stabilize the country.

With the security environment continuing to spiral downward, the UN evacuation of personnel in Iraq (and even after the approval of several Security Council resolutions) because the secretary general Kofi Annan deemed the situation in Iraq unsafe, many coalition partners (such Pakistan) refused to provide troops in Iraq without UN legitimacy. Thus again the failure to secure Iraq impacted post-conflict activities to the extent that interagency cooperation among critical American foreign policy institutions, and likewise with the UN and Atlantic coalition partners (and elsewhere), retarded postwar development in Iraq.

Nation Building

The failure to secure the country, the absence of institutional cooperation between State and Defense, and the misfortune of not including the UN and additional coalition partners in the postwar process, invariably affected US nation building efforts in Iraq. For critics of administration policy in Iraq, any failures associated with nation building began long before *Operation Iraqi Freedom*. Bush entered office with major opposition to nation building; such opposition reared its head during the 2004 Presidential Campaign where candidate Bush observed nation building in Kosovo is a wholly European responsibility and that US peacekeeping forces should be withdrawn. In the days after 9/11 the eventualities—the need to prevent al Qaeda's return—in Afghanistan and the war on terror in general quickly forced the president to rethink administration policy in this venue. With war on the horizon in Iraq the realities associated with potential threats to nation building should have been clear. The failure to implement a well-defined postwar strategy affected nation building and therefore postwar security in Iraq.

With the ever-decreasing security situation in postwar Iraq, foreign fighters, most notably those groups loyal to al Qaeda, recognized the porous environment could be exploited to enlist anti-American forces within the country and outside the country to participate in a jihad to end the US occupation of Iraq. Bin Laden recognized that a defeat in Iraq could deal a crushing blow to the US-led war on terror. At the very least by forcing the US to commit valuable resources in Iraq, bin Laden had hoped to stall the war on terror, thereby preventing the administration from moving to another phase which presumably translated to possible US intervention in Syria, Iran, or other countries in the region with a high concentration of al Qaeda fighters.

These issues not withstanding, the major flaws in US nation building were later exacerbated by the twin insurgency (one indigenous the other exogenous; they are twins only to the extent that both insurgencies are working toward the same goal—the withdrawal of US forces). The major variable that implicates the administration involves the issue of infighting. Just before the war commenced Pentagon civilians wanted to control postwar reconstruction, thereby stripping the State department of their traditional authority. With respect to reconstruction funding and distribution, this too was significantly but not completely controlled by the Pentagon. In the ensuing three-plus months after the war, the Pentagon ran the show despite internal protests from Powell. However, when the security situation declined, and reconstruction projects decreased, congressional dissatisfaction with the pace of reconstruction mounted. In time a number of events further eroded the nation building efforts in Iraq. First, under increasing domestic, regional and international pressure the administration made a major decision: reconstruction efforts were shifted from the Pentagon and were now under the purview of Condoleezza Rice. The second issue concerned the pace of the insurgency itself, which threatened and consistently attacked and killed many coalition supported workers, the result of which added to the decreasing pace of reconstruction projects. Third, yet another internal barometer concerned the bureaucratic red tape that in the end further slowed the reconstruction efforts. In the end, the period beginning in August of 2003 through July 2004 represented a critical period that was lost to set the tempo for nation building all over Iraq. Fourth, while Powell did regain significant control over reconstruction distribution (something mandated in the legislation from Congress), national building had made the inevitable turn for the worse, which only recently began to shift. Still, those tracking the pace of reconstruction argue that it is far behind the expectations of the Iraqi people which in the end represent the most critical variable.

Fifth, according to the Pentagon nation building consisted of three phases: stabilization, transition to democracy, and the transformation phase.[29] Though each stage has shown progression, the reality is nation building is far behind schedule. Similarly, the administration missed an opportunity to learn from history and from errors of their own making. Historically, in the wake of World War II, the US military oversaw two occupations successfully, one in Germany and in Japan. In both cases the Truman administration worked with two disparate military proconsuls to ensure that a clear set of procedures or postwar plans were ready. These plans in turn ensured success on both fronts.

Ironically, the Bush administration attempted to repeat the successes of Truman with two major nation building efforts: one in Afghanistan and in Iraq. The administration failures in postwar planning occurred not just in Iraq. In fact, what should have been its benchmark—successful nation building in Afghanistan—was anything but. The reality is that the administration had no detailed planning for postwar Afghanistan. Much of what was stated in the wake of the collapse of the regime of Saddam Hussein had been stated in Afghanistan following the collapse of the Taliban regime. Namely, the war ended faster than expected. Equally astonishing, we forget that the (in) stability in Afghanistan had a variable that was later present in Iraq: not enough US troops to secure the country which in turn slowed post-conflict activities. Complicating nation building in Afghanistan concerns the fact that critical resources—from special forces (particularly, civil affairs troops), Satellites, linguists, logisticians, and other personnel—were shifted to Iraq in the run up to and in greater numbers in the wake of the *Operation Iraqi Freedom*.

The administration's ad hoc approach to post-conflict activities worked in Afghanistan for two reasons: the planned Taliban/al Qaeda insurgency had not been effective primarily because of weather, and second, the *loya jurga* proved successful in seating a transitional leader. Pentagon civilians made a gross mistake: they assumed that ad hoc post-conflict planning and post-conflict activities in Afghanistan could have been replicated on a much grander scale in Iraq.[30] The fact is the insurgency in Afghanistan may have been delayed but three years since the end war the insurgency has delayed many reconstruction projects.

Finally, Bush had three opportunities to learn critical lessons with respect to postwar planning. On the first, the historic lessons of Truman in Germany and Japan were never understood and applied. With respect to the second, Clinton's failures in nation building in Bosnia and Kosovo were additional lessons that were also ignored. Finally, the administration had its own example of Afghanistan to utilize as benchmark for the much larger nation building effort in Iraq. The unfortunate reality

---

29   John Dean, "Nation Building in Iraq: Future Plans and Problems in the Postwar Period," http: writ.news.findlaw.com/dean/20030411.htm.

30   State Department Study Foresaw Trouble Now Plaguing Iraq," *New York Times*, 19 October 2003; Michael Elliott, "So, What Went Wrong?" *Time*, 6 October 2003, p. 30; John Barry and Evan Thomas, "The Unbuilding of Iraq," *Newsweek*, 6 October 2003; and, Gerard Baker and Stephen Fidler, "The Best Laid Plans?" *London Financial Times*, 4 August 2003.

is that while the military has conducted an after action review of military operations in both Afghanistan and Iraq, no similar efforts whether from the military or from a presidentially mandated commission was utilized to learn the lessons of US post-conflict activities in Afghanistan. If such procedures were in place there is little doubt that nation building in Iraq would have been significantly enhanced.

The Insurgency in Iraq: Welcome to the Jungle

The aforementioned sections collectively demonstrate that the Bush administration failed in all three areas of post-conflict activities that are prerequisites for defeating an insurgency. The conclusion herein therefore is that the insurgency—which includes indigenous Sunni Baathists, Sunni Islamists, Shiite radicals and the foreign fighters led by Zarqawi—have flourished in an environment absent the stability and security promised by the administration. In an ultimate irony having destroyed al Qaeda's main safe haven in Afghanistan, administration policy has produced a burgeoning sanctuary for terrorists within Iraq. Even worse for the administration is the war on terror lost its momentum, moral authority, and until there is stability in Iraq, the overall effort will remain stagnant for years to come.

These failures notwithstanding, the administration committed a number of mistakes that would further exacerbate the fledgling insurgency, which as it expanded, thwarted many reconstruction initiatives in Iraq and has accounted for far too many Iraqi civilian deaths and coalition casualties.

The most obvious oversight concerns the administration's failure to confront the insurgency during its infancy[31] proved to be a fatal decision that increased the longevity of the US occupation and forced the Bush administration to expend far more resources than anticipated.

The second miscalculation is symptomatic with the former. As was the case with an administration unwilling to accept blame, mistakes and disappointments associated with the misperceptions about the size, leadership, and support structure were blamed on intelligence. Though this time the military accepted their share of the blame, it had become commonplace to assert that CIA intelligence miscues in Iraq, particularly the agencies inability to discern the size, location, and leadership of the multiple anti-coalition forces at work in Iraq. These failures are themselves the result of

> Underestimation of the work needed to secure, stabilize, and reconstruct Iraq after Saddam Hussein's regime had been toppled. Security in Iraq is labor intensive because of the country's long borders and extensive territory, and the coalition did not deploy adequate forces to prevent infiltration of foreign radicals and criminals. Coalition planners believed that a significant portion of the Iraqi security forces—military and police—would sit out the war in their barracks and then reemerge to form the core of the post-Saddam military

---

31   Metz, "Insurgency and Counterinsurgency in Iraq," 25.

and police with new leaders at their fore. None returned, however, leaving a massive security vacuum that the coalition was unprepared to fill.[32]

In spite of the administration's efforts to scapegoat the CIA, the reality is that the administration's shoddy pre-invasion planning and their failure to adjust to postwar realities assisted in the growth and eventual lethality of the insurgency.

Third, not destroying Ansar al-Islam (the largest of Iraq's al Qaeda affiliates), much like the senior Bush's failure to destroy Republican Guard forces, in hindsight, is by far one of the single biggest errors made by the US military. This point is instructive. US Special Forces, along with Kurdish *pershmerga* militia, killed significant amounts of Ansar terrorists in Halabja, destroyed their base camp, and located and captured over one hundred fighters and their Kurdish supporters. Problematic for the US military is that several hundred Ansar terrorists escaped into the mountains in Iran where they regrouped, rearmed and later returned to Iraq, fanning out into smaller cells throughout country, with the main concentration hold up in Fallujah. In short, much like Saddam's forces that escaped only to return and fight another day, Ansar, which had been allowed to flee, returned to inflict major carnage upon Iraqi civilians (mostly Shiite), UN diplomatic personnel, and US military personnel in their Fallujah safe haven until they were defeated in the second US-led military operation destroyed this safe haven in the fall of 2004. A fourth problem emanating from the first (a stable security environment) concerns the inability to close Iraq's porous borders. The coalitions' inability to secure Iraq's borders laid the foundation for two problematic eventualities. On the first, jihadists from Saudi Arabia, Iran, Syria, various parts of Africa, Europe, and elsewhere, flocked to Iraq to join forces with Ansar al-Islam, in what became, oddly enough, a second Afghanistan. The second dilemma is a by-product of the first. In order for these forces, and the Baathists within Iraq to flourish, they required supply lines, safe houses, and a leadership cadre. Two countries, Syria and Iran (and Saudi Arabia), were the central nodes that provided these critical linkages to support the foreign fighters that entered through these countries and into Iraq to attack coalition forces. US efforts to confront these threats came in the form of direct diplomatic initiatives to Syria on the part of senior Bush administration officials or open threats to Iran's theocrats. These efforts have repeatedly failed. The administration has launched a series of military campaigns all along the Syrian-Iraq borders. In every case these operations have proved successful. The problem, however, is that because Iraqi forces were unable to sustain US battlefield victories, forcing CENTCOM to return to many of the same areas to again defeat insurgents in such areas as Al-Qaim and Talafar.

Fifth, a major US failure concerned a definitive strategy to confront the insurgency. In the years and months after coalition forces declared an end to major combat operations, the US military had a continuous problem: the absence of a doctrine to confront the insurgency. As a result of this issue once US forces rotated dissimilar

---

32   Ibid., 27.

forces in and out of Iraq, the disparate units utilized different tactics to capture, and when the opportunity presented itself, to neutralize insurgents all over Iraq. Though US forces remain successful in defeating the insurgent challenges, the failure of Iraqi defense forces to sustain coalition battle successes illustrates another dilemma: the slow pace of training Iraqi troops. The administration has worked feverishly to embed US units with Iraqi forces, or permit Iraqi forces to lead select missions, but the reality is the pace of such a transformation of Iraqi forces remains too slow and is behind schedule.

At the time of this writing US military casualties have exceed 2000. The intensity of the insurgent attacks on US, Iraqi defense forces, not to mention the ever-increasing attacks on Iraqi civilians (mostly Shiites), along with the growing American and international skepticism of Iraq's fledgling government to appeal to "all Iraqi's" has fostered fears of a quagmire. The resulting clamor has educed calls for the rapid withdrawal of US forces by the American polity and from members of Congress. This internal pressure comes at a time when President Bush is a vulnerable leader. With too few successes to speak of (outside of the recent constitutional referendum), the president has tried time and time again to demonstrate the importance of the mission in Iraq. Additionally, with the cost of war exceeding $200 billion dollars and a burgeoning casualty rate among US military personnel, the president has thus far been unable to reverse public opinion against the war.

The pressure for the withdrawal of US forces is not limited to isolationist elements. Indeed, many scholars have questioned the administrations strategy and the president's commitment to the war effort. There are some who see too many parallels with the Vietnam War, namely that the US military strategy to kill numerous insurgents by itself will fail in Iraq as it did in that infamous Indo-China War. In a bold effort, Andrew Krepinevich asserts that CENTCOM may do well to implement the "oil spot strategy." [33]

This strategy calls upon the US to withdraw their forces to the Kurdish north and the Shiite dominated south, making both "safe zones." The point of this shift in US military strategy is an effort to win the hearts and minds of Iraq's. Additionally, a component of this plan calls for focused spending and reconstruction in the safe zones, along with the support of Iraqi troops (whose training and participation would greatly increase) to quicken the pace of the initiative.[34] In time the strategy holds that eventually US and Iraqi troops would then mount sustained military operations in the four Sunni dominated areas in Anbar, Baghdad, Nineveh, Salaheddin provinces. Thus these areas would see a reduction in US troops until the north and south are secured.[35] Eventually, according to Krepinevich, the totality of US-Iraqi nation building efforts would thereafter resemble the "spread of an oil spot" ensuring that

---

33   Jim Krane, "US Requires to Retool Strategy to Win Iraq War," *Daily News*, 7 August 2005. Http://www.dailytimes.com.pk/print.asp?page=stor_6-8-2005-pg4... The information was retrieved on 7 August 2005.

34   Ibid.

35   Ibid.

all parts of Iraq would eventually receive the same concentration of US-Iraq activity. As interesting as this strategy sounds, Krepinevich warns that there are caveats: "America's effort in Iraq can only be salvaged with a costly turnaround in US military strategy that requires a long-term commitment to withstand the huge expense and higher rates of US combat deaths." The increase in combat deaths ensures that this strategy will never be instituted.

The problem with an administration that has made so many mistakes is that the president's options have been severely limited. Some scholars assert that one of the most interesting parallels concerns the fact that success in defeating the insurgency requires turning the clock back and doing what the administration did not succeed in doing in postwar planning. As Anthony Cordesman asserts, "Military victory in asymmetric warfare can be virtually meaningless without successful nation building at the political, economic, and security levels. Stabilization operations—Phase IV operations—are far more challenging than fighting conventional military forces.[36] Thus, with the administrations inability to institute a workable plan, and the insurgency continuing apace, combined with a weak transitional government, the administration is unlikely to accept the advice of instituting a workable nation building effort. Thus what Iraqi's are likely to see is an ad hoc policy geared to buy time until the Iraqi's themselves provide sustainable governance and Iraq's troops are able to supplant US forces, who if the ad hoc plan succeeds, will draw down their forces. One thing is certain, the insurgency will continue, and the US-led coalition forces will work to contain it; the unfortunate reality is US casualties will continue to mount and American forces will come to again reacquaint themselves with the slogan known all too well in Vietnam: "Welcome to the Jungle."

Conclusion

One of the great ironies of the current administrations failure to learn critical lessons from its predecessors (Bush I and Clinton), and even from itself (Afghanistan), is that regime change was to end the Iraqi threat once and force all. Successful in regime change the administration was unsuccessful in postwar planning, war termination and post-conflict activities, which collectively have made the Iraqi threat far worse than at any time during the three previous presidents combined. Several indices are instructive: the per month costs in Iraq exceeds that of the previous two administrations; the casualties figures far exceed those of the two previous administrations, and the administration has expended far more US resources in Iraq than the two previous administrations combined. Equally significant, the administrations war on terror is in a state of flux, due in part to the war in Iraq; the UN Security Council, which did not support the war effort, would be far more reluctant the next time this administration or any other administration seeks to utilize the international forum to justify UN intervention.

---

36   Cordesman, *The War After the War*, 41.

For the United States, even with a host of successful military operations in Iraq, intermittent reconstruction, historic democratic elections in Iraq, two issues will remain for this administration and a subsequent administration. The first concerns the negative relationships between critical allies (France and Germany); and consistent with this point, is that the US utilization of coalitions must itself change. The process of the declining use of coalitions began with sanctions fatigue under the Clinton administration and moved to an all-time low under the current administration. The second issue may be far more difficult to overcome. The United States, again despite the postwar successes in post-Saddam Iraq, continues to have a credibility problem. The absence of WMD in Iraq will forever stain any US-led coalition successes in Iraq. Moreover, future US efforts, whether in Iran and perhaps Syria, will force this administration or a subsequent administration to go the extra mile to convince not just the UNSC but also the international community that international intervention is warranted.

Finally, in the war councils in the run up to the war former Secretary State Colin Powell warned President Bush that if you invade Iraq you will own it and it will forever impact your presidency. It is clear that the president should have listened to the advice of the senior diplomat. In final analysis, President Bush finds himself in a similar but far worse predicament then his father. For the senior Bush the slogan in the aftermath of *Operation Desert Storm* was "triumph without victory"; oddly the younger Bush, in the event the situation in Iraq spirals downward and US and coalition forces withdraw without defeating the insurgency, we may too hear the same words: "triumph without victory." For 43 this legacy would be far worse for 41; that is the younger Bush was positioned to complete the unfinished business of the senior Bush. The resulting security dilemma in Iraq may produce an unusual reality: 43 had an opportunity to do what 41 and 42 were unable to do, end the Iraqi threat once and for all. The great irony in Iraq is this: in the absence of Saddam, the insurgent attacks, their all too numerous safe havens, the support structures in Syria and Iran, make the current security situation in Iraq far more threatening to US interests than during the Saddam era. Thus the burgeoning insurgency, its linkage to al Qaeda, threatens the war on terror, and a defeat for "W" in Iraq could dramatically undermine the war on terror and damage the president's credibility. The reality for "43" is fundamental, so goes Iraq so goes the president's legacy.

Index